For Time And All Eternity
THE STERLING AND ELLIE COLTON STORY

For Time And All Eternity
THE STERLING AND ELLIE COLTON STORY

Lee Roderick

PROBITAS PRESS

Los Angeles • Logan, Utah • Washington D.C.

Copyright © 2017 Lee Roderick
All rights reserved.

Names:	Roderick, Lee, 1941- author.
Title:	For time and all eternity : the Sterling and Ellie Colton story / Lee Roderick.
Description:	Los Angeles ; Logan, Utah ; Washington, D.C. : Probitas Press, [2017]	Includes bibliographical references and index.
Identifiers:	ISBN: 9780996185073	LCCN: 2017951863
	eBook ISBN: 978-0-9961850-6-6

For additional copies and eBook link to: Amazon.com or ProbitasPress.com

Subjects:	LCSH: Colton, Sterling D., 1929-	Colton, Eleanor R., 1931-	Spouses--United States--Biography.	Man- woman relationships--United States--Biography.	Mormons--United States--Biography.	Colton family--Family relationships.	Marriott International, Inc.--History.	Church of Jesus Christ of Latter-day Saints--Biography.
Classification:	LCC: E748.C696 .R63 2017	DDC: 920.009/04--dc23

Probitas Press, LLC
1830 East Canyon Ridge Drive, North Logan, Utah 84341
1.800.616.8081   *Visit ProbitasPress.com*

Printed in the United States of America
Sheridan Book Ann Arbor, Michigan

Also by Lee Roderick

Voices Behind the Voice of America
Leading the Charge
Gentleman of the Senate
Television Tightrope
Bridge Builder
Courage
True Wealth

To Our Wonderful Family

Joshua said, "Choose you this day whom ye will serve."
We have chosen to serve the Lord.
This book is written to help us be an eternal family.
We love you.

Contents

Acknowledgements		xi
Introduction		xiii
1	Colton Pioneer Heritage	1
2	Like Father, Like Son	11
3	Man of the House at Twelve	23
4	A Rich Ricks Heritage	35
5	Ricks Family Tragedies	45
6	The Education of Ellie	55
7	All-American Adolescent	79
8	Ellie Bonds with the Coltons	89
9	From Oilfields to Stanford Law School	97
10	Love Story for the Ages	109
11	Temple Marriage, Long-Distance Love	121
12	Colton Baby Makes Three	131

13	Exploring Europe	137
14	First Home	145
15	Taming Ellie's "Herd"	151
16	Recruited to Marriott	177
17	Marriott Soars	183
18	Sterling Named General Counsel	191
19	Sterling Builds Superb Legal Team	199
20	Marriott Sails Into Troubled Waters	207
21	Charity Begins at Home	211
22	Coltons Lead Football Team to the Top	219
23	Ellie vs. Equal Rights Amendment	231
24	Marriott Sales Pass $1 Billion	241
25	Daughters-in-law Join the Family	261
26	Marriott Resurrects Times Square	273
27	Grandchildren Arrive	279
28	Marriott Builds, Sells, Manages Hotels	289
29	Hugh Dies — The Torch is Passed	297
30	Sterling Leads the Split that Saves Marriott	305
31	"Ellie Has Made All the Difference"	315
32	Family Motto: "We Will Serve the Lord"	325
33	Mission Trumps Marriott	335
34	Payback Time	355
35	Welcome to British Columbia	367

36	Care and Feeding of 200 Missionaries	377
37	Last Months in Mission Field	389
38	Home Sweet Home	403
39	Safari in Southern Africa	413
40	President, Matron of Washington D.C. Temple	421
41	Angels in White	427
42	Faith of a Patriarch	431
43	Traveling the World	439

Epilogue	463
Appendix	465
Sources	483
Index	499

Acknowledgements

Sterling and Ellie Colton themselves were invaluable sources of information. They graciously welcomed me into their home in Bethesda, Maryland, for in-depth interviews, and furnished voluminous personal records.

The Colton children and their spouses likewise were supportive, especially Jeri Colton, who was a surrogate for her parents-in-law in reading the manuscript for accuracy, and Carolyn Colton, who coordinated photos and other facets with her parents.

Companions of Ellie's from school days in Idaho Falls offered insights into her early character. They included Marilyn Pond Bengston, Paula Stanger Stanley, and Shirley Stanger Berrett. Among helpful college friends were Norma Warenski Matheson and Joan Douglas Earl, whose husband George also was accommodating.

Among college buddies of Sterling's who were interviewed were two former Sigma Chi fraternity brothers at the University of Utah, Russell Fjeldsted and David Salisbury. Salisbury and Howard Edwards, another interviewee, were in the same law firm with Sterling in Salt Lake City and shared adventures with him, including horseback pack trips into the high and beautiful Uinta Mountains. Valuable information also came from two other Colton friends and adventurers, Glenn Potter and Frank Richards.

Sterling's first professional job after the Army was at Utah's oldest law firm, Van Cott, Bagley, Cornwall & McCarthy. Stephen Swindle at the firm discussed Sterling and supplied a photo copy of a useful out-of-print book called *The Van Cott Firm: First Century,* by S.N. Cornwall.

Close friends to both Sterling and Ellie who were cooperative included Angela (Bay) Buchanan, Ralph and Barbara Mecham, Ralph Hardy, Frank and Sally Johnson, Suzanne Garff Cooper, Steve and Martha West, Lynne Mella, Sue Huguely, Anca Croitoru, Fred Daniels, Abdul Walele, Marilyn Brinton, and Cole Durham.

Helpful friends who were also associates at Marriott International included Bill and Donna Marriott, Dick and Nancy Marriott, Ron and Debbie Harrison, Brad and Mary Jane Bryan, Francis (Butch) and Judy Cash, and Phyllis Hester. Other Marriott sources especially helpful included Fred Malek, Steve Bollenbach, Gary Wilson, Steve McKenna, Bill Kafes, Jim Durbin, Joan McGlockton, Michael Jarrard, Myron Walker, Ed Bednarz, Beth Schuster, Kristen McGregor, and Katie Dishman.

Associates in the Church of Jesus Christ of Latter-day Saints who worked with Sterling or Ellie in various capacities included Clayton Foulger and Brian Johnson. Accommodating former missionaries who served under Sterling and Ellie in the Canada Vancouver Mission included Tom Hawes, Troy Thurgood, Marianne (Muffy) Evans Cook, Annette Adams Esplin, Mary Jones, and David Williams.

Helpful associates who served under Sterling and Ellie as president and matron of the Washington D.C. Temple included Ed and Lois Scholz, and Chuck and Marlene Eckery.

Mary Limb, a computer master and good friend, came to my rescue day or night throughout the writing of the manuscript. Two sons, Justin Roderick and Eric Roderick, hosted me when doing book research in their respective regions, Washington, D.C. and Salt Lake City.

Finally, my bright, superbly capable wife, Yvonne, oversaw the production of this book and handled an assortment of family challenges, leaving me free to write it. To her and to those above and those unnamed who also assisted, my deepest thanks.

Introduction

Sterling and Ellie have completed each other perfectly for more than sixty years. That has made possible an enormous number of successes—as parents and grandparents, among friends and colleagues, in their professional and church activities, and including a broad array of individuals from all walks of life who are beneficiaries of their kindness.

Both grew up in families long on love but short on means. That led Sterling and Ellie into the workforce at young ages—he into the grain and hay fields and the animal herds on his family's ranch; she into a broad assortment of part-time jobs. Ellie's family did not own a car from the time she was seven; Sterling purchased his first car, a used one, after graduating from law school.

Years later, Sterling played a pivotal role, alongside CEO Bill Marriott, Jr., in positioning Marriott International to become the largest hotel company in the world. Sterling thought big. A company leader recalled a strategy meeting on Marriott's future. Sterling told the others, "We don't need to talk about any ideas unless they are billion-dollar ideas." Sterling was also widely regarded as the conscience of the company.

Sterling's efforts and the remarkable growth of Marriott produced affluence for his family. They have not flaunted their good fortune, living in the same home in Bethesda, Maryland, for a half-century. Sterling and Ellie stayed physically fit and adventuresome all their lives. They traveled the globe, on assignment from Marriott and on their own dime.

People who have known them invariably talk of Sterling's integrity and hard work—"I was born responsible," he has said—and Ellie's leadership ability and sunny disposition. Ellie's younger years were marked by a series of family tragedies, including the deaths of her father, grandfather, and three sisters, one of whom had two young sons and a newborn baby girl.

After the last funeral, Ellie returned to college questioning her faith. Her wise mother Annie did not try to talk Ellie out of her feelings; rather, she simply asked that before abandoning her beliefs, Ellie test them against other religions and beliefs.

Sterling's only regret with Ellie was that, concerned about financial stability, he waited five years to marry the girl he has often called "the best thing that ever happened to me." They met in the fall of 1949 and married in the summer of 1954. She was ready long before then, and openly dated other men, hoping to make Sterling jealous. To her chagrin he was utterly unmovable.

Sterling and Ellie's long courtship and post-marriage separation—compliments of the U.S. Army—produced a treasury of insightful and delightful correspondence, included in these pages.

Both of them descended from Mormon pioneer families, he in Utah's Uintah Basin and she in Idaho's Upper Snake River Valley. As a young boy, Sterling's namesake grandfather lifted him onto his lap and gave him a silver dollar, explaining they shared the same name. "Never do anything to dishonor it," counseled Sterling Driggs Colton. Today's Sterling Don Colton has fully honored that counsel.

Ellie loves literature, especially Shakespeare and the scriptures, and often cites passages from memory. An oft-quoted poem is by Omar Khayyam:

The Moving Finger writes; and, having writ,
Moves on: nor all thy Piety nor Wit
Shall lure it back to cancel half a line,
Nor all thy Tears wash out a Word of it.

Make today, this hour, and this minute count for something, Ellie suggests, for we cannot revisit it. She has lived her life that way, ever alert to the beautiful and the good—in people and in God's handiwork in nature. A field or backyard of blossoms, a lake set in an alpine forest, thrill Ellie. She has a gift for gathering flowers and harmonizing colors and shapes to create a work of beauty.

Sterling is as practical as Ellie is philosophical. He has been clear and comfortable in his beliefs and direction. On the first page of a thick three-ring binder summarizing his first forty years, Sterling wrote: "Principles that have guided my life. Love of: God our Eternal Father; our Savior Jesus Christ; our Family; our Neighbors; our Church; our Country; and Nature, Freedom, Freedom of Religion, Honesty, Integrity, Hard Work."

Ellie provides the fun. Her humor, sometimes irreverent, is a staple—including the advice to "never, under any circumstances, ask a woman if she is pregnant, unless you see a baby emerging from her at that moment."

The Coltons' best traits have been reflected consistently in the lives of their four children, seventeen grandchildren, and growing number of great-grandchildren. Their keys to successful parenting have included personal example and consistent communication and encouragement. "Remember who you are and what you can become" have often been the last words a child or grandchild has heard as he or she headed out the door.

Sterling and Ellie's handprints are seen to this day in the institutions they have served. Stanford Law School students benefit from a generous Colton gift, as do several other institutions of higher learning. The Coltons fund critical work of global importance in fighting for freedom of religion. They donate substantially to humanitarian programs, including those of The Church of Jesus Christ of Latter-day Saints. And privately they have rescued numerous individuals in need.

For all their other abilities, music has largely eluded them. A daughter-in-law observed that Sterling "sings vigorously and seldom varies his pitch. The result is a steady, low, Gregorian chant." Such critiques thankfully have not kept Sterling from leading and belting out song after song with others—whether on horseback in the high and beautiful Uintas, soaking in a rooftop hot tub in Cabo San Lucas, Mexico; or riding elephants in Thailand.

One wonders if Heaven could be any better than the life Sterling and Ellie have shared on earth. It is unthinkable that they will not be together for eternity to find out.

1

COLTON PIONEER HERITAGE

Sterling Don Colton one day would close a family circle at what is now Marriott International. His father Hugh started the circle in 1926 by proposing to a pal, J. Willard (Bill) Marriott, Sr., that they buy a franchise to sell root beer in the nation's capital.

Their nine-stool root beer stand would grow into the world's largest hotel company. Long before that, however, Hugh left Washington and returned to his roots in the Rocky Mountain West.

Those roots descended from eight prior generations of Coltons in America, starting with "Quartermaster" George Colton, born about 1620 in Warwick County, England.[1] He emigrated to the U.S. and settled in Massachusetts in about 1644.

Six generations later Sterling Don's paternal great-grandfather Philander Colton was born in 1811 in Clarence Hollow, New York. His family moved to Shelby, Michigan, where he met Polly Matilda Merrill. They were married in 1833; he was twenty-one, she sixteen.

Their lives and those of their posterity were changed forever after missionaries for The Church of Jesus Christ of Latter-day Saints taught and baptized them, Philander in 1838 and Polly a bit later. They relocated to Nauvoo, Illinois on the Mississippi River, the central gathering place for Mormons, who had been driven steadily westward by persecution and mob violence.

Church leader Joseph Smith and his brother Hyrum were martyred in June 1844, by a mob with painted faces, and the violence continued.

A year and a half later new church leader Brigham Young spearheaded the Mormon exodus from Nauvoo—a great saga in the opening of the American West. The first pioneers crossed the frozen Mississippi in February 1846, before 3,000 began the trek west.

Meanwhile hostilities between the United States and Mexico led the U.S. to declare war in May 1846. At the request of the Army, some 500 strong men among the pioneers joined a military march to Mexico. Brigham Young believed it was a chance for Mormons to prove their patriotism, and to earn hard cash to assist the pioneer effort.

One of the first to enlist was Private Philander Colton. The 2,000-mile trek, one of the longest military marches in history, was laced with unspeakable suffering from hunger, fatigue, inadequate clothing, stifling-hot days, and bitter-cold nights.

One recruit in Company B with Philander wrote that it was common "to eat head, heels, hide and tripe (stomach lining), and even the wool was pulled off from the sheep skins that had been used under the pack saddles and the thin hide roasted and eaten."[2]

Years later Philander told a grandchild of the intense suffering of these citizen-soldiers, who got so thirsty their tongues swelled and hung out of their mouths. The boy asked why he had endured all the hardships. "Without any hesitancy he replied, 'Because I know the Gospel is true.'"[3]

While Philander marched with the Battalion, Polly was left in a dugout in Iowa with five small children—reduced to four when their oldest child, twelve-year-old Charles, ran off to join his father in the Battalion. They were too far away to return him to his mother, and, besides, Charles had a beautiful voice and the troops enjoyed his singing at night around the campfires. Charles thus became the youngest member of the Mormon Battalion.

Following the march, Philander and Polly remained in Iowa more than two years before continuing on across the plains to Utah. It is believed they arrived in Utah by ox team and covered wagon in 1850, settling in Provo, about forty miles south of Salt Lake City. Philander built a five-room house and opened a brick yard.

On March 22, 1851, Polly delivered a son—apparently the first white male born in Provo. A man named Sterling Driggs was of great help to her and the children in Iowa, leading the Coltons to name their first son born in Utah after him. The son, in turn, became the father of Hugh Colton and grandfather of Sterling Don Colton.

Hugh's mother was Nancy Adeline Wilkins. Her parents were baptized into The Church of Jesus Christ of Latter-day Saints in New York. They also crossed the plains with other pioneers, arriving in Utah in 1850 or 1851 and settling in Provo. Nancy's childhood playmates included Sterling Driggs Colton.

As adolescents Sterling and Nancy courted and fell in love. On March 21, 1870 they were married by Daniel H. Wells, a member of the Church's First Presidency, in Salt Lake City in the Endowment House, a temporary temple for church members during construction of the Salt Lake Temple. They believed strongly in the Mormon doctrine that their marriage was for eternity, sealed by the holy priesthood, the authority to act for God. The ceremony was just one hour before Sterling turned nineteen; Nancy was a few months shy of seventeen.

Sterling Driggs was hard working and ambitious—traits passed along to his son Hugh and grandson Sterling Don. Among other livelihoods he was a freighter, collecting goods shipped along the Missouri River to drop-off points in Montana, and hauling them to Utah. He wanted his own cattle ranch, a dream that became feasible after he invested in a mining venture that paid off.

To establish a ranch, Sterling and Nancy moved thirty miles south of Provo to Mona, a scattering of small dwellings on Willow Creek. They acquired free land through the federal Homestead Act which offered up to 160 acres in exchange for improving the property. They built a crude log cabin and bought livestock.

Over the next six years Sterling and Nancy toiled indefatigably to wrest a living from the stubborn soil and cattle. Both were up and working six days a week—honoring the Sabbath on the seventh—from before sunup until after sundown—as Nancy reared four children, a daughter born in Provo and three sons in Mona. Later she often said those six backbreaking years turned her from a girl into an old woman.

Finally they tossed in the towel on Mona, when it was painfully clear their share of Willow Creek could not support a large herd of cattle. Sterling's eldest brother Charles Edwin had gone to the Uintah Basin in the far northeastern corner of Utah, and built a cabin there. He returned to report that it seemed ideal for raising cattle. The wild grass, he said, was as tall as a cow's belly.

In the spring of 1879 Sterling went to have a look for himself. Riding a mount and leading a pack horse, he traveled many days on the rugged trail to the Uintah Basin. ["Uintah" is the common spelling for the county and basin, while "Uinta" is the mountain range.] Although at first sight the basin looked barren, as Sterling rode down into the valley he found a number of small streams and rivers. There was abundant water and wild grass.

Six months later the Coltons relocated to the Basin, which is also known as Ashley Valley. How they accomplished the three-week journey is puzzling. They had four children ranging in age from a one-year-old boy to a seven-year-old girl, and records do not indicate they had outside help. Yet their caravan included two wagon loads of provisions, with four horses on each wagon; a total of about a dozen horses and from twenty-five to fifty cattle. They arrived November 13 or 15, 1879. It was snowing—a harbinger of the winter to come.

Trouble had been brewing for a year between Indians and a zealous Indian agent named Nathan Meeker on the White River Ute Reservation, in western Colorado near the Utah line, not far from the Uintah Basin. Meeker tried hard to turn the Utes from hunter-gatherers into farmers. He dismissed the value of their ponies, considered by Indians as their measure of wealth.

The last straw came in September—a month and a half before the Coltons arrived—when Meeker ordered that a race track be plowed under and the ground planted with some useful crop. In addition, he told the Indians they had too many horses and had to kill some.

Instead, Indians lassoed Meeker and dragged him behind a pony across the ground until nearly dead. They drove barrel staves through his body, staking him to the ground. Then they killed the ten other male employees and took the white women captive, including Meeker's wife and daughter.

The Meeker massacre ignited the Ute War.

Settlers scattered around Ashley Valley were advised to dismantle their cabins and haul the logs to the upper level of the valley—future site of Vernal—and reassemble them next to each other for a measure of protection. They created a three-sided fort of cabins.

Meanwhile an even more ominous threat loomed: a vicious, paralyzing winter that may have been the worst ever in Ashley Valley. It was called "the winter of the black bread," or simply "the hard winter."

The Coltons prepared well, and brought enough foodstuffs to see them through the winter. Others had little, including dozens of families arriving later than the Coltons. Many assumed they could purchase flour, sugar, and other staples locally. However, that spring's harvest had been poor, and there was little food to be had.

With no feed for sale, Sterling herded his horses and cattle to a river bottom, hoping they could fend for themselves until spring. The extreme snow soon blocked all entrances to the valley; no goods could get through. Sterling and Nancy refused to stand by and watch others starve. They shared what they had until they faced the balance of the winter on even terms with their neighbors.

Nancy "told a story that I believe to be true," said one of their children. "They brought flour in fifty-gallon barrels, and after they had shared their supply and the flour barrels became empty, my mother told how she would go there each morning and there would be more flour, and that continued for a two-week period prior to the time spring supplies came in."[4]

Early in 1880, as starvation loomed, five brave men vowed to break through to the outside world or die trying. Four horse-and-wagon teams left the valley, hoping to cross the northern mountains and reach Green River, Wyoming.

Time passed with no sign of the men. Then one day movement was seen at the top of the north rim. As the pioneers strained to see what it was, several other objects joined the first. The wagons were returning! Miraculously, no one had died and enough supplies were brought in to see the settlers through until spring.

In February Sterling set off to Brush Creek to check on his livestock.

What he found was disheartening. All his cattle were dead, many still standing up, supported by the crusted snow. The horses proved heartier; all were alive, though in poor condition.

As snow melted the Coltons planted vegetables and grain, harvesting about 3,000 bushels of grain. Sterling built a five-room log house in Maeser, outside Vernal on Ashley Creek. At last the future looked promising.

Uintah Basin had been part of Wasatch County. In February 1880 Uintah County was created. Among new officials, Sterling was appointed sheriff for five years. The job was high risk. Laws were few and disputes often were settled with guns, knives, or fists. It was the heyday of cowboy bandits in the area, including Butch Cassidy and his Wild Bunch.

Sterling was a good choice. He was scrupulously honest—sometimes to a ridiculous degree—as well as tough. Occasionally on the slightest provocation Sterling would haul off and slug someone.

His public duties sometimes endangered Nancy and their children, as when he would bring a prisoner to their cabin to stay the night before taking him on to jail in Vernal the next day.

Sterling was also fearless. One time he reached Vernal with an outlaw he had arrested for stealing cattle, and clapped him into jail. By next morning the man had broken out and was at a saloon, saying the "cowboy sheriff" would not take him again.

Sterling accepted the challenge. He mounted his horse and rode into Vernal. As he "stepped into the dimly lighted saloon from the daylight outside," wrote a historian, "his eyesight was temporarily affected and he saw a dim figure step away from the bar.

"At the same time he saw a flash and heard the roar of a six gun and his hat jumped on his head. Sterling drew and fired in one smooth motion and the man went down. The outlaw's bullet had hit the brim of the sheriff's hat. The outlaw was buried the next day."[5]

Sterling and Nancy Wilkins Colton had eight living children by 1900. Then in Nancy's forty-eighth year—eight years since her previous baby—they got a big surprise: Nancy was pregnant with their tenth child. Hugh Wilkins Colton, the only sibling given his mother's maiden name, was born January 11, 1901.

Nancy almost lost her life carrying Hugh to term, and was extra protective of him. For years his young age inoculated him from the harder toil on their ranch. His favorite duty was working with the horses. The larger ones pulled plows and other machinery, the smaller ones were ridden to round up cattle and sheep.

Hugh was a natural leader. In 1915 he graduated from the eighth grade in Vernal. He attended the next four years in Provo, at the high school division of Brigham Young Academy, which became Brigham Young University. He graduated in 1920 and that fall was called by LDS Church leaders as a missionary to the Eastern States Mission.

Also serving in that mission was J.W. (Bill) Marriott, Sr. They had a lot in common, including herding sheep for their families, and became good friends.

Sterling Don Colton's irrepressible mother was the ideal counterpart to his father Hugh. Margaret Baxter Maughan, known throughout her life as Marguerite, was born to an LDS family as prominent in Cache Valley—250 miles northwest of Vernal—as was the Colton family in the Uintah Basin.

Marguerite's great-grandfather was Peter Maughan, born to working-class parents in northern England, whose family joined the LDS Church in 1838. By then Peter was married to Ruth Harrison. Three years later tragedy struck when Ruth died after giving birth to their sixth child. That same year Peter and the children sailed for America in a shipload of other Mormons.

Arriving in the U.S., most convert immigrants continued on to Church headquarters in Nauvoo, Illinois. Peter, however, was impressed to first visit a former headquarters, Kirtland, Ohio. There he met Mary Ann Weston Davis, a young widow also recently arrived from England. In November 1841 they were married. She was a nurturing mother to his children, and bore an additional eight children with Peter.

One of the children born to Peter and the late Ruth Harrison Maughan was William H. Maughan, destined to play an important role alongside his father in settling Cache Valley. The large family crossed the plains by wagon, arriving in Salt Lake City in September 1850. They first settled in

Tooele, thirty miles southwest of the city, but had difficulty raising crops in the salty soil.

Six years later Brigham Young sent a scouting party led by Peter to Cache Valley, in northern Utah near Idaho and Wyoming. That was the start of settling the pastoral valley. The Maughans and their neighbors faced the same challenges the Coltons had faced in the Uintah Basin: deep snow and sometimes hostile Indians.

Peter Maughan died in April 1871, leaving his son William as the most prominent family member in Cache Valley. William was the civic and ecclesiastical leader in Wellsville, at the far south end of the valley. He was called to be Wellsville's first LDS bishop and served an amazing forty years, by some accounts the longest in church history.

At a time when polygamy was sanctioned by the Church, William had a substantial impact on the town's population—six wives and forty-eight children, divided exactly even between sons and daughters.

William's fourth child, born to his wife Barbara Morgan in October 1860, was William H. Maughan, Jr., a leading merchant in Wellsville and a member of its school board and city council, as well as the Utah State Legislature.

William H. married Margaret Wright Baxter in the Logan Temple on December 17, 1885. She was the daughter of Robert Baxter, a native of Ireland, and Jane Love Baxter, a native of Scotland, the country where they lived and joined the Church before emigrating to Utah. The sixth child of William H. and Margaret was Margaret Baxter Maughan, known as Marguerite, perhaps to distinguish her name from her mother's.

Marguerite was vivacious—beautiful, bright, creative, and with a lively sense of humor. She hated wasting time. When standing in line she sometimes charmingly crowded in front of others to shorten the wait. She was a student officer in her junior high school and in the high school section of Brigham Young College (BYC) in Logan. She also appeared in stage productions and was on BYC's debate team.

Marguerite taught school briefly in Wellsville, where she learned that not all families were as well off as hers. She began a program that gave each student an individual bottle of milk each school day.

In the spring of 1921, as Hugh was on his mission in New York, Marguerite graduated from BYC. That fall she enrolled at the University of Utah (the U) in Salt Lake City—the oldest state university west of the Missouri River. Marguerite continued to lead. She was elected vice president of Associated Women Students (AWS), serving for the 1924-25 school year. She was then elected president for the 1925-26 year.

In January 1923, weeks after returning home from his two-year mission, Hugh enrolled at the U. A friend lined him up on a blind date with Marguerite. For both it was love at first sight, and they commenced a romantic whirlwind courtship. Hugh graduated from the U in pre-law in the spring of 1925 and set his sights on law school in Washington, D.C. He wanted Marguerite by his side.

She could remain at the U another year, when she would be AWS president and earn her degree, or marry Hugh and head east. Marguerite chose Hugh and the East. They were married in the Salt Lake Temple on September 3, 1925, and immediately left for the nation's capital in a new Ford coupe. They rented an apartment and he landed a full-time job in a federal agency, working during the day and taking law classes at George Washington University in the evening.

Late the following year, Hugh wrote Bill back in Utah, proposing that they secure an A&W franchise to sell root beer in the nation's capital, which was uncomfortably hot in the summer. Bill responded positively. Hugh wrote him again in February 1927, saying "...this thing has impressed me for two years now...The more I think of it the firmer I become convinced that it is sound and will make money for someone that gets located right."[6]

Bill approached Roy Allen—the "A" of A&W—who lived in Salt Lake City after recently moving from California. Allen sold Bill and Hugh a franchise for Washington as well as for two cities in the general region, Baltimore, Maryland and Richmond, Virginia. Bill and Hugh each put up $3,000 to launch the business, Hugh borrowing his share from his older brother Don.

On May 20, 1927 they opened for business in a nine-stool root beer stand on 14th Street NW, selling ice-cold root beer at five cents a mug. It was an immediate hit. Two months later they opened a second stand in the heart of downtown government buildings, which also flourished.

Between the two openings, Bill went home to Utah, married Alice (Allie) Sheets, and returned to the capital. They stayed with the Coltons until finding their own apartment. While Marguerite taught school to help make ends meet, Allie worked in the business. She kept track of income and expenses in a simple notebook. At the end of each day—usually late into the night—she washed syrup off the nickels and dropped them into a bank night depository. Allie continued to help with the business daily until after the birth of Bill Jr. in 1932.

When the weather turned cool they added coffee and hot food to the two stands—including Mexican dishes cooked up by Allie, based on recipes she got from the chef at the nearby Mexican Embassy. Adding hot food led Bill to suggest they name their fledgling company "Hot Shoppes"—a fancy rendering of "Hot Shops."

During the first year of their fledgling business, from May 1927 to May 1928, Hugh and the Marriotts grossed $16,000. Business soared but Hugh did not. Money was tight and he was worn out by long hours at one of the Hot Shoppes, along with his full-time federal job, law school, and a new church calling as head of the local LDS congregation.

Alongside the weighty considerations in Washington was an alluring one beckoning from the Rockies: Hugh was homesick for the West, especially for his beloved horses. Bill tried to talk the Coltons out of leaving, confident Hot Shoppes would become a good business. In the spring of 1928 Hugh and Marguerite prayed hard about what to do. "My prayer was answered," said Hugh many years later. "The decision came loud and clear to come back home, to small-town Vernal."[7]

The two couples decided $5,000 was a fair price for Hugh's half of the business. Bill borrowed it from a local bank and gave the Coltons a check. Hugh finished law school around that time and prepared to head west.

Marguerite had her own reason for wanting to go home. When they left Washington she was pregnant with their first child, Sterling Don Colton. They could not know that one day in Washington he would pick up where they left off.

2

LIKE FATHER, LIKE SON

Sterling Don Colton was born in Vernal, Utah on April 28, 1929, a Sunday, at 4:30 a.m. It was good practice for the innumerable times throughout his life he would arise at that time and get to work.

Shortly before Sterling's birth Marguerite became ill, apparently with a cold or other minor ailment. Hugh, taking no chances, took her to the home of a local midwife, Nantie Richins, who lived at 350 West Main in Vernal. That is where their first child was born. A healthy eight and a half pounds, he was named Sterling in honor of Hugh's father, Sterling Driggs Colton, and Don in honor of Hugh's beloved older brother, Don B. Colton. Between the time he took Marguerite to the midwife's home and the birth of their baby, Hugh led a Boy Scout outing and almost missed the birth.

Hugh wrote his parents to say the baby "of course he is the finest child that was ever born. I am not as yet claiming that he is very good looking but they tell me that seldom real young babies are...it looks to me like he has his Grandmother's ears and they look mighty good to me. His eyes are now a very pretty blue, just like yours Daddy and he has black hair...I am so happy that the good Lord has blessed us so much during this experience."[1]

He added that "most of the excitement is over and all there is left is some tiredness. Marguerite and the baby are doing just as well as they possibly can...Marguerite does not look as though she has been sick at all. The color is in her cheeks just as it was before she took sick."

Four days later the birth was reported this way in the local newspaper: "Mr. and Mrs. Hugh Colton announce the arrival of a bonny baby boy weighing eight and one-half pounds. Mother and baby are doing nicely."[2]

That year 1929 is remembered for the crash of Wall Street. It began the Great Depression, which ended a profligate, devil-may-care period in U.S. history known as the Roaring Twenties. Other Americans born that year included the Rev. Martin Luther King, Jr., Jacqueline Kennedy Onassis, Arnold Palmer, and Grace Kelly.

Marguerite apparently took exception to Hugh's view that Sterling was not very good looking at first. She entered a photo of him in a Gerber Baby contest and won!

Six months after he was born, Hugh wrote to his father that Sterling "is now to the point where he recognizes us and occasionally shows us that he has a will of his own and will not be imposed upon, which pleases me a lot."

Hugh had graduated from George Washington Law School in the spring of 1928, shortly before he and Marguerite returned to Utah, and he was admitted to practice law in the District of Columbia and Utah. After returning to Vernal they rented a small home. Marguerite, who grew up in relative affluence in a home that often hosted important church and political figures, was a hit in Ashley Valley.

Clara Hall, a niece through Sterling's extended family, remembered the first time she saw Marguerite. Peeking through a cracked-open door, Hall said "I thought 'She has to be the prettiest person I have ever seen.' She had beautiful dark hair, and popping black eyes, and she was so tiny...And I fell in love with her that day."[3]

Marguerite became a leading activist in the valley, garnering support for such causes as a new library and new hospital. She was among a small cadre of influential women who came together twice a month, usually on Saturday afternoons, in an organization called the Beaux Arts Club. Its agenda included "promoting the intellectual and artistic development of members" and "participating in community activities."

Hugh had greased the political skids before returning home, and in November 1928 was elected Uintah County Attorney on the Republican ticket. The $930 annual salary covered only a small part of the Coltons' needs.

Hugh's legal fees were largely based on ability to pay, and many clients could pay little or nothing. But he never turned someone away for lack of funds. Hugh personified the country lawyer, in the mold of Clarence Darrow, Abraham Lincoln, and former Supreme Court Justice Robert Jackson.

Jackson described the role of the country lawyer in a classic essay:

> Such a man understands the structure of society and how its groups interlock and interact, because he lives in a community so small that he can keep it all in view...the circle of the man from the small city or town is the whole community and embraces persons of every outlook...this vanishing country lawyer...rarely declined service to worthy ones because of inability to pay...He never quit. He could think of motions for every purpose under the sun, and he made them all...the law to him was like a religion, and its practice was more than a means of support; it was a mission.[4]

Hugh's penchant for low or no fees was hard on other lawyers. Attorney Ken Anderton had difficulty starting his own practice because "people were used to the rates Hugh and his partner charged." An example was an elderly woman who had used Hugh in the past and now sought help from Anderton. "I spent about a half-hour with her. Then I sent her a bill for $15. She sent a check back for the $15, along with a note that said 'that's quite a bit of money for the time I spent with you.'"[5]

In 1923, five years before the Coltons returned to Ashley Valley, the region's economy and people were hurting. "Uintah Basin people were depressed," said a local history book. "Many had left the county and more were ready to leave. This land of promise had failed to be what advance publicity had represented..."[6]

Streams with abundant water flowed past them, but without adequate infrastructure not enough was captured and stored to slake a thirsty high-desert land. Unpaved roads and no railroad system meant there was no ready market for what they produced. "Their faith and morale were low, prospects for the future were dim, they would have to leave," summarized the history.

The Uintah Basin's economy was challenging in the best of times. It was narrowly based, resting primarily on farming, ranching, and the extraction of oil and gas.

As a result the Basin experienced frequent economic boom and bust cycles, especially when world oil prices were low.

In that year, 1923, some enterprising citizens launched an effort to turn the valley's fortunes around. They formed an organization called the Uintah Basin Industrial Convention (U.B.I.C.), a cross between a booster club and a chamber of commerce. About 3,500 citizens attended the first convention in 1923, seeking practical advice and inspiration to boost the economy and their morale.

The U.B.I.C. became an annual event. Six years after it was formed, State Senator Ray Dillman resigned as president and Hugh was unanimously elected to succeed him. The *Vernal Express* called Hugh "a young man, but he has had much public experience and will undoubtedly render good service."[7]

Hugh got to work immediately and lined up a blue-ribbon group of industry and political leaders to come to the Basin and suggest approaches to solve some of the area's challenges.

Utah was one of the hardest-hit states during the Depression and the Uintah Basin was one of Utah's hardest-hit regions. Utah's unemployment rate in 1933 was 35.8 percent, fourth highest in the nation. By that spring 32 percent of Utahns received all or part of their basic necessities, including food, clothing, and shelter, from government relief agencies.

"The first assistance given to the public in Uintah County," wrote a historian, "was administered by a committee" chaired by Hugh.[8] Local assistance continued until 1933 when the first relief program of the federal New Deal reached the Basin. It was the Federal Emergency Relief Administration (FERA) which assisted the unemployed and their families. Able-bodied adults were expected to work for the financial aid. FERA distributed $90,000 in Uintah County in 1934.

Meanwhile Marguerite was busy rearing a lively brood of children while volunteering service in church and community. She was called as a board member of the area Primary, the LDS Church's children's organization. If that wasn't enough, she also supplemented the family income as a substitute teacher in Vernal schools, as she had done in Washington.

The Coltons bought their first home in 1930 at 1st North 6th West in Vernal. Two years after Sterling's birth came his only sister, Nancy Carol, born February 7, 1931, who grew to be strikingly attractive. Two years after Nancy came a brother, Hugh Maughan, on April 20, 1933. Completing the family was John Phillip (Phil) Colton, a delightful, chubby-cheeked boy, entering the world on January 3, 1937.

In 1936 the Coltons moved to another house on 2nd West, selling the first to a recently widowed school teacher, Stella Harris Oaks. A son, Dallin H. Oaks, would become president of Brigham Young University and later a member of the LDS Church's Quorum of the Twelve Apostles.

The Coltons' newly purchased three-bedroom house was long and narrow, with a porch across the front outlined by cobblestones embedded in cement. The door inside the porch led to a living room which included a player piano, a couch, and several chairs. A floor heater in the dining room provided most of the house's heat. It had just one bathroom, with a cast-iron tub on four legs. The three boys frequently complained that Nancy took her time *and* theirs in the bathroom.

Nancy's room had a small floor heater. The boys' bedroom had a set of bunk beds, a single bed with a metal headboard, and a metal chest of drawers. But no heater. Sterling, Maughan, and Phil jostled each winter evening for the right to have the family dog, an Irish Setter named Boots, sleep on their bed for warmth.

A prominent relative who impacted their lives was Hugh's brother Don B. Colton, a quarter-century older than Hugh, and an important figure in church and in government. Don was an LDS stake president in Vernal—lay leader over six to ten congregations—when he was elected to the U.S. House of Representatives at virtually the same time Hugh left on his mission in 1920.

Don, married to Grace Stringham, served six two-year terms in Washington, ending in 1933. While Hugh was in the Eastern States Mission, headquartered in New York, Don visited New York City and preached powerful sermons there. Hugh periodically took the train to Washington to visit Don and Grace and their family, no doubt influencing Hugh's later decision to return to the capital for law school.

The Depression overshadowed the 1932 election. Incumbent President Herbert Hoover's promises to heal the economy had failed, and he led Republicans to massive losses at the polls. New York Governor Franklin D. Roosevelt swamped Hoover, winning forty-two states while Hoover won six. Democrats also picked up twelve U.S. Senate seats and a whopping ninety-seven House seats. One of the House seats was Don's.

After he was defeated for a seventh term, Don was called by church leaders as president of the Eastern States Mission from 1933 to 1937. He then moved to Salt Lake City and resumed practicing law.

Don's last calling for the Church was as president of its Mission Home in Salt Lake, where new missionaries were taught and oriented before departing for their respective fields of labor. In about 1936, Don and Grace invited Hugh, Marguerite and their children to spend Christmas at the mission home. Don and Grace's young daughter was with them, but the home was otherwise deserted.

The "home" actually was three separate homes in a row, facing east on State Street between North and South Temple. "It was a wonderful place to explore," recalled Sterling. "The large bedrooms were empty and the row upon row of made-up beds made great trampolines." They were allowed to sleep wherever they wanted; Sterling chose a large second-floor sleeping porch with an open view of the Salt Lake Temple.[9]

From a young age Sterling was spiritually sensitive. He looked back on this Christmas Eve as the first building block in his testimony:

> I will never forget my feelings as I looked across the pristine snow to the temple spires reaching to the star-filled heavens. It was the first spiritual experience I had. I knew this was the Lord's house and I resolved then that I wanted to live so that some day I would be able to go there.

Sterling learned to pray at his mother's knee. They had family prayers and blessed the food before every meal. Usually his spiritual promptings came through feelings of confirmation and assurance that the decisions he had made were correct.

One experience stood out. When Sterling was eight or nine, he and another boy, Glen Morrison, were helping to move cattle on Diamond Mountain, near Vernal. Leading the roundup was a colorful cowboy named Marcus Jensen. They stopped at a spring for a drink of water. As they remounted, Marcus's spur caught beneath his horse's tail. The mount reared back, throwing him to the ground on a rock, breaking his pelvis.

"We were just two little boys up there," said Sterling, "and didn't know where we were. We knelt down and asked Heavenly Father what we should do. A voice came to me, just as clear as could be. It said 'Ride north.' I left Glen with Marcus, who was on the ground and couldn't move, and rode north through the sagebrush.

"After I had ridden for some time, all of a sudden I saw a bright green pickup truck coming through the sagebrush. I told the driver what had happened. He drove to where Marcus was, loaded him in the truck, and took him down to the hospital."

Another indelible experience was with his namesake grandfather, Sterling Driggs Colton. Sitting in a chair on his front porch, he lifted Sterling Don onto his lap and gave him a silver dollar.

"'Do you know why I'm giving it to you?'" he asked. When I didn't, he said it was because we shared the same name: 'It's a good name. Never do anything to dishonor it.' His statement had a great effect on me. I have always tried to not do anything to dishonor his name." His storied grandfather was widely known as an honest man, noted Sterling. "I wanted to have the same reputation."

Sterling was a typical boy in other ways. Many families in Vernal had vegetable gardens watered by irrigation ditches. Sterling and his friends would follow ditches to the canals that were the source of the water. There they often found frogs, toads, snakes, and turtles, while watching older boys catch trout in the canal.

Sterling started kindergarten in September 1934 at Central Elementary School. He especially liked fire-escape drills, sliding down a large steel pipe from the second floor to the ground. His teacher was Bea Stringham, his Aunt Grace's unmarried sister. "She was outstanding," he wrote later, "and instilled in me at that early age a love for learning."

For his eighth birthday on April 28, 1937, Sterling's parents gave him an Indian pony that had been captured wild in the badlands south of Vernal. Blue in appearance, they named him Blue Cone. He had been broken to ride and was gentle with children; however, if an adult tried to ride him, Blue would buck as if in a rodeo. In the summer, Blue was kept in a pasture near the Vernal house and the children often rode him.

That started Sterling's love of horses, mirroring that of his father's. While Sterling became a good horseman, no family member or friend had the touch with horses that Hugh had. Long before actor Robert Redford popularized the term in the movie of the same name, Hugh was a "horse whisperer" with a sixth sense in understanding and working with horses.

In preparation for baptism at age eight, Sterling's teacher in Primary had her class memorize the Thirteen Articles of Faith, a succinct summary of core LDS beliefs. Sister Smith's incentive for those who could recite all thirteen was to give him or her a live rabbit. Sterling memorized the articles well before his eighth birthday and got his rabbit.

"This resulted in my having to build a cage and then feed the rabbit daily," said Sterling. It was a good lesson in responsibility, though one day the rabbit escaped from the pen and neighborhood dogs killed it.

On May 1, 1937, a Saturday, Sterling donned all-white clothing and was baptized by full immersion by a church elder named Russell Grey. The font, in the basement of the Uintah Stake Tabernacle, was the only one in Ashley Valley. "It had a large cover that had to be lifted off," Sterling recalled. "I can still remember the musty smell." In church services the following day, his father placed hands on Sterling's head, confirming him a member of the Church and bestowing on him the gift of the Holy Ghost.

The stately tabernacle had a large open room with a balcony on three sides. Sterling remembered that the balcony was a favorite seating place for boys who shot spit wads through straws at bald heads of men seated below. Decades later the tabernacle was renovated and rededicated as a small temple, the Church's holiest type of edifice, considered the House of the Lord.

Lack of funds for public services such as schools was noticed by young Sterling as early as grade school. He and other third- and fourth-graders met in an old brick building located south of Central

Elementary. "The heating and cooling system was erratic," he recalled. "There was a crack in one of the blackboards, with a vine growing in it."

Outmoded facilities did not deter Sterling's love of learning. There were two fifth-grade classes and Sterling hoped to be assigned to the one where most of the popular boys were going. Instead he was assigned to the other class, taught by Arthur Manwaring, from whom he learned a lot and was inspired to learn a lot more.

Sterling loved to read and set his sights on reading all the books in the Vernal City Library, a modest collection in a small room of a city building. Eventually, as Sterling aced nearly all his school classes, the rumor circulated that he had read them all. "Actually I fell far short of that goal," said Sterling, "but I did do a lot of reading."

At age eleven, Sterling spent a week with an aunt and uncle thinning sugar beets at their farm in Mendon, Utah. Although uncertain at that age what he wanted to pursue as a future career, he was *definitely* able to rule out sugar beet farming.

Hugh Colton's heart was not in a courthouse but rather on the farm and ranch in Maeser that had long been in the family. His parents, Sterling and Nancy Colton, herded cattle into the Uintah Basin and homesteaded there starting a half-century before. Apparently in the early 1900s they had switched to sheep, which offered two cash sources, wool and meat. Sterling sold part of the farm and its sheep to Hugh for around $2,000 on easy terms. In addition, Don leased another 300 acres of irrigated farm and pasture land to Hugh.

Hugh hired Wallace Caldwell to run the operation. He was a year younger than Hugh and was married to Hugh's niece, Nancy Mar Colton Caldwell. Hugh offered Wallace a modest salary and a small house on the property. Assisting Wallace on the farm were his own two sons and the Colton boys, led by Sterling as the oldest.

Although he started with sheep, Hugh's dream was to develop a fine cattle ranch, and he began to buy cattle systematically. He bought registered Domino Hereford bulls that did much to improve Uintah

Basin cattle bloodlines.

Each summer Hugh hired cowboys who drove the Colton horses and cattle onto Diamond Mountain, where they had a permit from Ashley National Forest to feed on the thousands of acres of brush and mountain grasses. It took several days to move the livestock about twenty miles. A cow herder was hired to spend the summer on Diamond Mountain, tending what grew to be about a thousand head of cattle, half of them owned by the Coltons.

Farm work in Vernal was rugged—freezing in winter, scorching in summer—and routinely backbreaking. The heaviest work was accomplished with draft horses that pulled the array of equipment used to plant, grow, and harvest crops.

Alfalfa hay was the principal crop on the Colton farm, along with wild grass hay. To plant, the land would be plowed, harrowed—broken up to level it, break up clods, and root out weeds—then seeded and irrigated. At harvest time the alfalfa would be cut with a two-horse mower with a five-foot cutter blade, then raked into ten-foot piles. Men with pitchforks turned them into five-foot piles which were left to dry for several days.

Then the men forked it onto horse-drawn wagons, where others on top would tromp down the hay. The horse would pull the wagon into the hay yard to a stack of hay that sometimes would be twenty-five feet high and ninety feet long. Sterling often was on top of this big stack of hay, given the particularly challenging and sometimes dangerous job of shaping the final stack.

Sterling worked with a pitchfork beneath a wicked-looking piece of equipment called a Jackson fork. The Jackson fork had four sharp tines and was connected to an A-frame by a rope and pulley. When lowered into a wagon stack it could pick up several hundred pounds of hay. A horse supplied the power to move the hay over the stack; then it was released, the hay cascaded down, and the fork bobbed free.

"There were numerous ways the Jackson fork could stab the people working with it," said one writer. "...the greatest danger awaited the man up on the haystack." When it was tripped to dump the hay, "the empty fork jumped into the air and danced wildly about...an unwary or slow-reacting stacker trying to maneuver on the uneven footing of a haystack could find himself entangled with the flashing steel tines."[10]

The stacker's job was not enviable even without the Jackson fork. "It was hot and dirty," recalled Sterling. "The hay heated as it dried and was very dusty. We worked in the hot sun and did not use sun screen. My nose would peel from the beginning to the end of summer. My legs were often raw from scratching."

Caldwell was a good psychologist. "When he sensed me tiring," said Sterling, "he often bragged on my skills, making me want to do it right."

3

Man of the House at Twelve

As the Coltons settled into their life in peaceful Ashley Valley, the world overseas was becoming less peaceful by the day. Tyrants were on the march.

In Europe Adolf Hitler, head of the Nazi Party, published *Mein Kampf* (My Struggle), a blueprint for seizing power and ridding Germany of what Hitler defined as "undesirables." In the East, Japan brutally invaded China in 1931, setting up a Japanese state and killing tens of thousands of civilians.

World War II began in Europe in 1939 when Germany invaded Poland. There had been a long run-up to war. The Soviet Union under Communist dictator Joseph Stalin had signed a non-aggression pact with Hitler, secretly calling for the two giants to carve up and absorb a number of east European countries.

President Franklin D. Roosevelt, prodded by Britain's Winston Churchill, tried to aid England in every way short of a formal military alliance. Most Americans, with memories of World War I still fresh, opposed entering the conflict. One result of America's isolation was a nation unprepared for war. In 1939 the regular army consisted of 188,000 soldiers—seventeenth largest in the world, after tiny Portugal. The U.S. also had 199,000 in the National Guard and 120,000 in the Reserve Corps.

Then as now, members of the National Guard answer to their respective state governments, who call upon them to assist with local emergencies. When mobilized for war they answer to Washington.

Some citizens, including Hugh Colton, saw the inevitability of war and took it upon themselves to prepare for it. Hugh had tried to enlist in World War I but was too young. Now, explained his son Sterling, "he felt a genuine duty to serve his country when it was threatened again."

In the late 1930s the War Department in Washington increased National Guard forces across the country. By 1939 the Uintah Basin was the only large region in Utah without a National Guard unit. Hugh led local leaders in petitioning for one, organizing an effort that resulted in ninety-two men completing applications to join the Guard. The Utah Legislature in March appropriated funds to establish an engineering unit in Vernal, and Brigadier General W.G. Williams traveled there, meeting with Hugh and other leaders.

About five weeks after Williams' visit, scores of men were sworn into the new Guard unit, and three officer candidates were chosen by secret ballot of all enlistees.

"Those mustered into the newly organized corps," reported the *Vernal Express*, "included Hugh W. Colton, temporary captain."[1] Frank Wright was elected temporary first lieutenant and T.R. Johnson temporary second lieutenant. Hugh was not an engineer but he was a natural leader of men.

Vernal was organized as Company B of the First Battalion of the 115th Combat Engineers Regiment. Members overall were free to continue their regular civilian pursuits, while participating in paid weekly drills over a forty-eight-week period and a two-week summer encampment. By June 1940 Hugh had completed requirements for a commission, and the regular Army officially awarded him the rank of first lieutenant.

The Utah National Guard was inducted into federal service on March 3, 1941. The average guardsman was twenty years old, single, and attending school. Hugh was forty, married with four children, and had a legal practice and a ranch to run. As an officer it was likely he would have better housing and other privileges in the U.S., making it possible for his family to follow him, which they did. Local citizens held a series of farewell socials and Hugh was released from the LDS Uintah Stake Presidency.

Company B left Salt Lake City on March 16, 1941, for Camp San Luis Obispo in California for a year of training. It had been the home of the California National Guard before it was taken over in 1940 by the U.S. War Department. It was a tent city for 19,000 enlisted personnel, with room for another 1,500 officers who were housed according to rank. The camp was still being enlarged; when it rained it became a sea of mud.

Hugh was billeted four miles away in the town of San Luis Obispo. Marguerite drove the rest of the family to California, renting a house in Arroyo Grande, a small community about thirty miles south of the military camp. Their yard had several large oak trees that Sterling loved to climb. Occasionally they had Sunday dinner with Hugh in the officers' mess on base.

The three older children, Sterling, Nancy, and Maughan, attended school in Arroyo Grande, with Sterling completing sixth grade. After the school year Marguerite and the children moved to an apartment in San Luis Obispo to be closer to Hugh. The apartment was across the street from a large hill, which the children found ideal for flying kites.

Hugh was in combat engineer training at Ft. Belvoir, Virginia and Marguerite and the children were in Sunday sacrament meeting in California on December 7, 1941, when Japan attacked Pearl Harbor. Many of the young men in the San Luis Obispo congregation were stationed at the nearby base. When a local church leader announced the attack, many of the men in the congregation left swiftly to return to duty.

"We certainly wish we could bring our daddy and be back in Vernal tomorrow," wrote Marguerite to a friend. "But we are all mighty proud of him, in his serving our country to free it of our terrible foes. All we can do is hope and pray everything will come out ok."[2]

Hugh's leadership ability was evident; he returned from Ft. Belvoir to San Luis Obispo as adjutant—staff assistant—to the commanding officer of the 115th Combat Engineers Regiment. He was then sent to

Los Angeles, tasked with helping to secure potential coastal targets of the Japanese. Hugh directed troops who sandbagged aircraft factories and other defense facilities in the Los Angeles area.

The critical importance of their work was underscored on February 23, 1941 when a Japanese submarine attacked the U.S. mainland—the first Axis ship to do so. The submarine, the I-17, surfaced a few hundred yards off Pismo Beach, within the Ellwood Oil Field west of Santa Barbara, and fired seventeen shells at the aviation fuel storage tanks on a bluff behind the beach. Residents along the West Coast feared an invasion was at hand, but it proved to be an isolated incident.

In May 1941 Hugh was officially promoted to captain. (Earlier he had been a temporary captain, elected by his peers in Vernal.)

Marguerite and the children followed Hugh to Los Angeles, renting an apartment.

Sterling turned twelve that year and Hugh had the privilege of ordaining him a deacon—the first of three offices in the LDS Church's Aaronic Priesthood.

In February 1942 Hugh was assigned to the 133rd Engineer Combat Regiment, stationed at Fort Lewis, Washington. This time Hugh and Marguerite decided it was time for Marguerite and the children to return to Vernal. The children finished the school year in Los Angeles and went home. With his father gone, Sterling found himself, at age twelve, the man of the Colton household.

While visiting his Maughan grandparents in Wellsville, Utah that year, twelve-year-old Sterling himself suffered bloodshed. He was chasing a cousin, Margaret Rae Sorenson, on his grandparents' front porch, when she slammed the front door closed. Raising his right arm to stop his momentum, Sterling smashed his arm through the plate glass door. Blood shot from his wrist like a fountain; he had severed the blood vessels and tendons in his right wrist.

Fortunately a Dr. Christiansen who lived two doors from the Maughans was home and they rushed there. He bandaged the wound and stopped the bleeding, then took Sterling to the hospital in Logan, about ten miles away. The injury was about as bad as it could be; there was nerve damage and the severed tendons had retreated up the arm. Searching for tendons, the medical staff wheeled a large anatomy book into the operating room and flipped through its pages as a guide.

Sterling suffered permanent nerve damage to his right index finger and right thumb, hindering such functions as his ability to write and handle balls and rackets in sports. Several years later a noted surgeon, Dr. Jack Clark, operated on Sterling's wrist at the U.S. Army Hospital in Salt Lake City, restoring some but not all of its function.

In 1943, Sterling began his freshman year at Uintah High School in Vernal. Judging from the school yearbook, the *Uintahn*, the following spring he had a lot of friends. Nearly every page is filled with signatures, many addressed to "Sonny," Sterling's nickname until college. Typical was this note from a girl named Dorothy: "Dear Sonny, I have enjoyed going to school with you and you are the sweetest boy I have ever seen. I'm sure you will succeed in life."

A page called "Scrapbook" is filled with random photos including one with Sterling's parents standing on the school steps with Principal Harold Lundell. Hugh, wearing his Army dress uniform, was on fifteen days of furlough from Fort Lewis, visiting home to wrap up personal affairs before heading off to the eastern U.S. and to war in Europe.

Hugh's first foray to Fort Lewis had been for a training session in the summer of 1940. Another soldier there at the time was Lt. Colonel Dwight Eisenhower, who would be promoted to full colonel early in 1941. Eisenhower was named chief of staff in the IX Corps, responsible for defense of the entire Pacific Coast. Later, of course, as a five-star General of the Army, he commanded D-Day, the Allied assault on German-occupied Europe.

Hugh likewise had risen rapidly in the ranks. In June 1942 he was promoted to Major and, by the end of that year, to Lt. Colonel.

Uintahn editors dedicated the 1944 yearbook this way:

> In every theater of war our boys are gallantly fighting for a cause that is right. They are fighting on battle fields while we here at home are doing all we can to bring an early victory...We are doing

essential war work, learning first aid, gathering scrap, and, above all, putting every extra cent into war bonds and stamps. Uintah sponsored many war bond drives throughout the year, and every student contributed generously...The fate of democracy rests on the outcome of this crisis. So to you, the brave boys of our fighting forces, do we dedicate this 1944 edition of the *Uintahn*.

Combat engineers like Hugh cleared the path for friendly forces to advance and blocked the path of the enemy. During World War II in Europe, arguably the most important role of combat engineers was to build bridges across the continent's numerous rivers and streams. The waterways were natural defenses the Nazis counted on to halt Allied advances or, at worst, to slow them down until superior German firepower could be brought to bear on the engineers themselves and the troops and armor massed behind them.

Combat engineers also built roads and buildings; devised electric and other power supplies; used explosives for construction and demolition projects; and cleared minefields using specialized vehicles. Other typical tasks included breaching and constructing trenches, tank traps and other fortifications, and constructing bunkers.

Years later General Norman Schwarzkopf, who in 1990-91 led Allied forces in Desert Storm—the first war with Iraq after it attacked and occupied Kuwait—said Army combat engineers are "traditionally considered the elite by everyone."[3]

In addition to specialized training, combat engineers have the same basic training as infantry troops, and are called upon as necessary to enter the line as infantry.

In March 1943, thirteen months after Hugh reported to Fort Lewis, the 1104th Engineer Combat Group was formed. On April 1 Hugh organized the 247th Engineer Combat Battalion, attached to the 1104th, and was appointed its commanding officer. Under his leadership the 247th would make outstanding contributions to winning the war in Europe. Two other combat battalions were also activated and attached to the 1104th, along with six general engineer service companies.

On May 20 Hugh was reassigned to the 1104th and appointed its Executive Officer, one step below Commanding Officer.

After his two-week furlough back home, on December 9, 1943 Hugh and other members of the 1104th boarded a train at Fort Lewis for a five-day trip to New York. A week later Hugh wrote to his sister Zora and her husband, saying, in part, "I can't tell you where I am but will do so as soon as possible." He added: "Received a letter from Marguerite today. They are all well. May the good Lord keep them that way. That is my one worry."[4]

On January 7, 1943, Hugh and 8,000 other soldiers boarded the *SS Mauretania*, a storied British troop ship more than two football fields long, bound for England. It docked at Liverpool on January 19. More than another year of training was still ahead before D-Day, when Allied forces would land in France to begin liberating western Europe.

During the next few months Hugh wrote letters home. At least two were to Sterling. In February Hugh encouraged Sterling to "continue your straight A record. Remember your school work must be your first consideration. Your basketball will do you much good too." He asked Sterling to write and tell him "about all the horses and cattle at the ranch."[5]

Exactly one month later he sent Sterling a second hand-written letter, tightly spaced on four pages. "Was glad to hear you received the 'superiors' you did but please don't be satisfied unless they are all superiors," wrote Hugh. "...bring your marks back UP this next period, huh? I have been so very proud to tell my friends about your 'straight A superiors and on the basketball team'...Don't let me down."[6]

Again Hugh asked Sterling how the horses and cows were doing. "When is Zar going to foal. Is Sunshine going to have a colt. Is Miss Dean—tell me about all of them—cows too. How much hay is left... How is Sun Dance and Highbrow—will they make good saddle horses for us? I hope so. We'll have some good ones so when I return we will have some real horses to ride together." Hugh added that Maughan, Phil, Marguerite, and Nancy could ride with them.

"Give my best love to your sweet Mother, sister and brothers. I love you all more than you'll ever know. Good night my Dear Son, 'carry on' until Dad returns. We will make up for lost time when I return, which I will do as soon as I can finish up a little fighting I must do over here."

Hugh would distinguish himself as a true war hero, notably for his courage under fire when building bridges that enabled Allied forces to pursue the Nazis all across Europe and into Germany. Operation Overlord—D-Day—was June 6, 1944. It was the largest single-day amphibious invasion of all time. Over twenty-four hours more than 5,000 ships disgorged 160,000 troops on the shores of Normandy, France. Not everything went as planned. Americans landed at two beaches, Omaha and Utah. Heavy winds pushed infantry and engineer units off course, with only five of the sixteen engineer teams arriving at their assigned locations. The heaviest casualties were taken by the infantry, tanks and engineers in the first landings.

Engineers cleared exits and marked heavily-mined beaches—tasks made difficult after the loss of much of their equipment. Nonetheless D-Day engineers succeeded in clearing six gaps, while suffering casualties of more than 40 percent.

Some forward elements of Hugh's 1104th Engineer Combat Group landed on D plus one, one day after Allied troops first landed at Normandy. On D plus five, five days after the original landing, Lt. Colonel Colton and several other leaders of the 1104th went ashore to arrange landing and operations for the troops and heavy equipment that continued to arrive for many weeks. Hugh was awarded the Bronze Star for actions there.

On July 7, under unrelenting German bombardment, the 1104th constructed four bridges over the strategic Vire River. Three days later the Group crossed the Vire and bivouacked in a farmer's field. That night the Germans counter-attacked in force, moving less than a mile from the Group's encampment and blasting flak-holes in its tents before being repulsed by Allied cavalry and armored divisions.

An AP correspondent called the crossing of the Vire "perhaps the best and most heroic job by American combat engineers in France."[7] He noted they were under the overall supervision of Lt. Col. Hugh W. Colton.

For his leadership in bridging the Vire, the Army awarded Hugh the Silver Star, the military's third-highest medal, for "gallantry in action against the enemy..." His engineers built a road on the far shore of the Vire, calling it "Rue de Colton" in honor of their chief.

Periodically Hugh and his men set aside rakes and picked up rifles. One instance was at the Wurm River near Aachen, Germany. The 1104th's units constructed five bridges across the thirty-foot-wide, slow-moving stream. There, the Group established its first command post on German soil. That night, working in a complete blackout under highly accurate incoming fire, the Group's 247th Engineers installed a bridge at Rimburg Castle. Military traffic began crossing the bridge within hours of its completion.

German shelling subsequently severed the bridge twice but engineers repaired it each time. With stiffening resistance, Hugh led elements of the 1104th into the line as infantry to contain German bunkers. Supported by a platoon of tanks, Hugh's forces more than held their own during the three-day assault, advancing more than two and a half miles and capturing some 300 prisoners.

Hugh's leadership and bravery came to the attention of Allied Commander Dwight Eisenhower. On November 5 General Eisenhower, in a written order from headquarters, promoted Hugh to full Colonel. Stephen Ambrose, one of the most respected author/historians on World War II, calls battlefield promotions such as Hugh's "the highest honor a soldier can receive."[8]

The last major natural obstacle between the Allies and Germany was the Rhine River. Beyond it lay the Ruhr Valley, a score of grimy cities whose tall smokestacks marked it as the enemy's industrial heartland. Crossing the Rhine had always been near the top of the Allies' goals. To reach the Rhine, however, the Allies first had to cross other rivers, especially the Roer, which was as wide as two football fields laid end to end.

In November and the first half of December 1944 the 1104th planned meticulously for crossing the Roer. Planning came to an abrupt halt, however, on December 16 when Hitler unleashed a last desperate attempt to turn the tide of the war. Germany launched a major offensive through the densely forested Ardennes region in Belgium, France, and Luxembourg. History would call it the Battle of the Bulge.

The surprise attack caught the Allies completely off guard. U.S. forces bore the brunt of the assault, suffering their highest casualties for any campaign of the war. Soldiers on every side of the battle suffered terribly from frigid weather, most of them sheltered no better than in frozen foxholes.

Inevitably, with more troops and weapons, and Allied planes controlling the skies when clouds lifted, Hitler's gamble was doomed. It ended on January 25 and was Germany's last major attempt to win World War II.

The 1104th resumed planning the crossing of the Roer. Three footbridges and three vehicular bridges would be laid early on, with others to follow. Footbridge components had previously been carried close to the water's edge under cover of darkness. The river was commanded on both sides by high ground. Engineers were fired upon by rifles, machine guns, and mortars as they assembled bridge components.

A fragment from a German shell tore into Hugh's jaw and exited through the opposite cheek. With so much at stake, he refused to leave to take care of a very serious wound. A medic stanched the blood the best he could and tied a wrap around Hugh's face as he continued to direct the bridging throughout that night and the next day.

Allied planes again weighed in. Artillery observation aircraft—as many as eleven at a time—crisscrossed the area, looking for sources of enemy fire, muzzle flashes from artillery or mortars. When spotted, Allied artillery zeroed in on enemy guns. The engineers' work nonetheless was perilous: thirteen officers and enlisted men with the 1104th were killed in the complex bridging operation, and another 116 were wounded, for 129 casualties.

Other engineer groups on other parts of the Roer also suffered casualties, but they were heaviest among Hugh's troops. Other officers said casualties in the 1104th could have been much higher without Hugh's bravery.

"Although wounded in the face by artillery fire early in the operation," wrote a superior officer, "Colonel Colton remained at the bridge sites almost constantly throughout the entire engineer phase of the crossing. Undoubtedly the crossing would not have been as successful as it was and casualties would have been heavier had it not been for Colonel Colton's personal supervision and presence at all phases of the crossing."[9]

His heroism on the Roer earned Hugh a Purple Heart for his wounds, and a second Silver Star—technically an Oak-Leaf Cluster—to wear alongside his first Silver Star. The citation noted he had supervised construction of seven bridges across the river, "contributing immeasurably to the advance of an infantry and an armored division. Colonel Colton's leadership and courage were an inspiration to the men under his command and reflect great credit upon himself and the Military Service."

Allied troops poured across the Roer and headed for the Rhine—the last major obstacle on the Western Front between the Allies and the heart of Germany.

Hugh's reputation spread, and commanders in other sectors began asking for him. In preparation for crossing the Rhine, British Field Marshal Bernard Montgomery built up an enormous arsenal and army group of five divisions—120,000 men. Montgomery's XVI Engineering Corps was commanded by Colonel John Wheeler. He tapped Colonel Colton on an urgent basis to train his rank-and-file engineers, who had no assault experience.

Hugh was at their side at the river bank for the multiple crossings necessary to transport the entire XVI Corps over the Rhine. The crossing cost the Corps 38 men killed, 426 wounded, and 3 missing. The figures were far lower than expected. The lead engineer of the XIX Corps wrote, "The success of the operation was materially improved by the numerous detailed decisions made by Colonel Colton on the river itself."[10]

The Americans had one more major river to cross, the Elbe. There they linked up with British and Russian troops. By prearrangement American and British troops held back as the Russians—who had suffered far more casualties in the war—were given the right to lead the assault on the last Nazi bastion, Berlin itself.

A correspondent for an American newspaper wrote in April, "With the crossing of the Elbe River by the Ninth Army comes the story of a Utah colonel who has distinguished himself as a gallant and courageous leader of a group of Army Engineers...He—Col Hugh W. Colton of Vernal—and his men were commended by a columnist in the Paris edition of the *New York Herald Tribune* as being 'the bravest men on the western front' after the writer had observed them build the bridges across the Roer River under withering fire and at heavy cost."[11]

On April 30, 1945 Hitler committed suicide in the *Fuhrerbunker*, along with Eva Braun, his mistress-turned-wife for their last forty hours, and propaganda minister Joseph Goebbels and his wife Magda. The Goebbles killed their six children before killing themselves.

Remaining German leaders surrendered unconditionally, prompting this message from the Supreme Allied Commander to Washington and London: "The mission of this Allied Force was fulfilled at 02:241 local time, May 7, 1945. Eisenhower."

Hugh was released from active duty the following January, just seven weeks shy of five years in the Army.

4

A Rich Ricks Heritage

Four hundred miles northwest of Vernal is the tiny village of Hibbard, Idaho—near Rexburg in the Upper Snake River Valley. There, in a small log farm house without indoor plumbing, a girl was born who would complete Sterling's life.

Eleanor Ricks fortunately came from resilient stock; she would need all the spunk she could muster for the challenges ahead.

Ellie's storied great-grandfather on her father's side was Thomas E. Ricks, born in Trigg County, Kentucky in 1828, to Joel and Eleanor Martin Ricks. Thomas was the seventh of ten children. Two years later the family moved to Silver Creek, Illinois. There, in 1840, LDS missionaries taught them, and the following year baptized family members into the Church. A month later the Ricks family moved to Nauvoo, Illinois, the central gathering place of the saints.

In the teeth of growing persecution of the Mormons, Thomas and his father helped construct the Church's second temple, in Nauvoo. As a sixteen-year-old in 1844, while breaking a horse, the horse fell, landing on Thomas' left leg. The accident stunted growth in the leg, leaving it shorter than the other. From then on he walked with a limp, later using a cane.[1]

On June 27, 1844 church leader Joseph Smith and his brother Hyrum were martyred in Carthage, Illinois. A year and a half later, in the dead of winter, new church leader Brigham Young led the first major group of saints across the frozen Mississippi River, heading west. In

April, after hunkering down in a winter camp, these vanguard pioneers began the final push beyond the western border of the U.S. and into what is now Salt Lake Valley.

The first pioneers started entering the valley on July 22, 1847. Immediately they dammed City Creek and diverted it onto sun-scorched land. Two days later, on the formal date of their arrival, the pioneers plowed a five-acre tract and planted seed potatoes. A week later the potatoes already were growing. That encouraging development was a harbinger of the bright future for potatoes north of there in eastern Idaho.[2]

The Ricks family was a year behind the first pioneers. They left Winter Quarters, Nebraska, heading for the Salt Lake Valley, in May 1848. A week later Indians raided their camp, stealing cattle. Thomas and some other youths pursued them. They were ambushed and Thomas was shot three times, once in the backbone and twice in the kidneys. The other youths, sure he was dead, returned to the wagon train and told Thomas' father the sad news.

Joel mounted a horse and left to retrieve his son's body. He found, however, that Thomas, though grievously wounded, was still alive. He took the young man back to camp and laid him in their wagon. There Thomas remained for the rest of the trek west as he recovered from his wounds. At one point Joel floated him across a river on a buffalo hide. They arrived safely in Salt Lake Valley.

Unlike a great majority of other pioneers, the Ricks family had accumulated some means to assist their travels, and shared it bounteously. They donated one of the first wagon teams that entered Salt Lake Valley with Brigham Young. They also assisted five more groups of pioneers to cross the plains and mountains to the Salt Lake Valley.

About 90 percent of pioneers made the journey in wagon trains. Many were aided by the Church's Perpetual Emigration Fund, loaned money to make the journey, on the promise to pay it back to help other pioneers coming behind them.

In 1856, with far more pioneers than expected gathering to the new Zion, Brigham Young initiated handcart companies—pioneers who would make the trek from a jumping off point in Iowa or Nebraska, pulling and pushing two-wheeled carts loaded with all their worldly belongings. From then until 1860 ten handcart companies made the arduous trek.

Two of the ten companies ran into disaster: the company led by James G. Willie, with 500 individuals, and one led by Edward Martin, with 665. Both left Winter Quarters in Florence, Nebraska too late in 1856 to reach Zion before they were overwhelmed and stranded by deep snow and bitter cold in Wyoming.

Brigham Young learned of their plight on October 4, and immediately called a meeting that evening to begin organizing a rescue effort. Young repeated the call the following morning during Sunday services, and again the next day, October 6, during general conference. "Many of our brethren and sisters are on the plains with handcarts," he said, "...and they must be brought here...Go and bring in those people now on the plains..."[3]

Thomas Ricks, now 28, had returned to the valley from a colonizing mission in Nevada ten days before President Young's clarion call. Thomas immediately responded. On October 7, the day after conference, he was among the first rescuers who headed east into the frozen Rockies with sixteen supply wagons. That was only the beginning of the need; before the end of October some 250 rescue wagons were on the trail in one of the great sagas of the American West.[4]

The Martin company had left Nebraska ten days later than the Willie company and included more women, children, and aged members. Thomas was one of the rescuers of these pioneers, who were about a hundred miles east of the Willie company.

Although exact numbers are elusive, it is generally believed that about 69 members in the Willie company perished on the trail, along with at least 150 in the Martin company. These numbers would have been far higher if rescuers, including Thomas, had not immediately obeyed Brigham Young's call to "bring in" their fellow pioneers.

Thomas had proven his faithfulness, and continued to help lead a highly ambitious colonizing effort. Young, as both territorial governor and church leader, foresaw a far larger earthly kingdom for the saints than what eventually became the State of Utah. He directed the colonizing of some 350 settlements in Idaho, Wyoming, Nevada, Arizona, and Colorado.

Thomas was commissioned to find a better route from picturesque Cache Valley in northeastern Utah to the Bear Lake Valley, forty miles eastward, through what is now Logan Canyon. The centerpiece of the latter valley is dazzling Bear Lake, a kaleidoscope of blue shades depending on the weather and time of day—about twenty miles long, half in Utah and half in Idaho. En route to Bear Lake, Thomas found a natural spring flowing from the interior of a large rock cave, which today bears his name, Ricks Spring.

In 1859 Thomas moved his family to Logan. He continued to play an important role for the Church, while becoming one of the region's leading entrepreneurs and public servants. He was a principal contractor for the railroad in building the grade and laying track from Franklin, Idaho to Butte, Montana.

Thomas accumulated substantial wealth—and proceeded to give almost all of it away in the undertaking for which he is best remembered: spearheading the settlement and development of the Upper Snake River Valley in southeastern Idaho. He was called to that mission in December 1882 by President John Taylor—who became leader of the Church upon the death of Brigham Young five years earlier.

Thomas was asked to colonize eastern Idaho from Pocatello north. Just two months later he arrived and was laying out the city of Rexburg.

The Snake River watershed, high desert with endless sagebrush taller than a man, did not appear inviting to settlers. It was a flat, wide-open frontier where bandits and hostile Indians were often a threat and law enforcement spotty. Sometimes the Ricks family itself was the only law. Settlers repeatedly lost livestock—the equivalent today of being robbed of cash.

On one occasion three rustlers stole nineteen horses and hid them in a canyon in Teton Basin. A citizen spied what they were doing and hurried to Rexburg and reported to Bishop Thomas E. Ricks, Jr.—son of Thomas E. Ricks the colonizer. Bishop Ricks called some men together who decided to send two deputies after the outlaws.

The deputies rode high in the basin, tied up their horses, and crept down the mountain close to the shack where the three rustlers were sleeping. At sun-up one of the rustlers, named Robinson, came out of the cabin, heading for the privy. A deputy about fifty feet away yelled "Put your hands up, Jim!" Robinson turned and dashed for the cabin as the deputies opened fire, hitting him in the leg.[5]

Back in Rexburg Robinson's leg was amputated in an attempt to save his life, but he died regardless. His two companions were sent to prison in Blackfoot. They escaped, fled, and were captured again and sentenced to twenty-five years in prison.

Another time three clean-cut, well-dressed, heavily armed "cowboys" arrived in Rexburg with a band of twenty horses, seeking hospitality for the night. They were invited to stay at the home of Brigham Ricks, one of Bishop Ricks' brothers. After they were bedded down in the dining room, a posse of about a dozen men from Sheridan, Wyoming arrived in Rexburg. The sheriff, named Ray, was directed to the home of Bishop Ricks, who told them where the bandits were sleeping.

When the rustlers rose the next morning at about seven, they were told breakfast was ready in a house across the street. Two of the men sauntered out into the open. As they reached a wood pile Sheriff Ray yelled for them to throw down their guns. One man took cover as the other sprinted back to the Ricks' home. As he returned fire from the doorway a sharpshooter cut him down. The dying bandit, George Munn, was just twenty years old.[6]

Thomas E. Ricks, Sr. proceeded to lay out nearly every settlement in what would become Madison County, Idaho. He built the first sawmill, the first grist mill, and first ferry service across the North Fork of the Snake River. He opened the first mercantile store and, most notably, founded an educational institution in Rexburg called Ricks Academy, which became Ricks College and today is Brigham Young University–Idaho.

Ricks spent his personal resources in developing the region and assisting the poor and needy who settled there. He had also practiced polygamy—sanctioned by the Church until 1890—and had five wives and over forty children, no doubt also straining his finances.

The savings he had accumulated during a remarkably productive life apparently were all gone before the end of it. "I was called here and have expended my means for the benefit of the people," he said in February 1890. "My means have been used up, and I am comparatively poor. But my faith has been increased in the Lord,..."[7]

LDS President Joseph F. Smith said of Thomas E. Ricks, Sr., "It may be a long time before we find another man equal in honor, mind, and unswerving loyalty to the cause of God and His people."[8]

Orson Ricks, son of Thomas E. Ricks, Sr. and his third wife Elizabeth Jane Shupe, was born April 23, 1873, when the Ricks family was living in Logan, Utah. The family stayed in Cache Valley until Orson was about ten, when they moved to Rexburg, Idaho and into a log house with one large room. Orson was the first person to be baptized in Rexburg. As an adolescent he herded cattle in the summer and attended school in the winter. He learned to love reading and continued to study and read all his life.[9]

Orson grew to be six-feet-one and, it was said, was strong as a bull. He married Margaret Agnes Archibald in the Logan Temple on May 20, 1896. Margaret's family had emigrated from Scotland in 1864 and crossed the plains in a covered wagon pulled by oxen. Orson was a stalwart in the Church, serving in many local capacities, including as bishop of the Hibbard Ward for eighteen years.

Orson and Margaret lived in Salem, several miles from Hibbard, for about a year after their marriage. In the fall and winter of 1897 Orson herded sheep for a brother as Margaret was staying with her parents in Rexburg. There, on November 14, 1897, Orson and Margaret's first child, a boy, was born.

Two months later their son was blessed in an LDS service and given the name Thomas Emerson Ricks. At the age of eight Emerson was baptized on December 3, 1905, after Orson chopped a hole through thick ice on a slough, big enough for both to fit in. Thomas Emerson Ricks would become Eleanor Ricks' father.

As a young man Emerson was handsome, with a penetrating gaze and a full head of hair combed straight back until it started to recede later in life. He was a good student, well liked by teachers and friends, and enjoyed sports as well as dramatics, appearing in many plays. There were just two teachers at Hibbard Elementary; each taught four grades.[10]

After finishing the eighth grade in Hibbard, Emerson enrolled in classes at what was then called Ricks Academy, founded by his grandfather in Rexburg. With not enough students in Hibbard to warrant a bus, Emerson rode his horse to high school each day. There he met an attractive coed with dark eyes, wavy hair, and a radiant disposition, named Annie Hutchings.

Annie also came from pioneer stock, who made their mark in southern Utah. Her mother was Sarah Edwards Hutchings, born in 1856 in Winfield, Yorkshire, England. Sarah's father, Annie's grandfather, Robert Edwards, Jr., whose lungs were bad due to the pollution in England, emigrated to the U.S. He worked for the Union Pacific Railroad and sent the earnings to his family. While her father was away Sarah helped support her mother by working in a needle factory and as a peddler.

Finally the money from Sarah's father and a contribution from a generous member of the Church gave the family the required amount and they left for America in 1869, when Sarah was thirteen. During the voyage Sarah's six-month-old baby brother died and was buried at sea. The family crossed the plains by railroad in 1869—the same year that the Union Pacific and Central Pacific Railroads met at Promontory, Utah, linking the nation east to west by rail. The family ended up in southern Utah at Greenville, Beaver County.

Two years later Sarah, at the age of fifteen, married John Charles O'Donnell. It was a troubled marriage and life was tough. John started to drink and gamble and frequently left Sarah alone to rear their children and try to make ends meet by milking cows and making butter and cheese to sell. After four years of desertion, Sarah and John divorced.

In April 1887 Sarah married William Willard Hutchings, Jr., who was born in Salt Lake City on November 23, 1851. His father had been called to help settle Beaver in southern Utah, where their family settled. William already had one wife, Agnes, but was encouraged by church leaders to take a second. This was three years before the LDS "Manifesto" in 1890, officially ending church support for polygamy.[11]

William's service in southern Utah was similar to that of the Ricks family in eastern Idaho—an ecclesiastical leader as well as enforcer of the law. He was deputy U.S. marshal in Beaver County for four years and then county sheriff for another fifteen. The latter post was tricky: As sheriff he was expected to crack down on polygamy, yet he himself was a polygamist.[12]

The family ran the Hutchings Hotel in Beaver, with the women engaged inside the hotel and William caring for the livery stable, an essential chore since all travel was by horseback, horse and buggy, or horse-pulled wagon.

William was spiritually sensitive and heeded the promptings of the Holy Spirit. A new addition was being added to the hotel and he had been gathering rose-colored rock for it at a hillside quarry. One night he dreamed that he had arrived at the quarry as usual and unearthed a large piece of stone which he was about to load on the wagon. A distinct voice said to him, "Step aside." He did so just as the stone turned over and rolled down the hill. He would have been crushed.

The next morning William left for the quarry, arriving just as usual. He was about to load a large piece of rock when the same voice said "Step aside." Having been forewarned, he quickly stepped away. At that moment the rock turned over and rolled down the hill.

William and Sarah had six children together, two boys and four girls. The youngest child, born March 5, 1898, was Annie Hutchings. Two of Annie's sisters died within months of their births—a sad precedent for Annie's own immediate family.

Annie was especially close to her next oldest sister Vie, nearly five years her senior, who had been hired to teach school in Hibbard, Idaho. Annie came north from Beaver to stay with Vie and attend Ricks Academy. Emerson and Annie were strongly attracted to each other from the start. They dated a number of times during the school year and appeared together in a play or two at the academy.[13]

On November 22, 1918, after a short courtship, they were married in Emerson's parents' home by Bishop Joseph Rigby. Emerson was twenty-one, Annie nineteen and a half.

The temples were closed at that time, postponing a temple marriage. On the following February 26, Emerson and Annie took the train from Rexburg to Salt Lake City and were sealed in that temple as husband and wife for eternity.

Emerson and Annie rented one side of a clapboard house in Hibbard for five years and owned a Model T auto. Their first two children were born in that house—Doretha on April 4, 1920 and Vie on March 4, 1922. Annie chose the name Vie in honor of her own sister Vie, who played an important part in Annie's life and who would be especially comforting and helpful to Annie as the Ricks family faced difficulty.

Orson leased 160 acres of one-time Homestead land in Hibbard from Joseph Rigby and he and his son Emerson farmed it together. The federal Homestead Act of 1862 offered 160 acres of surveyed government land for free, with the proviso that the taker had to improve the property. Rigby had met that obligation and now owned the land.

Emerson took naturally to farming; he loved the animals and being outdoors. He and his father forged a partnership. They borrowed $4,000 and bought the 160 acres of farmland Orson had been renting from Bishop Rigby, dividing the property in half.

The two men made a good team, and were also partners on a dry farm about twenty miles from Rexburg.

Orson and Emerson built a log house on Emerson's half, filling the chinks with cement to keep out foul weather. It had five rooms—a nice-size kitchen, a dining room, and three bedrooms. One of the bedrooms, for the only boy, Lloyd, was the size of a closet; the other children's bedroom was slightly larger with two twin beds squeezed together where four sisters slept. Ellie would be fourteen before she got a bed to herself.

The house had electricity but no indoor plumbing. It was cozy and Annie was thrilled. Some family members were less than thrilled, however, with the two unfortunate options they had for relieving themselves—the thunder mug or a two-hole privy about twenty-five yards from the house. "I learned to have great retention because I hated going out in the cold," said Ellie. In the summer Annie planted sweet-smelling flowers along the twenty-five yards to tamp down the odor.

Emerson and Annie's third child was Sarah Ann, an angel-faced, carefree little girl with dark hair, born on February 24, 1924. She was followed by Emerson Lloyd, who Sarah delighted in "mothering." When Sarah was three years old Emerson and Annie went on a short trip with Annie's sister Vie and her husband Joe Parker. They left the children with Grandpa and Grandma Ricks. While they were away, an epidemic of red measles hit Hibbard.

Some of the Ricks children caught the measles, including little Sarah, whose illness turned to pneumonia. One of Emerson's brothers was on a mission in Nebraska. The night Sarah died, Elder Robert Ricks saw her in a dream. "When she passed away, Robert saw a full-grown woman's spirit come out of Sarah's body, stand by the bed for a few minutes before disappearing through the room," wrote Lloyd Ricks. The next morning Robert told his companion that his niece had passed away during the night—confirmed by a letter from home a few days later.

Marie was the next child, born on August 6, 1928, followed by the sixth and last, Eleanor, on August 21, 1931.

5

Ricks Family Tragedies

Ellie Ricks was full of spark and spunk. How else to account for her prank, with another second grader, Charlie, after workmen had poured the foundation for the Idaho Falls LDS Temple?

This temple would be sacred to members of the Church, including Ellie herself when she was married there two decades later. But for a child the temple construction site was an adventuresome spot to pass another boring day in the quiet community. Ellie and Charlie pooled their pennies, bought a bottle of Coke, and buried it in the freshly poured cement.

Ellie's first seven years were spent in the log house in Hibbard. Water for culinary use was pumped outside and carried indoors. In the kitchen was a large wood-burning stove on which Annie did all the cooking and heated their only hot water. Family members washed up in a bowl kept by the front door. A celebrated event in Ellie's memory was the purchase of an electric refrigerator which replaced the ice box.

Family members took turns bathing once a week, on Saturday evening in a metal tub brought into the house. The children bathed in order from oldest to youngest: Doretha, Vie, Lloyd, Marie, and Ellie—three years younger than Marie and whose bath water was never hot. Their parents bathed after the children had gone to bed.

Money was scarce but the family did not go hungry. Annie made bread and other baked goods; Ellie did not taste store-bought bread until years later in school.

Annie grew a large garden and bottled its production each fall—peaches, apricots, raspberries, applesauce, plums, huckleberries, and jams and jellies galore. She also bottled a variety of vegetables, from the garden or gleaned in the woods. The foods were all kept in a root cellar under the back porch.

Emerson was a wheat farmer, so they always had hundred-pound sacks of flour and cracked wheat. They also had a variety of farm animals, including cows that were milked morning and evening. The milk was poured through a separator to divide the cream from the milk. The milk provided butter and cheese; extra milk was sold in large silvery cans to the Nelson-Ricks Creamery, the only dairy in nearby Rexburg.

As an adult Ellie had fond memories of farm life. "My mother was an expert gardener and grew beautiful flowers," she recalled, "including lilac and snowball bushes, bridal wreath, roses, peonies, petunias, sweet peas, dahlias, and other varieties." Flowers would remain special to Ellie all her life.

"Besides that we had dogs, cats, horses, cows, pigs, chickens, and turkeys—and lots of room to play and explore. It was a wonderful place to grow up."

Emerson and his father Orson together grew wheat on a dry farm near Tetonia, about twenty miles east of Rexburg, parallel to and in the western shadows of the Teton Range. Dry farming or dryland farming, as its name suggests, is a risky proposition. It is common to regions that receive little water but have soils that, when tilled, turn up earth more moist than the top couple of inches. Dry farmers typically plant drought-resistant seeds deep in the ground to take advantage of natural moisture. Grain crops can thrive with little water, but still require a minimum. Prolonged droughts are deadly.

"A dryland farmer plants and prays," summarized a national reporter after visiting eastern Idaho. She quoted a local grower on the challenges of a dry farmer: "He's looking to the heavens, saying 'Come on, big guy! Give me some rain!' And if it happens, it happens. And if it doesn't, he can lose his whole crop." Fluctuating prices are another vagary faced by farmers.[1]

Orson and his wife Margaret lived down the lane about a quarter-mile from Ellie's family in Hibbard; Ellie and her siblings often could be found there, playing or helping their grandmother with chores such as shucking corn or shelling peas.

While her siblings were in school or busy in other activities, as the baby of the family, Ellie's closest companions were Mike, a cute little mutt, and Old Bob, a very sharp sheep dog. Together they sought whatever fun they could find or create.

Also as the youngest, Ellie often got to go with her father in his pickup truck to the farm. Emerson and Ellie had a secret pact. "There was an Evans Ice Cream store on the way, and when we were alone in the truck he would never pass it without stopping for ice cream," said Ellie. "Then he would stop for gas and buy me a 'guess what?'"—two pieces of salt water taffy in a box with a prize inside. Cost: five cents. With family money always an issue, Ellie agreed with her father to keep the treats a secret. "He had a great sense of humor and I loved being with him."

On the farm one day with her grandfather, Ellie was riding on a grain drill being pulled by a tractor driven by her father. The grain drill was used to plant seed by digging furrows in the soil and then releasing seed into the furrows. When the seed mechanism that dropped the seed got stuck, Orson loosened it with a gloved hand. Ellie, also wanting to help, imitated her grandpa, trying to pry the device loose— and screaming as it severed her finger, leaving it dangling by a small bit of skin. Emerson leaped from the tractor, wrapped a cloth around her finger, and carried Ellie to the car, rushing her to the hospital in Rexburg.

The doctor wanted to amputate, but Emerson said no. "That's her ring hand," he pointed out, telling the doctor to patch it together the best he could. For six months Annie applied a poultice to the finger twice a day. It healed almost completely; the only lasting evidence of the injury was an extra thick fingernail.

Ellie looked forward eagerly to Sundays. In preparation for the Sabbath, men in their ward came to the Ricks' house for Emerson's free haircuts. Her grandfather Orson, bishop of the Hibbard Ward, was known for his kindness and punctuality; Sunday meetings always started on time. Ellie's father was Sunday School superintendent.

Ellie's Junior Sunday School teacher was her grandmother Margaret Archibald Ricks. Ellie loved to be with her at bedtime when Margaret unloosened her long hair from a twisted bun and brushed and combed it. Margaret was an excellent cook but lost her sense of smell to diphtheria when she was fourteen; as a result she could barely taste.

"I loved to go to church because of her," recalled Ellie. She would line up the children in a row. "Songs I learned from her have stayed with me all my life, including 'Jesus Wants Me for a Sunbeam,' and 'Give Said the Little Stream.' Often the class would end with Margaret giving the children homemade sugar or raisin-filled cookies.

"I thought going to church meant lots of hugs and a cookie, because that's what we got every Sunday. She started me out loving church."

Grandma Ricks was also the center of the family's social life. A lot of aunts, uncles, and cousins lived nearby and, recalled Ellie, "Grandma used any excuse for a party."

For Christmas each year, her grandmother had one particular tradition that Ellie loved. Grandmother filled a big washtub with small toys, and then placed the tub behind a table cloth. Each toy had a string attached and each child got a turn to pull on a string tied to a toy. Ellie continued this delightful tradition, called Jack Horner's Corner, with her own children and grandchildren.

On occasion Grandpa Ricks, also Ellie's bishop, gave her a dime. The following Sunday she would return a penny as her tithing. "He made me feel like the most generous person in the world."

As the baby of the family, Ellie later admitted she had been spoiled.

She often tagged behind the two siblings closest in age, Marie, three years older, and their only brother, Lloyd, five years older. Ellie idolized her sister Marie. "I was her shadow and I looked up to her as the kind of person I wanted to be. She was a very fun, very sharp girl."

As siblings can sometimes be, Marie and Lloyd didn't always want their little sister Ellie tagging along. On one occasion, Ellie coaxed her two siblings into letting her help hunt for magpie eggs. Marie and Lloyd agreed, but only if Ellie could pass "the test"—catching the eggs standing on the ground as they were dropped to her from high in the tree. Magpies are nuisance birds; they eat the eggs and even the baby chicks of other birds, including chickens and ducks. A local agency paid a penny or more for each magpie egg turned in. The two older children climbed a tree to a nest full of eggs. They called down to Ellie to catch the eggs as they dropped them one by one.

It was mission impossible. After the first several eggs splattered on the ground, Marie and Lloyd yelled at their little sister and ordered her to go home. She left crying. The shortest way home was through a pasture where several old bulls eyed her intently. Decades later she still shuddered at the memory.

In the fall of 1937 six-year-old Ellie started school in the first grade. Her teacher was her Aunt Vie, Annie's faithful sister, who had come from Idaho Falls to live with them temporarily.

Ellie learned the Pledge of Allegiance on the first day of school and proudly repeated it to her parents that evening. "Annie, isn't she wonderful!" said her father.

Those were his last words that Ellie heard. Two days later her beloved father died of a lingering kidney ailment.

Ellie then learned why Aunt Vie had come to stay with them. It was to help the family, after Emerson's condition, unbeknownst to Ellie, turned grave. He had suffered from poor health for several years, but his condition was not regarded as critical until the previous Sunday evening. He died at home on Wednesday morning, September 29, 1937, at age thirty-nine. The attending physician wrote "acute nephritis" on the death certificate—inflammation of the kidneys, often caused by an autoimmune disorder that affects major organs.²

The custom at that time was to have the body in an open casket for viewing in the home of the deceased, prior to the funeral. Relatives filed by the casket, kissing Emerson on the cheek or forehead. Someone lifted Ellie up for her turn, but it frightened her and she refused.

Grandpa Orson checked in on Annie and the children every day and tried to run the farm alone. But the strain was too much. Also in poor health, he died the following September, less than a year after his son, from a heart attack. Orson had come to Madison County with his family as a boy of ten and died at sixty-five.

Grain prices were down and the family was heavily in debt when Emerson and Orson died. Annie had to make a living for the five children and herself. Her sister Vie, married and living in Idaho Falls, suggested she relocate there to have family nearby. Idaho Falls was significantly larger than Rexburg and more diverse, though Mormons were the majority by far in both communities.

In 1938 Annie sold the farm and their car to purchase a small home at 610 H Street in Idaho Falls—a quiet street that cut diagonally through a rectangular block. She never had a car again. The home had white siding and a backyard for a garden. A set of cement steps in front led to the main floor; another set on the west side led downstairs.

The house had two bedrooms on the main level and several small rooms downstairs. Ellie was delighted to share the front bedroom on the main level with her sister Marie. Most thrilling to her, their home had indoor plumbing.

Annie was a good seamstress, doing alterations for a department store and sewing almost all of her children's clothing. At night she worked in a potato dehydration plant, where water was separated from potatoes which were reconstituted as powdered mashed potatoes or potato chips. Annie had a beautiful voice and often sang or hummed while working at home; Ellie believed it was to keep up her own spirits. Annie taught the children not to waste anything. "We never left a light on that wasn't being used," recalled Ellie. "All meals were home-cooked."

Annie was righteous and faith-filled, setting an inspiring example for her children. As busy as she was at home, Annie regularly served others in their congregation as a volunteer leader in Relief Society, the LDS women's auxiliary, or Primary, the children's organization. After an LDS temple was built right across the street from her home, she regularly volunteered there as well.

Ellie longed for the time when her mother's life would be easier. "How can you stand it without Dad?" Ellie asked her mother on occasion. Annie answered: "When you have happy memories it's a lot easier…The people I feel sorry for are those whose marriages have gone sour. Your father and I had a great love affair."

Annie had an even disposition, despite the stress of earning enough money to cover the family's needs. On one occasion while she was at work, Ellie invited a friend, Maxine, to their home. They had a large sack of corn that Ellie's brother Lloyd had grown, and they heated a big skillet to pop it.

"What would happen if we popped all this without a lid on?" wondered Ellie. They decided to find out, oiling the skillet and filling it full of corn. Within minutes the kernels began to burst, spraying popcorn in every direction. "Just then Mom arrived home and came in the door," recalled Ellie. "I looked at her and said 'uh oh.'"

"But she just started to laugh, and said 'I've always wanted to do that myself!' She was just wonderful."

Ellie began second grade at Riverside Elementary, about five blocks from their home. The two-story brick building, dedicated in 1908, was almost entirely rebuilt two years before Ellie enrolled. It included seven classrooms upstairs, six classrooms and several offices on the first floor, and an auditorium and teachers' bathrooms downstairs. Students answered nature's call in a line of outhouses behind the school.

Classes at Riverside had two levels of learning—Level B for less-well-prepared students and A for higher achievers. As a new and unknown student, Ellie was assigned to the B level, but was soon promoted to A. The principal, a Mr. Bush, took a liking to Ellie, and encouraged her development. By the sixth grade, when Bush momentarily stepped out of a class he was teaching, he called on Ellie to watch the other students. "He and my uncle, Joe Parker, made me feel that I could do anything I wanted to do," said Ellie.

Ellie had many natural gifts but music wasn't one of them. For music time, her third-grade teacher had divided the class into canaries, blue birds, and robins. "Then she'd say, 'Okay, this time we'll just have all the canaries and blue birds sing,'" remembered Ellie, "and the other robin and I just looked across the room at each other."

In June 1940 Marie and Lloyd went with a busload of children to Logan, Utah, a drive of about two and a half hours, to perform service in the LDS temple. One of the temple rites is baptism for the dead. Mormons believe that worthy members can be baptized by immersion vicariously for relatives and others who are deceased. The deceased, on the other side of the veil, then can decide for themselves whether or not to accept the gospel of Jesus Christ represented by the baptism.[3]

After all the children were baptized several times, they boarded the cold school bus, hair still wet, for the long drive home. They arrived in Idaho Falls well after sundown. It was cold when they were dropped off at the church and Marie and Lloyd walked home.

Marie caught a cold and soon she was in bed. When it worsened she was admitted to the hospital. There, on July 13, three weeks after the outing, she died of pneumonia.

The opening song at Marie's funeral was "Though Deepening Trials."[4]

There was no time for Annie to sew a dress for Ellie. Instead her Aunt Opal Ricks took Ellie to a store, buying her a dress, almost the only store-bought dress Ellie ever had as a youngster. "I was thrilled to have a store-bought dress, but felt guilty about liking it so much because it was such a sad time."

Marie's death was a traumatic experience for Ellie. Ellie had been Marie's shadow her entire life and she was devastated without her big sister.

In 1937 the Church had announced it would build a temple in Idaho Falls—a very big deal among Mormons, who hold their most sacred ceremonies in their temples. This would be the Church's eighth functioning temple.

Ground was broken in December 1939 right across the street from the Ricks' house. The foundation was excavated the following year, and work on the structure itself began in 1941. Ellie and her little friends had great fun climbing the tall mounds of sand and gravel and sliding down. That's when she and Charlie entombed the bottle of Coke in the foundation—each promising to never tell another soul.

The seven acres of temple grounds included a pond with gold fish. On a dare, Ellie ran to her house, less than a hundred yards away, donned her swimming suit, and climbed into the pond, intent on catching a fish. Soon, around the corner came Brother Waller, a German convert.

"You get out of there," he demanded, "and don't you forget or I'm going to tell your mom!"

U.S. entry into World War II in December 1941 suspended temple construction. The temple was completed soon after the war ended and was dedicated in September 1945.

Ellie—in an early example of leadership—organized a "victory club" to aid the war effort. Pupils met once a week. The others marched around the school auditorium as Ellie banged out on the piano the one song she knew, the *Marines' Hymn*.

"*From the Halls of Montezuma
To the shores of Tripoli…*"

The Victory Club collected foil, among numerous things in short supply. Sources for foil included cigarette stubs that had foil wrapped around them, many of which they found near the hospital. "We proudly turned them in to a community collection place," said Ellie.

Her patriotism was spurred by the silver and gold stars in the windows of families whose son, father, or brother was serving overseas. Silver meant a loved one was missing in action; gold meant he was confirmed dead. Ellie vividly remembered being in the home of a friend, Marilyn Thompson, whose window displayed a new gold star.

"Marilyn's sister got married just before her husband went overseas," said Ellie. "When I went to their house her sister was just sobbing; I felt so bad for her." Ellie made a mental note of the stars she saw as she walked around town. She also saved the front page of each *Post Register* newspaper with a headline about the war.

Ellie long remembered the rationing during those years. Instead of creamery butter their family had to settle for an ersatz substitute, a whitish margarine with an unpleasant taste. Ellie stopped putting anything on her bread or toast—a habit she carried into adulthood.

Ellie had to work for every dime she got. She started baby-sitting at age eleven, worked in a department store, and ushered in a movie theater.

6

THE EDUCATION OF ELLIE

In 1943 Ellie enrolled in the seventh grade at O.E. Bell Junior High School. The two-story red-brick building was on the other side of town, about a mile from the Ricks' home. Ellie and many other students walked to school.

Ellie began taking piano lessons from a Mr. Summers. Later that school year he organized a piano recital for all his students. As a beginner, Ellie tried to beg off, but he insisted. In preparation for the recital, held at a church across town, Annie re-made one of her other daughters' dresses for Ellie, and had her wear nylon hose attached to garters.

The fashion of the day was bobby socks and sweaters. Ellie felt extremely self-conscious as the recital began. She was second on the program, following another beginner. Ellie poised over the keys, ready to play a very simple tune called "Spring." She tried to begin—then tried and tried again, but was utterly unable to recall what came next.

Some girls giggled. Reddening in frustration and anger, Ellie tried one more time and, in her words, "pounded it out."

Ellie returned to her seat by her mother, on the verge of tears. Annie wisely didn't say anything. Last to play was Marilyn Pond, adorable in bobby socks and sweater, who performed magnificently. As Marilyn finished, Ellie urged her mother to leave at that moment.

On the long walk home the Ponds drove up beside them and

rolled down a window. "Like a ride?" asked Mr. Pond. Ellie and Annie answered at the same time. "No," said Ellie, as Annie drowned her out: "We'd love one!"

The Ponds, like the Ricks family, did not have a lot of money; both parents worked. As they drove, Marilyn asked if Ellie could spend the night at their house and walk together to school the next morning. "She would love to," answered Annie. They drove to the Ricks' and Ellie changed into school clothes. Mr. Pond then took his wife home and drove the girls to a drug store where he bought milkshakes.

That night in bed the two girls talked for an hour before falling to sleep. What began as a terrible evening ended as a great blessing to Ellie. Her close friendship with Marilyn would be lifelong.

The extent of Ellie's childhood world was Idaho Falls and surroundings. She occasionally spent time with her family in Yellowstone National Park, whose West Yellowstone entrance is about 100 miles from Idaho Falls, and in Jackson Hole, Wyoming, about ninety miles from Idaho Falls, near Grand Teton National Park and world-famous Three Tetons.

The summer Ellie turned eleven, in 1942, another kind family, the Claytons, expanded her world significantly. Ellie's sister Vie was now married to Howard Andrew and they lived in Santa Monica, California, where he worked at a Douglas Aircraft factory building war planes.

Mr. and Mrs. Clayton dropped by the Ricks' home and invited Annie to join them on a trip to California, including a visit to Vie and Howard.

"That sounds really tempting!" answered Annie.

Ellie, standing nearby, said "Oh Mom, if you're tempted can I be tempted too...please, please?"

Mr. Clayton said "I think that's a great idea!"

With no freeways at the time, the two families drove through every town en route to Santa Monica. Stopping in St. George, southern Utah, they went to a drug store. Ellie enthusiastically ordered a double-thick chocolate malted milk, something she had never had.

It was prepared in a tall metal quart container. The "soda jerk" poured out a small glassful and sat the container next to it on the counter. "It was the best thing I had ever tasted," recalled Ellie, "and I sipped it very slowly."

Back in the car Mr. Clayton said, "What's the matter, Ellie, don't you feel well?"

"I feel wonderful," she answered.

"But you only drank a small glass of your malt."

Ellie was stunned. She didn't know all the rest in the container was also hers. "I mourned the rest of that long, hot day as we crossed the Nevada desert."

California pulled Ellie out of her funk. Before the day of canned or bottled orange juice, fruit stands along highways across the Golden State offered fresh chilled orange juice. They stopped at a stand and each drank a pint. "Only then could I forget my neglected chocolate malt back in St. George."

From there it was all wonderful: The visit with Vie and her family; seeing spectacular homes in Bel Air and Beverly Hills; playing in the Pacific Ocean surf and walking barefoot on the beach; eating at a famous restaurant with a waterfall inside.

They drove the coastline to San Francisco. Although the Pacific Coast Highway, or Highway 1, would not be completed and officially dedicated until 1962, enough of the route was open to offer spectacular scenery all the way to the Bay area. For good measure they crossed the Golden Gate Bridge four times, and had thrills driving up and down San Francisco's roller coaster roads.

"My world was never the same again," said Ellie. "It was more interesting and full of wonder."

Marilyn Pond, pretty, with brown hair and blue eyes, was the first of five girls in school who would form a tight friendship circle and remain friends for life. Marilyn was a straight-A student, talented in music and theatrics, with a sparkling personality that drew others to her.

Decades later Marilyn said about Ellie, "We were best buds." She recalled Ellie as one who "always tried her own way, always smiling... she was original, with her own style. To this day if I were in trouble, she'd hop a plane and be here to help."[1]

The three others in their circle likewise were attractive, smart, and popular, Paula Stanger among them. "Ellie and I both came from parts of town that were not in elite areas. She was creative and fun." Paula recalled that the group loved having sleepovers at the Ricks' home. Ellie's mother left them alone to entertain themselves.[2]

Shirley Stanger, Paula's cousin, was also in the group. "Ellie was one of these happy, effervescent people who was eager to help however she could," recalled Shirley. "She was efficient at everything she did, in the best of taste. She had a great sense of quality, not quantity."[3] Shirley was one year behind Ellie in school and followed in her tracks. She was president of the high school pep club the year after Ellie, and later joined the same college sorority and followed Ellie as president of the chapter.

Elayne Heaton was the fifth member of the circle. Her time was divided between school, her girl friends, and a boyfriend she went steady with all through junior high and high school. After high school she would be the first to marry.

Ellie dove into junior high with gusto. Among many other activities, she sold advertisements for the school newspaper. A regular customer was her Uncle Joseph Parker, married to her Aunt Vie. Ellie recalled him as a man with a great sense of humor, similar to Milton Berle, television's "Uncle Miltie" whose dry wit lit up television screens in the 1950s.

"He sold real estate," said Ellie, "and took out an ad every time I went to his office for our junior high newspaper. I'm sure not one person went to him for real estate from that ad, but he was really sweet to me."

Junior high was one of the happiest times in Ellie's life—but also the time of her greatest trial. In her mind a dark cloud hovered over their family in the form of a man named Alpha R. Jaques. Born in 1876, he had moved to Rexburg with his family, who were farmers, when he was eight years old. Jaques had married a woman in the Salt Lake Temple who died thirty-five years later in 1940.

By every account he was a nice man, though humble in circumstances. He was a handyman who helped others at their homes when not on duty as a janitor at the LDS Hospital in Idaho Falls. Ellie met Jaques during her first year in junior high as he mowed their small lawn at 610 H Street. He began to take Annie to baseball games and other activities. Ellie was alarmed at the possibility that Mr. Jaques saw Annie not just as a friend but as a possible marriage prospect.

"He was an old man, twenty-one years older than Mother, and I couldn't stand him," said Ellie. His English was not grammatically correct and Ellie considered him an embarrassment. When her mother announced she was going to marry Alph, Ellie turned on her heel and headed to a bank of the Snake River, a favorite place when pondering something important.

Her mind firm, she returned home and laid it out for Annie: "You know I do not like the man you're marrying, and I will never call him 'father.' I will always just call him your husband." Annie answered, "You're not going to be around here much longer and I don't want to stay home feeling sorry for myself. I now have someone to share life with." She and Alph were married in August 1944.

Ellie said she was not rude to her new stepfather, but simply ignored him as much as possible. Part of Ellie's uneasiness was that she didn't want any man to try to replace her father. And, she explained, "I wanted my mother to marry someone who had enough money that she wouldn't have to work anymore." Another concern in Ellie's mind was that Annie would end up taking care of a sickly old man as Alph aged.

Years later she acknowledged that Alph was "a good man who adored my mother," and was always kind to her. "I think I was just so sorrowful for my other losses that I could not accept him."

Ellie was the only family member who felt this way about Alph. Ellie considered living with her grandmother, who told her in no uncertain terms that she should be ashamed for making Annie sad after all she had been through. Ellie's siblings likewise accepted Alph, as did Ellie's future husband.

Annie and Alph were together twenty-six years before Annie died first, in April 1970. Ellie telephoned Alph to offer condolence. Alpha Jaques lived three years more, dying in July 1973 at ninety-six.

Years later Ellie acknowledged that she was wrong to treat Alph the way she did. "I regret that I was so insecure myself at that time that I couldn't accept him."

As an eighth-grader in 1945 Ellie stole the show when the junior high put on a play called "Growing Pains." It portrayed a series of amusing incidents in the lives of adolescents, reported the local newspaper, "including their first romance, the first dance, automobiles, etc. The play is very typical of American family life."[4]

All the other girls tried out for the pretty, popular girl role—except Ellie. "She tried out for the homely, gawky girl with thick glasses and buck teeth, and it was the cutest part in the show," said Marilyn Pond, who had the lead role as Terry McIntire, a teenage tomboy agonizing over her first romance.

The production ran twice in the junior high auditorium—which was filled to capacity. *The Post Register* said "Growing Pains" was "excellently cast" and "thrilled" the audience. Its headline was "Brilliant Performance Given by Students."

A month later, in March 1945, O.E. Bell Junior High released an honor roll. About one-tenth of the student body of just over 1,000 were honored. Highest honors in the eighth grade—for earning straight A's during the semester—went to five students, including Marilyn. Among those receiving high honors—at least two A's and the rest not lower than a B—were Ellie, Paula Stanger, and Elayne Heaton.

The following year O.E. Bell sponsored another production, a three-act comedy called "Her First Flame." Marilyn Pond was student director and Ellie and Elayne Heaton were in the cast.

Ellie inherited a strong work ethic from her parents. Annie

insisted on a clean house and enlisted Ellie to help keep it that way. Every Saturday Ellie cleaned—vacuuming, dusting, washing windows, washing clothes and hanging them out to dry, among other chores. Annie also was a marvelous cook and a master gardener—other traits picked up by Ellie.

 The potato is Idaho's iconic symbol, for good reason. More of the ubiquitous vegetable is grown in Idaho than in any other state.

 The mighty Snake River has been called the mother of Idaho's potato industry. It winds its way across southern Idaho in a 550-mile arc, plunging a mile downward in its course and transporting silt left from volcanoes that erupted in the region millions of years ago. Most Idaho potatoes are grown in lower-lying fields along the Snake. Other ideal local conditions for potatoes include warm days and cool evenings, and a well-developed irrigation infrastructure.

 Despite continual upgrading of technology—for planting, weeding, uprooting, and storing potatoes—Idaho and other states for generations have relied on students to harvest them. All the investment in time and capital can be lost if potatoes are not harvested before freezing weather sets in.

 That is why, for two weeks in the fall, usually October, middle and high schools throughout potato country have dismissed students as well as adult personnel for "potato vacation." Some students in fact used the time to vacation. Others who genuinely needed the money, like Ellie, took the two weeks seriously to earn money they probably couldn't earn in any other way.

 "It's the most money a teenager could make," recalled Ellie. "If you went back to school without a sunburned face, people would think you were a sissy." Student workers typically earned about $25 during the two weeks in Ellie's day.

 Gatherers worked in pairs; Ellie and Marilyn Pond were partners. Each used a bucket on opposite sides of a row. Tearing away vines and dirt clods, they deposited potatoes into their buckets. When a bucket was full they deposited its contents in large sacks lying at intervals along each row, and returned to the back-breaking work.

"We greatly looked forward to lunch time," said Ellie. "We talked all day long—about a lot of things, including boys, teachers, and our future. I started to develop a philosophy of what I wanted out of life."

Ellie worked in the potato fields each autumn in the seventh through tenth grades.

Ellie entered Idaho Falls High School in the fall of 1946 when she was fifteen. The school had three grade levels, tenth through twelfth. Boys and girls increasingly were on each other's minds. Three of her best friends went steady. Ellie did not, explaining that "I never knew someone I wanted to go steady with."

She did not date a lot, but usually had dates for major school dances. Some of the boys were not Mormon, worrying her mother that they may not share the family's moral standards.

Although Ellie never got serious with a boy in high school, at least one other guy felt serious about her. Decades later at a high school reunion Richard Gillis (Gil) Hahn, a noted oncologist at the Mayo Clinic, approached Ellie. "He came up to me and said 'Do you realize you were the only girl friend I ever had in high school?' I said that was news to me!"

No doubt one memorable image from long ago came to both of their minds. Hahn, strikingly handsome as a student, and Ellie were both in the dance club. During the club's annual show they were performing as a pair. As a flourish at the end of their number, Gil flung Ellie into the air. Her body flew but her skirt did not. Gil was standing on it. "It came right off," recalled Ellie, who ran red-faced off the stage as the appreciative audience hooted and applauded.

Ellie was in a variety of high school clubs and leadership positions. As an entering sophomore Ellie was elected class vice president, one of four officers, and Paula Stanger was elected secretary. The following year Ellie chaired the Junior Prom.

In her 1947 yearbook, called *The Spud*, a boy named Richard autographed, "Dear Ellie, you are a wonderful person, one who ranks at the very top of my list of character, personality, friendliness and many other wonderful traits."

Other students who signed Ellie's yearbooks often commented on her perpetual smile. "Don't ever lose your grand smile or wonderful personality," wrote Aleen in 1948. Ray wrote that "It's girls like you that guys want to marry."

Richard—probably an A student in vocabulary—perceptively wrote, "A person can always know that your smile is always meant in a sincere manner and not cluttered with the hypocrisy of flirting. You have an efficiency and dependability not characteristic to most girls, yet you still maintain a feminine delicacy that makes you extremely attractive."

In addition to academic classes, many students, including Ellie, were given an hour of release time each school day to attend a program of religious instruction called Seminary. Students met in an LDS facility across the street from the school.

"The Church has been my guiding light," said Ellie. "I have been very blessed with good teachers in Sunday School and other church organizations."

On September 15, 1950, Ellie's brother Lloyd married Jean Hart, whose parents owned Hart's Bakery. The company had outlets in three states, including a large bakery in Idaho Falls at 350 North Yellowstone Avenue. It could bake 2,400 loaves of bread in two giant ovens every thirty-five minutes.

Ellie was hired as a cashier in a small retail outlet next to the bakery, called Jack and Jean's. (Jack was Jean's brother.) Ellie walked to the store, crossing the railroad tracks and highway. She worked there during her senior year of high school and each summer when home from college. Customers in Yellowstone Park were a major outlet for the baked goods, which were distributed in a fleet of trucks and trailers, one of them driven by Lloyd.

A famous couplet Ellie liked to quote from bakery days was this:

"As you ramble on through life, brother, whatever be your goal, keep your eye upon the doughnut and not upon the hole."

About school, Paula Stanger said, "Our senior year we were big fish in a little pond. All of our group were student officers and club leaders." Occasionally that year she and Ellie went home for lunch and skipped school in the afternoon. "Instead we went to the banks of the Snake River and just sat and talked," said Paula. "We didn't get in trouble for it."

On one occasion, however, Ellie and four other girls did get in trouble. One of them "borrowed" her family's Jeep, and they ditched school. They drove north of Idaho Falls to a public pool and, recalled Ellie, "had a good swim." Returning home was not as trouble-free. They avoided the highway and stuck to side roads. By then the sun was low in the western sky and, as they drove through Rigby, it briefly blinded the driver. The Jeep careened off the road and down the shoulder. A barbed wire fence was all that kept them from ending up in the canal. Elayne Heaton's leg was badly gashed by the fence, and the Jeep was not drivable. The high school gave all five girls a grade cut. In Ellie's case that B marred an otherwise straight-A report card, costing her a ranking of Highest Honor that semester.

Ellie's leadership ability flowered as a senior. She was elected president of the prestigious Pep Club, which, up to that time, she considered "not very nice and hard to get into." She opened its doors wider to aspiring members.

One of the Pep Club's activities was during Halloween. Club members blindfolded students and had them touch liver and other slimy substances. "I thought this is so dumb; what we should do is have the pep club make more pep for the school." For starters, she told members that, whenever there was a game, they should all wear orange and black that day—the colors of IF High, whose symbol was a tiger. Members agreed and got many other students as well to wear school colors on game days.

Ellie also led club members in doing community service. "That was my first experience when I realized I had leadership ability, because I talked them into doing it. The teachers all thought I was amazing."

Ellie was also amazing in the classroom. She loved history and was an excellent writer. "She wrote a little essay comparing a field of waving grain to a group of ballet dancers," remembered Paula Stanger. "It was so good that the teacher was stunned."

Most of Ellie's teachers in the 1940s were single women whose husbands served in or did not survive the war. She credited three high school teachers for imbuing her with the love of learning:

Gladys Buckley, who taught Latin and "made all the students so excited about word derivation, where words came from. She always pushed me to work harder." Among the Latin words that Ellie learned was the conjugation of the word "damn" (damno, damnare, damnavi, damnatum), which Ellie memorized and recited and used to her advantage for the rest of her life, claiming that this was classical swearing.

Ethel Rottman, who taught English, instilled in Ellie her love of poetry and prose, beginning a lifelong love of literature. Ellie had an uncanny ability to recall and recite what she had read. Rottman wrote in Ellie's senior yearbook, "It's sorry I am to see you absent from IFHS."

The third teacher, who influenced her the most, was Mae Neuber, who taught American and world history. Neuber, slender with wavy blonde hair, dedicated her life to teaching 5,000 Idaho Falls students over four decades, from 1927 to 1968. Neuber created Ellie's love of history.

In 1951 Neuber started a world history class, restricted to college-bound seniors. Among class members was Rodney Merrill, one of many students she prepared to enter and excel in the nation's top colleges and universities. In 1962 Merrill was a senior at Harvard. Members of the graduating class were invited to nominate high school teachers "for significant impact on their students." A total of 350 teachers were nominated. Of that pool, a Harvard faculty committee chose four, including Mae Neuber.[5]

Ellie would leave the Snake River Valley, but the valley would never quite leave her. A friend wrote in Ellie's senior yearbook, "I won't say goodbye because remember you told me to always say just 'so long.' So long Ellie."

67

Vernal, UT 1929

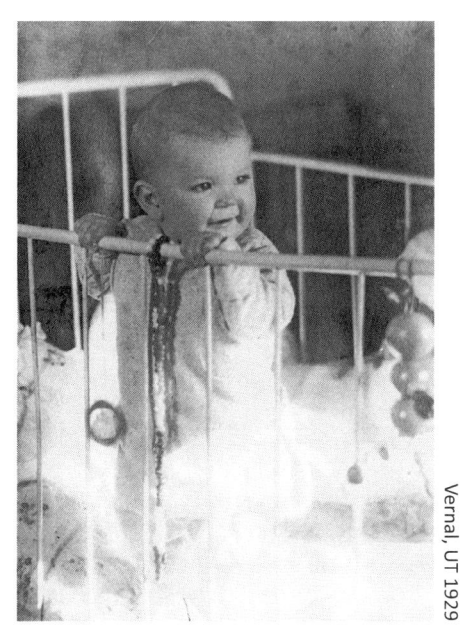

Sterling, an early-morning riser from the start, checks out what work awaits him today.

Vernal, UT 1929

Baby Sterling held by his mother.

Vernal, UT 1934

Sterling's kindergarten class with teacher Bea Stringham. Sterling is on the far right in back row.

68

Sterling, Marguerite, Maughan and Nancy.

Extended Colton family gathering at home of Hugh and Marguerite. Sterling is in overalls.

Sterling posing on fairground "bucking bronco."

Sterling had soft, kind eyes as early as his fourth-grade school picture.

Marguerite with Maughan, Nancy, Sterling and Phil.

Captain Colton and family as he prepared to ship out to Europe. (l-r) Phil, Nancy, Hugh, Sterling, Marguerite and Maughan.

Sterling at 16.

Sterling in a school play. Uintah girls had eyes for Sterling, but he rarely dated in high school.

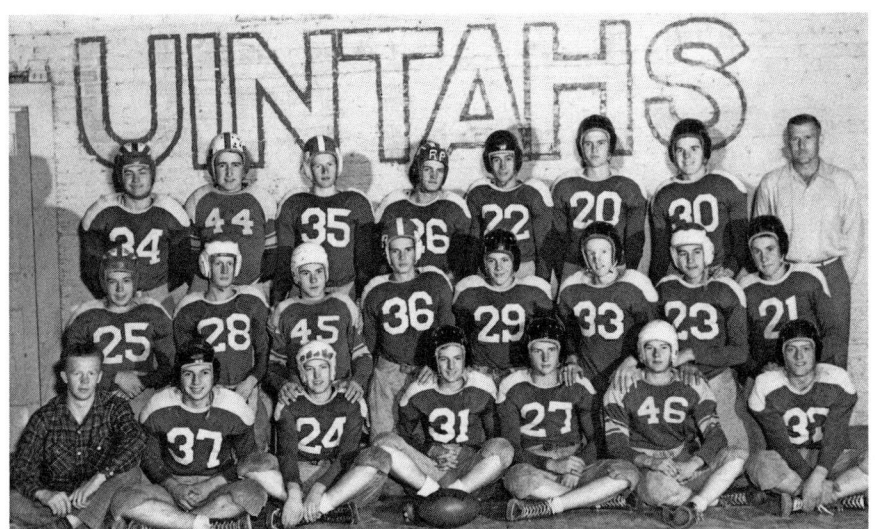

Sterling was a straight-A scholar all through high school while involved in numerous activities. He played end on Uintah High's football team (#30) and center on its basketball team (#11).

72

Vernal, UT 1947

Family Christmas with special friend Kate Forrest Adams, widely known in the Uintah Basin as "Mother Adams." Her philanthropy blessed the lives of local boys going to war and children she treated to parties, movies, and other activities. (l-r) Nancy, Sterling, Phil, Hugh, Marguerite, Mother Adams and Maughan.

73

The log farm house where Ellie was born. It lacked indoor plumbing.

Baby Ellie with cat.

Three generations of Ricks men: Ellie's grandfather Orson, father Emerson, and brother Lloyd. Orson farmed together with Emerson and died less than a year after his son.

Sister Marie (l), three years older than Ellie, with Ellie, cats and little mutt Mike, Ellie's closest companion.

Ellie (r) and older sister Marie with Ellie's other closest companion, sheep dog Old Bob.

First grade. Ellie is in first row, far left. Ellie learned the Pledge of Allegiance on her first day of school and recited it to her parents that evening. Two days later her father Emerson died from a kidney disease.

Ellie tending cousins outside their log home.

Ricks family home in Idaho Falls. Annie sold their car to help buy it, and never owned another car.

The Ricks family after moving to Idaho Falls. Annie is at top right, next to daughter Doretha. Lloyd and Vie (Annie's daughter, not sister) are next, with Ellie at bottom.

77

Idaho Falls, ID 1945

Ellie at 16.

Idaho Falls, ID 1947

Annie, Ellie and Mike.

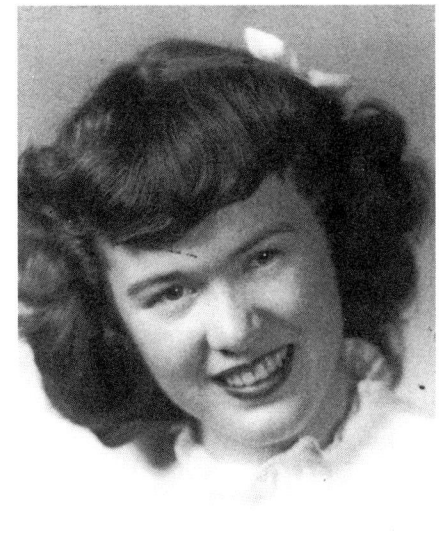

The Ricks family during World War II: Doretha, Annie, Lloyd, Ellie and Vie.

Idaho Falls, ID 1945

Ellie in Idaho Falls High School Pep Club uniform. She was club president.

7

All-American Adolescent

Back in Vernal, Hugh returned home to a hero's welcome, picking up where he left off as a husband and father, and a country lawyer, farmer, and rancher.

He may well have been Utah's most decorated serviceman. His awards included two Silver Stars, a Bronze Star, Purple Heart, Croix de Guerre from France, Order of Leopold from Belgium, and Legion of Merit for "Outstanding Leadership" in eleven months of combat. He had been promoted to full colonel on the battlefield on the direct order of Supreme Allied Commander Dwight Eisenhower.

The war was over in much of the world but not in the Pacific. Allied leaders pivoted away from Europe and toward Japan, whose fanatical leadership guaranteed a terrible blood bath when Allied troops attacked the Japanese home islands. U.S. Military leaders estimated that, in such attacks, American deaths would reach a quarter-million. Colonel Colton was among those facing the peril: He was not released from active duty until January 12, 1946, five months after Japan's surrender.

Sadly, President Roosevelt did not live quite long enough to see the surrender of Germany, dying on April 12, 1945, less than one month before V-E Day (Victory in Europe Day) on May 8. His successor Harry S. Truman held the fateful decision of dropping newly invented atomic bombs on Japan, and did so in early August, the first on Hiroshima and the second on Nagasaki, with unheard of destruction.

Sterling was in the U.S. Army Hospital at Fort Douglas, Utah, on

August 15, where a surgeon operated on his misshaped right hand, trying to give it more mobility—only partially successful. Suddenly Sterling heard sirens, horns honking, and shouting. Japan had just surrendered unconditionally. "I will never forget the cries of joy as bells rang and sirens blared" on V-J Day (Victory in Japan Day), he said.

Sterling had proved his mettle during the nearly five years his father was in the Army. He grew to be six feet tall, had worked hard at the Colton ranch, earned excellent grades at Uintah High School, and competed in a variety of sports and leadership. There seemed to be very few wholesome youth activities in Vernal in which Sterling was not involved.

In Hugh's absence Marguerite contributed to the war effort. She organized and led the Uintah Service Association, a group of women who corresponded monthly with about 350 servicemen from the valley fighting in distant lands. An excellent cook, she stretched a dollar about as far as it would go in those lean years, creatively dressing up almost every scrap of food left from one meal to be served at another. She refused to use an electric dishwasher or clothes dryer. She also earned cash by substitute teaching.

Marguerite also got high marks for overseeing the farm and ranch. "Marguerite was something else," said Lowell Caldwell, a son of farm manager Wallace Caldwell. "Not just with her family but she spent a lot of time on the ranch. Nancy did too."[1]

Ralph Siddoway, a close friend of Hugh and Marguerite, said, "The brains of that ranch for five years was Marguerite Colton...She isn't a country girl, far from it. She was cultured and refined, and a college-educated city girl. She didn't know how to catch a pig, didn't know how to sell the livestock....She learned how."[2]

When the war ended in Europe, Sterling was sixteen, Nancy fourteen, Maughan twelve, and Phil eight.

Like both parents, all four children were hard workers. In later years Phil explained, "Dad had some characteristics that were very tenacious. I'm sure that's what made him a good soldier. When we got sick he would tell us, 'You can stay in bed and get lots of rest and it will take seven long days to get better. Or if you get up and work hard, sweat, and keep going, it will be just one short week.'"[3]

Farm manager Wallace Caldwell had two sons, Larry, five months younger than Sterling, and Lowell, three years younger. Sterling worked alongside them. They did men's work as boys. "As the oldest son in our family I felt a responsibility to work hard while Dad was in the Army. We had an old steel-wheel tractor but couldn't get gas for it during the war, so we did the heavy work with horses."

Like numerous others during the war, the Coltons had learned the value of teamwork and frugality. With most able-bodied men away at war, boys like Sterling, along with older men and many women, took their places in the fields and factories. Harvest time in the fall was a grand community affair. Teams of men and boys went from farm to farm harvesting hay and other crops.

Although Sterling worked hard, it was not always with pleasure. On one occasion he was planting seed corn with a two-horse corn planter. It was a hot day and he dozed off as the horses continued walking. When the corn sprouted it was in meandering lines all over the field, instead of straight lines easy to irrigate.

"I learned the importance of doing things right the first time," he said. "The people in the valley still talk about the Colton boy who couldn't plant a straight row."

With the family farm in Maeser, five miles west of Vernal, Hugh decided they should also have a cow at home to supply fresh milk and to teach the children discipline.

Wallace Caldwell had a buckskin-colored Jersey delivered to an old shed a hundred yards southwest of the Colton home.

"I was the only one who milked Bossy," said Sterling. "The other boys were too young at the time. I'd come home from basketball practice late at night and have to go out through the snow—which seemed three feet deep from November until April—to milk the cow." Each time he washed the udders with warm water before milking her. In appreciation, Bossy often tried to kick over the milk bucket or at least put a hoof in it.

Uncharacteristically, Sterling said, "I hated that cow and she didn't like me very much either. The cow would be mooing. The neighbors said, 'That Colton boy will never amount to anything—he can't even milk his cow on time.'" Sterling also had to scoop out the shed floor and throw fresh straw on it with a pitchfork.

During his freshman year in high school Sterling did a project as a member of Future Farmers of America (FFA). He raised a calf in the shed with Bossy, then in the spring took it along with other FFA calves to an auction in Salt Lake County. He got a good price for the calf, setting the money aside to help pay for college.

It was easier for a boy to stay out of trouble in Vernal than in most places. It was a small community with more pranks than crime—including the time some boys reportedly led a cow into the principal's office and left her there for the weekend. Outdoor privies were tipped over for fun, occasionally while occupied, and farmers sometimes complained that watermelons had gone AWOL from their fields.

Uintah High School had a leadership society called Boys' League, comprised of three boys from each class. Sterling was one of the three freshmen in 1943-44, standing a head taller than one of the other two freshmen and nearly two heads taller than the other one. He was secretary of the FFA, substitute center on the Ute varsity basketball team and starting center on the junior varsity, called the Papooses.

As a sophomore Sterling was president of the FFA, on the debate team, second-string center on the basketball varsity team, an end in football—they played six-man football in a league of smaller schools—and performed in the annual school play, "Sky Road," wearing a pilot uniform.

Hearts were lightened across the globe on V-E Day, May 8, 1945, when Nazi Germany unconditionally surrendered its armed forces to the Allies, formally ending World War II in Europe. V-E Day coincided with the end of the school year, reflected in the dedication of the school's yearbook, the *Uintahn:* "To a world of everlasting peace...peace not only among the nations of the world, but also among ourselves in the role we play in the great drama of life."

The *Uintahn* also carried a prayer written by American author and poet Stephen Vincent Benet, which had been read at the United Nations three years earlier by President Franklin D. Roosevelt. It ended this way:

> We are all of us children of earth—grant us that simple knowledge. If our brothers are oppressed, then we are oppressed. If they hunger, we hunger. If their freedom is taken away, then our freedom is not secure. Grant us a common faith that man shall know bread and peace, that he shall know justice and righteousness, freedom and security, an equal chance to do his best, not only in our own lands, but throughout the world. And in that faith let us march toward the clean world our hands can make. Amen.

As a junior Sterling was on the prom committee, in the Boys' Pep Club and FFA, was sports editor of the *Uintahn*, played end on the football team and center on the varsity basketball squad.

He also got his pilot's license that year, enticed by the discounted flying lessons offered by the Civil Air Patrol, who were looking to grow their ranks. Sterling flew long enough to take one solo flight, flying over Ashley Valley and Diamond Mountain, where the Coltons ran their cattle. With limited funds and limited time, Sterling's flying days were short-lived.

Also as a junior, Sterling had a principal role in the annual school play, "Lost Horizon," based on the novel by James Hilton. Sterling played Charles Mallinson, a British vice-consul and one of four people on a plane that crash-landed near Shangri-la. The other three, including the play's lead character, British consul Hugh Conway, fell in love with Shangri-la, where people didn't grow old, and wanted to remain there. Mallinson chafed to return to the outside world. Hugh Conway, who strongly opposed Mallinson, was played by Sterling's good friend Glade Sowards.

That spring, heading into their senior year, Sterling and Sowards opposed each other for real, this time for student body president of

Uintah High. Sowards won. Sterling then ran for senior class president and won.

Sowards went on to have a distinguished career. He was on the Vernal City Council and then was elected to the state legislature, serving a decade in the House of Representatives, including as Speaker, and another eight years in the Senate. He helped expand his family's half-dozen businesses, and served as an LDS stake president and regional representative before his death in 2001 at age seventy-two.

In his senior class photo Sterling is shown wearing glasses, albeit with fashionable frames so small the glasses are inconspicuous. As a senior he was again sports editor of the *Uintahn*, on the debate team, student council, and in two school plays. He was also starting center on the football team, on the basketball first team as a guard, and on the tennis team, a sport he continued to play his whole life. Music was the only major extracurricular in which he didn't participate. "I realized early on that music was not one of my talents," said Sterling.

Sterling attended and graduated from Seminary—the LDS Church educational program for high school students—and was called to be Sunday School superintendent in his ward at the age of seventeen.

A girl named Dorothy was one of many students signing Sterling's yearbook. "Dear Sonny," she began, "...I guess you know how brilliant you are, I really admire you. I'm sure you'll be a great success and I hope some day you find some cute little gal and settle down. I'll be up to see ya at the U next year."

One of his debate partners, named Rita, wrote: "Dearest Sterling, Well I'm certainly going to miss you next year...Sterling you are one swell kid and I like you a lot. Good luck up at the University darling, good luck in readjusting too. Well success, I know you'll have it, 'cause you couldn't have anything else with your working ways. Love, Rita."

The captain of the football team, Richard Peterson, wrote, "You sure are one of the best leaders this school has ever had and I look up to you for being such a good sport and having the ability to try all athletics."

Sterling down played his athleticism. "I was not an outstanding athlete but I did enjoy participating. One of the advantages of going to a small high school was that there were opportunities for someone who was dependable and would show up for practices. "The coach of Uintah's football, basketball, and track teams, Frank Wright, perceptively wrote this in Sterling's senior yearbook: "Success is not always measured by how much we play the game but how we play it. I have enjoyed you participating on the teams I have coached. I admire your determination and wholehearted efforts towards the team and I know what it takes to do the kind of job you have done for me. Simply, Thanks. Coach."

Sterling picked up various awards along the way. In the spring of 1945 and 1946 he and his partners won debates held at Carbon College in Price, Utah.[4]

Sterling praised the teachers he had at Uintah High, especially Stella Harris Oaks, who directed the plays he performed in, taught speech, and introduced students to the arts and good literature. Sterling credited her with sparking his lifelong interest in reading and learning about the world and its cultures. Stella Oaks had been widowed when her doctor-husband died, leaving her with three children under the age of eight. The oldest of the three, Dallin, was a freshman at Uintah High when Sterling was a senior.

"Sterling was a favorite student of my mother," Dallin recalled many years later. "I remember him as one of the two or three leaders of the high school. He was a leader in everything going on in the school...just a person that I admired very much."[5]

Dallin H. Oaks became the eighth president of Brigham Young University and a member of the LDS Church's Quorum of the Twelve Apostles on May 3, 1984.

Sterling advanced at the customary ages in the Church's Aaronic Priesthood. He was ordained a deacon at twelve, a teacher at fourteen, and a priest at sixteen. For his faithfulness he also received a special Aaronic Priesthood Certificate signed by the Presiding Bishopric at Church headquarters.

Sterling led the senior class as president, graduating with eighty other students on May 15, 1947. In addition to earning all A's throughout high school, he lettered in football, basketball, tennis, track, debate, and drama.

Sterling had always had many friends of both sexes, but never a "girlfriend." He could recall only two dates during his school years. One was when he was in the eighth grade and a female friend's friend was visiting from Provo; Sterling took her to a matinee movie. As a high school junior he took a girl named Rachel Calder to a school dance. He and some male friends occasionally went stag to dances at local dance halls.

After graduation in 1947 Sterling worked at the ranch for the summer. Hugh didn't pay him wages. Instead, when Hugh needed cash to pay for college for Sterling or another family member, he typically sold a bull or a horse to come up with it.

That fall Sterling enrolled at the University of Utah in Salt Lake City, the state's flagship public university. "Academically it had the best reputation," he explained. Both his parents attended the U and three friends in his class likewise were going there, Glade Sowards, Bill Siddoway, and Dorothy Anne Witbeck.

There was a lot of bustle on campus; the university was bursting at the seams as hundreds of veterans, many using the GI Bill of Rights, enrolled. Sterling rented a room in the basement of a house across the street from Carlson Hall, the freshman girls' dormitory. He shared the room with Ralph Harding from southern Idaho, who later served two terms in the U.S. House of Representatives as a Democrat from Idaho's Second District.

Sterling took his meals at Ma Bradley's, a large boarding house near campus where his Vernal friends Glade and Bill lived.

Sterling registered as a banking and finance major, arranging a schedule that would enable him to complete requirements for graduation in three years rather than the customary four. Later he considered that a mistake. "I did not obtain a well-rounded education." Most of his classes were at the Annex, a World War II building at Fort Douglas, about two miles from his apartment.

Sterling studied hard and, as in high school, got excellent grades.

In winter quarter 1947 he got straight As, earning eighteen credits in six classes—economics, business, math, English, health education, and physical education. He was elected to Phi Eta Sigma, the nation's oldest and largest honor society for freshman college students in all disciplines. It was the first of many college honors to come his way. He joined the U's debate team, whose makeup reflected students who would go on to make public names for themselves beyond college.

Three days before Christmas in 1947, the U sent twenty-six debaters, including Sterling, to a western states tournament. Also included were Glendon Johnson, who became administrative assistant to U.S. Senator Wallace F. Bennett from Utah; Bennett's son, Bob Bennett, later a U.S. senator as well; Mark Cannon, who became administrative assistant to Supreme Court Chief Justice Warren Burger; and Don Lind, a future astronaut.

Sterling worked on the ranch again following his freshman year at the U. Returning for his sophomore year in the fall of 1948, he was "rushed" by Phi Delta Theta Fraternity, which his father had belonged to. He was not comfortable with the group then in the fraternity, however, and, the following spring joined Sigma Chi Fraternity. His close friend from Vernal, Glade Sowards, also joined Sigma Chi.

There Sterling met and mingled with men who became lifelong friends, including David Salisbury, a future law partner and pack trip companion; Bill Marriott, Jr., the son of his father's partner when they started what became Marriott International; Scott Matheson, a future governor of Utah; Jake Garn, a future U.S. senator; and M. Russell Ballard, a future member of the LDS Church's Quorum of the Twelve Apostles.

"For a farm boy from Vernal," said Sterling, "there was much to learn from this rich blend of men associated with the fraternity." Sterling moved into the Sigma Chi house that fall and lived there three school years. He was on the second floor in a four-bed bedroom.

Fraternities and sororities were leadership as well as social clubs. "Greek" groups competed in wholesome activities such as playing in intramural athletics, achieving the best grade-point averages, building the best homecoming floats, and performing humanitarian service.

Sterling was inducted into Beta Gamma Sigma, a business school honorary society; was on the staff of the campus newspaper, the *Utah Chronicle*; and again on the debate team. He also received the Church's higher priesthood that fall, when he was nineteen and a half. On September 26, 1948 his father laid hands on Sterling's head and bestowed the Melchizedek Priesthood on him, ordaining Sterling an elder, one of the offices in that priesthood.

During Sterling's second year on the debate team his partner was Ralph Mecham, who would become a lifelong friend and colleague over many years in the Washington, D.C. area. Mecham was one year older than Sterling and earned a bachelor's degree in political science at the U—a precursor to a number of high-level political and government jobs.

In spring 1949 Sterling was elected president of the U's junior class, to begin serving that fall.

8

ELLIE BONDS WITH THE COLTONS

Ellie, after graduating from Idaho Falls High School, faced the decision of where to attend college. Her best friends were going to one of three schools—the University of Idaho, Brigham Young University, and Utah State University—and each coaxed Ellie to go with her.

She sought other help to decide. "I just made it a matter of prayer. One morning I woke up and said, 'You know, Mom, I really feel I should go to the University of Utah.'" It was the most expensive choice, but Annie said, "If that's the way you feel, then you should. We'll find a way to make it work."

Nancy Colton, Sterling's sister, made the same decision, though it was a natural choice since her parents and all her siblings had already gone there or planned to do so. Nancy was set to live in Carlson Hall, the U's oldest dormitory, for freshman female students. Sterling drove his sister there in a borrowed car. Family money was tight and, although a big man on campus, he did not have a car until years later. He relied on his parents or friends to take him the 170 miles between Vernal and Salt Lake City. Occasionally he hitchhiked.

On September 18, 1949 Sterling and Nancy pulled up and parked behind Carlson Hall, and then went inside for Nancy to check in. They returned to the car and got her luggage, Sterling carrying it inside. At the same time as they got on the elevator from the back of the building, Ellie got on from the front. All were going to the third floor. When the elevator opened, Sterling dropped Nancy's suitcases, picked up Ellie's, and carried them to her room, leaving Nancy to carry her own. "I liked him right away!" said Ellie.

"I was just a farm boy from Vernal but I knew a good thing when I saw it," said Sterling. "I have been carrying her things ever since. Ellie's mother sent her to the university to find a husband. I was fortunate that she was not very picky and chose the first boy she met."

Sterling added, "I didn't know it then, but that chance meeting would lead to an eternal relationship that has been the best thing that has ever happened to me. Ellie is spiritual, intelligent, beautiful, and fun to be with."

Shortly after arriving, Nancy and Ellie climbed a tree in back of the dorm and for the next two hours shared their life stories. "She told me how proud she was of her father," said Ellie, "and how they missed him during the years he was involved in World War II. She said he spoiled her in a very nice way." Nancy and Ellie bonded from the start and became each other's best friend.

Several weeks later Sterling phoned Ellie and asked her to go to a movie—with his roommate, Rod Kump. They double-dated. "I think he was just checking me out first," said Ellie. On Sterling's arm that night was Dorotha Sharp, a very pretty junior. "His date was this beautiful blonde from Salt Lake. I thought 'Oh well, he likes blondes so I'm not in the picture.'"

Ellie's concern proved to be unfounded when the following week Sterling took her to a Sigma Chi party. As he walked her from the frat house to Carlson Hall, the dorm light blinked, signaling that the girls had five more minutes. "We had our first kiss," said Sterling. "She was a good kisser"—so good that Ellie's hat fell off. She scooped it up, took her shoes off, and ran to the dorm, just before the doors closed for the night.

A month after meeting for the first time, Nancy invited Ellie home to Vernal for the weekend. Maughan, sixteen, and Phil, twelve, were told that Ellie was Sterling's girlfriend, and to behave themselves.

"The first morning in their home I woke up with something licking my face," recalled Ellie. Opening my eyes in alarm, I faced an Irish Setter named Rusty, eager to get acquainted. Great laughter came from the doorway, where the brothers had coached him!"

Ellie loved Sterling's family from the start. "Marguerite was a fantastic cook, kept the place sparkling clean, and knew how to order her kids around. She had a very warm personality and was very involved in the town, making the most of improving the cultural life in her small community. She had many friends and was greatly respected."

The traditional Homecoming Dance at the U was a big event. As Junior Class president Sterling was deeply involved in planning and organizing it. Time got away from him and he neglected to get a date. The night before the dance he asked Ellie to go with him. She had already turned down several offers and was so unhappy at being taken for granted that she turned him down.

Instead, Nancy asked one of Sterling's fraternity brothers, Des Barker, to drive the two girls to Utah State University, ninety miles north in Logan, where Ellie's high school friend Paula Stanger had lined up dates for them.

A few weeks later, Ellie invited Sterling to the Carlson Hall Christmas formal dance. "She was strikingly beautiful," he recalled. "She was wearing a black strapless formal her mother made. It certainly caught my eye." The orchestra left at 11 o'clock and couples who had cars disappeared at that time. Sterling and Ellie genuinely enjoyed dancing and they kept dancing, with Sterling singing "Blue Moon" over and over. They decided "Blue Moon" would be their special song.

Ellie pledged Kappa Kappa Gamma and Nancy pledged Chi Omega, considered the top two sororities on campus. Sterling's fraternity brothers had also taken a liking to Ellie; early in 1950 she was chosen one of fifteen finalists for the coveted "Sweetheart of Sigma Chi."

In 1950 the U was one hundred years old. To help celebrate its centennial, Sterling requested and was given the State Capitol as the venue for the Junior Prom. A society columnist wrote about the evening under the headline "Brilliant Prom Rates 'Raves.'" She observed that "Sterling Colton and Elinor [sic] were doing a tango when Jerry Smith and Shauna Smith (not related) accidentally bumped into them."[1]

Sterling was mentioned in another society column two months later. Along with his many other activities he had joined the Army Reserve Officers' Training Corps (ROTC). It meant that he would be obligated to serve several years on active duty after completing his education. Meanwhile it would help pay for college.

In April the ROTC service branches on campus held their first annual "Combined Operations Prom." A columnist wrote that Sterling was at a table with Kathryn West, a freshman member of Alpha Chi Omega.[2]

Sterling continued to win awards and honors. Skull and Bones, a highly selective honorary organization for Junior men, named him one of its eight members for 1950. He also was named to Tau Kappa Alpha for excellence in debate. Sterling seemingly had touched every base and won every school honor by the spring of 1950 when he filed to run for the most prestigious honor of all, student body president.

There were two other candidates for president—Burton Cassity, a handsome, blond-haired member of Pi Kappa Alpha fraternity and also a member of Skull and Bones; and Richard Clayton, also blond, a former Air Force pilot who was active in debate and theater and belonged to Delta Phi, comprised of returned male missionaries. Neal A. Maxwell, another Delta Phi who one day would become a member of the LDS Church's Quorum of the Twelve Apostles, chaired Clayton's campaign. That was fortuitous for Clayton, as Maxwell was an eloquent speaker and writer, who authored dozens of inspirational and educational books in his lifetime.

The election for a total of seventeen student body offices was unusually lively, with creative signs popping up all over campus. Cassity dated one of Ellie's sorority sisters, who told the Kappas they should vote for him. Ellie, who had dated Clayton as well as Sterling, rejoined that they should vote based only on the best person for the job.

In what a newspaper called the "heaviest primary balloting in University of Utah history," more than 2,500 students went to the polls. Sterling and Clayton were the primary winners for president. In the general election a week later Clayton beat Sterling by nearly 500 votes—1670 to 1191.[3]

Ellie and Sterling found they had a lot in common. They were from rural backgrounds, were ambitious, and adventuresome. Both loved to read and dreamed of traveling to exotic places—dreams later realized together.

Both were deeply committed to their religion. For all their leadership and other talents, neither was musical. Both were physically attractive with engaging personalities, yet prior to college neither had dated a lot.

College life and Ellie suited each other. She soon made many friends, especially among the sixty or so girls in Kappa Kappa Gamma. Sterling's mother Marguerite helped establish the University of Utah chapter of the sorority as a member of Lamba Phi Lambda which evolved into Kappa in 1932.

"She was such an outstanding student, very well-liked," said Kappa member Norma Matheson of Ellie. Matheson, whose maiden name was Warenski, was two years ahead of Ellie in school. Ellie "was wonderful, effusive, positive. She had a great sense of humor, a great laugh."[4]

Norma, who later married a fraternity brother of Sterling's, Scott Matheson, who served as Utah's governor from 1977-85, recalled a time when she was taking an ornithology class. "I was really enthusiastic about birds. Ellie and I were sitting under a tree talking when one flew over and deposited its droppings on my head. Ellie couldn't stop laughing."

Another Kappa, Joan Earl—Joan Douglas when at the U—and her husband George remained good friends with Ellie and Sterling through the decades. Occasionally they got together for a picnic or dinner.[5]

For a small-town girl from an overwhelmingly Mormon community, some aspects of the sorority were jarring to Ellie at first. The LDS Church's Word of Wisdom proscribes the use of alcohol, tobacco, tea, and coffee, but some sorority sisters indulged in all those substances. Ellie did not like it when the smoky haze thickened inside the Kappa house, but she quickly learned to regard her sisters for character traits other than such personal choices, as did Sterling his smoking brothers in Sigma Chi.

Kappas are one of the oldest Greek-letter societies. "In spite of their reputation for being sophisticated," said the 1951 U yearbook, *Utonian*, "the Kappas are a lively lot. They refuse to let prettiness pass for personality…" The 1953 *Utonian* said "It takes a prim, pure, old-fashioned girl to be a Kappa…" Both slogans seemed to fit Ellie well.

Nancy Colton and Ellie continued to grow close, Nancy determinedly taking it upon herself to keep Ellie and her brother together. Ellie had other allies as well. One evening two pretty Chi Omegas, Dorotha Sharp and Cathy Pearson, were on the Sigma Chi porch flirting with Sterling. Across the yard, hidden in the bushes of the Alpha Chi Omega house, one of Ellie's sorority sisters listened to their conversation.

"She ran home so fast she was out of breath," recalled Ellie, "as she told me everything she had seen and heard." The sisters at the Kappa house had an understanding, said Ellie, that whenever they saw one of their boyfriends with another girl, they would report it immediately.[6]

During the summer of 1950 following their freshman year, Nancy visited Ellie and her family in Idaho Falls. It was a time when the Ricks family suffered another major blow.

Vie Ricks Andrew was Ellie's beloved older sister who had helped nurture Ellie when she was growing up. Vie and her husband Howard had two little boys, Garrett and Rodney, when Vie gave birth to a daughter, Marie. There were serious complications and Vie was in the hospital when Nancy arrived in Idaho Falls. Learning Vie needed a transfusion, both girls donated blood.

The technician who drew the blood was very handsome, making the procedure more appealing for the two friends. Nancy and Ellie were on beds opposite each other, bantering as their blood dripped into collection bags. "Nancy said, 'My blood is bluer than yours,'" recalled Ellie. "'This means you should marry my brother!'" The technician laughed at the repartee.

Nancy left Idaho Falls while Vie was still ill. Doctors were puzzled. They thought some of the placenta may have been left after the birth, but checked and ruled that out. Meanwhile Vie was sent home, on the condition that Ellie would be there to help take care of the two boys. Their mother Annie had baby Marie. Vie was at home for about two weeks when she passed away. Doctors later decided she died of aleukemia, an acute form of leukemia characterized by a low white blood cell count and loss of normal bone marrow function.

"I was stunned by the death of Vie, leaving two little boys and a month-old baby girl," said Ellie. "Why had the Lord not responded to our fasting and prayers? Why couldn't a mother with three little children be saved?

My mother, in the struggle with her own grief, taught me a great lesson.

"She said, 'We can't second guess the Lord. Instead we ask for strength to carry on.' To help find that strength she asked me to join her again in fasting and prayer—this time to ask the Lord to help us be so grateful that we could share part of our lives with Vie, that we would not be bitter, but have strength and wisdom to help Vie's husband and children."

Vie's widower husband Howard kept the two boys to raise and Annie quit her job and remained at home to rear Marie. A couple of years later Howard remarried and took back Marie. That was very hard on Annie, yet she demonstrated a kind heart and stoicism, traits often mirrored by Ellie.

Annie wrote to Ellie, "I'm afraid it won't be too long before Nanny and Grandpa will be heart broken over giving up our little sunbeam. But I feel if Howard can find a good girl who will be good to the children and help ease his heartache, that one more adjustment and sorrow added to the many I've had must be added to the hills I must climb and I hope the Lord will always give me faith and the will to overcome them."[7]

"I went back to the University of Utah at that time with a very sad heart because my sister Vie had been my champion all along," said Ellie. "I was back for only a short time when I was told my Uncle Joe had also died." Joe Parker was married to her Aunt Vie. Ellie was fond of Joe, an outgoing man with a keen sense of humor. By then Ellie's college classes had begun and she was unable to return to Idaho for her uncle's funeral.

The Ricks family years earlier had lost Ellie's father, Emerson, and grandfather Orson, a sister Sarah Ann—born before Ellie—and another sister, Marie, who died at the age of thirteen. Vie and Joe extended that tragic toll.

When Ellie returned to the U she moved into the Kappa Kappa Gamma house, living there for the rest of her three years of college. She was fortunate to find space; the house had only five bedrooms—another five were added in 1963—and accommodated about twenty young women. Preference was given to out-of-state students like Ellie. Ellie and other girls with more seniority got to live at the front of the house, whose windows overlooked the street.

The red-brick home was located north of campus at 33 South Wolcott

Street (1455 East), in a well-established neighborhood called Federal Heights. It had been purchased by Kappa's predecessor, Lambda Phi Lambda, for $8,000 in 1929, and remodeled a decade later at a cost of $15,000.

The housemother, Mrs. Coates, was a stately woman who had a small living quarter near the front door—a good vantage point to keep track of the sisters, who had a curfew of 10:30 p.m. during the week and midnight on weekends. "She was a very proper woman," said Joan Douglas Earl. "We loved her and wouldn't think of being out after curfew."

"None of us had cars and there were no buses," said Douglas, who was two years behind Ellie in school. "That meant we had to walk a lot." Still absorbing World War II veterans, classes were scheduled from 7 a.m. to 10 p.m. Quonset huts and other "temporary" buildings were renovated to become classrooms, offices, and dormitories. They were hot in summer and cold in winter.

All the sorority sisters met at the house for formal dinners, served on long tables, each Monday evening. Afterward they were required to linger together while coffee and tea were served from a silver tea set, and remain until excused by chapter leaders. They hired two houseboys at a time who served the meals and cleaned up. One houseboy during that period was Maughan Colton, Sterling's younger brother. "We all had crushes on them," said Earl, who called Maughan a "quiet, cute kid."

Kappas competed in building homecoming floats, having the best combined academic grades among sororities, and performing at the U's annual Songfest. For casual breaks they frequented such places as the CI (the College Inn), Fernwood Candy and Ice Cream, or A&W Root Beer.

On April 1, 1951, students and others had a unique new place to frequent for lunch or dinner in Salt Lake City. The prices were right and the food excellent. What's more, you could stay in your auto and a carhop would take your order and bring it to you. On that day the first Marriott Hot Shoppes in the West opened for business at 5th South and Main.[8]

Sterling and Ellie were among the thousands who patronized it—never dreaming that Hot Shoppes foreshadowed their own future.

9

From Oilfields to Stanford Law School

World War II did not end cleanly. For all the blood and treasure lost by tens of millions of servicemen and civilians alike, the seeds of future conflicts were sown before hostilities ended in Europe and the Pacific.

Three allied powers—the U.S., Britain, and the Soviet Union—met in Potsdam, Germany from July 17 to August 2, 1945 to carve up what remained of pre-war Germany west of a newly created line between Germany and Poland. France later acceded to the agreement.

Germany was divided into four occupation zones. Although its capital Berlin was fully within the Soviet zone, Berlin itself was also divided into four zones. The Soviets would not allow access to Berlin by vehicle. The Berlin Airlift followed, supplying West Berlin residents with necessities to survive. The foiled plans of Moscow and its puppet regime in East Berlin led to the infamous wall dividing the city.

On the Pacific front, the Korean Peninsula had been part of the Japanese empire since early in the twentieth century. After World War II it was left to the Americans and Soviets to decide Korea's future. In August 1945 the State Department recommended that the peninsula be divided at the 38th parallel—a demarcation that stuck—with the Russians occupying the area north of the line and the United States occupying the south.

On June 25, 1950 some 75,000 soldiers from the North Korean

People's Army poured across the 38th parallel, igniting the Korean War. North Korea was supported by China and the Soviet Union. The United Nations Security Council, meeting in emergency session, called for an immediate ceasefire. Two days later it announced the formation of U.N. forces to be sent to Korea.

Washington did not wait for the U.N. to act, fearing that, should the North's aggression succeed, China, the Soviets, and international Communism as a whole would continue attacking across national borders.

By July American troops were on the way to Korea, but not with an enthusiastic send-off. "If the best minds in the world had set out to find us the worst possible location in the world to fight this damnable war," said U.S. Secretary of State Dean Acheson, "the unanimous choice would have been Korea."[1]

The Korean War technically never ended. Instead, after three years of fighting, an uneasy armistice was signed. American military casualties totaled about 128,000 including 37,000 deaths, with another 5,000 missing in action.

For the fourth time in history the United States turned to conscription to fill military ranks. (The other three were the Civil War, World War I and World War II.) Congress passed and the President signed into law the Selective Service Act of 1948, requiring all men between the ages of eighteen and twenty-six to register for the draft. About 20,000 were drafted in 1948 and another 10,000 in 1949.

From the outbreak of the Korean War in 1950 to the armistice that suspended armed conflict in 1953, 1.5 million servicemen were drafted. Another 1.3 million volunteered, usually choosing the Navy or Air Force.

With the writing on the wall, Sterling joined the Army Reserve Officer Training Corps (ROTC) at the U. He wouldn't serve active duty until he completed his schooling, and then as an officer. During summer 1950 Sterling attended two weeks of camp at the U.S.

Army Artillery School at Fort Sill, Oklahoma. It was not a pleasant experience—hot and dry with a lot of creepy critters including chiggers, centipedes, tarantulas and rattlesnakes. The men were housed in tents with cement floors.

He and fellow Vernal native Dallin Oaks crossed paths again. Sterling taught the gospel doctrine class in the LDS branch while at Fort Sill, and handed it off to Oaks, who was there with a Utah National Guard unit for summer training.

By the spring of 1950, Sterling had completed his bachelor's degree with honors in banking and finance, finishing in three years as planned. That fall he started law school at the U's S.J. Quinney College of Law. Still living at the Sigma Chi house, he was again involved in student activities and chaired Sigma Chi's fall rush—when potential members visit fraternities and coeds visit sororities.

Sigma Chi attracted an impressive pledge class. It included young Bill Marriott and his roommate Bruce Haight, who lived in an off-campus apartment. Bill had one of the sportiest cars on campus, a red Ford convertible, and was diligent and studious. He worked part time at the new Salt Lake Hot Shoppes and joined the Navy ROTC.

On the romance front, Sterling and Ellie continued to date; Sterling exclusively with Ellie and Ellie with a string of suitors. Two dates with Ellie that stood out in Sterling's memory were a hike up Red Butte Canyon and another occasion when he gave Ellie three roses.

Ellie focused on what she wanted to do after college, and changed her major to elementary education. She and Nancy Colton joined Spurs, a national service organization for sophomore girls and one of the hardest-working groups on campus. They read to the blind, collected funds for charities, sold tickets to events, marched with the band, and assisted other campus activities.

By the fall of 1951 Sterling and Ellie had been seeing each other for two years. "I was very much interested," he recalled, "and didn't date anyone else, but I didn't think I could afford to consider getting married." Years later he would regret his decision to wait.

With money tight, Sterling sought out jobs that paid well, often because they were unattractive to most others. One that fit this description was the oil fields, including Red Wash Field near his hometown, Vernal. The area has one of the world's largest deposits of oil shale and tar sands. Exploratory drilling began as early as 1900 but was not commercially successful until 1949, when Sterling first worked there.[2]

For four successive summers—as well as at Christmas and other holidays—Sterling labored in the oil fields of Utah, Colorado, Wyoming, and Nebraska. Usually he was on drilling rigs, work that was hot, dirty, and dangerous, but paid well with a lot of overtime, which he welcomed.

The work on rigs involved running a large revolving drill bit into the ground. It was attached to three heavy thirty-foot connected pipes. Periodically workers pulled the pipe to the surface, replaced the drill bit, and ran it back down the hole. A drill team normally consisted of a driller and three or four deckhands.

Laboring in the oil fields in 1950, Sterling reported to Ellie, "We work seven days a week and often 16 hours a day. Most of the time we work all night and sleep all day...This would be a terrible life to live for long. Honestly, these men live only from one day to the next, with no thought of the future other than getting a new car." He added, uncharacteristically, "They (most of them) are the lowest type of human I know."[3]

A year later, on August 21, 1951, Sterling sent Ellie another letter from the oil fields. His conscience obviously had bothered him. "As to the fellows I work with," he wrote, "I must take back what I said previously about their companionship being poor, for they really are the salt of the earth and would give you the shirt off of their backs if you needed it."

In the summer of 1951 Sterling found a mentor in the form of "Tex" Henry, a driller who had spent most of his life in the oilfields. "He was rough, tough, and foul-mouthed," recalled Sterling, "but he took pleasure in providing work for college students working to pay for their education. One adventure in the oilfields was with Tex and Nyle Merkley, the younger brother of one of Sterling's high school friends.

Tex and Nyle got a job working on a drilling rig at White Valley, west of Tremonton in northern Utah, and invited Sterling to go with them. The drilling was in hard rock and penetration was very slow. The crew ran three shifts: The morning shift pulled the drill pipe to the surface; the afternoon shift ran it back into the hole; the night shift often had nothing to do but to clean up and sleep. After a few weeks drilling stopped, putting the three out of work.

They drove to Casper, Wyoming, headquarters of Loffland Brothers, one of the world's largest contract drilling companies, and landed jobs. The oilfield, in Sidney, Nebraska, was shallow and sandy. Drilling was easy. Rather than repeatedly pulling pipe, they spent most of the time adding new pipe to drill deeper. They worked very hard and often were shorthanded, getting a lot of overtime and making a lot of money. The downside was that they were always dirty and tuckered out.

At the end of summer, Sterling left Tex and Nyle in Sidney and took a bus home to Vernal. Next stop: Palo Alto, California and Stanford University. Sterling had decided that, given all the distractions at the U, he needed a change of scenery and a more rigorous intellectual challenge if he was to succeed at the practice of law.

He had applied for and been accepted into Stanford Law School, where his need for challenge would be met completely. Stanford would do for Sterling's brain what the hay fields and oilfields did for his body—stretch and grow it close to what seemed the maximum possible.

When Sterling entered Stanford Law School in 1951 he needed help to make ends meet. Help came in the form of the Henry Newell Scholarship, set aside for law students from Utah, and later the

Chalmers Graham Scholarship.

Sterling moved into Crothers Hall, a small, fairly new men's dorm, and held a series of part-time jobs: working at the library and dry cleaners; clearing dishes for one meal a day at the freshman men's dorm—in exchange for eating all his meals there at no cost—and supplying coffee and donuts at the law school. He also received a stipend from the ROTC, which he continued at Stanford.

He entered Stanford Law one year before two luminaries graduated in 1952—Sandra Day O'Connor, who became the first female U.S. Supreme Court Justice (1981-2006); and William Rehnquist, who became Chief Justice of the Supreme Court (1986-2005).

By everyone's reckoning, Rehnquist was by far the smartest student in law school and was his class's valedictorian. Rehnquist and O'Connor were, however, but two of a remarkable law school group at Stanford from 1948 to 1953, which also included two U.S. presidential candidates, a governor, a Secretary of State, an assistant to the U.S. President, a member of the President's Cabinet, and several CEOs of major corporations.

Professor George Osborne—fearsome and cantankerous—welcomed Sterling and other newcomers this way: "Look on your right and on your left, and realize that probably one out of the three of you will not graduate." Sterling at the same time was encouraged by two other Utah Sigma Chis who had preceded him to Stanford—future Utah Governor Scott Matheson, and David Salisbury, one of the smartest students on campus, who would end up in the same law firm as Sterling and join him on a series of lifetime adventures.

Leading law schools later in the twentieth century would become known as hotbeds of political activity, typically leaning leftward. When Sterling started at Stanford in mid-century, however, it was a placid place; few students were politically active and those who were tended to be conservative. Rehnquist and O'Connor were nominated for the high court by two conservative presidents from California, Richard

Nixon and Ronald Reagan, respectively.

Stanford Law faculty as well as students were almost entirely white males. "We only had three females in our starting class, and I can't remember any minorities," said Sterling. One factor in the campus atmosphere at the time was that about half the students were veterans. There was little interest in public interest law and legal aid, perhaps on the part of some men who felt they had already fulfilled their duty to country and society.[4]

Organized activities in the school included the Law Forum, the Moot Court program, and the *Law Review*. The latter was launched at Stanford in 1948 and is among many such publications in law schools, participation on which is a standard way of identifying top students. Candidates to staff the Stanford *Law Review* were selected from the top 20 percent of the class. Sterling excelled in his first year and was named a member of the *Law Review* Board of Editors. "I never worked as hard as I did at Stanford and never learned so much," he said.

Frank Church, later a U.S. senator from Idaho, who transferred to Stanford in 1942 after a year at Harvard, said, "The formulation of the law was more open to exploration at Harvard, but I learned more law as such at Stanford...The sheer volume of substantive law that Stanford choked down our throats was quite adequate to prepare us for the bar."

Scott Matheson, who spent his first two years at the University of Utah Law School before transferring to Stanford, said, "Everyone at Stanford was capable, outstanding, aggressive, and successful. The intensity nearly killed me."[5]

Sterling observed that "It was not as hard to get into the law school then" as it is now in the twenty-first century, "but it was more difficult to graduate. Now if you get in you are pretty much assured you will graduate if you don't really goof up." Graduates then had to take the California bar exam. Overall passage rate at California law schools was about 50 percent—compared with 90 percent at Stanford.

One facet keeping Stanford students on edge was that many courses did not have tests during the term; everything depended on a student's performance on the final exam. "The end result was that most of us studied very hard," noted Sterling. Classes whose professors made the biggest impression on him included torts, constitutional law, contracts, criminal law, and wills.

Stanford students were brainy but were still students. There were activities outside class, such as intramural football and poker. Occasional pranks helped keep the atmosphere breathable. During Sterling's era someone fashioned big black feet and hung them on Hoover Tower; someone also sneaked into the faculty library and put a goldfish in the water cooler. Magnified by the glass, said one student, "it looked like a shark."

It is doubtful that Sterling was ever accused of such capers. He was a focused student and serious though light-hearted person. There are thousands of lawyer jokes but probably few if any that fit him. Sterling loved humor and enjoyed people who spun it, but it was not his personal style to do so.

Most of Sterling's diversion in law school came compliments of local LDS Church members who became warm friends. The local stake president was David Haight, Mayor of Palo Alto, who later became a member of the Church's Quorum of the Twelve Apostles. Sterling attended the Palo Alto Ward, which also included the Taylor and Mary Rich Peery family, who had him to Sunday dinners a number of times.

"We loved having students over," said daughter Nancy Peery Marriott, a teenager at the time. "They were fine examples to us. Sterling was no exception; he lived up to his name 'Sterling.' He was warm and friendly and a most kind man."[6]

Nancy later married Richard E. (Dick) Marriott, also a Sigma Chi at the U and a future leader of the worldwide Marriott enterprise, founded by his father J.W. Marriott and Sterling's father Hugh.

Ellie provided Sterling's biggest diversion that fall. Nancy Colton and Bill Marriott were good friends. When she learned that Bill was driving to Palo Alto, home of his roommate Bruce Haight, to attend a big football game, Nancy poured on the charm: "How about taking three adorable coeds with you? That way it won't be such a long, dull ride."

Bill readily agreed. His interest was Stanford's big game with the University of California-Berkeley; Ellie's was seeing Sterling; Nancy's was keeping Ellie's interest in her brother alive. Back in Utah, Ellie was a dating machine. Whenever she started to like a guy, Nancy stepped in and reminded Ellie that her true love was in Palo Alto. Also along for the ride to California was Nancy's sorority sister Beverly Clark. The four Utah students piled into Bill's new two-tone blue Oldsmobile 88 and headed west.

For Bill and other football fans the game that year was indeed a big one. After a disappointing season in 1950, Stanford fired its coach and hired Chuck Taylor, a former Stanford All-American. Stanford reeled off nine straight wins without a loss that season, and was ranked No. 3 nationally. Unfortunately for Stanford fans at this year's big game, Cal upset Stanford, 20-7.

After the game, Sterling borrowed a car and drove Ellie to San Francisco, thirty miles north. He had a special and, for Sterling at the time, very expensive treat in store—dinner at the exotic Omar Khayyam restaurant

Sterling and Ellie entered the building at 200 Powell Street and descended the stairs, turning left into the Rubaiyat Lounge with its velvet banquettes and low Persian lamps. Beyond was the cavernous, sumptuously appointed Omar Khayyam restaurant. A host wearing a fez bowed slightly and led them to a curtained chamber surrounding a low table, decorated with individual wall hangings from *Arabian Nights* and inscriptions from Khayyam's *Rubaiyat*.

The delicious food was a mix of Armenian, Middle Eastern, and African cooking. Altogether an unforgettable evening.

The Stanford-Cal game was Saturday, November 24, 1951, still warm in California but cool and cold in Nevada and Utah. With the weekend wrapped up, Bill and the three girls left for Salt Lake City. The Olds didn't make it that far. It blew a gasket in the water line crossing the Nevada desert and, with steam pouring out of the hood, crept to a stop. Bill, already feeling ill, apparently from mononucleosis, was thoroughly perplexed.

"It was twenty degrees below zero," he recalled, "we had a broken water hose. I was so young at the time, it was very scary."[7]

The closest town was Winnemucca, a small community whose claim to fame was having a bank that was robbed of $32,640 by Butch Cassidy and his Wild Bunch on September 19, 1900. Bill found a sympathetic state trooper who arranged to have his car towed all the way to Salt Lake City.

Ellie enjoyed most of the weekend with Sterling—but not all of it. Soon after returning to Utah she wrote and thanked him for "a perfect Thanksgiving to remember." Then she dropped the other shoe. "But, Sterling, in reviewing the events, I'm left quite confused at your inconsistency...I'm not trying to tie you down to anything—it just seemed a little strange that the only time you acted like you liked me at all—was when we were alone Saturday night.

"Are you ashamed to let other people know you like me...by being as indifferent as possible? Or did you feel a strong obligation because I came down?????"[8]

Sterling responded in a rambling four-page letter that was written between midnight and 2 a.m. when he was obviously weary. "I have no wonder that I left you confused with my inconsistency," he wrote. "I constantly find myself wondering as to what I do believe. I am sorry that too often have I subjected you to these inconsistencies, this indecision that belies me." He also blamed it on selfishness. What he was sure of, he wrote, was that "so many of my most fond memories are centered around you."[9]

Perhaps in an attempt to deflect their differences with humor, a number of Sterling's letters to Ellie during the last quarter of 1951 began with this salutation: "My Dear Miss Ricks:."

She responded with a friendly, conciliatory letter. Under the circumstances, wrote Ellie, "there couldn't help but have been some strain between us at Thanksgiving." She acknowledged that, "I was a little unfair to ask for the justification of your inconsistency when I was already aware of the situation.

"This is for sure—that it wasn't or isn't due to your selfishness—'cause in the time I have known you, you have shown less selfishness than any one else of my acquaintance."[10]

As an ROTC member Sterling was asked to be in the color guard to post the flag for the Rose Bowl, held each year on New Year's day in Pasadena, California. He had arranged to be in Vernal for Christmas and planned to drive to Salt Lake and fly to Los Angeles the day before New Year's.

There was an unusually heavy snowstorm, however, and the rural route between Vernal and Salt Lake became impassable. He arrived too late in Salt Lake to catch a flight to Los Angeles. Instead he decided to visit Ellie. He arrived at her apartment unannounced, learning she already had a date for the evening. "She became very nervous when I didn't show an inclination to leave before her date was scheduled to arrive."

Leave he did, returning the following afternoon to help Ellie hang drapes. She thanked him in a letter, admitting she wasn't sorry he missed the Rose Bowl, since it gave them an opportunity to be together before his return to Palo Alto. Sterling gave her a pair of moccasins and a book of poetry for Christmas. The moccasins, to her dismay, were many sizes too small; Sterling had guessed the size based on his mother's and sister's small feet.

Ellie loved the book. In thanking him she quoted a stanza in it from "An Essay on Man," by Alexander Pope:

Know then thyself, presume not God to scan;
The proper study of Mankind is Man...
Born but to die, and reas'ning but to err;
Alike in ignorance, his reason such,
Whether he thinks too little, or too much;
Chaos of thought and passion, all confus'd;
Still by himself abus'd, or disabus'd;
Created half to rise, and half to fall;
Great lord of all things, yet a prey to all;
Sole judge of truth, in endless error hurl'd:
The glory, jest, and riddle of the world!"

In the same letter, in her typical humor, Ellie said she had decided to "marry for money and have a maid do all the scrubbing of floors, cooking, making beds, etc. etc. so I can dedicate my time to basking on a warm beach and reading all the things I've wanted to read!"[11]

10

LOVE STORY FOR THE AGES

Sterling and Ellie's love story is one for the ages.
It was nourished and forged early on from long distance. They spent far more days writing to each other than being with each other—Sterling from summer oilfields in the West and Midwest; from Stanford Law School; and in the Army, posted stateside as well as 5,000 miles away in Europe. Ellie wrote back from Utah and Idaho.

Their correspondence explored nearly every facet of their personalities, and gave them a breadth of insight into each other that they may not have acquired in any other way. The letters formed a small stream before Sterling entered Stanford Law School in 1951. They became a river from then until he graduated in 1953.

The letters later became a flood, after they married, starting in December 1954 when they communicated for four months between Germany and Idaho.

Ellie came into her own during 1952-53, her senior year at the U. She was elected president of Kappa Kappa Gamma, the *Utonian* yearbook reporting that she had "a beaming smile and cultured diplomacy."[1] In her photos with the Kappas that year, Ellie wore her hair in a bang that curled like a fishhook toward her right eye.

She used her diplomacy, among other ways, to introduce a new activity in the sorority—inviting select foreign women students to join Kappas once a month on a Monday for their chapter dinner.

"Kappas were proud of their activities this year," said the *Utonian*, "from campus leadership to helping with the National Election… they were happy crews working and playing together as their crowned queens and year's activities unfolded." Looking back on the year, however, Ellie acknowledged that, "It isn't always fun to 'be in charge.'"

Ellie's hometown newspaper reported that she "was recently chosen president of the Delta Eta chapter of Kappa Kappa Gamma sorority at the University of Utah. She will be official representative at the national convention in Hot Springs, Va. this summer. She is active in campus affairs, was an officer in Spurs, a sophomore honorary group."[2]

Ellie and another Kappa, Irma Ward, traveled by train to Virginia for their national convention. It was the first time either had been east of the Rocky Mountains. "We had a great time at the convention and afterwards in New York City, where I saw my first Broadway show, 'South Pacific,'" said Ellie.

The acquaintance whose personal example had the strongest influence on both Ellie and Sterling was Lowell L. Bennion, a great humanitarian and practical philosopher. "He reached my heart more than anyone else," said Ellie. Following the deaths of family members, Bennion comforted Ellie, assuring her that one day she would see and be with her loved ones again. Sterling added that Bennion was "the most Christ-like man I have known; he had a profound influence for good in my life."

Bennion was married to Merle Colton, a first cousin to Sterling. He was a prolific writer of short books and articles, and his outlook on life was reflected in the lives of Ellie and Sterling and numerous others. Material possessions had little attraction for Bennion, who preached that the simple, unadorned life was the one most likely to be peaceful and happy—and the life most acceptable to God.

Bennion emphasized daily acts of kindness and Christian service along with study of scriptural doctrine. Outside class he was more likely to be found with a shovel and hammer than with a stack of books, more likely to be clearing a widow's sidewalk of snow, or repairing a roof. He routinely invited students to join him in such weekend projects; over the years thousands did.

At the age of just twenty-six in 1934 he helped found and direct the first LDS Institute of Religion, at the University of Utah. It was a program of religious instruction for college students, a companion to Seminary at the high school level. LDS Institutes are now found at many colleges around the world. Sterling and Ellie were both active in the LDS Institute program at the U.

At the end of an Institute class during her year as Kappa president, Bennion pulled Ellie aside and asked how they could attract more Greek students to give Institute a try. Not long afterward, when Ellie entered his classroom door she was trailed by about thirty other Kappas. "I just told them this was something we were going to do," she explained.

Sterling, in the journal of his college years, recorded a set of widely quoted lines by Bennion that summarized the great man's philosophy of life:

> *Learn to like what doesn't cost much.*
> *Learn to like reading, conversation, music.*
> *Learn to like plain food, plain service, plain cooking.*
> *Learn to like fields, trees, brooks, hiking, rowing, climbing hills.*
> *Learn to like people, even though some of them may be different... different from you...*
> *Learn to like to work and enjoy the satisfaction of doing your job as well as it can be done.*
> *Learn to like the songs of birds, the companionship of dogs.*
> *Learn to like gardening, puttering around the house and fixing things.*
> *Learn to like the sunrise and sunset, the beating of rain on the roof and windows and the gentle fall of snow on a winter day.*
> *Learn to keep your wants simple and refuse to be controlled by the likes and dislikes of others.*[3]

Sterling's discipline and self-denial were stunning. He went all through high school, college, and law school without ever owning a car. He asked others for rides or even hitchhiked. Sterling didn't purchase his first car, a used one, until after graduating from Stanford Law School. More significantly, he found Ellie, the love of his life, in the fall of 1949, and yet, wanting to be solvent, waited five years to marry her.

Ellie herself was reared in a family that knew privation. After the untimely deaths of her father and grandfather, Ellie's mother Annie sold the family car to buy a home in Idaho Falls. The family never owned a car again. Annie bottled fruits, vegetables, and meats, and all meals were homemade. She hand-sewed virtually every piece of clothing worn by Ellie and her sisters. For Ellie, the youngest sibling, that usually meant altering an older sister's clothing to fit her. Ellie, like Sterling, worked to earn every cent she received.

Ellie continued a steady correspondence with Sterling, who was heading into his last year of law school. Periodically she included poetry, sometimes whimsical verses she created. For Valentine's Day in 1952, Ellie wrote:

Someone thinks you're wonderful,
Someone thinks you're true;
Someone thinks you're brilliant,
And that someone is you![4]

While sobered by being halfway through college and not knowing what would come next, Ellie felt that "the period of friendship we have had has added so much to my life and has helped me so much to try to be a better person…I really do appreciate your strong character and ideals and your crazy ways," as well as "your attention and thoughtfulness when we're alone." But she was still bothered by "your indifference when we're around other people."

She added this P.S.: "I just remembered—a year ago from today I was really mad at you…Try and figure that one out!" Ellie apparently referred to a time when she wanted a committed relationship with Sterling, but he was not ready for one. His hesitancy reflected not his feelings for Ellie, which were real, but his rigid sense of responsibility: neither that time in his life nor his finances were prepared for a long-term commitment.

Thanksgiving weekend 1952 again found Ellie with Sterling in Palo Alto. His reaction later reflected his growing affection for her—which apparently still hadn't been communicated clearly to Ellie. "Golly,"—a youthful term sprinkled in his letters—"it seems that I had a dream and oh such a wonderful dream, but it seemed to pass so quickly," he began… "I have gone over every moment of your sojourn in sunny 'Calif.' countless times. Thanks again for coming."[5]

In that same letter, perhaps persuaded by Ellie that his actions weren't consistent with his feelings, Sterling said, "I have decided conclusively that I am not normal—I don't know what it is but something is wrong somewhere. Think I should see a psychiatrist?"

Ellie quickly reassured him. "I have decided conclusively that you are normal — a slight deviant, characteristic of most of us this age. Your insistence on your individuality might make you more individualistic, but I still think you're an okay kid!!"[6]

Sterling and Ellie spent several exhilarating days together over the year-end holiday, eliciting the warmest letter yet from Sterling. "The three days I was able to spend with you added much to my already overflowing store of memories," he wrote. "…much of what I am or ever hope to be is tied up very closely with you, because much of my growth, mentally, spiritually and emotionally is so closely associated with you as to be a part of me."[7]

But Sterling was still dogged by doubts. "Sometimes I feel that I dwell too often in this area of reverie, and either refuse or am afraid to deal in realities and the decisions which of necessity go hand in hand." Regarding their relationship, "much as I have tried to analyze it and reach some decisions regarding it, I still find myself in the same dilemma of uncertainty.

"…I feel that my treatment of you has been anything but thoughtful. I have often wondered why you continue to put up with me and my many idiosyncracies [sic]." As usual he signed off "as ever, Sterling."

Again Ellie reassured him. "I too have often wondered why I put up with your idiosyncracies [sic] — all I know is I look at you as a total personality — I like you for what you are — not for what you aren't!" In the same letter Ellie said she went to the U's Junior Prom with another guy, adding: "I kept my shoes on the whole time this year!"[8] The reference apparently was to the time Sterling had walked her from a Sigma Chi party to Carlson Hall. When the lights blinked, signaling the doors would lock in five minutes, Ellie and Sterling lingered long enough for a kiss, then Ellie removed her shoes and sprinted to the dorm.

Finally, more than three years after first bumping into each other in a dormitory elevator on the U campus, the word "love" crept into their vocabulary. After spending a romantic evening together ushering in the new year, 1953, this magical word appeared repeatedly in a letter of Ellie's:

> I'm sure love in its fullness is quite a mystery to me; however, I do know there are some things that I do love and will always love about you: your belief in the fundamental dignity of man, your unwillingness to accept things without investigation, your ambition and desire to work, your consideration for others, your thoughtfulness which seems to come so naturally, your sportsmanship, and so many other things…I love you for the happy memories of the past that you have been such a part of.[9]

Sterling's response has been lost to history, but we know he reciprocated because of another letter from Ellie two months later. It began in an entirely new way: "Hello, my Love (alias Sterling Don Colton)," and included, euphorically: "All at once it occurs to me that you really do want me around — and I have such a wonderful feeling that I want to immediately tell you that I love you, too — and can think of no better existence than to spend it with you."[10]

Sterling's last full-time semester at Stanford was the summer of 1953, enabling him to graduate a year early from law school, as he had done in earning a bachelor's degree at the U. His riveted focus and grueling work had earned him a coveted position on the *Stanford Law Review* and landed him in the top ten percent of the class of 1953. By the end of school he was relieved and thoroughly exhausted.

"I hope I never have to go through another quarter like the last one, it was by far the most difficult that I have ever had," he wrote to Ellie, adding that he probably took too many classes. "By the end of test week I was really a physical wreck."[11]

For one of the few recorded times in his life, immediately after finishing finals Sterling impulsively set out on what he called "one of the most enjoyable weeks I have ever spent." It was like air escaping from a badly over-inflated tire. Three college friends, Chuck Stewart, Dick Janapaul, and Vince Jones, were great travel companions as they all headed south from the Bay area. Vince's car had radiator trouble as night came on, forcing them to putter along at twenty-five miles an hour and stop repeatedly at service stations between Salinas and Bakersfield, where it was finally fixed.

From there they drove to ritzy Palm Springs, where the four had chipped in to reserve a motel room. Unfortunately the registration was in only two of their names. Sterling and Dick "spent a major part of our time eluding the manager or trying to convince him we were just visiting," said Sterling—ironic, given that one day he would be the top attorney for a hotel chain, enforcing rules and the law against such offenders.

"We kept on the go for three days," reported Sterling to Ellie, "swimming, sun, sports car races, sun, playing tennis, sun, horseback riding, sun, night clubbing, and more sun." Tartan is "great sun tan lotion, but unfortunately we ran out of it and bright ones that we were, we failed to get any more." The result was sunburns all around, and "I am still feeling the consequences...but believe me I enjoyed every minute of it."[12]

Sterling passed the Utah and California bars, and later the District of Columbia bar. Sterling's degree was a Bachelor of Laws; several years later Stanford changed it to a Juris Doctor.

Ellie graduated that spring from the U in elementary education with a minor in history. During her last quarter she took two classes that reflected lifelong passions: Shakespeare and tennis. That fall she taught fifth grade at Edison School in west Salt Lake City.

During that summer Sterling's dad took the young couple to a horse show in Ogden. "How do you tell a good horse?" Ellie asked innocently. "Same way you tell a good woman," answered Hugh. "Check out her legs, her teeth, and her breeding possibilities." Ellie's face turned bright red.

That evening, a beautiful starlit night, Sterling and Ellie were sitting in a car on a hillside overlooking Salt Lake City. "Let's see," teased Sterling, "good teeth, nice legs, and the breeding possibilities are fascinating!" Lacking the money for an engagement ring, and following fraternity tradition, he asked Ellie to wear his Sigma Chi pin. She said yes.

"It was the happiest day of my life," said Sterling, "and the most meaningful event in my life." They planned to marry the following April.

As a student in ROTC, Sterling owed Uncle Sam the next three years of his life. He was commissioned a second lieutenant in the Army Field Artillery and ordered to report for active duty at Fort Sill, Oklahoma on January 1, 1954. He purchased his first car, a used, four-door, brown Ford, from Showalter Motor Company in Vernal. Near the end of the year he drove from Vernal to Fort Sill and reported as ordered.

Although there was an uneasy truce in Korea after three years of war, hostilities there or elsewhere could break out again at any moment. It was the height of the Cold War and Washington was determined to stop further Communist territorial gains.

Sterling was being trained as a forward observer, a particularly hazardous assignment. Their job was to find enemy cannon firing against friendly forces and report its location to U.S. units who could take defensive action. In World War II more than half of battle casualties were caused by artillery fire, and "forward observers overwhelmingly suffered the vast majority of all artillery losses."[13]

Three days after arriving at Fort Sill, Sterling wrote "Dearest Ellie" to say "I miss you so much tonight. I love you so much and would give anything to be with you tonight for a few moments to hear your voice and be able to hold you for a few minutes."

Ellie's letters, always filled with love, sometimes included humor and advice as well. She said she loved him "in many different ways. Even your faults (Don't be shocked—you do have some, you know!)"[14] She included a poem by Sara Teasdale:

They came to tell your faults to me,
They named them over one by one,
I laughed aloud when they were done,
I knew them all so well before,
Oh, they were blind, too blind to see
Your faults had made me love you more.

Sterling's law school education came to his rescue at Fort Sill. A regular army officer named Major William (Bill) Keogh had been sent to Stanford to be trained as a lawyer. Keogh met Sterling at Stanford and they became friends. Learning that Sterling too was at Fort Sill, Major Keogh requested that he be transferred to the military's legal arm, the Judge Advocate General's Corps (JAG). While most of his artillery classmates went to Korea, Sterling joined JAG.

He was ordered to report to the JAG Legal Center and School, located on the campus of the University of Virginia in Charlottesville. The concentrated three-month course meant a postponement of wedding plans. The school is accredited by the American Bar Association to award master's degrees in military law. Although directed by the Army, the center trains and teaches legal officers of each branch of the service.

While there, Sterling was promoted to first lieutenant.

The center was commanded by Colonel Charles Decker, a regular army officer in line to become a general. Military students lived and went to class in university facilities that were not meant to be used in the area's hot summers. Sterling and other class members had difficulty staying awake in suffocating classrooms.

One day the Army's top lawyer, Judge Advocate Major General Eugene Caffey was visiting from Washington. As he lectured, a number of class members dozed off.

Suddenly General Caffey stopped in mid-sentence and roared to JAG Commandant Decker: "Get that man!" Class members woke with a start as Decker rushed to the back of the room to a raised row of seats. He grabbed a lieutenant by the collar and said "This one?" The startled lieutenant cried out in a fear-induced high-falsetto voice, "No! not me."

Fortunately for him, Caffey said "No, the one on the end." The offender was promptly taken from the classroom. "We thought for sure he would be sent to Korea," recalled Sterling. Thanks to some sympathetic officers, however, he was assigned instead to a post in San Francisco.

Near the end of the three-month course, class members were taken to the Supreme Court in Washington and sworn in to practice before the highest court in the land.

That spring Ellie's hometown newspaper ran a story under the headline "Eleanor Ricks to Marry Utah Man," accompanied by a photo of Ellie. It said Annie Ricks Jaques "announced the engagement of her daughter, Eleanor Ricks, to Lt. Sterling Don Colton, son of Mr. and Mrs. Hugh Colton of Vernal, Utah. An August wedding is being planned...in the Idaho Falls LDS Temple."[15]

Later that month the newspaper on its society page ran a three-column photo of Ellie with two other women, examining items in a "hope chest." The caption said the chest holds "priceless linens and home items" and that Ellie "shows the bejeweled and traditional 'blue

Love Story for the Ages 119

garter' she will wear to her friends, Mrs. Harrison Dennis and Mrs. Lloyd Ricks."[16] The latter was married to Ellie's brother Lloyd Ricks.

Ellie was giddy with anticipation as wedding day neared. Working again at Hart's Bakery in Idaho Falls, she wrote Sterling to say, "Received a letter today – and as usual (they're my barometer, you know) it put me in even a better mood – I gave the customers bigger frosties – added the thirteenth donut to the dozen occasionally, etc. etc."[17]

Upon completion of JAG school, Sterling was given leave to be married. While driving across the country to his hometown in Vernal, Utah, he came upon a thunderstorm in Kansas. "I drove over a hilltop to find a large circus truck overturned in the middle of a dugway," he said, "with barely enough room on each side for my car to squeeze by." His car almost made it through, but struck the truck a glancing blow, putting a large dent in the right front fender and pushing it against the tire.

It was Sunday and difficult to find an open repair place. Finally Sterling was able to find an open service station where the attendant was able to pull the fender off the tire. However, the wheel was out of alignment, causing excess wear on the tires, two of which blew out before Sterling got to Vernal. He was tired and dirty by the time he reached home. Waiting inside was a special surprise: Ellie! He hadn't seen her in nearly six months and didn't expect to then. But he was thrilled, though also tired and dirty.

On July 29, 1954, Ellie met with the bishop of the Idaho Falls Fourth Ward, who happened to be her brother Lloyd, to be interviewed for a temple recommend. In the interview, a bishop asks a series of questions to determine compliance with church standards. Ellie passed the interview, as well as the following one with the local stake president.

Sterling went through the same procedure on August 2 with the bishop of the Vernal First Ward, William Wallace, and stake president Archie Johnson.

Sterling and Ellie left Vernal the first week in August 1954, heading to Idaho Falls for their wedding. They stopped in Salt Lake City to purchase rings, after Sterling borrowed part of the down payment from his brother Maughan.

While driving from Salt Lake to Idaho Falls, Ellie asked Sterling when he was going to ask her to marry him. The closest he had come was a year earlier when she had agreed to wear his Sigma Chi pin. Sterling pulled to the side of the road and stopped the car. Kneeling in some lava rock, Sterling popped the question. She said yes.

That was a pattern for their marriage: He would be the mainstay and she, with laughter and love, would trim the sails.

After a lot of stops and starts over five years, their future together at last looked golden.

11

TEMPLE MARRIAGE, LONG-DISTANCE LOVE

Sterling and Ellie arrived in Idaho Falls the evening of August 5 and walked around the temple grounds, seeking assurance from Heavenly Father that they were doing the right thing. Each received a strong spiritual confirmation that indeed they were.

They were married the following morning, August 6, 1954. Dressed all in white, they participated in temple ordinances, making a series of covenants to obey God's commandments. Then, in a specially appointed room, with a few LDS family members, including Sterling's parents and Ellie's mother, and close friends seated nearby, Sterling and Ellie knelt across an altar and were sealed as husband and wife for this life and for all eternity. Performing the ceremony was temple president William L. Killpack.

Afterward Sterling's parents hosted a luncheon for the wedding party in the Rose Room of the Hotel Rogers in Idaho Falls. That evening Ellie's mother hosted a reception in the hotel's Emerald Room. Maughan Colton was best man; Phil Colton and Lloyd Ricks were ushers. Shirley Stanger and Paula Stanger Vanderford attended Ellie.

The new couple spent that night at a motel on the Snake River, within sight of the temple. The next day they left on their honeymoon to Banff and Lake Louise, Alberta, Canada. The pristine area in the Canadian Rockies held special charm for Sterling, who had grown up close to what his father Hugh invariably called the "high and beautiful Uintas."

Sterling's car wasn't fully repaired yet and it vibrated when they drove over about fifty miles an hour. A benefit, he decided, was that when Ellie was driving, it acted as a governor to control her "hot foot."

They stayed in a small cabin near Yoho Valley Lodge, close to spectacular Takakkaw Falls, which is many times higher than Niagara. They hiked and rowed a boat on Lake Louise with its turquoise-blue water.

Ellie learned something important about Sterling. While steady and fairly predictable, within him beat the heart of an adventurer. They rented horses and rode mountain trails, where they spotted a young bull moose. Sterling dismounted, gave his horse's reins to Ellie, and left with his new camera to take pictures of the moose. Ellie was not pleased that he was gone a long time—especially later when they discovered he had taken more pictures of the moose than of the bride.

After the honeymoon they returned to Idaho Falls and then to Vernal for a large open house in his parents' flower garden. The new couple stood before a flower-covered trellis to greet guests. "The bride was lovely in a summer gown of white cotton embroidered in red," reported the local newspaper.[1] Two-hundred guests were treated to a buffet on a table decorated with white gladiolas and two crystal swans.

Looking back on that time, Ellie told a later congregation, "The day we were married in the temple I became a believer in miracles. One, that I had actually found someone who loved me and I loved him at the same time, and two, that we were both eager to make an eternal commitment to a most challenging, interesting, and satisfying relationship. My desire to keep those eternal covenants has been a powerful motivation."[2]

Sterling's sister Nancy wrote to Ellie shortly after the wedding, welcoming her dear friend into the family: "Oh, what lucky people we are to have such a wonderful addition. Good Old Ster, I knew he'd pull through!"[3]

Following the open house Sterling and Ellie headed east to Fort Sill, Oklahoma, where Sterling was stationed while awaiting a long-term Army assignment. They rented a furnished apartment in Lawton, adjacent to the base. It was hot and dusty and they lacked good air conditioning. Ellie often put on her bathing suit early in the day to help stay cool. Each evening when Sterling returned they went for a swim in the base's large pool. Ellie started a bug collection, eventually zapping and mounting nearly forty species.

After a lifetime of living frugally, Ellie continued to economize. They invited a bachelor officer friend of Sterling's to dinner. Ellie bought a pot roast, cutting it in two and cooking half of it. By the time it was ready it had shrunk, leaving little meat for anyone. The next time they had company, recalled Sterling, "she more than compensated by cooking for each guest the largest steaks I have ever seen."

Ellie also decided to save money by moving into a less desirable apartment. She overlooked giving advance notice to the first landlord, however, and they ended up paying rent to both places for months.

Soon after arriving at Fort Sill, James Cullimore, a Regional Representative of the Church, called Sterling to be a traveling representative throughout Oklahoma. His assignment was to befriend unmarried young LDS adults and encourage them to participate in church meetings and functions. Meanwhile the Coltons became active in the LDS branch on base. An LDS branch is like an LDS ward, but typically with a smaller membership.

Though the epitome of graciousness, Ellie knew nothing about military protocol for spouses of officers, and was nervous at the thought of attending social functions. To put her at ease, the wife of the JAG Corps commander took Ellie under her wing and offered to tutor her. Ellie was very grateful. At a large reception Ellie stayed close by her side as the woman introduced Ellie to the wives of senior officers.

Also at the event was the wife of the LDS branch president, who Ellie didn't recognize. Watching Ellie being fussed over and having Ellie not speak to her, the woman decided Ellie was a snob and a social-climber. She proceeded to create stories and make nasty comments about Ellie behind her back.

About a month later the Coltons were delighted when Sterling received orders transferring him to Germany. Ellie hesitated, however, to leave with bad feelings between her and the branch president's wife. There was another newlywed couple in the apartment across the hall with whom the Coltons had bonded tightly. Ellie confided to the wife her hurt feelings from the raw relations she had with the LDS woman.

The neighbor suggested that Ellie choose one of her prized possessions and go visit the woman and give it to her as a goodbye gift. Ellie pondered that idea and prayed for a forgiving heart. Finally she chose a favorite vase in which she had grown a fantastic plant from a sweet potato, and went to the woman's home. "She was surprised to see me on her doorstep," recalled Ellie.

"I told her I was sorry we were leaving before we had had a chance to be friends, and that if I had offended her in any way, I was sorry." Before Ellie left there were tears and hugs and words of forgiveness from both women.

Sterling left for Germany the first week in December 1954, a pivotal time in Germany's history. At the end of World War II nine years earlier, four powers—the U.S., Great Britain, Soviet Union and France—divided Germany into four occupied zones. The U.S. Seventh Army occupied the Western Military District of the American zone. The Seventh was created in the war as I Armored Corps under General George Patton.

In March 1946, given the belief that major Allied disputes were settled and peace achieved, the Seventh Army was deactivated. Subsequent hostile actions by the USSR set off alarm bells in freedom-loving nations, led by the U.S., which mobilized again to defend against a potential aggressor.

In 1949, faced with the prospect of further Communist expansion, the United States and eleven other Western nations formed the North Atlantic Treaty Organization (NATO) to provide collective security against the Soviet Union. The Soviet Union in 1955 formed a rival alliance, the Warsaw Pact.

The new Seventh Army was rebuilt, starting in 1951, headquartered at Stuttgart-Vaihingen, Germany. The size of the Seventh was to be increased four-fold, to assure effective opposition against possible aggression. It would largely be made up of young men who had been drafted into service, had little experience beyond basic training, and often did not understand why they were in Germany.

Within a year 100,000 young Americans arrived in the command—even though adequate facilities, equipment, and training were not ready for them. Also of concern was the conduct of soldiers with the German people. Their deportment was critical to the goodwill of local citizens and the success of working relationships with the West German government at every level.

Allied servicemen were ordered to obey local laws while in Germany, though they could not be prosecuted in local courts for crimes committed against German citizens, unless authorized by occupation authorities.

That was where the Judge Advocate General's Corps played a critical role. When a soldier broke a local law, occupation officials almost always preferred for JAG to prosecute the accused. Sometimes the result was a harsher penalty than a soldier likely would have faced in German courts.

The Seventh Army grew from 44,000 men and two divisions to 170,000 men and five divisions. Multilateral relations continued to improve, and on May 5, 1955 the Allies ended the occupation of West Germany. Four days later West Germany formally joined NATO, since then becoming Europe's most powerful country resisting the expansion of Russian hegemony.

In an early letter to Sterling in Germany, Ellie recited his strengths, "fundamental honesty, integrity and good will"; vowed to put their marriage above any other earthly concern; and accurately predicted that "someone with as many qualities as you have for good, will be expected to do many things, both for the Church and the community…I want to be there to help you in some way because I love you." She advised that they be perfectly honest with each other and "share as many mutual interests as possible."[4]

A downside to Sterling's new posting was that he and Ellie would be separated for an unknown period of time, while he settled in Germany and arranged for Ellie to join him. Christmas was just around the corner when he left for Europe, and Ellie was blue without him. She stayed with his family in Vernal for a few days after he left, then returned to Idaho Falls to teach school.

While Ellie was in Vernal, Marguerite tried to cheer her up, plying Ellie with a great assortment of hats as a diversion. Hugh did his part by driving her around the area, including to Diamond Mountain. They were accompanied by a cattle herder who, recalled Ellie, "bathed once a year, whether he needed it or not." By the time they reached Little Brush Creek, Ellie felt nauseated. They stopped the truck and she vomited.

Phil Colton, Sterling's younger brother, was especially kind, offering many acts of service and helping to entertain her. Repeatedly in her letters to Sterling, Ellie mentioned that Phil "seems just like a brother to me."

In Idaho Falls Ellie visited her doctor, who told her she was pregnant. She called Hugh and Marguerite with the news. Hugh wasn't surprised, telling her, "I knew when you got sick there what the problem was." He suggested they name the baby Little Brush Creek.

Sterling was thrilled at the news. He was assigned to Seventh Army Headquarters in Vaihingen, and moved into bachelor officer quarters until Ellie could join him. She was delayed by the pregnancy and dependent on Army procedures and timing. It was not clear how soon she would be in Germany.

Sterling's reputation for hard work was well deserved. But occasionally he roamed off the base and into local society. "I went with two other officers on a slumming tour of Stuttgart last night," he wrote, "and we didn't return until about 1:30 this morning.

"We visited several of the German gasthauses [taverns]. Boy I created a minor international crisis when I asked for something non-alcoholic." The friendly bar maid explained that they had nothing like that. "They hurriedly had a meeting of waiters, bar tenders, etc. and came up with a fruit cocktail concoction that wasn't bad."[5]

Returning to base that night, Sterling was not through. "We spent some time in the officers club where they had some good music, good floor show and cheap drinks, but it was jammed."

During their four-month wait Sterling and Ellie talked longingly of the future, in scores if not hundreds of letters. Sterling wrote that he hadn't neglected writing her more than a single day in a row; Ellie also wrote virtually every day. Sometimes one of them would go several days without a letter, then receive three or four at the same time. An obvious change was that, once hesitant to express his love in writing, Sterling now was as effusive as Ellie.

> Ellie: "I thought, even though it is early to be telling, that it would be fun to tell your parents about the coming addition, in a Christmas package." [12/10/54]

> Sterling: "Dearest Sweetheart, Is it true!? Or am I just reading between the lines?...It is almost unbelievable to me that we are to become parents. I do ask our Father in Heaven that I may prove worthy of being your husband and the father of our child...I love you so much. I have so many wonderful memories, and they all involve you. How your funny little nose crinkles up when you laugh. How you used to go sulk and yet would have such a hard time doing it." [12/18/54]

> Ellie: "I'm terribly ambitious for you – not for you to make any sort of splash in the world – but to develop yourself into a great man – not necessarily one that everyone knows about – but a few of us who know you well – will know what obstacles you have overcome – what temptations – what false pride, etc. So far I think you have made a fine record – and I pray that I may add and not detract from your future – and that because of me – you will be better and your future greater because I'm your wife instead of someone else." [1/2/55]

> Sterling: "Oh happy day, five letters from my one and only...This makes me so happy that I'm sure the entire office wonders what I've been drinking on the days I receive letters from you." [1/03/55]

> Ellie: "I just can't believe that I'm so lucky to have you for my husband. I love you so much it hurts – it hurts terribly not to be with you – not to be able to look forward to having you come home at the end of the day...not to be able to reach out and find your arms." [exact date unknown]

Sterling: "Oh how I do miss you. The few months we were together I realize they were the happiest that I've ever had and I want you to be with me always. I promise that there will never be another separation like this if I can help it." [1/12/55]

Ellie: "Mother and I went through the temple...it was all so much more clear and meaningful tonight. When you were there – I was so excited about being married – and so interested in looking out the corners of my eyes to find you, that I didn't get too much out of the ceremony." [1/14/55]

Sterling: "It means so much to me to be able to hear from you and know all is well, for my whole life is centered in you – Without you it seems meaningless." [1/06/55]

Ellie (quoting Shakespeare): [1/24/55]

> *How like a winter hath my absence been*
> *From thee, the pleasure of the fleeting year!*
> *What freezings have I felt, what dark days seen!*
> *What old January's bareness everywhere!*

Sterling: "Please stop worrying about your physical condition. I'd love you no matter how you looked. It is not your figure I'm in love with other than the fact that I love every bit of you and that love grows every day." [1/15/55]

Ellie: "It seems strange that our love should grow when we're apart – but it does – every letter brings you nearer and dearer to me. I keep thinking I can't possibly love you any more than I do now – but I know every year I can look back and say, 'I love him even more this year!'" [1/18/55]

Sterling: "I bought Dr. Benjamin Spock's book on child care so I'm ready to settle down for the night and learn what's expected of an expecting father. It says here 'The father often feels he is left out of this having a baby business.' …Well, I must learn how to pin the diapers so good night my love." 1/20/55]

Ellie: "So the father often feels left out, huh?…it's wonderful you're reading up – cause you'll be a wonderful father! I'm afraid of little babies until they're about 2 months old. I wish Joan would hurry and have hers – so I could pay more attention to what they're like… All my love to my Favorite husband, sweetheart, lover, companion, friend, critic, and correspondent." [1/26/55]

Sterling: "I really do miss you so much that it is almost unbearable. You have really bewitched me. I can't live without you…with all my love, hoping you'll be with me soon, never to leave again." [1/25/55]

Ellie: "You now have a greater proof of my love than anything thus far. I let them shoot me twice in each arm. It's the bravest thing I've ever done – if you only knew my phobia for needles…I have to go back for the next two Fridays. Sob!" [1/21/55]

Sterling: "I don't know why your [sic] so frightened of that little needle. Think of all the soldiers and little kids who take shots – actually mine gave me very little trouble and I've received the same ones you'll be taking – so don't worry about it." (Exact date unknown. He apologized in a follow-up letter, writing, "I'm really sorry to hear that the shots had such an adverse effect upon you.")

Ellie: "I've missed you more than anyone's ever been missed – and feel like a girl who's never been kissed. Oh these poetic moods – I just can't squelch them…The port of call – it came today – and I've been shaking with excitement ever since. How I want to hurry and be with you. March seems like an eternity away." [2/10/55]

Sterling: "I love you more than ever and am counting the minutes until you'll be in my arms…Just think, in a week you'll be in New

York – then only 14 hours and you'll be in Germany…It seems too good to be true. The last three months I've been merely marking time." [March 1955]

In another letter in this series, Ellie explained why she had stuck with Sterling several years earlier when he did not give her much encouragement. "When you'd give me a bad time – I'd try to think of all the things I didn't like about you – and end up liking you more," she wrote on January 30, 1955.

"…ever since the first thought of eventual marriage entered my head I began to formulate the qualities I wanted in a husband…I couldn't help but be drawn to a person who had these qualities all wrapped up in an attractive form…Oh – so many times I'd wonder if that Sterling Colton was so special after all – and was I paving the road to spinsterhood by saving my special feelings for him?"

The big debate in her mind was "whether it was better to love or be loved – at times I would decide on the latter and look again at my other beaux." As she pondered the reality that she was married to "my true love," she saw "that it wasn't enough to love or be loved – but for real happiness it took both of these…When I thought of these things how blessed I felt."

Throughout their separation, Ellie's humor never deserted her. And she couldn't help but send some of it poetically: "I'm counting my calories – honest and true…and find I'm deficient in vitamin 'U'!" Sterling rarely if ever had been on skis, and told her of a harrowing trip down a steep mountain. She responded: "Be careful on those skis – Keep your eyes open when you sneeze! And write to me often – please!"

Her orders from the Army finally came through in mid-February. The Army shipped off their clothing and household goods to Germany and authorized her to fly by Western Airlines to Salt Lake City, and by United Airlines from Salt Lake to New York. From there she flew to Frankfurt and into Sterling's arms.

12

COLTON BABY MAKES THREE

As Sterling settled into his work with the JAG Corps during the last days of 1954, the war in Europe had been over for nearly a decade. Blessed with freedom, West Germans had made great strides in rebuilding demolished cities.

East Germans, on the other hand, were largely controlled by Moscow, which carted off many of their factories to Russia right after the war and chained its citizens to Communism. There was little incentive for individual initiative, and stark differences became apparent between the blossoming West and moribund East.

A major task after the war had been to prosecute members of the Nazi leadership and others who shared responsibility for the Holocaust and other war crimes. In 1944 the U.S. Joint Chiefs of Staff had created the War Crimes Office as a division of the Office of the Judge Advocate General. Although other branches of the U.S. military have their own JAG sections, the Army JAG corps coordinates the prosecution of war crimes.

Sterling and other JAG officers dealt with the U.S.'s own service personnel, accused of breaking military rules or local laws. Prior to Sterling's era, defendants were subject to the Articles of War. Then, in 1950, Congress overhauled and updated the system, creating the Uniform Code of Military Justice (UCMJ), signed into law by President Harry Truman the following year.

JAG Corps members were assigned to preside over, prosecute, or defend individual service members accused of criminal or civil offenses.

In about two-thirds of the courts-martial to which Sterling was assigned, he represented the accused. In the others he represented the U.S. Government as prosecutor.

Most defendants were young men of low rank, though a number were sergeants. A major problem for these young men was the alcohol content in German beers, higher than in America, which contributed to drunkenness, rioting, fighting, and stealing.

The Seventh Army evolved into the United States Army Europe (USAREUR) during the 1950s and 1960s, and had troops stationed throughout the European Continent. JAG staffing was either feast or famine. The lion's share of Sterling's work was in Vaihingen, but during the last half of his stay Sterling traveled to more than a dozen German cities to participate in courts-martial.

Ellie was about six months pregnant when she arrived and looking "very matronly," he confided to his journal. Married officers were housed in new apartments, completely furnished with china, crystal, and fully equipped kitchens.

Their third-floor walk-up also had a maid's quarters; Sterling had already hired Frau Vencura to live there. She was a lovely, well-educated German who had been forced by the Russians to leave her home in East Germany. She was very grateful to be with them and Ellie was delighted. The apartment faced the parade ground, from where Ellie could watch Sterling walk to and from his office each day.

The Army had taken control of many resort hotels and other recreational facilities, which were available to service personnel at relatively low cost. On New Year's Eve while Ellie was still stateside, Sterling went with several bachelor officers to Berchtesgaden, Hitler's onetime playground, to ski.

"I had not been on skis before I rented skis during this trip," said Sterling. "They took me to the top of the mountain. I didn't think I would ever get down."

As usual, Sterling's reputation and leadership ability brought him to the attention of local church officials. Lt. Colonel Theodore Curtis, a Mormon chaplain, called Sterling to be president of the LDS Servicemen's Branch (which also had a small number of servicewomen). They met each Sunday in USO facilities in a railroad station near the center of

Stuttgart. Members came from a number of military installations in the region and attendance varied considerably, depending on activities of the units involved. German saints in the area had their own chapel near the USO.

Soon after Ellie arrived in Europe in 1955, she and Sterling took a short trip to England to visit museums and Shakespeare's sixteenth-century birthplace at Stratford-Upon-Avon. While in London, LDS Chaplain Curtis took them to Hyde Park, famed for its tolerance of free speech, where Mormon missionaries had preached in the open air for more than a century. At Curtis' invitation, Sterling mounted a traditional soap box and proceeded to preach to passersby and those who stopped to listen.

It was an exciting time and place to be young and in love and adventurous. Western Europe was abuzz with activity as countries continued to rebuild from the war. Relatively inexpensive merchandise of every description was available on base. The military had shipped the Coltons' car to Germany at the government's expense and gas cost them just thirteen cents a gallon.

Ellie's mother Annie had continued to make almost all of Ellie's clothes, including peddle pushers, calf-length trousers popular in the 1950s and '60s. Soon after Ellie arrived, large with child, the Coltons took their first European trip, Ellie wearing peddle pushers. For comfort while traveling, she unbuttoned them.

When they reached the Italian border, Sterling took their ID papers into a small building for clearance. Ellie got out of the car to stretch. She had forgotten to button up, and, with border guards standing nearby, her pants dropped to her ankles. The guards called to other guards to see this American woman whose underwear flapped in the breeze as Ellie pulled up her pants and scrambled back inside the car. The guards were still pointing her way when Sterling returned. Red-faced, she ordered him to leave ASAP.

They did not have a fixed agenda, content to find places and things of interest as they traveled. They arrived in Siena, Italy on the same day as the *Palio*, a horse race through the center of the city, held twice a year. Sterling saw another wonderful opportunity to use his new camera.

Leaving Ellie in the car, he went off to chase horses.

Sterling was gone longer than he realized. In her condition Ellie needed to go to the bathroom more often than usual. The longer he was away the more desperate she got. With no public facilities nearby, Ellie importuned a little monk in a brown cassock for help, without success. She was beside herself by the time Sterling returned, and he was in the dog house.

Ellie was still game for more adventure. Reaching Florence, they found its famous cathedral, completed in 1436, being renovated. Scaffolding surrounded the Cathedral of Saint Mary of the Flower, but hearty visitors were welcome to climb the scaffolding. Ellie insisted on doing so, and climbed all the way to the top of the dome, taller than the length of a football field.

They were mesmerized by the marble sculpture of David, located nearby in the *Galleria dell/Accademia*. Michelangelo created his seventeen-feet-tall nude masterpiece between 1501 and 1504. The Coltons resolved to name their first son after David who, as told in the Old Testament, slew Goliath.

The Coltons' attempts to economize did not always produce good results. Their hotel room in Rome was a renovated bathroom, with a lingering odor. They usually ate as cheaply as possible. They did, however, splurge on the small, wild and expensive strawberries available in Italy that Ellie in her pregnancy craved.

Driving to Naples, they visited nearby Mount Vesuvius, best known for its eruption in 79 AD that destroyed and buried several Roman settlements, including Pompeii, and killed about 16,000 people. On a beautiful blue-sky day they took a ferry to the Isle of Capri and the Blue Grotto, a natural sea cave rendered beautiful by the sun peeking in. Also aboard was a group of high school students, singing beautifully at the top of their lungs. Sterling and Ellie were enchanted.

On the Fourth of July 1955, the Coltons drove to Berchtesgaden in the Bavarian Alps with another JAG couple, Robert and Jane Pennington. Adolf Hitler had vacationed there starting two decades before he ignited World War II. Leading up to war the Nazis renovated the site as a second impregnable chancellery—the first was in Berlin.

German engineers had also built a teahouse atop a nearby mountain peak as a gift to Hitler for his fiftieth birthday. The Allies called it the "Eagle's Nest."

The two JAG couples climbed to the Nest—probably not wise for Ellie, who was due to give birth at any time. On their drive back to Vaihingen, Ellie said the baby was unusually active. That night she felt severe pains but didn't want to wake Sterling, who had a trial the next day. When her water broke, she stopped hesitating.

It was the middle of the night when Ellie woke Sterling and told him their baby was coming. Sterling flew out of bed and started gathering everything Ellie would need at the hospital. He was about to run out the door when Ellie suggested it would be a good idea to first put on some clothes.

They were more than thirty miles from the U.S. Army Hospital at Bad Cannstadt. Quickly getting into the car, they took off fast over cobblestone roads as Sterling silently wished he had completed a fathering course. Arriving and checking in, a Women's Army Corps (WAC) nurse assured them that, since this was Ellie's first child, there was no hurry. She put Ellie in a waiting room and sent Sterling to the fathers' waiting room. (In that era fathers were not present when their babies were born.)

Ellie soon realized her baby was not going to wait. In fact he was already coming out—feet first. Ellie called to the WAC nurse, who screamed, in a terrified voice heard throughout the hospital, "Help!"

Sterling knew Ellie and their baby were in peril. He dropped to his knees, praying as he had never prayed before. "I asked the Lord to somehow spare Ellie and our baby." At that instant the hospital's commanding officer, an OB/GYN specialist, came through the front door. He immediately saw the circumstances and took charge, delivering a healthy boy on July 8, 1955. The nurse had not known where the doctor was, but God knew.

About ninety-seven percent of babies are born head-first; baby Colton was in the three percent who arrive breech—buttocks or feet first.

Within weeks, in a Stuttgart Servicemen's Branch sacrament meeting, Sterling, assisted by other priesthood holders, blessed their little boy and gave him the name Sterling David Colton. He was the third Sterling D. Colton in the family, and would not be the last.

On August 6, their first wedding anniversary, Ellie taped together several sheets of blank paper and hand-wrote this:

> "I love you: For making this the <u>happiest</u> year of my life. For <u>not</u> bringing disillusionment to my dream of marriage. For arranging for my arrival in Germany to be a <u>happy</u>, <u>exciting</u> experience. For making me feel <u>glamorous</u> during those tedious awkward months of late pregnancy. For being <u>understanding and patient</u>, when I was irritable or thoughtless. For eating <u>quietly</u> all that indigestible food. For your <u>memorable performance and sweet tenderness</u> at the birth of our first child. For being the <u>kind of man</u> I would wish our sons to be. For being the <u>kind of husband</u> I would wish our <u>daughters to marry</u>. For all these reasons plus a <u>million</u> more — I love you even more than last year.
> <u>Happy Anniversary</u>.

David was an active, imaginative little boy who filled their home with sunshine. With Ellie's mother on the other side of the ocean, the Coltons' next-door neighbor, a nurse named Jane Dominique, was a godsend. She patiently answered all Ellie's questions and repeatedly assured her she was a good mother.

13

Exploring Europe

Another Colton, Sterling's sister Nancy, was also in Europe. She had helped keep Ellie and Sterling together during their five-year courtship. Once when she saw Ellie dating someone else at the U while Sterling was at Stanford, Nancy drew a cartoon and sent it to Ellie, signed "In defense of family honor."

Ellie wanted Nancy to be maid of honor at her wedding in August 1954, but by then Nancy was in Europe and unavailable. Following graduation, Ellie and Nancy both taught school for a year, Ellie in Utah and Nancy in Redwood City, California. At the end of the school year Nancy and a girl friend set off in search of adventure.

Her hometown newspaper reported that Nancy and Faye Knudson "left early Tuesday morning to drive to Washington, D.C., where Nancy will visit her brother Sterling [in JAG School in Charlottesville] and will then go on to New York City to spend a week before the... girls leave for a vacation in Europe."[1]

Nancy and Faye visited Italy. Then they decided to find jobs to afford more European travel. They took a train to Madrid, Spain and visited the *Edificio Espana*, a new twenty-story building that housed, among other organizations, the U.S. Navy's construction arm. Stepping off an elevator, they spotted a tall, handsome stranger and asked if he spoke English.

"A leetle," said Bob Bradley, "but not very well. I'm from San Jose."

They asked how to find the person in charge of Navy construction. Bob courteously in perfect American English told them how to find the admiral.

"After work that day," said Bob, "a friend and I saw them on the street and I asked how their meeting had gone." The two women were optimistic they would be hired. "As they had just arrived in Madrid, we invited them to dinner," said Bob. "It was, of course, purely an act of kindness and had nothing to do with the fact that I found Nancy so attractive."

Robert (Bob) Louis Bradley was twenty-nine, six years older than Nancy. A native of California, he served in the U.S. Army Signal Corps for two years, then graduated in electrical engineering from Santa Clara University. He went to Europe in 1952 as Nancy had—for a vacation, and also decided to stay. He was hired in Paris by the American construction firm building bases in France for NATO.

The company and Bob moved to Spain in August 1954 to construct air force bases. He arrived in Madrid just two weeks before Nancy. The two young women were hired by the Navy office, and Nancy and Bob started seeing a lot of each other. Within a few months they were engaged to be married. The news was hard on Nancy's parents who, like most practicing LDS parents, hoped their children would marry in a temple, which required both bride and groom to be members of the faith.

In a letter to Sterling, Nancy explained that they probably would marry in Europe. She was not big on elaborate wedding ceremonies and accompanying festivities. More important, wrote Nancy, "In a big way, it's probably best that this proposed ceremony take place over here," in Europe, since "the problem of not having a temple marriage would undoubtedly take any joy mother would have out and leave it a tragic proceeding..."[2]

They could not marry in Spain because of a conflict with the Catholic Church. Instead they traveled to Tangiers, in the north of Morocco, and were wed at the American Consulate on February 21, 1955.

Nancy and Bob loved to travel and did a lot of it, in a sporty Porsche convertible. Often they had another passenger, Paella (Pah/EH/yah), an English bulldog named for a Spanish seafood dish. Nancy gave Paella to Bob when they were courting. Bob's career specialty, supervising heavy construction on major projects, guaranteed a lot of relocating, as they made more than a dozen major moves between and within Europe and the U.S. over the coming years.

Sterling and Ellie welcomed Bob without reservations, encouraging Sterling's parents and siblings to do the same. In the spring of 1955, Sterling and Ellie were the first Colton family members to meet Bob. He and Nancy drove from Madrid to Vaihingen. Sterling found Bob impressive-looking and "very personable."

Several months later, with two-month-old David and Frau Vencura in tow, Sterling and Ellie drove to Bern for the dedication of the Switzerland Temple. Church President David O. McKay dedicated it on September 11, 1955. Also on hand was the 360-voice Mormon Tabernacle Choir and thousands of members and missionaries from across the continent.

It was the Church's first temple outside the U.S. and Canada and the ninth operating temple. The temple immediately preceding the Bern Temple was the one across the street from Ellie's childhood home in Idaho Falls, dedicated in 1945.

Marguerite, having overcome her initial shock, made arrangements to go to Spain to properly welcome her new son-in-law into the family. In early September 1955 she set sail for Gibraltar on the *Andria Doria*, the largest, fastest, and ostensibly safest ship of the Italian Line. Ten months after Marguerite's trip it was struck by another ship and sank in the north Atlantic, with fifty-two killed.

From Gibraltar, Marguerite flew to Madrid to spend a month with the Bradleys. They had moved into a new apartment that Marguerite loved. In a letter to a close friend, Marsale Sidoway, she said, "Here I am sitting on Nancy and Bob's beautiful terrace. Boxes filled with roses, dahlias, morning glories, and many more beautiful flowers…Bob and Nancy have a gorgeous apartment and have been so wonderful to me. We have been to some beautiful places nearly every day."[3]

"I put on my best behavior," said Bob, "and I think I passed the test. At least she certainly did. She was a great lady and curious about everything," including a bullfight they took her to. Bob added, "That was my first introduction to the Colton family—it was a great one and just got better and better through the years." The Coltons loved Bob and took him to their hearts.

Marguerite was about to leave to tour southern Spain and Italy. She wrote, "It's really going to be hard to leave Nancy and Bob."

She rendezvoused with Sterling, Ellie, and her first grandchild, Sterling David, in northern Italy. They toured Italy then drove through Switzerland on the way home to Vaihingen. "It was all I had ever dreamed it would be, majestic snow-capped Alps, glittering lakes, long rivers, good roads, beautiful cities, and especially friendly people," she wrote to her friend. She gave David an oil rub each day and fed him cereal each morning. "Oh! What fun," she wrote.

They toured a half-dozen other countries, alternating nights tending David. Marguerite and Ellie went to the Paris Opera. Ellie thought she saw a familiar face and asked, "Well, how are you?" The slender woman graciously replied, "I am fine; how are you?" Ellie then realized she was talking to actress Audrey Hepburn. For his night out with his mother, Sterling took her to the *Follies Bergere* for a show that likely shocked the two Mormons.

Marguerite visited Austria, returned to Madrid for another week with the Bradleys, then flew home to the United States, landing in New York. She had been gone more than three months. Maughan, who had been in ROTC, was now a second lieutenant in the Army. He met his mother in New York and they drove to Vernal. Maughan subsequently was posted to a base near Munich, periodically visiting Sterling and Ellie.

The Bradleys welcomed their first child into the world, a daughter named Robin, on May 1, 1956. Sterling and Ellie went to Spain to visit them for the first time, while an LDS couple named Allred stayed in their home with David. They left their car in Barcelona and took the train from there. Bob and Nancy were delighted to greet them—especially when they saw that Ellie was again pregnant, news the Coltons had not yet shared with their families. The two couples got along well.

When going to a late dinner at a restaurant, they saw Spanish surrealist painter Salvador Dali, with a much younger woman on his arm. Their visit also coincided with one by former American actress Grace Kelly and Prince Rainier of Monaco. Their wedding, on April 19, 1956, was watched on live television by a worldwide audience estimated at thirty million. As it happened, the Coltons were now in Madrid at the same time as the royal newlyweds, and their itineraries overlapped.

After visiting the Prado, Spain's national art museum, Sterling and Ellie stopped for lunch at the Hotel Ritz. The prices almost cost them their appetites. "The only thing we could afford was a bowl of gazpacho soup," recalled Sterling. While eating the cold soup, the Rainiers came to the restaurant and were seated at the table next to them. Waiters rolled out several carts filled with the restaurant's finest cuisine, as the royal couple selected their meal. The Coltons ate their soup very slowly to take it all in.

That evening Sterling and Ellie went to the Madrid bull fights, where the Rainiers were honored guests and sat above them in the best seats. The next day the Coltons took the train to Seville and toured the Alhambra, a palace and fortress complex. While there, the Rainiers appeared yet again, moving officials to temporarily close part of the site to additional visitors.

The Coltons took the train back to Barcelona and drove home to the base in Vaihingen. While they were gone, David took his first step, and they resolved not to leave him again. They thought he was slow in talking, but when he began, to their surprise, he did so in sentences. His first words were said outside: "Look a bird up there."

Frau Vencura left the Coltons to relocate closer to family. They hired a new German maid, Lydia, who was energetic but not as refined as Frau Vencura. She loved to take David for afternoon walks in the sunshine. One time when Lydia returned home with David, Ellie smelled beer on his breath. Lydia explained that, during their walks, she often stopped at gasthauses and let David sample the local beverages. David was active enough even sober. On one occasion he jumped from a steam heater in their apartment, hitting his head and requiring several stitches.

The doctor who delivered David advised Ellie that, if she had another baby, she should leave for the hospital at the first sign of labor. Ellie did so during the first week in August, arriving at the Bad Cannstadt Hospital in time to paint her fingernails before giving birth to a beautiful baby girl on August 6, 1956. This time there were no complications. Carolyn's arrival was on the same day as Sterling and Ellie's second wedding anniversary.

The next morning as Ellie recuperated, her spirits were lifted further when she saw Sterling and David on the other side of a window—families were not allowed in the maternity ward. David carried a red rose for Ellie and a pink rose for Carolyn. A few weeks later Sterling blessed Carolyn in the LDS Servicemen's Branch and gave her the name she would be known by on church and civic records, Carolyn Colton.

One advantage of the military was that the cost of having babies was very low—covering only what the mother ate in the hospital. David cost them $12.90; Carolyn cost $10.50.

Early in 1957 Colonel Theodore Curtis, the Mormon chaplain, released Sterling as president of the local Serviceman's Branch and called him to be Area Coordinator for U.S. servicemen in southern Germany. He and Ellie spent many Sundays visiting small congregations throughout the region.

Sterling's three-year commitment to the Army ended in 1957. The four Coltons returned to the United States in April, on a large propeller-driven airplane from Rhein-Main Airbase, a U.S. installation on the south side of Frankfurt Airport.

Before leaving Germany they sold their old brown Ford to a man in the LDS branch. Ellie had dreamed of returning home with a new red Mercedes, and was going to teach school while in Germany to pay for it. The arrival of David and Carolyn torpedoed that plan, however, and instead the Coltons ordered a new blue Ford station wagon with no frills: stick shift and manual crank windows. It was to be picked up near Fort Hamilton, New York, where Sterling would be discharged from active duty.

Sterling was released at Fort Hamilton, after being awarded the Army of Occupation Medal (Germany) and National Defense Service Medal. A Utah newspaper announced their return. "Welcomed back to Salt Lake City after 2 1/2 years with the U.S. Army are Mr. and Mrs. Sterling Colton and their two children, David and Carolyn," said *The Salt Lake Tribune*. "...Mr. Colton was serving as a 1st lieutenant with the Judge Advocate General's offices in Stuttgart, Germany."[4]

Halfway home to Utah, Sterling and Ellie discovered that two-year-old David had figured out how to open the rear window, and had been throwing things out of the car, including silver baby gifts.

During the latter months of Sterling's service in Germany, David Salisbury had written to see if he would be interested in joining one of Salt Lake City's most prestigious law firms, Van Cott, Bagley, Cornwall & McCarthy. Sterling was a couple of years younger than Salisbury and had followed in his footprints—as a fraternity brother at the U and law student at Stanford. In his class at Stanford, Salisbury had ranked No. 2—sandwiched between No.1 William Rehnquist and No. 3 Sandra Day O'Connor, both future Supreme Court justices.

Sterling received feelers from several prominent San Francisco law firms as well. He and Ellie liked San Francisco; they had been away from their families for a long time, however, and felt it was time to be closer to their roots. Salt Lake City was midway between Vernal and Idaho Falls, facilitating travel to both hometowns.

After pondering and praying about it, the Coltons agreed that the Van Cott firm was a good next step in their lives, perhaps for the rest of their lives.

They had a joyous reunion with Sterling's family in Vernal, and afterward with Ellie's family in Idaho Falls. After living so far away, it was wonderful to be home.

14

First Home

The Coltons rented a small house at 1244 Ashton Avenue. Years later it disappeared, making way for a new interstate highway.

They quickly made friends in their neighborhood and in the Highland Park Ward. Sterling was called to be leader of the M-Men program, for single men between the ages of nineteen and twenty-six. Their bishop was H. Burke Peterson, who would later become a general authority as First Counselor in the Presiding Bishopric and then a Seventy.

Little David continued to challenge them. He climbed on everything, including the garage roof. Once he escaped the backyard by climbing down trees, then followed neighbor boys to Forest Dale Park, several blocks away. Once he arrived home in a police car. Another time Sterling came home to learn that David had run into the street and been hit by a car. An ambulance took him to a hospital, to where Sterling rushed. Fortunately David's injuries were not life-threatening. "How he made it to adulthood is a miracle!" said Ellie.

The law firm Sterling joined, Van Cott, Bagley, Cornwall & McCarthy, was the oldest firm in Utah, formed in 1874, more than two decades before Utah became a state in 1896.

Most of its attorneys were commercial litigators. Other areas of emphasis included estate planning, taxation, business transactions, intellectual property, banking and finance, real estate practices, and energy and natural resources. The firm began as Bennett, Harkness and Kirkpatrick. The name changed several times to reflect its principals, and acquired its final name in 1948.

Sterling's first office with the firm was in the Walker Bank Building. Soon afterward Van Cott relocated to the second floor of American Savings and Loan, on the east side of Main Street between South Temple and 1st South. Members of the firm pitched in and did most of the moving themselves to save money.

Sterling was a natural fit at Van Cott. "We've always looked for top academic credentials, of course," said Gregory Williams, the firm's president in 2016. "We also look for people who we think will be hard workers and work well with others."[1]

Most of the firm's lawyers, including Sterling and his good friend Dave Salisbury, made their marks not in the courtroom but in quiet offices where the financial well-being of individuals and organizations was often decided.

Salisbury, said lawyer-historian S.N. Cornwall, "is one of those rare lawyers in whom clients place the utmost confidence in the handling of their taxes, their trusts, their wills, and in the planning and administration of their estates."[2]

Sterling was a superb attorney, said Salisbury. "In addition to knowing the law," he explained, "Sterling was just extremely likable, friendly, and non-pretentious. He was a good friend to a lot of people."[3] Sterling and Salisbury practiced together for nine years and were lifelong friends.

After returning to Salt Lake City, Sterling joined a JAG Reserve unit based at Fort Douglas, near the University of Utah. The unit met one night a week and required a two-week summer camp. It provided supplemental income but cut into family vacations by using all the annual leave allowed by the firm.

Summer camps for Sterling were at JAG School in Charlottesville or Camp A.P. Hill, both in Virginia; at the Presidio in San Francisco; or the Oakland Army Terminal in Oakland, California. Sterling was promoted to Captain in 1958 and Major in 1965.

In July 1958, the Coltons purchased their first house, at 1605 Princeton Avenue, a historic neighborhood on the east bench, full of maple trees, convenient to East High School and the University of Utah. All the houses were made of brick, including their small one-story, twenty-five-year-old house. They bought it for $14,950 at an interest rate of 4.75 percent, financed through the GI Bill of Rights.

On 1,205 square feet, it had a kitchen, family room, three bedrooms and one bathroom. It also had a detached garage. They had no furniture, but borrowed some pieces and found others at local thrift stores to get started.

"It was the house of my childhood," recalled Carolyn Colton, almost two years old when they moved in. They ate most meals on a white formica-top table in the kitchen; the dining room was for Sunday dinners and special occasions. Carolyn's bedroom had blue shag carpet and a dresser, rocker, and miniature kitchen cupboard which Ellie painted in shades of blue. "I loved it," said Carolyn.

Flowers and flower-arranging have always been important to the Coltons, especially to Ellie and Carolyn. Ellie grew a flower garden on one side of the house, and taught Carolyn how to pick gladiolas and arrange them

They were in the Bonneville Ward of the Bonneville Stake. Joseph Wirthlin, later a longtime member of the Quorum of the Twelve Apostles, was their bishop. It was a strong family ward with many others about their same ages. Ellie was called to teach the Laurels, young women ages sixteen and seventeen, and Sterling became president of the elders quorum.

Sterling and Ellie developed a warm relationship with other couples in the ward, forming a book study group that met on Sunday evenings, and taking a variety of trips. Two memorable group outings were to ski in Vail, Colorado, traveling once by car and once on the Denver & Rio Grand Railroad. "It seemed like we never stopped laughing," recalled Sterling.

On one trip they stayed in a lodge that had open log rafters. Sterling and Ellie's room was next to that of George and Joan Earl.

After a long day of skiing they were all tired and looked forward to a good night's sleep. There was a problem, however. In the room above the Earls' was a rowdy bunch of young guys, drinking and whooping it up into the night. Finally George could take it no more. He went to the fireplace in the common room, got a log, and banged on the ceiling above their bed.

A thick blanket of dust and debris from the rafters rained down on both couples. Sterling scurried out of bed and dashed into the Earls' room, fearful it was an avalanche or other calamity. Decades later, the Earls still teased Sterling about how much clothing he had on when he sprinted into their bedroom.[4]

Sterling sometimes occasioned laughter with his attempts at being a handyman. "Some wives have 'honey-do lists,' we had an 'Uncle Phil-do list,'" quipped Sterling. Uncle Phil, Sterling's brother, would often be asked to do home repair projects at Sterling and Ellie's house. The Coltons' house on Princeton Avenue only had one bathroom, whose toilet constantly was clogged with items thrown in by the children. "The plumber came so often the children started calling him 'Uncle,'" said Sterling.

One of Sterling's classic handyman mishaps was when he tackled a toilet project. After a stoppage one winter, Sterling decided to fix the toilet himself. Investigation convinced him the problem was a plastic cup. He poked a flexible plumber's whip down the toilet to remove the cup, with no success. "Then I had the brilliant idea that if I removed the toilet bowl and took it outside, I could apply a torch and melt the cup."

After considerable effort, he removed the bowl and took it out into the freezing night. When he applied the torch, the porcelain toilet bowl broke. They were without a toilet for several days, with only a hole in the floor to use when nature called. Ellie and their children urged Sterling to call their "Uncle Plumber," which he finally did.

Ellie's brother Lloyd stayed with the Coltons occasionally. He volunteered to help build a bedroom in their unfinished basement. One Saturday they decided to install floor tile. Sterling was in his "work clothes," including black socks, wingtip Florsheim shoes and khaki shorts, eager to help. As he lifted the can of black tile adhesive to read the instructions, the lid fell off and the adhesive poured down his hairy legs and shoes. "Our children still remind me of my 'skills'," said Sterling.

On November 5, 1958, Bradley Hugh Colton joined their family. He was born in Salt Lake County Hospital, where Ellie's doctor, George Veasy, practiced. The day before his birth was the national midterm election day, in the middle of President Dwight Eisenhower's second term.

That evening Sterling and Ellie were listening to the radio. Republicans were losing badly when Ellie announced they needed to go to the hospital. Sterling seemed reluctant to leave, hoping the GOP would make a comeback as more states reported in. "You can stay and listen to the results," she told him, "but I'm going to go have a baby!"

That moved Sterling to action. Brad was born healthy and strong, and they took him home to join their family on Princeton Avenue.

A few months later Sterling was at the chapel on a church assignment. Ellie was getting ready for bed when she noticed that Brad was struggling for breath. She hurriedly called Dr. Veasy, who lived several blocks away, and he came right over. "Brad has instant pneumonia," he told Ellie. "We need to get him to the hospital immediately."

Dr. Veasy told Ellie she didn't have time to change from her dressing gown. She called their next-door neighbor, Olene Walker—who decades later would become Utah's first woman governor—and asked her to watch David and Carolyn and contact Sterling. Dr. Veasy raced to the hospital as Ellie nursed Brad to keep him calm. As they entered the emergency room, "Brad went limp," said Ellie, "and I was afraid he was gone."

Sterling said, "When I reached the hospital they had Brad in an oxygen tent used for TB patients. I can still remember the terrible wheezing sound the machine made as it pumped oxygen in and out. He was naked except for a diaper; his little chest would nearly touch his backbone each time he struggled for breath."

Sterling first embraced Ellie, then put his hands into the oxygen tent and held Brad to give him a father's blessing. "I pled with the Lord to save our little boy. I promised that we would do everything we could to see that he grew up loving and serving the Lord." After the blessing, Sterling received a strong feeling that Brad would survive.

No doubt Ellie, whose Ricks family suffered multiple premature deaths, felt déjà vu as her son barely clung to life. She and Sterling prayed harder than ever before. Gradually Brad improved, and within a week of the emergency they were able to take him home. Doctors instructed them to keep him in steam for several months. They did so in their own bedroom, where the steady steam separated wallpaper from the wall. A tiny price to pay for this precious son, who would grow up to enjoy excellent health and become an all-star athlete.

Ellie faced another trauma in the wake of Brad's birth. Doctors told her that she had a congenital gene that damaged her ears whenever she was pregnant. Ear tissue turned bone-hard, costing Ellie some of her hearing. An ear doctor and her obstetrician warned Ellie that having more children risked losing the rest of her already damaged hearing.

She and Sterling had planned to have at least one more baby, and they prayed hard to know what to do. They felt strongly that their family was not yet complete, and Ellie again conceived. On August 20, 1960 a third son, Steven Ricks Colton, was born at Salt Lake County Hospital.

As feared by doctors, Ellie's hearing got worse. When Steve was about a year old, Ellie had her first ear operation, which helped only a little. A half-dozen years later, Ellie learned of a new type of ear surgery. A doctor who practiced it operated on her left ear. The surgery was a devastating failure, damaging the nerve. Ellie lost all hearing in that ear, along with her equilibrium.

Ellie refused to give up. She went to other ear specialists, from Los Angeles to Washington, D.C. Each doctor confirmed there was nothing to be done to restore hearing in the damaged ear.

To her chagrin she was forced to start wearing an "ugly hearing aid." A third operation restored her equilibrium but not her hearing. While continually hunting for the best hearing aids, Ellie otherwise was stoic. "I was determined not to let it make a difference in the things I wanted to do. I loved my husband and children and was determined to have a happy home."

Ellie found a silver lining in the cloud. "The hearing aids have gotten better. I've been able to manage fine with just one ear, and when I don't want to hear I turn it off and I have a quiet world. I'm never disturbed in my sleep at night by any sound, so there's a silver lining to everything."

15

Taming Ellie's "Herd"

Sterling's legal excellence was applauded by peers. He was made a Van Cott partner in 1961, just three years after joining the firm, and in 1965 was elected chairman of the Tax Section of the Utah State Bar.[1]

He worked long hours, usually leaving the house around 6:30 a.m. and returning around 6:30 p.m. He ate dinner with the family, then sat on the living room couch reading the daily newspaper, often falling asleep while doing so.

"During that time it was hard to see Dad relax," said their oldest child, David. "In fact, it was hard to see Dad very much at all." Brad echoed the same sentiment. On Sundays, much of Sterling's time was consumed in church callings, and his vacation time was dedicated to the Army Reserve.

The one time they had his attention was when the family drove to his hometown, Vernal, and Sterling morphed into his younger cowboy self. "There was always a transformation," said David, "when Dad put on his cowboy hat and boots."

Steve said "I was in awe when Dad was around horses. He always knew just how to put the bit in the horse's mouth and tighten the cinch. He was a cowboy!" As they rode together, Sterling—whose tuneless voice was not always welcomed elsewhere—would lead them in songs.

Favorites included:

Riding in the West and it looks like rain,
And my darned ol' slicker's in the wagon again.
Come a ti, yi, yippy-yippy, ay, yippy, ay
Come a ti, yi, yippy, yippy, ay.

Someone's in the kitchen with Dinah
Someone's in the kitchen I know
Someone's in the kitchen with Dinah
Strumming on the old banjo, and singing
Fie, fi, fiddly I O
Fie, fi, fiddly I O
Fie, fi, fiddly I O
Strummin' on the old banjo.

Her mother's name was Cleo,
Her father's name was Pat.
They called her Cleopatra,
Now what do you think of that.

They enjoyed other recreation in the Vernal area, home of Dinosaur National Monument with its numerous unearthed fossils. "We would often go white-water rafting there," said Steve. One year when he was in elementary school they went down the river. "Dad was trying to control the boat when his hat blew into the river," recalled Steve, "and I remember him calling out to Mom, 'Oh Mommy, Mommy, catch my hat.' We laughed so hard to see our normally in-control dad unable to control the river."

Sterling's parents, Hugh and Marguerite, fed and fussed over their grandchildren and always made them feel special. "When I close my eyes and think of Grandpa," said Carolyn, "a picture comes to my mind of Grandpa wearing his cowboy hat and a smile, while sitting on a log with his horses nearby in the 'high and beautiful Uintas.' There was no doubt he was having a wonderful time. When Grandpa smiles, his eyes twinkle and warmth and kindness spill out."

Grandma Marguerite was kind to everyone around her, and greatly loved by the Colton children. Years later a woman told Carolyn that Marguerite had been her Primary teacher. Marguerite noticed that the little girl, who came from a poor family, didn't wear slips or underwear. Soon afterward a bag of underwear was left on their porch, and she knew it was from Marguerite.

When there was a funeral, a birth, or hard times for a family, Marguerite often appeared on the doorstep with one of her famous angel food cakes. She also made a variety of candy, mostly to give away, and taught her daughters-in-law and grandchildren to make it.

Marguerite always sent birthday cards with cash in them to her grandchildren. She grew beautiful flowers; whenever her children or grandchildren stayed overnight, there were fresh roses at their bedsides. "When we came for a visit," said Carolyn, "she would immediately have me come sit with her on the couch, talk to me about the menus, and give me spoonful samples of anything she had prepared ahead of time.

"When she was older and we would be coming for a visit—especially for Thanksgiving—she would set the table days in advance. Sometimes we would laugh that we had to dust off the dishes before we ate. She would fix us a magnificent meal but barely sit to eat it. She would be in the kitchen doing dishes before we finished."

Sterling's frugal ways were a reflection of how his parents lived. Marguerite seldom bought things for herself. She didn't use her dishwasher, saying she "didn't want to wear it out." One of Hugh and Marguerite's other sons gave her a microwave as a gift. She used it as a breadbasket.

When it came to disciplining their four youngsters, Sterling and Ellie typically had far more bark than bite. "Dad would not get mad at us very often," said Steve. "When he did he would take off his leather belt and snap it to get us worried, and have us touch our toes. I would be crying even before I touched my toes; sometimes that would be enough punishment. At other times I would get the sting."

Ellie called the children her "herd." Once when Steve was an adolescent, Sterling was set to punish him, but Steve took off running and outraced his father. "I hung out in the woods for an hour, then slid back into the house. Dad had cooled down by that time and I was free." Ellie was less feared. She used a wooden spoon, one time breaking it on Steve or Brad as they laid on the floor laughing so hard that Ellie forgot why they were in trouble.

Another time, while living in Salt Lake City, Ellie smelled smoke coming from their garage. She opened the door to find a group of wide-eyed boys, including David, who wasn't eight yet, smoking their first cigarettes.

The boys, she learned, had shoplifted a pack from a nearby store, with David standing lookout to be sure no mothers saw them. Ellie promptly marched the boys to the store, where they apologized to the owner and agreed to save money to pay for the purloined pack. Then she taught David—who one day would become an attorney—the meaning of "accessory."

One day Ellie heard a fire alarm on a nearby street pole, followed by the wailing of a fire engine. At that same time David dashed into the house, into his room, and crawled under his bed. Ellie got David, a kindergartner, from under his bed and asked if he had anything to do with the fire alarm. His chin quivered as David admitted that, at the urging of some older boys, he had indeed set off the alarm. He now feared he might go to jail, like in *Curious George*, a popular children's book.

Ellie marched him to the fire station, where the chief asked David if he had pulled the alarm. He stepped forward and, like a captured spy, said: "My name is David Colton. I live at 1605 Princeton Avenue," and also gave the telephone number. The chief explained that while they were busy chasing a phony fire, a real fire might break out elsewhere, damaging property and possibly lives because they could not respond promptly. That seemed to get David's attention.

In an annual log, Ellie reported on her and Sterling's major pursuits during those years. Repeatedly she wrote: "Sterling working long hours in law firm…Eleanor washing laundry and changing diapers."

Ellie recalled once going out behind the house, kneeling in despair, and "praying that God would keep me from killing these kids." There was some respite for Ellie starting in 1960 when she noted "David goes to Kindergarten." Carolyn started kindergarten in 1961, Brad in 1964, and Steve in 1965.

Ellie was the Pied Piper of Princeton Avenue. There were numerous children in the vicinity and routinely they ended up at the Coltons', whose house was in the middle of the block. The backyard had a swing set, tetherball set, and a small grass area. A neighbor's cherry tree leaned over a fence into their yard, and the children gorged on its fruit each fall.

Ellie organized all sorts of games and activities, along with parades and parties. Carolyn especially treasured the activities manufactured by Ellie. "Mom would organize games of red rover, freeze tag, or jumping and other challenges. On several occasions such as a farewell to a family, she would organize a neighborhood parade where we would dress in costumes and pull our wagons, ride bikes, or march up and down the block.

"Our family had our own 'penny parade.' Mom would lead us children on a walk. When we came to a corner one of us would flip a penny, and if it landed heads up we would turn right; if tails, we would turn left. Mysteriously we would always seem to end up outside the Fernwood Ice Cream store."

Ellie loved animals ever since living her first years on a farm. The Coltons had a series of pets. Smokey was a very smart Siamese cat who lived in their basement. Each morning at daybreak she popped out of the clothes chute that was between the basement and the main floor, waking the household.

Sterling's Aunt Barbara had a great fear of cats. Occasionally she visited their home. Perhaps Smokey sensed her fear, for several times on Barbara's visits Smokey leaped stiff-legged into her lap, almost giving her a heart attack.

One morning in their basement bedroom the boys woke up to find Smokey giving birth to a litter of kittens at the foot of their bed.

Sterling's sister Nancy had given her husband Bob an English bulldog when they were courting. Paella had grown old and blind in one eye as the Bradleys moved around the world for Bob's work. ("The ugliest dog I have ever seen," Sterling confided to his journal.)

The Bradleys were too tender-hearted to put Paella down, and the Coltons agreed to take Paella off their hands. Ellie let Paella attend

David's birthday party in their backyard. A balloon burst on Paella's blind side. Frightened, he bit the belly of a child, fortunately not hard enough to break her skin. Ellie decided it was time to put Paella down; she loaded him and the children in the car and took him to a veterinarian who euthanized Paella.

Other pets included Licorice, a Yorkshire Terrier that barked a lot; guppies, hamsters, frogs, birds, and snakes. One Christmas day a friend showed up on their doorstep with a young basset hound, which had been won in a Hush Puppy contest. The children instantly fell in love with the long-eared, sad-faced hound and would not let their parents say no to the proffered gift, which they named Casey.

One day when Ellie was driving, Casey stuck his head out the window. Apparently he saw something interesting and stretched toward it, tumbling out of the car. "Casey fell out," one of the children screamed. Ellie turned around to look and ran into a telephone pole. Casey was not injured at all, and came trotting up the street to see what all the commotion was about.

Sterling and Ellie did not disagree on many things. One of the few was Ellie's driving, with Sterling often telling her to slow down and be more careful. The blue Ford station wagon bought new in 1957 served them well for almost a decade, but took a lot of abuse. As it accumulated dents and scratches the car assumed a character all its own, so Ellie gave it a name: Bluebell.

Driving Bluebell one day, Ellie encountered road construction. Trying to avoid the excavated trench on her left and the building on her right, she got too close to the building, crushing the passenger-side front door. They didn't have car insurance, and with money tight, they decided not to have it repaired. "She became known as the lady with the bashed-in Ford," quipped Sterling. From then on, front-seat passengers had to enter the driver's door and slide across the seat.

"I remember the car stuffed with kids and pets and Mom working the stick-shift as it chugged and sputtered up the hills," said Carolyn, "with Mom and all the kids chanting 'Come on Bluebell!'"

Ellie drove it so much that the salt from the snow-covered roads corroded a hole in the floorboard, and Ellie warned the kids not to stand on the floor. The kids, led by Dave, tied a piece of fishing line around a pencil and dropped it through the hole, watching through the back window as it bounced down the road. Useful to the end, Bluebell finally was driven to Vernal and into Ashley Creek to help with flood control.

Ellie often experimented with new recipes. Once for a large dinner party she spent considerable time making a pâté appetizer from scratch. She placed it on a table in the basement, with crackers. A half-hour before guests were to arrive, someone noticed that Casey the basset hound had eaten a large portion of the pâté.

Ellie had inherited a heavy glass pitcher from her mother. It reminded her of Annie's hospitality. Even when the Ricks were poor in Idaho Falls, her mother would always fill it with something for guests, usually lemonade. Now it was Ellie's turn to be the perfect hostess, which indeed she was. She was a superb cook, making the meals herself, from appetizer to dessert. Whether friend or stranger, a guest could always count on being warmly welcomed into their home.

As the four children grew, they were given increasing responsibility for helping Mom pull off numerous dinner parties—for Sterling's work colleagues; for personal friends or family; and for numerous couples or individuals who the Coltons perceived could use a friend and some cheering-up.

"I have many memories of being her 'slave labor,'" said Carolyn. On one occasion Ellie was working hard to prepare dinner for Sterling's law partners and spouses. The Coltons had just installed new drapes in the living/dining room. Dave and Carolyn got into an argument and were wrestling to sort it out. They rolled across the drapery, pulling it off the wall, rods and all. "Mom was so mad she sent us to our rooms," recalled Carolyn, "saying 'I don't want to see you until your father gets home!'"

After awhile Carolyn tiptoed out of her room. Peeking through the swinging kitchen doors, she softly sang a Primary song: "Mother so gentle and kind and true, I love you, I love you." That broke the tension. Ellie said she hadn't been feeling so gentle or kind. Then she laughed, gave Carolyn a hug, and continued preparing dinner.

"The greatest snow on earth" is a popular reason to live in or visit

Utah, home of the 2002 Winter Olympic games.

When David turned eight he wanted to ski. Sterling and Ellie enrolled him in a ski class, then decided they should learn as well. Sterling planned to take Wednesdays and Saturdays off for skiing. In trying to economize, he bought a cheap used pair of extra-long skis for himself. He soon learned that was a mistake. Long skis are harder to control than short ones.

A neighbor, Gene McCoun, an expert skier, agreed to teach the three Coltons and his wife Diane how to ski. Sterling found that his good intention to ski regularly was difficult to keep. While David, Ellie, and Diane skied weekly and became good skiers, "I was never able to ski well," said Sterling. He decided, however that "skiing is a wonderful family sport."

A couple of decades later the Coltons purchased a completely furnished three-bedroom condominium in Park City, Utah to facilitate getting away summer or winter and enjoy skiing and other seasonal activities.

Another outdoor activity that pulsed in the Colton DNA was adventuring into Utah's tallest mountain range, the Uintas, in the vicinity of Vernal. They rise to King's Peak at 13,528 vertical feet and have hundreds of lakes teeming with a variety of fish. In the 1950s Hugh and a friend or two began going by horseback and pack horse into the Uintas; they continued to do so the first week in August for thirty-five years. As Sterling and Ellie's children got older, they too were welcomed into the club, but never during the first week in August, which was just for Hugh and his buddies.

In 1962 Sterling and his good friend David Salisbury—both of whom grew up riding horses—packed into the Uintas. Neither, however, had experienced taking pack horses with them. The tent carried by a horse was lost somewhere along the way because they failed to tie a proper diamond hitch. In addition, they lost a horse, which wandered the mountains for several weeks before finding her way out.

The following year Sterling and David went again, with two friends this time, and taking with them a couple of men from the U-Bar Ranch, a pack trip outfitting company. Although it was August, it snowed.

One of their friends, Ed Morton, didn't have boots, so he wrapped his feet in plastic bags. A year later Sterling and David, accompanied by four other individuals, took another pack trip, this time following the Duchesne River, an eighty-mile tributary of the mighty Green.

The next year, 1964, it was back to the Uintas with a dozen people: four couples, including Sterling and Ellie, and four children, including Dave Colton. This time the Coltons got more than they bargained for. The children announced a competition to see who could catch the biggest fish. The group spent most of a day looking for Carat Lake, which reputedly had some of the biggest fish in the Uintas. Shortly before dusk the others headed back to camp while the Coltons decided to search over one more mountain. Voila! There it was.

The sun had set by the time they reached the lake; although it was fast growing dark, they cast their lines in. Immediately fish gobbled the bait, and David reeled in the biggest fish of the trip. The lure of sure success glued them to the lake edge as the black of night enveloped them. They continued to bait their hooks, as Sterling would later say, "by braille."

Finally, with a creel brimming over, they decided it was time to go. Finding the camp in unfamiliar territory and pitch dark was the next challenge. They mounted and set off in what they believed was the general direction. "We often couldn't see the next horse and were only guided by sparks from a horseshoe hitting a rock," said Sterling. Finally, traversing a ridge, they were relieved to see the light of a friendly campfire.

As others huddled around in the firelight, David emptied his creel of prize-winning trout on the wooden camp table, to a lot of "oohs" and "ahhs." An adventure and memory never to be forgotten.

Though formal family vacations were relatively few when living in Utah, the family took at least two trips to southern California in the early 1960s. One was to Disneyland, where they stayed a block away at the Peter Pan Motor Lodge for about $20 a night.

Keeping four children together at the crowded amusement park was not easy. Brad, about seven, loved to watch people. He would stop and stare as the rest of the family continued walking. At one point he was simply missing. As the rest of the family retraced their steps, a trolley bus passed. Waving to his family from the back of the bus was Brad. Sterling sprinted after the trolley and retrieved their son.

The other California vacation was to Capistrano Beach in Orange County. They rented a beach house with family friends, the Russells. Carolyn and her good friend Robin Russell wore matching outfits—white tennis-like skirts and red, white, and blue striped tops. Ellie dressed the three boys in Beach Boy T-shirts, bright with large horizontal stripes, to help spot them in a crowd.

The Colton and Russell children built a huge mermaid sand sculpture and collected hundreds of starfish. Sterling carried the star fish back over a long stretch of beach to their beach house. Then—as Earl Russell teased him—he boiled the starfish to kill the fishy scent. "Greater love hath no man," Carolyn remembers Russell saying. They returned to Salt Lake with the starfish, opened a stand on their front lawn, and sold them.

Sterling and Ellie provided church leadership during their nine years in the Bonneville Ward. Sterling was elders quorum president; was ordained a seventy by S. Dilworth Young, an LDS general authority; and became a Bonneville Stake missionary. Ellie taught the Laurels in the Young Women's program; was a Cub Scout leader; and a Junior Sunday School coordinator.

The Coltons taught their four children to be charitable and to give service wherever needed. Many individuals in need passed through their lives and home. In 1964 they sponsored a University of Utah student from India, Nashir Jesung. He was a Zoroastrian, one of the world's oldest monotheistic religions.

His mother summoned Nashir back to India so she could pick out a wife for him. Nashir, however, ended up choosing his own wife in India. He returned to the U.S. with his wife, graduated from the U in engineering, and took a job as an aeronautical engineer in Los Angeles.

The Colton parents used a combination of example, psychology, and persuasion to have their four children act properly. One Sunday David decided to boycott church. "He said he didn't like it and didn't want to go," recalled Ellie.

Rather than make a fuss, the rest of the family went to services. After church they made a rare stop at an ice cream store, going home with large ice cream cones. "Gee, we sure missed you," Ellie told Dave. "That's all we had to say. He was in church the following Sunday."

"Where my father was perhaps the rock, my mother was the one that kept the spice in our lives," said Dave Colton many years later. "They both have a wonderful sense of humor, but she particularly. With three boys she had to have a good sense of humor."[2]

Dave said, "I've got two of the best parents in the world for me. They have been wonderful examples. As a son of a father who had a very busy profession, you always felt like you didn't get enough time with your dad, but as I've looked back at the time that I had, my father taught me phenomenal lessons...As far as parenting skills, probably the best and most important thing was their consistency.

"We always knew where they stood, and it didn't take anything more than my mother crying to let me know that I'd really stepped over the line...The transition from physical discipline to the 'I'm disappointed in you, Dave,' started when I was about eight or nine. That's all I really needed to help me get in line."

Dave paid homage to Ellie. "She knew that by having children her hearing would be impacted, and yet she chose to have kids. She has taught us that adversity can be best dealt with by keeping the right perspective."

Carolyn noted her father's frequent compliments to her mother. "Ever since we were little my dad would always say, very vocally, 'Isn't she beautiful! Isn't she wonderful!' and 'Look at how beautiful your mother is.' They have a sign of three taps that means 'I love you,' so there was a lot of tapping going on."[3]

Her mother likewise always spoke highly of Sterling. "She would say how wonderful and kind he was. Growing up I don't remember hearing arguments between them. Their method of disagreeing was quiet, not with ugly words or dramatics. They both have each other on pedestals. It was a peaceful home."

Brad recalled that Ellie was a Cub Scout leader when he was in the program, and that "she was an amazing mother, involved in everything her children participated in." Of Sterling, Brad said, "When I sit back and think of our Heavenly Father, it is easy to visualize Him because I have an earthly father so close to that. I have always felt unconditional love from both parents."[4]

What the Colton children learned inside the home prepared them well for the choices and temptations awaiting outside. "They just had great expectations of us," said Steve. "In later years we constantly went to high school parties where there was smoking and drinking. Brad and I were never even tempted to do it because we knew the amount of respect and the expectation our parents had for us."[5]

Carlson Hall, University of Utah freshman girls' housing, where Sterling and Ellie first met. Later, the X marks the spot of their first kiss.

Sterling and Ellie at a Sigma Chi formal.

164

Another Sigma Chi formal. Sterling and Ellie are on the right.

Salt Lake City, UT 1950

Sterling (second from left) decorating the Sigma Chi house for Homecoming.

Salt Lake City, UT 1950

Sterling (second from left) with Stanford Law classmates (l-r) Chuck Stewart, Dick Janapaul and Vince Jones.

Palm Springs, CA 1953

165

Ellie and Sterling, just married, outside Idaho Falls Temple.

Wedding reception, August 6, 1954. (l-r) Ellie's stepfather Alpha Jaques, Annie, the newlyweds, Marguerite and Hugh.

Ellie and Sterling cutting their wedding cake.

166

Honeymoon moose. Ellie claimed Sterling took more photos of the moose than of the bride.

Banff, Canada 1954

First apartment, with Ellie standing in front.

Fort Sill, OK 1954

Army drills at Fort Sill. Sterling is third from right.

Fort Sill, OK 1954

Apartment on third floor.

Stuttgart, Germany 1955

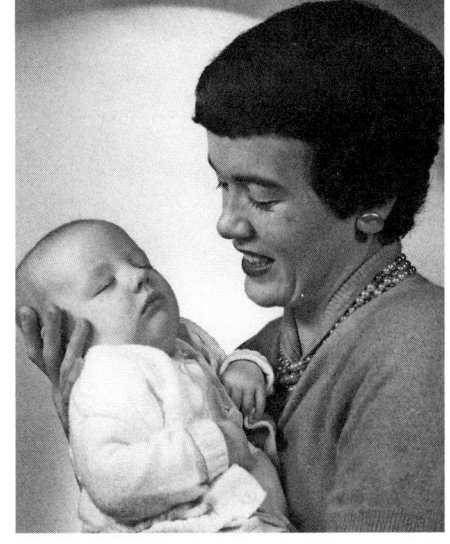

First baby Sterling David.

Stuttgart, Germany 1955

Serviceman's branch of The Church of Jesus Christ of Latter-day Saints. Sterling is at far right; Ellie is not pictured.

Stuttgart, Germany 1955

Marguerite visits Germany to meet first grandchild, Sterling David.

Stuttgart, Germany 1955

David and Ellie, pregnant with Carolyn, watching from apartment for Sterling to come home.

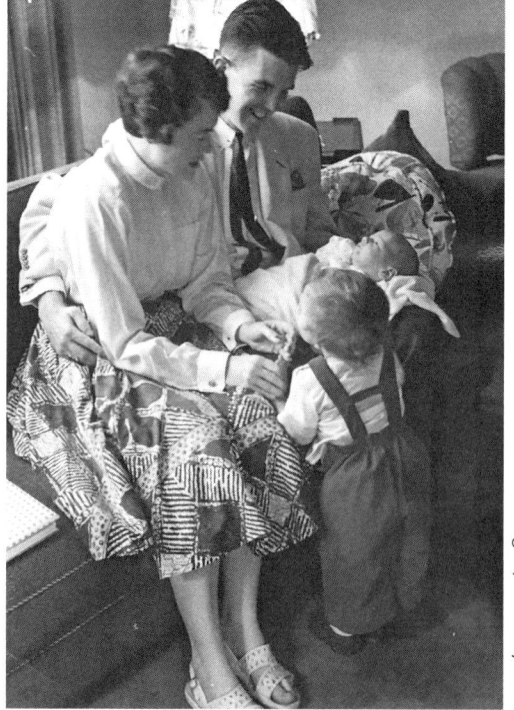

Stuttgart, Germany 1956

One-year-old David greets his new baby sister Carolyn.

Stuttgart, Germany 1956

Ricks family reunion. (l-r back row) Howard Andrew, Sterling, Ellie, Doretha and Don Lindholm. (l-r front row) Marie Andrew, Jean Ricks, Annie Ricks Jaques, Alpha Jaques and Lloyd Ricks.

Idaho Falls, ID 1957

Neighborhood parade organized by Ellie. Carolyn sits in the middle wearing black hat, David stands in gray hoodie.

Salt Lake City, UT 1959

Thanksgiving. (l-r) Sterling's brother Maughan, Marguerite, Hugh, Brad, Dave, Ellie and Carolyn.

David, Carolyn, baby Steve and Brad.

Christmas. (l-r) Sterling, Steve, Brad, Carolyn, Ellie and Dave.

Warming up for Christmas caroling with friends in study group. Sterling and Ellie are both on far right.

Sterling has a tight grip on Brad and David in Canyonlands National Park, on the way to California.

Carrying box of starfish kids collected at the beach to boil and take home as souvenirs.

Children sitting on "Bluebell" after trip to California. (l-r) Carolyn, Dave, Brad and Steve.

Dave, Carolyn, Brad and Steve.

Playing with Brad in front yard. Note Sterling's tennis outfit with black socks and dress shoes.

174

On a boat to Catalina Island, California.
(l-r) Carolyn, Dave, Ellie, Brad and Steve.

Backyard of 1605 Princeton Avenue. (back to front) Ellie, Carolyn, Brad and Steve.

175

Family portrait. (l-r) Brad, Dave, Sterling, Steve, Ellie and Carolyn.

Salt Lake City, UT 1966

As they moved from Utah to Maryland, the Coltons stopped in St. Louis to visit the Phil and Bobby Colton family. (l-r) Ellie, Bobby, Brad, Carolyn, cousin Marci, Dave, Sterling, cousin Nancy and Steve.

St. Louis, MO 1966

16

RECRUITED TO MARRIOTT

In the fall of 1965, J. Willard (Bill) Marriott, Sr.—founder, along with Sterling's dad Hugh, of what became Marriott International—called Sterling. He and his wife Alice (Allie) were in town from Washington to attend the Church's semi-annual general conference. They were interested in seeing some sites in Park City, twenty-five miles east of Salt Lake, and asked if the Coltons would take them there. Sterling and Ellie of course said yes.

"It quickly became obvious that what they really wanted to know was if we'd be interested in coming to Washington, D.C. to work for them," recalled Sterling. "We indicated that we were flattered, but we were Westerners and had never considered living in the East." The Coltons wanted to be close to their aging parents, and Sterling's future at his law firm was bright.

The Marriotts asked the Coltons to pray about it and not make up their minds before checking out Washington first-hand. In March they flew Sterling and Ellie to the nation's capital and put on a full-court press, putting them up at the fairly new Key Bridge Marriott; treating them to wonderful restaurants; and furnishing front-row seats at a basketball tournament to watch their alma mater, the University of Utah, play the University of Maryland.

As the Marriotts hoped, the Coltons were dazzled. "We realized it was a wonderful opportunity, but were concerned about being far away from our families, and giving up what we had worked so hard for," said Sterling. "We prayed mightily, asking what we should do. We both received strong assurances that we should accept the Marriotts' most gracious offer. It was a decision that would dramatically change the course of our lives and the lives of our children."

A big plus, in Sterling's view, was an exciting new trajectory in his professional life. He would use a full range of his legal skills, and learn new ones, safeguarding programs and large tangible projects from beginning to end. It would be a stark contrast to his current law practice, where Sterling toiled anonymously in taxation and estates—issues of vital interest to individual clients but not the sort of work that makes one's heart beat faster.

The acorn—a nine-stool root beer stand—planted by Hugh and Bill Sr. four decades earlier in the nation's capital had grown into a strong oak tree.

J.W. and Allie had two sons, J.W. (Bill) Marriott, Jr. and his younger brother, Richard E. (Dick) Marriott, also a key company executive. Like Sterling, both had attended the University of Utah and joined Sigma Chi. In fact, Sterling, said Bill, was one of the main reasons he was attracted to the fraternity. As their company sought new legal assistance, Allie was the first to suggest they try to woo Sterling and Ellie to join them in the East.

"I agreed he'd be a great choice," said Bill, "but I never envisioned that he would take the job. We were a tiny company when he came, with just six hotels." He added that "Sterling became my best friend," and was "too good to be true."[1]

After Hugh and Marguerite Colton sold their half of the business in Washington to J.W. and Allie and returned to Utah in 1928, the Marriotts built the third Hot Shoppe later that year at Georgia Avenue and Gallatin Street NW. It was one of the first drive-in restaurants in the East, similar to eateries Bill and Hugh had known in Utah. The small building was perched in the middle of a parking lot, with a bright orange roof to attract passing motorists, and became a model for future Hot Shoppes.

In 1929 Marriott was officially incorporated in the state of Delaware as Hot Shoppes, Inc. By 1933—in the teeth of the Great Depression, which brought most of the U.S. economy to a standstill—the Marriotts opened three more Hot Shoppes across the city, for a total of six. The following year the company opened a Hot Shoppe in Baltimore, Maryland, its first restaurant outside Washington.

Hot Shoppes specialized in "comfort foods" such as its original Mexican cuisine and barbeque, along with steak sandwiches, grilled cheese, and ham and eggs.

In 1937 Hot Shoppes pioneered airline catering, at Hoover Field, just south of Washington at the current site of the Pentagon. The new In-Flite catering division began by furnishing box lunches to American, Eastern, and Capital airlines, and later hot meals to many airlines. In-Flite would grow into one of the most important Marriott divisions.

In 1939 Hot Shoppes launched food service management with an account at the U.S. Treasury building. During World War II, Hot Shoppes fed tens of thousands of men and women who flocked to Washington to work in defense plants and government complexes. Following the war, in 1947 the first industrial cafeterias run by Hot Shoppes were opened at the Ford Motor plant in Virginia and the General Motors plant in Georgia.

Public regard for the company was reflected in 1953 when Hot Shoppes, Inc. stock went public at $10.25 a share. It sold out in two hours of over-the-counter trading.

Marriott headquarters moved in 1955 from the District of Columbia to 5161 River Road in Bethesda, Montgomery County, Maryland. The eleven-acre site previously had been a warehouse complex.

By the 1950s, Hot Shoppe menus reflected growing competition and took on a more modern-looking profile. When Sterling joined Marriott in 1966 as assistant general counsel, it was the high-water mark for Hot Shoppes eateries. By 1964 seventy-three Hot Shoppes restaurants and cafeterias were open in thirteen states and Washington, D.C. The combined operations were cooking more steaks than any other American institution except the U.S. Army.[2]

Also in 1964 the company changed its name to Marriott-Hot

Shoppes, Inc. Three years later it renamed itself Marriott Corporation. The last Hot Shoppe was also built that year. Meanwhile, in 1965, came Marriott's first fast-food restaurant, Hot Shoppes, Jr., starting in a Washington suburb and offering a fifteen-cent hamburger.

For its first three decades Marriott was a restaurant and innovative food-services operation. In the mid-'50s it began to evolve into a worldwide hospitality enterprise, managing a broad portfolio of hotels and related facilities. The restaurant arm of Marriott would shrink over time.

In 1955 ground was broken at Twin Bridges in Arlington, the Virginia side of the Potomac River, for the company's first "motor hotel." Plans called for 365 air-conditioned rooms equipped with telephone, radio, and television, along with a swimming pool and recreation area; a Hot Shoppe restaurant; barber shop and variety store. The Annual Report called Twin Bridges "The world's largest motor hotel owned and operated by Hot Shoppes, Inc., combining motel convenience with hotel luxury."

The hotel, opened in 1957, featured a drive-in registration desk, enabling guests to register in their automobiles. Bicycle attendants guided guests to their rooms.

In 1959 the second Marriott hotel opened, at Key Bridge in Arlington. The third hotel was the Dallas-Stemmons Marriott in Texas, opened in 1960.

Then followed the Philadelphia Marriott in 1961; Atlanta Marriott in 1965; and Saddlebrook, New Jersey Marriott in 1966. Consistently good results reflected in part the great care taken in choosing hotel sites. Near bridges worked well; company leaders figured that roads may move, but bridges never will. The growth strategy also targeted suburban locations near airports and major convention cities.

J.W., Sr., whose own father went bankrupt in the Great Depression, continued to favor restaurants, something he could get his arms around. He was against the kind of debt required to build large hotels. When asked how he dealt with company growth, J.W. famously replied, "I sleep like a baby; I wake up every hour crying."

In the forward to his book, called *The Spirit to Serve*, Bill Jr.

recounted that "A few minutes after the ribbon was cut to open the first Marriott hotel (Twin Bridges) in January 1957, the phone rang in the freshly painted lobby. The caller asked young Bill Marriott if the Marriotts would like to buy the new 48-room Disneyland Hotel in Anaheim, California. When consulted, Bill's dad replied: 'Heavens, no! We probably won't be able to make this one work.'"[3]

Bill Jr., however, saw hotels as the wave of the future, and chose to learn on the job by personally managing Twin Bridges. "Had I had my way," said Bill, "we would have plowed our energy into building the hotel division faster and sooner than we did. I felt confident that the future promised to be a bright one for new, aggressive hotel companies."[4]

In 1972 J.W. stepped down as chief executive officer and the Board of Directors elected young Bill to take his place. Once he had the reins in his hands as CEO, Bill knew that "to achieve the magnitude of growth that would move Marriott to the next level, debt financing was vital. I talked, my father listened; he grimaced, I borrowed."[5]

Contention between father and son, which became heated at times behind closed doors, would be a significant challenge to Sterling as he joined Marriott. His strong interpersonal skills sometimes were just as useful as his legal skills. He was completely trusted by both father and son as well as by colleagues and board members.

"Sterling was the rock of common sense," said Gary Wilson, who was Marriott's chief financial officer from 1974 to 1985. "Bill (Jr.) was the new CEO and his father was chairman. The brain trust also included Allie Marriott and Sterling. We'd all sit in the River Road office of the chairman and talk him into things he should do."[6]

Wilson, who later held similar positions at Disney and Northwest Airlines, said "Sterling basically tested our ideas from a legal and common sense view; we really operated as a team. You couldn't get anything approved without Sterling's OK."

He added that Sterling "really understood what we in finance were trying to do. Once we convinced Sterling, then Bill would listen to Sterling. Sterling was like Bill's rabbi."

Sterling joined Marriott in the best of circumstances for a corporate attorney. "In my early discussions with the Marriotts it was mutually agreed that it was of the utmost importance that the company always be in full compliance with the law," said Sterling.

The result: Sterling gave Bill Marriott his opinion on thousands of legal issues over the next three decades. According to both Sterling and Bill, there was not a single instance when Bill did not accept Sterling's recommendation.

17

MARRIOTT SOARS

In the summer of 1966, after accepting the job at Marriott and when the four children were out of school, the Coltons packed up their Chevrolet Kingswood Estate gold station wagon and headed east on U.S. Route 40 to Vernal and a delicious trout breakfast fixed by Marguerite—and from there to the nation's capital.

Their home on Princeton Avenue was left in the hands of a realtor. Also left behind, to be shipped later, was Casey, their long-eared basset hound.

Arriving in Washington, they spent the first few days in the Key Bridge Marriott before moving into a rented house on Onondaga Avenue in Bethesda, Montgomery County, Maryland. It was about a mile from Marriott headquarters. The Coltons became part of the LDS Chevy Chase Ward, which met in a lovely red-brick building on Western Avenue, the border between the District of Columbia and Maryland.

The Marriotts also belonged to that ward, including J. Willard and his wife Allie, and their two sons and families—J. Willard (Bill), Jr., his wife Donna and their three sons and one daughter; and Richard E. Marriott, his wife Nancy, and four daughters. Chevy Chase was the mother ward in the area; many other wards had formed from parts of it as church membership grew. Older members fondly remembered Sterling's parents, who lived in D.C. early in their marriage in the 1920s.

Soon after joining the ward the Coltons were asked to present a mock family home evening on reverence in the annual sacrament meeting Primary Program. When it was eleven-year-old Carolyn's turn to speak, some twelve-year-old deacons on the front row—including her brother David—made faces at her.

"I forgot my lines, then I started to laugh nervously," she recalled. "Dad cleared his throat, his signal for us to behave, and Brad started laughing. I continued laughing. Dad cleared his throat again and Steve started laughing. Dad cleared his throat. Then Mom started laughing. We just couldn't control ourselves, so they continued the rest of the program without us."

Sterling said, "I could only imagine what my parents' old friends who were in the congregation were thinking." Not to speak of his two new bosses—J. W. and Bill Marriott, Jr. "Dad just shook his head," said Carolyn.

Several years later, when the children were in junior high and high school, occasionally reverence at the dinner table was also a problem. Sterling would call on a family member to say the prayer. As he or she did so, it was not uncommon for someone else to snigger, triggering a chain reaction around the table.

"I hope Heavenly Father has forgiven our irreverence," said Carolyn many years later.

Then there were Ellie's capers. For instance, once when spaghetti, a family favorite, was on the menu, Ellie came to the table with a long noodle hanging down from each nostril. "Anybody got a Kleenex?" she asked.

On another occasion Ellie made two pies for dessert and she asked Steve which kind he wanted. "Whichever is easiest," replied Steve, something he had heard his father say. "That's not what I asked," pressed Ellie. "Now listen carefully. Which one would you like?" When Steve gave the same response, she promptly squashed a whole pie in his face. Steve and Ellie still chuckle over this.

Ellie was called to be one of two counselors to Donna Marriott in the ward Primary. Ellie's warmth, hard work, and administrative skills assured that she would be called on again and again for leadership. Soon after serving with Donna, she was called to be a counselor to Wanda Painter in the ward Relief Society. Sterling was called to serve in the presidency of the Washington, D.C. Stake Seventies Quorum.

After driving around on Saturdays looking for a home, the Coltons found an ideal one on Greentree Road in Bethesda. The backyard ended on the Cabin John Creek Watershed, about twenty-five square miles of woods that would never be developed. The creek, which eventually empties into the mighty Potomac River, teemed with several species of fish, and the woods with wildlife, including deer, raccoon, beaver, and many varieties of birds.

Ellie loved to walk; in her correspondence with Sterling years earlier, she wrote of the exhilaration she felt after a long walk. The woods backing up to this home had some rough, irregular trails, made mostly by deer or kids, waiting for others to be created.

Sterling likely felt at home by a familiar sound coming from the other side of the creek. It was a herd of cows whose bells jangled as they gathered to be milked at a dairy farm.

The Coltons offered $82,000 for the home, substantially below the asking price. The owner initially rejected the offer, but months later called and sold it to them at that price. At this writing, more than fifty years later, they live in the same house.

The woods became Ellie's sacred spot. Many years later she said, "I try to go for a walk in those woods every day that time and weather permit. There is a special private place which I consider my sacred grove, where I have pled for understanding and courage.

"On days that I can sincerely seek to know who I can help and how I can help, the answer comes before I get back up the hill. Some days I am too selfish to follow through—but in every case, when I respond to the promptings of the Spirit, I am blessed."

Montgomery County's per capita income has been one of the nation's highest for many decades. One benefit to residents is that its public schools are also some of the best. In the fall of 1967 the three younger Colton children enrolled in Seven Locks Elementary School, just 400 yards from their home, with no major streets to cross. David began seventh grade at Herbert Hoover Junior High.

One neighbor was the Jack and Joanne Kemp family. He was a former NFL quarterback and a prominent politician, serving as a Republican congressman from New York, a Cabinet secretary, and the GOP's vice presidential nominee in 1996.

Other neighbors included broadcast journalist Roger Mudd, Democratic Senator Daniel Inouye from Hawaii, several members of the U.S. House, and other prominent people in government, athletics, and business. Their next-door neighbors were IBM executive Bob Torgler and his wife Mary Ellen. Several decades later the Coltons' son Brad and his wife Melanie purchased the Torgler house.

Ellie on occasion was asked what she did professionally. "I read," was her standard answer. She in fact continued to read whenever time permitted, and joined a women's reading group. Her favorite books: the Bible, Book of Mormon, anything by Shakespeare, Pasternak's *Dr. Zhivago*, and Tolstoy's *War and Peace*.

The Coltons were befriended by many people, including the Marriotts. During the Coltons' first winter in the east, Dick and Nancy took them skiing in New Hampshire, where a number of Marriotts have vacation homes. "Dick is adventuresome and makes things happen," said Ellie. "He took us snowmobiling on Lake Winnipesaukee, going lickety-split."

Sterling and Ellie rode horses at the Marriott family's awe-inspiring ranch, Fairfield Farm, in the Blue Ridge foothills of Virginia, and cruised the Caribbean with Bill and Donna Marriott.

Several decades later, said Nancy, "Sterling has always had a dear place in my heart. Both of them have been very supportive of Dick and me, even when it wasn't convenient." Sterling has "a gift of having great empathy; he's kind and without guile. He has great wisdom and his priorities are always in the right order."[1]

Of Ellie, Nancy said, "She is a very thoughtful person, and goes out of her way to help people in a quiet way. She's someone you can always count on, very loyal, and lighthearted without being frivolous." Nancy said Ellie often made this toast: "Here's to you and here's to me. If we should ever disagree, here's to me!"

Sterling's first year with Marriott marked forty years since his father Hugh and J.W. founded the company. During the first year of their fledgling business, from May 1927 to May 1928, Hugh and the Marriotts had grossed $16,000.

In fiscal year 1967 when Sterling joined the company, Marriott-Hot Shoppes had sales of $146 million and profits of $6 million. Both increased more than 18 percent over the previous year, maintaining the company's growth rate of more than 15 percent a year. Marriott had 9,600 employees in 1964, 12,500 in 1966, and 19,700 in 1968.

Those numbers, impressive by themselves, would be dwarfed during Sterling's three decades at Marriott. And, next to Bill Marriott, Jr., who headed the company during most of that time, arguably no person was more responsible for its growth, reputation, and success than Sterling Colton.

"All through the years Sterling has been a great confidant and a great friend and a solid, solid guy from every standpoint," Bill told an interviewer. "Good sense, good judgment, handled all kinds of difficult matters...He made just a tremendous contribution to the company in every respect. He had a good feel for my father and he also had a good feel for me. He knew as much about the company, what caused the company to be successful, as anybody....He was just terrific."[2]

Marriott had a buttoned-up but friendly culture. J.W. stressed: "Take care of our employees and the employees will take care of our customers."

When Sterling came aboard, Marriott's legal team of a half-dozen attorneys was headed by Frank C. Kimball as general counsel and now Sterling as assistant general counsel. Kimball, an excellent attorney, had assembled a real estate department that gave Marriott outstanding locations for future facilities.

At the time it was popular in legal circles to regard in-house counsel as second-class lawyers. Marriott, with Sterling as point man, helped dispel that notion by bringing aboard, one by one, an excellent cadre of attorneys. The company's dynamic growth gave it the resources to compete with private law firms for the best attorneys.

By the end of Sterling's years at Marriott, a national reporter wrote,

"Wave goodbye to the days when partners at major firms sneered at in-house corporate legal departments as being the second string. These days, many corporate law departments are considered first class."[3] At Fortune 100 companies, general counsels were making as much as $1 million in compensation and stock awards.

Diversification was the watchword at Marriott. In food service alone the company had eight operating divisions: Marriott In-Flite Services; Motor Hotels; Food Services Management; Cafeterias; Hot Shoppes; Hot Shoppes Jrs.; Thruway Sales along interstate highways; and Specialty Restaurants.

By the end of Sterling's first year, Marriott was operating 206 units, an increase of nearly 40 percent over the previous year's 150 units. Its footprint reached into sixteen states and the District of Columbia. A major acquisition during the year was Big Boy Restaurants, a chain of twenty-two coffee-shops in the Los Angeles area, which gave the company its first restaurants in that state.

Sterling assisted Frank Kimball with the legal work required to acquire flight kitchens and airport feeding facilities in San Juan, Puerto Rico; St. Croix, Virgin Islands; and Caracas, Venezuela. They were Marriott's first foreign acquisitions.

Three major hotels were under construction, the Boston Motor Hotel on the Massachusetts Turnpike; the Chicago Marriott at O'Hare International Airport, and the Marriott next to the Houston Astrodome.

"Our constant program of diversification," wrote J.W. and Bill jointly in the 1967 Annual Report, "puts us in a stronger position than ever to capitalize on the future growth of the economy...We are taking advantage of the American family trend toward more informal dining," adding a dozen new Hot Shoppes Jrs. Average sales of the chain were higher than any others in the 18-cent hamburger business.

In an industry where as many as one of two new restaurants fail in the first few years, failure was rare at Marriott. A key reason was meticulous quality control. J.W. often was on the road, visiting restaurants to ensure they were clean and orderly, a trait followed by Bill as well. Another secret to success was note cards with precise recipes and instructions for everything served at the restaurants. They assured uniformly good food and limited waste.

As Sterling dug in at Marriott, Ellie was engaged with the children, planting a variety of flowers and other foliage, and turning their house into a home on Greentree Road. In their guest bathroom Ellie hung a hand-towel with this inscription: "Do you want to talk to the man in charge or to the woman who knows what's going on?"

With miles of woods behind their backyard, and twenty-foot-wide Cabin John Creek floating past, the Coltons created a lot of fun and adventure. Dave and some friends had rigged a rope swing on the far side of the creek.

One wintry day Ellie couldn't resist trying it. She and some of the children crossed the creek on a fallen log. Grabbing the rope, Ellie swung out over the creek. The rope slipped from her grasp and she plunged into the icy water, about four feet deep. The children remember her coming up sputtering and laughing all the way home.

In 1974 Casey, their beloved basset hound, got cancer. As Sterling took Casey to the vet's to have him put down, Dave searched the newspaper and found a litter of Irish Setters. "The boys got in the car and went to look at them," recalled Steve. "We chose a female pup and named her Kelly of Shannon the Fourth."

A year later they bred Kelly and she delivered thirteen pups of her own. They kept one male, naming him Moses.

A church couple who would become especially close to the Coltons were the Mechams. Ralph Mecham and Sterling had been on the debate team together at the University of Utah; Barbara Mecham and Ellie found they had many things in common, including having children who were similar in ages. The two women began taking monthly trips to Pennsylvania Dutch country and other places in the region, hunting for antiques and farmers' markets. In the fall they frequented orchards, returning home with station wagons full of peaches and apples.

"She is one of my very closest friends," said Barbara. "We could talk about what we thought was wrong anywhere, telling each other things that will never be repeated."[4] Ellie quipped that the money they spent on gas was cheaper than therapy. They often exchanged homemade gifts; Ellie's usually involved flowers.

When LDS congregations become large, they are divided periodically, creating new congregations from parts of old ones. In 1968, two years after their arrival, church officials divided the Chevy Chase Ward to create a new Potomac Ward farther north in Montgomery County. The Coltons were part of the new ward, leaving behind many friends in the Chevy Chase Ward.

In December 1970 Sterling was ordained a high priest by Washington Stake president Wendell G. Eames. High priest is one of two offices in the LDS Church's Melchizedek Priesthood; the other is elder. Most active adult male members of the Church hold one of these offices. Sterling also was called to be assistant high priest group leader in the new ward.

If the new Potomac Ward wanted a chapel of their own, they had to earn it. That meant raising 30 percent of the cost from members, either through cash or donated labor. The rest would come from Church headquarters. But another problem loomed first: Finding a suitable site. An ideal location was on the corner of Falls and Glen Roads in Potomac, Maryland. However, despite repeated overtures, the older couple who owned the 3.8-acre site would not sell.

"That's when I asked Sterling to take the lead in approaching them again," said Ralph Mecham, bishop of the ward at the time. "He handled negotiations masterfully. The couple really took a liking to him. He was able to do what a lot of people could not do over the years, and we closed the deal."[5]

Ellie was not surprised. "When I traveled with Sterling, I can't tell you how many people said he's the first attorney they trusted."

Church members saved building costs by contributing labor during construction. Mecham recalled that Sterling and Ellie worked alongside other members of the new ward during evenings and on Saturdays to build the chapel.

18

STERLING NAMED GENERAL COUNSEL

Even a small snowfall overnight in the Washington area usually meant schools would open late. When it snowed really hard, some government offices and even some businesses also opened late or stayed closed.

So when Marriott financial wizard Stephen Bollenbach arose one morning, looked out his bedroom window, and saw tons of snow, he knew nobody would be showing up for work. "I just went back to bed," said Bollenbach.

At that same time another Marriott executive was *walking* the three or four miles to work—on snowshoes. Sterling Colton, a country boy at heart from snowy Uintah Basin, Utah was not to be denied by a little weather. He may have been the only one in the executive suites that day, but he saw his duty and, that evening, could write in his journal that he did it.

"I always had huge respect for Sterling," said Bollenbach. "Very smart, very honest, very hard working."[1]

Francis (Butch) Cash, who rose to be a senior executive at Marriott, worked with Sterling for eighteen years. "I've worked with hundreds of the best lawyers in the country. Sterling is the best business lawyer I have ever seen. Many other attorneys are good in their areas of technical expertise. Sterling's strength is that he never gets lost in the trees. He always gets the right answer."[2]

Sterling was "great at managing people," added Cash, and could have chosen to have other attorneys handle all the nuts and bolts of business deals. "Instead he sometimes did a deep dive" to make a deal work. Cash recalled specifically Marriott's purchase of a food-service company in the Midwest, a deal worth a relatively small $15 to $18 million, that Sterling handled.

"Thinking over my eighteen years at Marriott, anything of substance that happened—land development, buying a hotel, many other things—the Law Department had a major impact. Sterling was always involved and always had excellent judgment, not only from a legal point of view but from a business view as well."

The 1960s were a watershed era in the nation's history, marked by widespread social unrest. The year 1968 was especially traumatic.

The war in Vietnam raged as protest demonstrations convulsed college campuses. At the end of January the North Vietnamese launched the Tet offensive, taking the war from the jungles to the cities. Three weeks later came the highest U.S. casualty toll of the war: 543 Americans killed and more than 2,500 injured. The Tet offensive was a major turning point in citizen support of the war.

On April 4 civil rights leader Martin Luther King, Jr. was assassinated at the Lorraine Motel in Memphis, touching off rioting and an orgy of destruction in major cities, including Washington, D.C. and Baltimore, Maryland—on both sides of Marriott headquarters.

"Ellie and I went to the top of the Key Bridge Marriott and watched the fires burning all along 14th Street in Washington," said Sterling. "It was very unsettling." The District of Columbia fire department reported nearly 1,200 fires between March 30 and April 14, damaging or destroying 283 housing units and 1,590 commercial buildings. The board of trade estimated a loss of $40 million in tourist trade in April and May.

On June 5, 1968 Robert Kennedy was shot in Los Angeles while campaigning for the Democratic presidential nomination; he died the following day. The assassination of the forty-two-year-old liberal icon touched off more demonstrations.

Republicans, at their party convention in August in Miami Beach, peacefully nominated Richard Nixon for President. Later that month Democrats met in Chicago for their quadrennial convention, which was anything but peaceful. Torn over the war, delegates were rowdy inside the hall and faced riots and tear gas outside, as Chicago police overreacted to crowds of demonstrators.

The Summer Olympic Games were held in Mexico City in October, boycotted by thirty-two African nations protesting South Africa's participation. The image best remembered from the games was that of two African-American medal winners, Tommie Smith and John Carlos, raising their arms in a black power salute as the "Star-Spangled Banner" played.

Despite all the trouble, Marriott experienced the greatest one-year sales increase to date—35 percent, rising from $146 million in 1967 to $197 million in 1968. Net income rose $7.4 million, a gain of 23 percent. Those numbers were achieved despite estimated losses in sales of $1.4 million in the Washington area because of the unrest.

"...good management is important in any corporate activity," wrote J.W. and Bill in their Annual Report, "but for a growth company it is absolutely essential...There is no doubt that Marriott's success is due in large measure to the exceptional quality of our management group as well as to the loyalty of our more than 20,000 individual employees,..."[3]

Franchising was the fastest-growing phase of the food service business, they explained, "because it combines the knowledge, experience and financial strength of a chain operator with the drive and profit motivation of the individual operator."

A famous cowboy saddled up for Marriott that year, when the first company-operated Roy Rogers Roast Beef Sandwich restaurant opened in Fairfax, Virginia. Rogers and his wife Dale Evans were on hand. Nine additional units were planned on the East Coast in 1969.

Marriott's expansion abroad increased during the year. Sterling represented the company in acquiring airline kitchens in Lima, Peru; Santiago, Chile; Buenos Aires, Argentina; and Sao Paulo and Rio de Janeiro, Brazil. During a three-week trip to the region, Ellie accompanied Sterling to each country. The company also acquired 75 percent control of the De Montis companies, headquartered in Rome—the largest independent airline caterer in southern Europe.

Food service remained Marriott's principal business, with food and beverage accounting for about 90 percent of sales.

Because of Sterling's ranching background—he occasionally said he still had hay seed in his ears—he was put in charge of the Marriott family's Fairfield Farm, a working ranch in the Blue Ridge foothills near Hume, Virginia. J.W. Marriott, Sr., bought a piece of the farm in 1951, later adding onto it to make 4,200 acres. J.W. spent numerous hours on horseback or Jeep traversing its trails. Sterling, Ellie and their children had many happy times at the ranch.

One that wasn't so happy for all was when the Colton children were horseback riding at the farm. Carolyn and Brad were riding the same horse, with Carolyn in the saddle. Dave was riding a horse ahead of them and grabbed a tree limb. Unfortunately a hornets' nest was attached to the other end. "The hornets poured out of the nest and covered Brad, with over fifty bites on one arm alone," recalled Sterling. "Brad jumped off the horse and started running and slapping."

Looking back on the incident, long after Brad was fully recovered, Sterling remembered how funny Brad looked running around and slapping the air.

J.W. and Bill, in the 1969 Annual Report, noted the impact of swiftly rising costs on the company. "The number of employees is approaching 25,000 and inflation in wage scales continues to affect our costs," they wrote. "Our extensive building program is occurring at a time when construction costs are soaring, and our needs for financing to help support this new construction have been accompanied by record interest costs. Food costs, as every homemaker knows, are rising.

"Difficulties have been particularly severe in our airline catering operations. Low airline profits have caused pricing problems, and airline strikes and air traffic delays were pronounced in our fiscal 1969." Climbing costs would be a company theme for years to come.

Fifteen Marriott-owned Roy Rogers Roast Beef restaurants were opened on the East and West Coasts during the year. In addition, the number of franchised Roy Rogers fast food units nearly tripled in 1969, from 34 to 92. The singing cowboy, still popular at age fifty-eight in 1969, personally attended twenty-two of the openings.

In 1970 Frank Kimball retired and Sterling was named vice president and general counsel. Sterling's name appeared for the first time in the 1970 Annual Report, as an "Officer of the Corporation."

In 1966 Marriott had five hotels—two in Washington, and others in Dallas, Philadelphia, and Atlanta. By 1970 it had eight additional ones, in Saddlebrook, New Jersey; Scottsdale, Arizona (Camelback Inn); New York City (Essex House); Acapulco, the company's first international hotel; Boston, Chicago, Crystal City and Dulles International Airport, the last two near Washington.

The company now had 5,800 hotel rooms, more than half opened in the past three years, and its occupancy rate was the best in the business.

Restaurant operations now included 46 Big Boy coffee shops, 72 fast food units, 63 food service management units, 28 Hot Shoppes restaurants, 37 cafeterias, and 17 terminal and toll road units. Those numbers paled compared to franchised units, which included 579 Big Boys and 131 Roy Rogers Roast Beef restaurants.

In Sterling's early years, restaurant growth outpaced all other Marriott businesses. Marriott's trend-setting In-Flite food services benefitted from increasing operations abroad as well as more air travel in general. Before the jet age, airplanes accounted for less than 75 percent of travel between the U.S. and other countries. By 1970 they accounted for more than 90 percent. The company had 29 In-Flite kitchens and related food services in the U.S. and 39 in Europe and Latin America.

"Airline meal and service prices in the United States are still low in relation to climbing costs, particularly labor" wrote J.W. and Bill in the 1970 Annual Report. "...We won't compromise our food and service—so we have the challenge of finding new ways to offset steeply rising wage and benefit costs."

With the largest airline food service in the world, Marriott was the first independent caterer to meet the extraordinary food service demands of the new 747 Jumbo Jet. The plane, with the distinguishing hump-like upper deck, had two and a half times greater capacity than the Boeing 707. It could be configured to hold up to 660 passengers or to remove the seats and serve as a cargo plane.

For about seven years after the Coltons moved to Maryland, Ellie drove the children to Utah and Idaho to visit grandparents, other relatives, and friends. For the cross-country trek they drove Highway 70, from Maryland to St. Louis on day one, to Denver on day two, and to Vernal, Utah on day three. They left at daybreak each day.

When Ellie got too tired to drive safely they found a rest stop and put a blanket on the ground for her to sleep. Two of the children were posted to guard her, while the other two played. They stopped at a motel before dark each day, trying to find one with a swimming pool.

Sterling could not be away from work long enough to make the drive to and from the West. Instead he flew out one way and then drove the family back to Washington.

In 1968 Ellie's mother Annie visited Maryland from Idaho Falls. The family showed her historic sites and spent a thrilling day at the Marriotts' Fairfield Farm. As a gift, Annie planted a rose bush in the Coltons' front yard. It is still a living reminder of her love of flowers and gardening.

Two years later, in 1970, Annie passed away on Easter Sunday, following an operation for a brain hematoma. She had been an outstanding woman of faith, perseverance, and service to family, friends, and the Savior. Ellie was with her mother in Utah where Annie was being treated at the time of her passing. Sterling and the children flew to Salt Lake City, then drove to Idaho Falls for the funeral. "I have never stopped missing her," said Ellie decades later.

Ellie recalled in a talk that Annie was just thirty-seven when Ellie's father died, leaving their farm in deep debt, common to most farmers during the Depression. "She also had no marketable skills," said Ellie, "and five children to care for. She often worked at two low-paying jobs at a time. She was fiercely independent, a strict tithe payer, and a devoted church worker. She believed if she did her part, the Lord would do his."

Sterling and Ellie maintained strong ties to their siblings, including Sterling's brothers Maughan and Phil and his sister Nancy, and their families.

The Colton family owed a great debt to Maughan, who was four years younger than Sterling. Maughan loved the soil and devoted his life to improving and running the Colton ranch, in which all of them had a stake. Remaining in Vernal also meant he shouldered the lion's share of care for their parents, Hugh and Marguerite, as they aged.

Maughan had been a prominent multi-sport athlete and coach in the Uintah Basin, and wrestled for the University of Utah, where he earned a business degree. As an Army officer he served in Europe. Maughan married Colleen Simper in 1961, in the Salt Lake Temple. Colleen became a prominent Utah educator and advisor to the governor's office. They had three children, Kimberly, Shawn, and Kellie.

Phil, eight years younger than Sterling, devoted much of his career to helping stop the proliferation of nuclear weapons across the globe. As a key staff member at the International Atomic Energy Agency, traveling to more than 100 countries, he shared the 2005 Nobel Peace Prize awarded to the IAEA. Phil served an LDS mission to Germany and later was an Army officer, with active stints that included Desert Storm in 1991.

Following his marriage to Barbara (Bobby) Snyder in 1962 in the Logan, Utah Temple, they both graduated at the same time from the University of Utah. Phil also did graduate work at a number of universities, including the Massachusetts Institute of Technology. They had four children—Nancy, Marci, Jeannie (who died three days after birth), and John—and spent a significant amount of their lives abroad.

Phil and Bobby and their children were particularly close to Sterling and Ellie's family because both families often lived in the same vicinity, first in Utah early in their marriages, and later in Montgomery County, Maryland.

Although Sterling and Phil's sister Nancy and her family spent many years abroad, Sterling and Ellie went out of their way to also stay close to them. For Christmas in 1969 they visited Nancy and Bob and their children Robin, Bobby, and Elizabeth, living in Puerto Rico. On Christmas Eve Sterling baptized Robin into the LDS Church in the Caribbean Sea. Later, in Cannes, on the French Riviera, he also baptized Elizabeth.

19

STERLING BUILDS SUPERB LEGAL TEAM

When Sterling took the reins of the Legal Department as general counsel in 1970, his fellow attorneys were delighted. During his previous four years at Marriott, he had earned a reputation as a rock of integrity. Many colleagues, including Bill Marriott himself, called Sterling the "conscience" of the company.

Sterling emphasized treating every individual with dignity, and taught his legal team to never do anything in Marriott's name that was dishonest or unethical. He succeeded to a great degree. In three decades at Marriott, Sterling only fired one attorney, and successful suits against the company were rare.

"Some of the lawyers in his department were so glad they could be mentored by him," said corporate executive Ron Harrison. "They considered him a father figure, and had an affection for him that you usually would only see in a family. He was a tutor in all aspects of the law as well as family."[1]

The company's most explosive growth would coincide with Sterling's twenty-five-year leadership of the Law Department.

During the 1970 fiscal year, sales increased 22 percent and profits 24 percent. Marriott aimed for annual levels of 20 percent and usually achieved them.

Marriott employees tended to remain with the company for many years, sometimes decades. Sterling began with a corps of eight attorneys who were assigned to key corporate functions including financing, trademarks and copyrights, labor relations, and litigation; and to Marriott's three primary businesses: restaurants, In-Flite services, and hotels. As the company expanded, so did its legal team.

Sterling assigned a lead attorney to work with the head of each major division. The attorney, however, remained independent of the division and reported directly to Sterling for personnel matters such as paychecks and promotions. As the need for additional attorneys grew, the lead attorney of a given division worked with Sterling to find candidates.

Sterling had two basic responsibilities—first, to administer the Legal Department, including preparing budgets, hiring and firing, and handling other personnel matters; and second, to practice law himself and advise other attorneys in doing so. He much preferred the second duty.

"I worked on a myriad of administrative matters," was a typical sentiment in his journal. "I find that I enjoy the practice of law, but the administration of a law department is not as enjoyable, but necessary." In addition, Sterling routinely consulted with senior management and the company's board of directors.

When Bill Marriott was in town, he typically held an executive staff meeting on Monday, with the heads of all departments, including Legal. Bill's meetings were decision-oriented, and included a written agenda and minimal small talk. Sterling often held an afternoon departmental meeting the same day.

Sterling had an open-door policy. An employee was welcome to visit with him without first going through a lower-level manager.

Whenever a new hotel or other major project was on the horizon, an inside team was formed, including someone from Legal, to work together on the project from start to finish. "Our secret was assembling the right team to get the work done," said Sterling. He quietly backstopped the other attorneys, recording in his personal journal the projects he had worked on that day. It was not unusual for him to list eight to ten such projects in a single day. Sterling's priority interest, given the high cost involved, was full-service hotels.

"We did as much legal work as we could in-house," said Sterling.

"The more experience our lawyers got, the more proficient they became." An exception was litigation. When Marriott was pressing or defending a lawsuit, Sterling found it wise to hire local attorneys familiar with local legal personalities and procedures. A Marriott attorney coordinated the outside attorney.

Ed Bednarz, an attorney hired by Sterling, made these comments about him: "Sterling was pretty close to the ideal boss. When you first met Sterling, there was a little bit of intimidation. His appearance was like meeting a bishop. But very quickly his humanity comes through. He assesses you, and once he decides to give you the job, he immediately trusts you, and believes that you are competent."

Ward Cooper, another attorney hired by Sterling, is still at Marriott twenty-eight years later at this writing. "Sterling was a great leader," said Cooper. "He helped set the tone, and his close association with Bill Marriott gave the Law Department great stature. People in our department gravitated to doing the right thing. Lawyers are the keepers of the conscience. Sterling set that tone."[2]

"Sterling was closely involved in the three best decisions Bill Marriott made," said Bradford (Brad) Bryan, who joined Marriott in 1980 from a high-level position at IBM. "They were, first, to split the company; second, to not build a hotel in Las Vegas; and third, to not buy Denny's, which would have cost us a billion dollars we couldn't afford."

Bryan, who directed Marriott's worldwide architecture and construction, observed that most others around Bill hesitated to disagree with him. "Not Sterling. Bill had such trust in Sterling, because he knew Sterling would always tell him what he honestly thought."

Bryan added that "I have always found Sterling a very special person. He is a great listener, has a positive demeanor, and is honest. He could be very direct, but direct with grace. I never heard him raise his voice. Although firm on legal and business issues, he was always constructive with his comments."

On a personal level, Bryan noted, "Ellie was by Sterling's side in every one of those situations. She is tied so closely to that good man.

How many others would love to have that kind of relationship?"

Mike Jarrard was in the Law Department for a dozen years, starting in 1976. He had prior experience in construction law and Sterling assigned him to help Marriott's Architecture and Construction Department. "What an impressive guy Sterling was," said Jarrard. "He was very straightforward, a hard worker. He had the respect of everyone in the Law Department."[3] Jarrard and other attorneys mentioned the popularity of the annual staff Christmas party hosted by Ellie and Sterling, usually at their home.

Sterling's nature was to be conservative with money, whether his own or that belonging to Marriott or other organizations he helped lead. A few attorneys mentioned their salaries were not as high as they might have been.

Myron Walker, who may have been the first attorney hired right out of law school by Marriott, was the company's seventh attorney when he began in July 1970. He assisted Steve West, associate general counsel, first in real estate and franchising and later in mergers and acquisitions. As a new attorney, Walker said his salary was relatively low when he was hired.

"However," he added, "when we had the most serious real estate recession in 1989 that the company had ever faced," Sterling's prudence in keeping salaries conservative in the Law Department helped buy credit with top company leaders. Some departments were closed and virtually all the others had to let employees go—except the Law Department.[4]

"During that time, Sterling did everything he could to keep lawyers" who were working faithfully, and tried to help others who elected to leave. "The result was that we did not have anybody laid off," said Walker.

Walker added that "Sterling was and is a very smart guy. Wonderfully educated, good instincts. A very capable lawyer." He was loyal to a fault to the Marriott family and to the company, said Walker. His example of hard work could be daunting.

"Sometimes he overworked himself, especially in the early years."

Walker recalled a time when Sterling showed up at the office directly from the airport after flying all night from Europe. "He collapsed in the hallway," said Walker. "Someone helped him up and we suggested he go home."

Sterling's dedication to Marriott impacted his family. He worked later into the evening than most colleagues, and was hesitant to take personal time off during work hours. Brad Bryan remarked to Sterling that he sometimes left during the day to watch his children's games. "Sterling later said he wished that he had gone off during the day to watch his kids," said Bryan.[5]

Steve McKenna, who joined Marriott in 1973, became associate general counsel for hotel development. "Sterling is a gentleman," said McKenna, "friendly, gracious, and as I discovered in working with him, exceptionally decent. I had a very good feeling about him from the first time we met. Not a stuffed shirt, not at all threatening."[6]

McKenna played a major role in the construction of a company jewel, the Marriott Marquis Hotel in New York's Times Square.

"Once Sterling gave us an assignment, he trusted us to run with it," said McKenna. "I had a completely free hand, but kept Sterling closely informed. Building the Times Square hotel was hard, bone-crunching work, but also very rewarding." McKenna needed a piece of information from Sterling on a weekend. McKenna apologized for calling him at home, but Sterling "could not have been nicer."

On Washington's Birthday weekend in 1979, as Marriott was relocating to new quarters in Bethesda, the capital area was hit with a paralyzing snowstorm. "Although it was a legal holiday, we had to be ready to open for business the next day," recalled McKenna. "I'll never forget the sight of Sterling in a two-piece suit and tie, working like a maintenance man. I can still see him with a ratchet wrench putting together a steel table."

McKenna said, "A guy who worked for me came down with AIDS. Sterling went to his house to help him. He is the perfect, God-loving Christian. He and I come from completely different religions. I was born and raised a Catholic. Sometimes people have asked me, 'Do you know any saints?' I'd say 'Yes, Sterling Colton.' I'm convinced that he and Ellie will end up in one of the highest houses of the Lord."

William (Bill) Kafes, a highly respected former lawyer at Marriott, speaks of Sterling in similar terms. "I have said it publicly: Sterling is the finest man I have ever known. When I first started talking to him he came across as the principled person that he is. He was the kind of person anybody would want to work for. I do not think he has ever disappointed anybody."[7]

Marriott's Legal Department protected the company well. "We never had any major legal problems," said Kafes. "We are not a regulated company, so we don't have the range of issues that, say, an airliner might have."

Kafes' tenure at Marriott—1972 to 1994—was close to Sterling's. A graduate of Yale Law School, he was hired to help ensure compliance with securities law. Later he dealt with outside financing and served for eight years as Corporate Secretary. He found Sterling "loyal to everyone; extremely loyal to his church, to Bill Marriott and Bill's father; to the people in his department." As others also noted, when the company faced hard times, "every department was told to slim down. Somehow he was able to not fire a single attorney."

Sterling, strongly encouraged by Bill, also led Marriott's efforts in the area of social responsibility. When he was named general counsel in 1970, Sterling wrote, "I became more involved in increasing opportunities for minorities, women, and the handicapped." It was a fitting assignment, given his strong humanitarian nature. Under his leadership Marriott made great strides in social responsibility.

Three years later the National Rehabilitation Association awarded Marriott the 1973 Organizational Award for its record in employing the physically and mentally handicapped. Marriott was the first corporation to earn the NRA award.

"We've had a story to tell about profit growth, new investment, new jobs created, more taxes paid, etc.," wrote Bill Marriott. "The business purists say *this* is social responsibility. And of course it is. But we run a little deeper at this company. There's more to us than those results at the bottom line."[8] Among progress cited by Bill:

Marriott created an advancement program, especially for employees at the low end of the pay scale. More than 2,100 workers, mostly minorities, have progressed into better-paying positions, including management.

Minorities now comprise a relatively high 13 percent of management.

Women likewise have a greater role in management, comprising 14 percent of supervisory and professional positions.

All individuals in our management training program spend 40 percent of class time on our own course stressing sensitivity to minority groups.

Marriott is one of the first companies to shift deposits into minority-owned banks to help them get a foothold.

In 1970, Marriott's Annual Report listed one woman in executive ranks—vice president Allie Marriott. In 1994, Sterling's last full year at Marriott, there were six women executives.

Progress in the Legal Department, which Sterling directly controlled, was even more pronounced, starting with a determined and creative outreach. By 1994 at least a dozen of the department's fifty-three attorneys were women; a handful of minority lawyers also had been hired, including the department's top tax lawyer, an African American. The paralegal and other staff members also were diverse.

Sterling's leadership led to the establishment of a day care center at company headquarters in about 1990. Among users was Joan McGlockton, an attorney Sterling hired in 1987. A graduate of Duke with a law degree from Harvard, McGlockton was at a private firm just two years when she became acquainted with Marriott and two men she greatly admired—Steve West, who became her immediate supervisor, and Sterling.

"Sterling is one of the finest people I have ever met," said McGlockton. "I felt like he was an excellent attorney, someone I wanted to work under. He was a wonderful mentor who had much to teach me." She called the environment "intellectually stimulating." Sterling named her Corporate Secretary.[9]

McGlockton expressed gratitude for the day care facility at headquarters providing such close proximity to her daughter Lauren. "I could see my daughter at lunchtime, at nap time, and at any other time."

20

Marriott Sails Into Troubled Waters

Sterling was an exceptionally hard worker at whatever he did, and his work ethic rubbed off on his children.

"I just grew up being responsible," said Sterling. From the age of twelve he had been the man of the house and a key worker on their ranch for nearly five years when his father was in the Army.

"Dad didn't tell us we had to work," recalled Sterling's son Dave, "he just started in Saturday morning and didn't stop until the end of the day, and Mom did the same thing. We learned that was what you did and you did it side by side until the job was done.[1]

"I think the only time my father ever touched a vacuum was Saturday mornings at about 6:30 a.m. outside our bedroom doors. It was his way of telling us we had chores and it was time to get up. Once we got those done we could do the other things we wanted to do. It wasn't an issue of whether your bed should or shouldn't be made. You just got up and made your bed, and that was what you did."

The LDS Church has a worldwide welfare system to help members who are going through difficulty. Sterling, like many other members, contributed time to keep it humming. Bountiful Farms was the regional welfare project for the greater Washington area. It was a modern, scientific dairy farm, located about 90 miles from the District of Columbia on the Atlantic eastern shore of Maryland. It produced enough milk to fill the daily requirements of 20,000 people.

On one Saturday David was with Sterling and others at the farm.

David was sweating hard inside a hole he was digging, while several others above told him how to do it better. "I suggested that one of the supervisors come down," said Dave. Sterling overheard him and said sternly, 'You get your job done and let them worry about their jobs.'"[2]

"That was a great lesson in working," said Dave. "When you have a task you do what you're asked to do and do your very best." He acknowledged that "whenever we had projects like that, Dad was also down in that hole with us, shoveling just as hard as we were. He taught us that working could overcome a lot of obstacles."

Dave said the farm manager seemed to delight in assigning lawyers like his dad, along with high-rollers like Bill Marriott, to shovel manure out of the cattle shed. "When those two worked in the cow shed," noted Dave, "it had to be some of the most expensive poop that was ever scooped."

Sterling had a lot of experience to draw on in encouraging their children to not fear hard work. "He told us about 'roughnecking' when he worked in the oil fields. They would bring their mattresses out to the rigs, so they could catch some sleep whenever possible," said Steve. "I always said there are people who are a lot smarter than me, but I can work as hard as any of them because of the example of my parents and grandparents."

Bill had become company president in 1964 when he was just thirty-two. Marriott's Board of Directors took a chance when they chose Bill, seeing in him the potential to be an excellent leader. He was elected CEO in 1972, then chairman of the board in 1985, the year his father died.

"He's not ego-driven," explained Sterling. "He is genuinely very concerned about people." A former Marriott senior vice president, Clifford Ehrlich, sometimes took sensitive issues to Bill. "His craving to understand made him an extremely good listener," said Ehrlich. "When you walked out of his office, he'd leave you feeling that you were the best human relations guy in the world. He wanted you to go out thinking you could conquer the world."[3]

Sterling had the same quality, said Ehrlich. "He reminded me of the old E.F. Hutton commercial—'When E.F. Hutton talks, people listen.' When Sterling voiced an opinion, people listened. His sage judgment came through...We avoided lots of pitfalls because of him. I have rarely known a leader as bright, practical, and principled as Sterling."

Phyllis Hester, Bill's executive assistant for twenty-five years at this writing, confirmed what many other Marriott people said about Sterling—that Bill listened especially closely to him. "Bill had all kinds of confidence in Sterling. If he thought Bill was about to do something he shouldn't do legally, Sterling would say 'You can't do this.' Bill would always listen."

Although hotels were Bill's first priority, he also guided the company into new areas, not all of which proved to be profitable. In 1971 came Marriott World Travel, a travel agency that seemed a natural given the company's current and planned ventures abroad as well as in the U.S. The effort ran into headwinds from established travel agencies, many of which stopped sending clients to Marriott units. The company closed Marriott World Travel in 1979.

Marriott acquired twenty-four Farrell's Ice Cream Parlour restaurants and forty franchised Farrell's, which also proved difficult to run profitably.

These were the two big Marriott headlines in 1972: The company is getting into the theme park business and the cruise ship business. Marriott acquired two ships from Sun Line—the *Stella Oceanis* and *Stella Maris*—and 45 percent interest in a third ship, the *Stella Solaris*, then being constructed. Smaller than most cruise ships sailing today, they were luxury vessels with a capacity, respectively, of 310 passengers, 180 passengers, and 650 passengers. Sun Line ships sailed in the Aegean, Mediterranean, and Caribbean Seas.

Sterling and Ellie joined Bill and Donna Marriott and Jon and Karen Huntsman on a Caribbean cruise on the *Stella Oceanis*, the ship's first cruise under the Marriott name. Stops along the way were at Tobago, St. Croix, St. Lucia, and up the Orinoco River. When a storm came up, Ellie was one of the relatively few who did not get seasick. "Only being able to hear in one ear saved my equilibrium," she said. "There is always a silver lining!"

Some Marriott leaders reasoned that cruise ships were a good fit for Marriott because they were just floating hotels and restaurants, and Marriott was expert in managing those. It was not to be that simple. A foreign war, high fuel costs, and other uncontrollable factors complicated the picture. "Mrs. Marriott voted against the acquisition," said Sterling. "It was the only time I can remember her voting no to an action taken by the Board of Directors. She was right."

"Marriott lost important money running Sun Line Cruises to the Greek Islands," said *Forbes*. "In fiscal 1975 alone, with the Cyprus crisis boiling, Sun Line ran $5.8 million in the red and caused Marriott its first earnings decline in 15 years."[4]

The company, in its Annual Report, explained the rare downturn this way: "The combined impact of serious recession and inflation, and the loss of Sun Line cruise business due to the Greek-Turkish war on Cyprus, caused your company's earnings to decline by 12% in fiscal 1975—the first decline in 15 years."

Marriott's decision to build "Marriott's Great America" theme parks, inspired by Disneyland, was arrived at similarly to its entry into cruising: We have experience building and running restaurants, hotels, and other large projects, so we can do this.

"Our pattern at the time was to diversify into related businesses, especially if they were food-oriented," said Sterling. "What we found out was that it was difficult to specialize in too many areas, and that we were better off sticking to a few things we did really well. We didn't understand that fully until after these ventures."

The company previously had three primary businesses—restaurants, In-Flite catering, and hotels. Now it had five, including theme parks and Sun Line Cruises, the last two tiny compared with the others.

21

CHARITY BEGINS AT HOME

Sterling and Ellie were very generous and helped many, many people through the years.

For a number of years there was a man known as "Happy" who lived in a small shack along Seven Locks Road, close to the Coltons' home. Happy, who only had one eye, was a hard worker who did odd jobs for people in the area, but had no car.

"There never was a time when we saw Happy walking along the road that Dad didn't stop and give him a ride," said Dave. "At first I was uncomfortable because he was poor and wasn't necessarily that clean. But my dad loved him and taught me that it doesn't matter what circumstances you are in, you love everybody and you help them, and that was just the way Mom and Dad spent their life."

Steve added, "When we dropped Happy off at his destination, it was not unusual for Dad to give him a few dollars." In addition, their family helped Happy find work, including odd jobs at their house.

Through the years the Coltons took into their home a number of individuals in need. One of them was a teenage seaman from Tanzania, Africa. Abdul Nasser Walele was a crewman on a Greek ship that docked in Baltimore Harbor in 1989. Abdul, pleasant and soft-spoken, knew little English when he went ashore and never returned to the ship. His impossible dream was to somehow become an American.

Abdul had $60 to his name when he visited a shopping center in Silver Spring, Maryland. In an empty shopping cart he spied a woman's day planner. In it were her phone number and address, along with credit cards, a set of car keys, and a wad of twenty and fifty dollar bills. He called the woman, Beth Pagley, and she drove to Silver Spring the following day to collect the day planner and invite Abdul home for dinner.

Beth happened to be friends with the Coltons. She introduced Abdul to Sterling and Ellie, who took him under their wing. Five years later he returned to Tanzania and came back legally. Sterling and Ellie enrolled him in Ricks College, a two-year school in Rexburg, Idaho, founded by Ellie's great-grandfather many years earlier. After Ricks, the Coltons sent Abdul to Utah State University, where he earned a bachelor's degree in computer science and soon afterward became a U.S. citizen. Today he and his wife Sophia have a beautiful little family and he works for a computer company in Phoenix.

Another recipient of Colton kindness was Angela Marie (Bay) Buchanan who, at age thirty-two was the youngest person to serve as U.S. Treasurer. She did so in the Reagan presidency after she was treasurer of his primary campaigns in 1976 and 1980.

During her term as U.S. Treasurer, from March 20, 1981 to July 5, 1983, Bay's signature was on all U.S. paper money. Afterward, Bay became a well-known political commentator who also managed the three presidential campaigns of her famous brother Pat Buchanan.

Not well known are the details of Bay's private life—details made significantly happier by Sterling and Ellie. "The depth of their compassion is remarkable," said Bay. "I wouldn't be where I am today without them." Sterling, she added, "is the best man I know."[1]

Bay and Pat are from a strong Roman Catholic family in the Washington area. In the 1970s, while in California, Bay studied the LDS Church and considered becoming a member. However, she knew no Latter-day Saints back home in the D.C. area. At the Republican National Convention in 1976, Pat introduced her to a Mormon friend, who also was a friend of the Coltons.

Sterling called Bay out of the blue and invited her to dinner at their home—the first of many such dinners through the years. That began a long and warm friendship. "They took me under their wing and became like my Mormon parents, introducing me to other members," said Bay, who was later baptized into the LDS Church.

Bay's parents had difficulty accepting her conversion. "It was tense in my home," said Bay. "Whenever I went back to Washington I'd go to the Coltons, where I could relax."

When she and then-husband William Jackson were married in 1982, Sterling flew to California and performed the ceremony. "While I was in California, I'd sometimes get a letter from Sterling when that was exactly what I needed," she said.

Bay had three sons and gave their second son the middle name of "Colton." As an adolescent he told Bay he wanted a marriage like the Coltons'.

An activity that involved Sterling one-on-one with each of his boys was the annual Cub Scout Pinewood Derby. Although in theory the boys themselves, with a little adult supervision, carve the car from a piece of wood and attach the wheels, in reality many if not most dads do a good deal of the work. This practice is so common that some packs have a separate Pinewood Derby for adults.

Sterling did not know this when David was the family's first Cub Scout. "David's car was a disaster!" remembered Sterling. "One of its wheels fell off in the middle of the race. "When Brad's turn came, we became much more involved, and he won! The next year we were concerned for Steve but his car took first place, beating Brad's car that had won the year before."

The Coltons loved family vacations, including a week spent in the Uintas with several friends in 1973, on a pack trip led by their grandfather Hugh. "Fantastic experience!" wrote Ellie in a journal. "All cooking was done over a campfire, no Coleman stove. We had a chance to practice what we taught at the annual LDS Girls Camp."

Hugh arranged in advance to rendezvous with a sheep herder in the mountains who had freshly butchered a lamb for their dinner. "I made the best lamb stew ever," Ellie wrote. "Grandpa was impressed with my creative cooking. We all loved watching Grandpa Hugh handle the horses like a pro and telling us many stories of adventure" in the Uintas. "The entire horseback trip was filled with never to be forgotten memories."

Football had a powerful impact on the family. When Dave was on his school's junior varsity team, Ellie helped save him from the initiation and hazing that was often the lot of JV players. "She always put extra food in my lunch," said Dave. "I'd pick out the biggest guy on the varsity team and give him extra food each day. So when they came around to haze me, he always said 'Don't bother Colton.'"

Dave made the varsity team but lacked prior experience. Brad and Steve followed a few years later. Both had played in the Beltway Football League. When they reached high school they were well prepared to shine on the gridiron.

One incident in the family's life was no laughing matter. When Steve was fourteen he was shooting starlings in their backyard with a pellet gun. Starlings were considered pests and legal to shoot. He went back inside the house through their walkout basement, carrying the gun, which was pumped up with as much compressed air as possible. A pellet is essentially a bullet, powered by compressed air rather than gunpowder.

The gun was wet from dew in the grass. When Steve started to put it down, the gun slipped out of his hands. As the butt hit the floor, it fired and, said Steve, "I felt a blast of air in my face." He continued, "I fell back and covered my face with my hands. To my surprise, my hands were covered with blood." Looking in a mirror he could see blood spurting from a hole in his upper cheek by his left eye.

Ellie, the only other one home, was preparing dinner when Steve came upstairs. Calmly she touched the wound and believed the pellet had not entered his head. She told Steve to go downstairs to see if the pellet was lodged in the ceiling. Doing this and finding no hole in the ceiling, Steve returned upstairs and Ellie called a neighbor, who was a nurse. When Steve asked if the nurse could come to them, Ellie replied, "She's doing us a favor. You run down there."

Steve at that point was feeling woozy and lay down on the bathroom floor, with his feet sticking into the hallway. Suddenly he felt his feet lifting up, not sure if he was dying. He opened his eyes to see his mom lifting his feet. When Steve asked what she was doing, she replied, "In first aid we learned, when the face is red, raise the head; when the face is pale, raise the tale."

Uncle Phil, Sterling's brother, came by about that time and

recognized the seriousness of the situation. He and Ellie sped Steve to the hospital. The emergency room doctor also did not think the pellet was in Steve's head. An X-ray showed otherwise. It had missed his optic nerve by about a third of an inch, and missed likely killing him by about a tenth of an inch. As the enormity of the danger to Steve sunk in, Ellie scarcely slept for two days.

Because of her hearing loss, Ellie normally had no trouble sleeping. She was totally deaf in one ear and more than half deaf in the other. Her high-tech hearing aid was a godsend—when she wanted to hear. She took it off at night, and as a result her sleep was almost never disturbed. Sterling often snored loudly, although his snoring never disturbed Ellie.

Sterling and Ellie insisted that when a child was out late in an evening, he or she was required to report in when they returned. "When Brad and I came home we'd go to Mom and Dad's bedroom," said Steve. "We'd take turns saying 'Dad, we're in.' But he would keep snoring. Then we'd say, 'Mom, we're in,' and she couldn't hear us either. We could always tell them that we reported in, but I don't think we ever woke them up."

For all her light-heartedness, Ellie was serious about values, the Savior, and "What I want my children to remember about home." She listed ten things:

That their father and mother loved each other.
That the reason our home was a happy one was because we all worked to keep it so. That we tried to teach by example that anything worth doing was worth doing well.
That each child was given every possible opportunity to develop his own personality.
That each child was entitled to some privacy and his personal possessions were inviolable if kept in the place allotted them.
That books in the house were to be read, enjoyed and shared.
That we believed in hospitality in spite of any extra labor involved and that our friends loved to come see us.
That personal and family prayer were an important part of each day.

That Sunday was the happiest day in the week because we went to church together, then came home for an afternoon together with father in the midst.

That music and laughter were heard often in our home.

That though father and mother worked hard and long at their respective jobs, they took time to keep informed on current events and to be of service to others.

The Colton children were starting to stretch their wings. David, Brad, and Steve were advancing in the Church's Aaronic Priesthood, open to worthy young men starting at the age of twelve. All three were good athletes and played football for Winston Churchill High School. Carolyn, also at Churchill High, advanced in the LDS Young Women's program and was on Churchill's pom pom squad. All four children got drivers licenses at sixteen.

In 1970 Ellie was called as president of the stake Young Women's organization, a program open to all LDS girls between the ages of twelve and eighteen. Ellie was her typically creative and warm self toward her fellow co-workers and the young women, who adored her.

The program is divided into three age ranges—Beehives, ages 12-13; Mia Maids, 14-15; and Laurels, 16-17. Ellie had two counselors, and each age group had at least one instructor. Young Women met together for an hour each Sunday and once during the week. Ellie and other leaders guided each young woman in accomplishing these objectives:

Strengthen her faith in and testimony of Heavenly Father and Jesus Christ.

Understand her identity as a daughter of God.

Be worthy by obeying the commandments and living gospel standards.

Receive, recognize, and rely on the promptings of the Holy Ghost.

Prepare for her divine roles as a daughter, wife, mother, and leader.

Understand and keep her baptismal covenants.

Ellie often spiced her talks with humor to make a point. "Never lick a steak knife," she told the girls and their leaders. "A person who is nice to you but rude to the waiter is not a nice person." Ellie, who loved to dance, said "Nobody cares if you can't dance well. Just get up and dance!" And she offered this advice: "Never, under any circumstances, take a sleeping pill and a laxative on the same night."[2]

Camping was part of the Young Women's program but it was difficult to locate a suitable summer campsite for the girls each year. Ellie embarked on a quest to find a permanent site. After three years of searching she found the perfect place where a girls' camp could be developed for the thousands of young LDS women in the region. It was about sixty miles north-northwest of Washington, in Catoctin Mountain Park, Maryland. Nearby was Camp David, the country retreat of the President of the United States.

Ellie was overjoyed when leaders of the Washington, D.C. stake purchased the idyllic site. Before it could be fully developed, however, those leaders changed and new stake leaders were called. The new leaders did not like the idea, believing the site would not be used enough to warrant ownership. They sold the property, crushing Ellie's dream. There are now fifteen to twenty stakes whose leaders pay to rent various campsites in the region when they could have rented this one from the Washington, D.C. stake, thereby helping to cover its cost.

Ellie no doubt was spirited in making a case for retaining the property. Afterward she wrote in a journal, "I learned you do your best when called and close your mouth when released. (The last part is the hardest)."

In a church talk, Ellie said, "I am the mother of teenagers." She continued:

> This means the house often smells of Bengay and gym shoes. It means one always doubles the recipe for cinnamon rolls if there are to be any left for the next day. It means 'Semper Paratus"—Always Prepared—like when you hear 'Mom, is it all right if I brought a few guys home for lunch? and you look up and see a third of the football team. It means yelling your head off at a game or a track meet...forgetting all about lecture No. 36, titled 'Winning

isn't everything!'

It means hair rollers, gallons of shampoo...all kinds of fingernail polish, of knowing just where to look for the missing bubble bath bottle. It means slumber parties with wall-to-wall sleeping bags that don't get used until morning.

It means trying to discipline your own scolding tongue to give more words of reassurance and encouragement...to realize what a competitive world they live in and although they need to be corrected and reprimanded at times, they need to come home to a place where they are loved, accepted, and forgiven of the fact they are not perfect.

It means wanting to reach out and shelter them from any painful experience, but knowing from your own growing pains that the failures, the insults, the feelings of inferiority, the disappointments can be the motivation, the stepping stones to being a better, finer person.

...It means feeling exasperated and like a failure some days when the house seems like the city dump...and the next day being thrilled by something they do that is so thoughtful, so generous, so decent. It means just when their minds start reaching out to explore new ideas and their souls search for the truth, you panic lest they should choose the wrong path and you find yourself on your knees pleading for help. You remember you had to find your own personal relationship with God. So must they.

22

COLTONS LEAD FOOTBALL TEAM TO THE TOP

Sports were a highlight in the Colton family's life. A colleague at Marriott said "Sterling is one of the most humble people I know—except when it came to his kids." When Brad and Steve played high school football, "Every other Monday in executive staff meeting he would tell us all about the latest game. We loved it."[1]

Despite a heavy travel schedule, Sterling almost never missed Brad and Steve's football games, sometimes arriving with luggage in a taxi bringing him directly from the airport. Ellie was equally enthusiastic.

The children inherited athletic genes from Sterling and Ellie. Sterling was a multi-sport athlete in high school and for decades he and Ellie played a lot of tennis. They also stayed in shape by exercising and jogging or taking long hikes.

Churchill's football team came together in a remarkable way in 1976 and 1977. All the ingredients for success were there: a legendary coach, strong parental support, and a group of exceptional athletes. The coach, Fred Shepherd, would teach and coach football at Churchill for twenty-seven years, turning out more than 200 players who went on to play college football and nine who reached the National Football League.[2]

In all those twenty-seven years, Churchill won the state championship just twice, in 1976 and 1977. Both times the Colton boys were major contributors. At the first of the season, a potential problem arose over Sunday practices. Brad and Steve prevailed upon

Coach Shepherd to excuse them from practicing on the Sabbath, promising extra effort on all the other days of the week.

Another conflict arose for Brad and Steve, who were weary from burning the candle at both ends of the day. They were tempted to give up early-morning Seminary—the Church's daily scriptural education program for high school students. Their teacher, Tom Ladd, struck a bargain. He would attend each of their football games if they would keep coming to Seminary. Tom kept his word, even sitting through pouring rain.

Quarterbacking the team was Jeff Kemp, son of former Buffalo Bills quarterback and New York congressman Jack Kemp. The Kemp family also lived on Greentree Road, down the street from the Coltons. Jeff went on to play at Dartmouth College and for several teams in the NFL.

Other standouts on the team were Brian Holloway and Eric Smith. Holloway, a six-foot-seven defensive tackle, later played for Stanford and was a first-round pick by the NFL's New England Patriots. Smith, a quarterback and safety at six-feet-five, played basketball rather than football in college. Smith was a basketball team captain at Georgetown University, when the Hoyas played for the national championship in 1982.

Coach Shepherd helped develop young men who were responsible off the field as well as on. Brad, a nose guard and middle linebacker, was a senior and team captain in 1976 when Churchill won its first state championship. He was named the game's MVP. Twenty-five colleges later tried to recruit Brad for their football teams.

Fred Shepherd's policy was to play only seniors. He made an exception for Steve, the only junior starter on the team. Steve played outside linebacker and was a team captain in 1977.

Shepherd was named Maryland Coach of the Year for 1976. He retired from coaching at Churchill in 1996 and later moved to Aiken, South Carolina.

Grandpa Colton, Sterling's father, wrote to his Maryland family days before the 1976 championship game. "We are cheering from this end that the boys will win their game Saturday. If they were anywhere in UTAH we would get there to see them (we wish so much that we could) but Washington is a little too far away."[3]

Sterling and Ellie scrambled and arranged for Hugh to fly to Maryland in time for the title game. Hugh said it was a thrill of a lifetime.

Ellie played an important role in Churchill's state championship seasons, helping to organize parents and build team spirit. Families took turns feeding the seventy-five players, coaches, and trainers on Friday night in their homes, and fixing them breakfast in the school cafeteria on Saturday morning before a game.

Ellie's reputation as a great cook was widely known; players often asked Brad and Steve when she was baking cookies or her famous cinnamon rolls. When the team ate dinner at the Coltons, Ellie and Sterling fed them huge bowls of stew and gallons of milk. Each guest also got a half-loaf of homemade whole-wheat bread and honey-butter.

The Bulldogs and their families were so determined that they were going to win the state championship that, at the first of the year, Ellie organized the mothers to each prepare a hand-sewn monogrammed quilt block to be made into a state championship quilt at the end of the season. They completed the quilt and presented it to Coach Shepherd.

Brad and Steve also starred in basketball. The LDS Church sponsored local and regional tournaments, with the Potomac Ward winning the Southeast Regional Tournament three years in a row. The championship games were played in Orlando, Florida; Atlanta, Georgia; and Washington, D.C.

Ellie made her presence known at games. She found a fog horn with a black rubber ball on one end, which, when squeezed, sounded the horn. If a player started arguing with a referee or otherwise was being a bad sport, Ellie squeezed the ball to get him back in line. She was a special threat to players, having learned to read lips to compensate for loss of hearing. Brad and Steve warned the other players to watch what they said.

When traveling to regional games, a number of Potomac Ward families went along, making it a grand occasion. Before leaving for the

Atlanta tournament, Ellie lectured the traveling youth that "we should all set a good example of sportsmanship." During one game a man from Maryland kept yelling obnoxiously. At one point he screamed at the referee, "Throw the bum out!"

Ellie had heard all she could stand. She jumped to her feet, pointed at the man, and yelled, "You are the bum he should throw out!" Then she looked at the amazed faces of the youth sitting around her and quickly exited the gym. Ellie went into the empty kitchen and softly wept at her outburst.

Ky Skidmore, one of the Laurels, came into the kitchen and put her arms around Ellie. "It's okay Sister Colton," she said. "We know you are just a hypocrite who's trying." Ellie often told that story on herself.

On June 9, 1978, the Coltons were at Steve's high school graduation, held at the Kennedy Center in downtown Washington. Carolyn, a student at BYU, was a summer intern for Utah Democratic Representative Gunn McKay, whose Capitol Hill office was about a mile away from the Kennedy Center. When the Congressman received a telegram from Salt Lake that day, Carolyn hurried from McKay's office to the Kennedy Center to share it with her parents and other members of their LDS ward in attendance.

It announced that the top leadership of the LDS Church—the three-member First Presidency and the Quorum of the Twelve Apostles—had met the day before and had received a revelation that henceforth, "every faithful, worthy man" in the Church would be eligible to hold the priesthood. It meant all blessings of the Church were open to all members in good standing, including black males who formerly were denied the priesthood.

It was an electrifying moment in Church history. That evening, Sterling wrote in his journal that, "I'm very pleased. I had never understood the reason for the doctrine and had reconciled myself to the belief that the policy would be changed when the people were prepared to have it changed."

Steve had this reaction: He threw his mortar board high into the air and ran around bear-hugging his football teammates who were African-American.

Church officials repeatedly called Sterling to leadership. With no local paid ministry, Mormon leaders work hard and closely together to tend their flocks in all the ways a paid minister in another church does. Sterling was a model of energy, compassion, and dedication.

"One time we were sitting quietly as a bishopric, working through things," said Clayton Foulger, a bishop for whom Sterling served as a counselor. "I said something about 'What could we do better?' Sterling immediately said, 'Oh, we can do a lot of things better.'"[4]

"Sterling is loyal, helpful, everything you could ever imagine in a counselor," said Ralph Hardy, a bishop in the region who Sterling also served as a counselor. "He is smart, quick, and wise—not afraid to give you unvarnished advice. I remember him saying 'I don't think you want to do that,' with a velvet glove." Hardy recalled that when Sterling assisted at a Boy Scout camp, he showed up in a full scout uniform bought for the occasion.[5]

The women's auxiliary in the Church is the Relief Society. One of its primary functions is in fact to provide relief and comfort to members who are sick or otherwise afflicted. Relief Society leaders act quickly when someone is in distress. However, said Hardy, when Sterling was a bishop, Relief Society leaders told him that "almost without fail, when I got there, Bishop Colton had already been there."

Sterling's voluminous journals document his extraordinary efforts to serve fellow members. At the age of twenty-six he was president of the Stuttgart Army Branch in Germany—equivalent to bishop of a ward in areas with more Mormons. He later served as a counselor to a stake president, three times as a counselor to bishops, and twice as a bishop. His callings as a bishop lasted a total of ten years.

Sterling's first term as a bishop began in 1979, in the Washington, D.C. singles ward, comprised of young men and women between the ages of about eighteen to thirty. Serving with him as counselors were Greg Prince and Brian Johnson, and later Steve Seiberling. The ward met in the Chevy Chase meetinghouse on Western Avenue, the border between the District of Columbia and Maryland.

Sterling as a bishop represented the church on WRC, a popular talk radio show in Washington. Sitting in the studio with host Mac MacGarry, Sterling clarified a number of questions regarding the church. Among them:

> Although members are called "saints," we're not beatified or canonized. "Saints" means followers of Christ, as it was used in the New Testament.

> Just as there was Moses and other prophets in the old world...we had prophets upon this continent as well, through whom the will of the Lord was made known. Their teachings were reduced to scripture that appears in the Book of Mormon.

> Temples are open to members in good standing. After an open-house period for the public, they are dedicated to the work of the Lord. We welcome people of all faiths to worship with us each Sunday in chapels.

Being spiritual advisor to young single adults is a challenging assignment. Yet the calling, said Sterling, was "the greatest thing that ever happened to me...the Lord has said that if He calls us He'll prepare a way for us to do His will...those jobs are hard because you're counseling and working with people who have problems, you see their sadness, their sorrow, their despair and despondency.

"And as you work with them on those things it's not easy. It's painful and it would be much easier to play tennis or go fishing or something than to be involved in the service of the Lord and fellow man. But as you serve, and as I have served, I found that my testimony has grown and grown and grown...We are here to serve one another and we need to help one another to return to our Father in Heaven.

"Let me assure you that we all need that help sometimes. You look to the side and might think all these people, they don't have any problems...*Everyone* has problems. They're different; some are financial, some are spiritual, some are physical, some are social...the Lord's plan is for us to help one another, first as family and then as friends and brothers and sisters in the gospel of Jesus Christ."

One ward member was Yvonne Maddox, who had converted from Catholicism a few years earlier. "Bishop Colton and Ellie were fabulous," said Yvonne. "Every time he came to the pulpit we could feel the love of the Savior through him. A pure conduit."

Yvonne added, "As for Ellie, her ready smile and winning wit touch the heart. Years later, when Bishop Colton was again my bishop, this time in a family ward, Ellie taught the gospel doctrine class. One day as I sat on the front row, I noticed she was wearing a hearing aid. After class I thanked her for the wonderful lesson and said I didn't realize she had a hearing problem. She quickly answered, 'Well, you know these bodies are just meant to self-destruct!'"

In the singles ward, Ellie was beloved especially by its women members. In a talk, Ellie remarked, "I have found what Portia said in the *Merchant of Venice* to be true: 'If to do were as easy as to know what were good to do, chapels had been churches and poor men's cottages princes' palaces...I can easier teach twenty what were good to be done than be one of the twenty to follow mine own teaching.'

"I feel very strongly that no matter what age one is or what sex or whether one is single or married, personal righteousness is life's central challenge...I believe the ultimate measure by which we shall all be judged is our love of God and one another."

Sterling served the first time as bishop for five years. After his release in 1984 he was called as a counselor to Dennis Simmons, president of the Washington, D.C. North Mission. Sterling was then a counselor to Bishop Clayton Foulger of the Potomac South Ward, starting in 1987.

Sterling began his second term as a bishop in the Potomac South Ward in 1989. As head of a congregation of several hundred members, Sundays were anything but a day of rest. Sterling rose early and usually was at the meetinghouse by 7 a.m. He met with his two counselors and the ward clerk and executive secretary. Other leaders joined them for ward council, including the high priest group leader, elders quorum president, ward mission leader, and presidents of the Relief Society, Young Men, Young Women, Primary, and Sunday School.

All of this was before the three hours of general meetings for members. These meetings include the main worship service, called sacrament meeting; Relief Society for women; two adult priesthood quorums for men; three adolescent priesthood quorums for boys; three classes for adolescent girls; Sunday School for those aged twelve and over, and Primary for those younger.

Sterling's responsibilities as bishop included counseling members; blessing those ailing in body or spirit; interviewing and determining worthiness to enter a temple or serve a mission. He also issued calls to members and, usually with other priesthood holders, laid hands on the head of a newly called member to encourage faithful service and to give them a blessing.

Near the end of the year Sterling conducted "tithing settlement" for all members. He met confidentially with each member, for each to declare if he or she was a full tithe payer—10 percent of income—and, regardless of their tithing status, Sterling encouraged generous giving.

Sterling continually prayed for guidance to minister to others in need, and he conducted his life to deserve the companionship of the Holy Spirit. Like leaders in every walk of life, some bishops are more energetic than others. Bishop Colton was at the tireless end of any scale.

Among families Sterling was especially close to was the John and Gail Evans family, who were stalwarts in the Potomac South Ward. A daughter, Marianne (Muffy) Evans, at the age of three had contracted rheumatoid arthritis (RA), a chronically painful disease that attacks the joints and is rare in children.

Muffy, a bright, pretty blonde-haired girl, had a particularly bad form of RA. The disease wore away the cartilage in her joints, leaving bone against bone and putting Muffy in constant pain. Through the years doctors replaced a number of joints with artificial parts, including both hips and both knees.

Sterling followed Muffy's development closely, as the family's home teacher—called by ward leaders to watch over assigned families—and later its bishop. On one occasion, Sterling wrote in his journal, "I visited Muffy Evans. She is feeling a little better."[6]

In March 1992, Elder Dallin H. Oaks, a member of the Quorum of the Twelve Apostles, visited Sterling and Ellie's ward and gave Muffy a health blessing, noted Sterling in his journal. "Elder Oaks gave Muffy Evans a blessing that she may recover to be able to attend BYU this fall."[7] Muffy attended and graduated from BYU, with a bachelor's degree in therapeutic recreation.

On Saturday, August 15, 1992—the day before a typical Sunday—Sterling and Ellie drove to rural Maryland and bought five bushels of peaches. Following Sunday services, they delivered peaches to ward members, including a man named Les Taylor, who was critically ill, and to a man named Jack with an eye problem that required a patch. They visited a young family whose son had mononucleosis and, assisted by the father, gave the boy a healing blessing.

Sterling also stopped by to see a man who had ruptured an ear drum waterskiing. That evening a member brought to the Colton home a woman who was in great pain from dental surgery. Sterling and the other man gave her a blessing.

On Tuesday Bishop Colton visited Les, writing that "He can't last much longer." Two days later, on Thursday, wrote Sterling, Les "passed away at 2 p.m. It was a blessing...It was a beautiful day to go. I spent several hours with the family making the funeral arrangements." On Friday he designed the printed program, "then handled a crisis" at one of the local hotels. The following Monday, Sterling conducted Les' funeral.

The end of Sterling's service as bishop this second time came in January 1993. Replacing him was Ron Harrison. Ron was the global design officer for Marriott at the time, whose group designed and renovated facilities across the globe. He was married to Bill and Donna Marriott's only daughter, Debbie.

"After Sterling was released and I was called as bishop," said Ron, "he invited me to sit down and go over the membership. I blocked out an hour, which I figured was long enough to learn about the welfare cases. It didn't take an hour—it took eight hours! He had comments about every single individual in the ward. He exemplified one-on-one ministry to those big and small."[8]

Sterling's legacy as bishop lived on for years. His daughter-in-law Melanie Colton, married to Brad, recalled when they moved into the ward shortly after Sterling was released. "I met three families with stories of remarkable service by my father-in-law," she said. "There had been one year during his tenure as bishop when three baby boys endured long hospital stays, two from drowning accidents and one who had contracted meningitis.

"The Ashtons, Foulgers, and Finlaysons had to deal with months of the kind of stress I cannot imagine. Sterling made routine visits to the hospitals before or after work. He offered his time, his prayers, and his tears throughout the year. I heard years later from different family members the gratitude they felt for their dear Bishop's love and concern during such a difficult year. Brad was called to be the bishop of the same ward to replace Ron Harrison. He felt he had large shoes to fill with the example of service his father set."

On Sunday, January 24, 1993, Sterling wrote, "It was the first Sunday I have had at home for years when I didn't have to prepare for church meetings. Ellie and I were able to ride to church and sit in sacrament meeting together. It has been a long time since we have been able to do that."

The Coltons were also exceptional neighbors. In the spring of 1985 a neighbor named Dennis Garff, also a member of the Church, drowned tragically in the Potomac River, leaving a widow, Suzanne, and three young children.

"When Dennis died, they were there for me in every way," remembered Suzanne. "I was in great grief. I remember Ellie telling me, 'It's been said that if you could take all your troubles and put them in a bag in the middle of the room, and others did the same, you may not want to exchange bags with someone else.'"[9]

The LDS Church has a women's program called "visiting teaching," and a men's program called "home teaching." Generally two women are assigned as partners to visit several women members once a month. Men are also assigned to visit the homes of several families once a month. They are to share a spiritual message and be available to help with family needs.

Following her husband's death, the Potomac South Ward assigned Ellie as Suzanne's visiting teacher and Sterling as her home teacher. They went far beyond any assignment to help Suzanne and her daughter and two sons. "I feel with both of them I could confide any challenge or worry I had and ask their advice. No confidence would be betrayed, and they would always have my best interests at heart."

Ellie frequently dropped by with apples she'd picked or homemade candy or something she had baked. The Coltons often had the Garffs in for dinner, including at Easter, when they would hide Easter eggs in the woods for children to find. "They always worked as a team," added Suzanne. While Ellie was cooking, Sterling would remove furniture from the living room and set up tables. And he always did the dishes.

Suzanne recalled that, as young mothers, she and some other women in the ward asked Ellie to give them practical advice on marriage. "Ellie said 'Concentrate on what you love about your husband and why you married him.'"

"The first Halloween after Dennis died, I was at Ellie's for a luncheon. I commented on the fantastic witch Ellie had on the center of her dining room table. She picked it right up and insisted I take it home. Every year when I put out Halloween decorations, I think of Ellie and her generosity and kindness."

The first winter after Dennis' death the Coltons offered them their condo in Park City, Utah. "It was for me to take my family on a ski trip during the children's winter break," said Suzanne. "That got us all into skiing as a family…I couldn't play football with my teenage boys, but I could ski with them!"

Several months after Dennis' death, Suzanne sent Sterling and Ellie a card. "Your tremendous help and caring got me through the darkest days of my life," she wrote. "Sterling — all the many hours you spent at our home during the week of Dennis' tragic death, calling, coordinating, checking on things, making arrangements. I appreciate it so.

"Ellie, the flowers for the service were absolutely perfect...I knew you would understand what I wanted but I could never have pictured anything so creative and gorgeous. I know it was a labor of love."[10]

23

ELLIE VS. EQUAL RIGHTS AMENDMENT

In 1974 Ellie was called to be Relief Society president in the Washington, D.C. Stake. That would lead to some of the most exhilarating as well as challenging experiences of her life—and thrust her with trepidation into the national spotlight.

There was a buzz across the region for the 20,000 or so Mormons, as their magnificent new temple rose on a fifty-two acre site in nearby Kensington, Maryland. Hundreds of thousands of visitors toured the tall, six-spire temple for a month and a half, before it was closed to the public and dedicated by Church President Spencer W. Kimball in November.

One of Ellie's first assignments as Relief Society president was to prepare a luncheon for President Kimball, a man small in body, soft in speaking, but enormous in spirit. Learning he liked fish, Ellie and her colleagues prepared a gourmet meal with halibut casserole, Korean salad, herbed bread and fresh strawberry pie. The evening before the luncheon they set the tables beautifully in the Chevy Chase meetinghouse and left, knowing they were ready. They returned the next morning with the food, to find that basketball-playing boys had moved everything.

"We tried to subdue our unkind thoughts of their lack of kindness," wrote Ellie in her journal, "and hurried and put everything back in order!" They were ready "in the nick of time and calmly, sweetly served a delicious meal" to President Kimball, several other general authorities, and local leaders. Lenora Romney, mother of Mitt, was one of the scheduled speakers. The night before the luncheon she called Ellie and said she was too sick to attend. Ellie herself gathered some thoughts and spoke in Lenora's place.

The United Nations called 1975 International Women's Year (IWY). The U.S. Congress voted $5 million to help fund state women's conferences as well as a National Women's Conference to be held in Houston in November 1977. Militant feminists were in the driver's seat, led by liberal New York Representative Bella Abzug, who was appointed by President Jimmy Carter to head the national women's commission preparing for Houston.

Abzug, nicknamed "Battling Bella," vowed to steer into U.S. law a host of new pro-feminist legislation, notably the Equal Rights Amendment to the Constitution. ERA had been around a long time. The brainchild of suffragist Alice Paul, it had been introduced in every Congress since 1923 and was routinely included in the platforms of Republicans as well as Democrats.

ERA had lain dormant for most of the half-century since 1923, until a version was passed by the House and Senate in 1972 and sent to the states for ratification. Three-fourths of the states—thirty-eight—had to approve the amendment within seven years for it to be added to the Constitution. The proposed amendment said simply: "Equality of rights under the law shall not be denied or abridged by the United States or by any state on account of sex." It was obvious the courts would be kept busy interpreting the ERA.

About six weeks before the Houston conference, Ellie got a phone call from Washington, D.C. Stake president W. Donald Ladd. He asked her to attend a meeting at the home of Eleanor McGovern, widow of former Democratic Senator and presidential contender George McGovern of South Dakota. The meeting was billed as an opportunity for IWY leaders to bring opposing women's groups together. President Ladd suggested to Ellie that, if given the opportunity, she should explain the Church's stand against ERA.

"Brother Ladd," said Ellie, "I am not sure I understand that myself."[1]

He suggested she had three days to find out. Ellie, stunned, retired to her own sacred grove in the woods behind their house to meditate and pray. Then she got to work, calling two people—a member of her stake Relief Society Board, Marilyn Rolapp (later Brinton) to accompany her to McGovern's, and a friend in Salt Lake City, Nona Dyer, to send information on the Church's position.

The information from Salt Lake arrived the following morning. It included a statement from the Church's First Presidency opposing the Equal Rights Amendment. Included in the statement:

> There are additional rights to which women are entitled. However, we firmly believe that the [ERA] is not the answer…It could indeed bring them far more restraints and repressions…We fear it will even stifle many God-given feminine instincts. It would strike at the family, humankind's basic institution…Passage of ERA…could nullify many accumulated benefits to women in present statutes… We recognize men and women as equally important before the Lord, but with differences biologically, emotionally, and in other ways. ERA, we believe, does not recognize these differences.[2]

The night before the McGovern meeting, Ellie and Marilyn pored through the stack of information until nearly 11 p.m., with Ellie mentally exhausted from cramming and insecure because Sterling was out of the country. Their children came through in his stead. Carolyn called from BYU to offer advice and suggest some comforting scriptures.

Steve, a senior in high school, came to her room. "Since Dad is gone," he said, "would you like to have a prayer with me? And he offered this short, sweet, simple prayer on my behalf that was engraved in my heart. I left my home that morning feeling like I could handle any challenge that would come to me."

"We were ready to spar with Bella or anyone else," said Ellie. But any anxiety was wasted this day. They arrived at McGovern's to learn that the leaders of the conference had cancelled the meeting, believing it would be "counterproductive" after all to meet with the two Mormon women and other anti-ERA representatives.

Ellie and Marilyn's preparation by no means was in vain. They now better understood the large issues involved and were far better prepared to debate them.

Soon afterward Abzug held another press conference announcing twenty-six goals for the Houston conference, also to guide the state conferences. Abzug warned against "subversive" groups who disagreed. The LDS Church was on her list.

The labeling of the Church by Abzug and others angered Ellie. "I asked myself why should one woman have the power to decide for all women? I became so angry that I wrote a letter to *The Washington Post*." A journalist friend edited Ellie's letter, which the *Post* ran instead as a column on its editorial page.

"I resent being told I am against women's rights if I'm not for ERA," wrote Ellie. "I am *for* women's rights. I am for correcting inequities." She explained that her mother was widowed during the Depression and had to "work day and night to rear five children. It is wrong for women not to receive equal pay for equal work."

"There has been a steady stream of legislation and judicial decisions to improve the legal status of women during the past 10 years. Enough, I feel, to prove that we can continue to make progress without locking ourselves into an amendment so vague even constitutional lawyers can't predict its consequences...We can better correct inequities with specific legislation."[3]

The Washington Post was considered required reading by almost anyone of influence in the national capital area, and was the nation's most comprehensive and authoritative news source for all things political. Breaking into print in the *Post* gave Ellie more confidence as she contemplated what to do next. It also led to many lively conversations with neighbors and others over ERA, the hot-button issue of the day.

As 1979 approached—the seven-year deadline for state passage of the ERA— proponents were still three states short of the required thirty-eight. Champions of the amendment in Congress, egged on by ERA proponents, decided to change the rules and extend the deadline by three years. They did so even though no successful amendment to the Constitution had ever required more than four years.

By then, four of the states ratifying ERA had since voted to rescind their approval. Pro-ERA leaders supported an extension of three years to add states to ERA's column—while refusing to allow states who had already voted for ERA to rescind their votes.

Ellie attended some ERA hearings on Capitol Hill, learning first hand how politics can render some people uncivilized. She created a homemade button out of a red paper plate, which said "Stop ERA Extension." Pro-ERA women wore green buttons.

"When I timidly stepped on the elevator to the House Chambers," she wrote, "I was taken aback to hear a woman say to a group of green-button wearers, 'We don't need to ride with her.' They stepped aside to wait for the next elevator. This experience was repeated on three other occasions!"[4]

In August 1978 Ellie was there when the Senate Subcommittee on Constitutional Rights debated the issue. It was chaired by Senator Birch Bayh, a Democrat from Indiana and strong ERA supporter. He had arranged for several panels, including at least one on which all four witnesses supported extension of the amendment. The four included Sonia Johnson who, with a few friends, had formed "Mormons for ERA." The Church was a strong foe of ERA and Bayh obviously hoped to blunt its effect by parading a pro-ERA Mormon woman at the hearing.

Johnson was a mother of four and the organist for her ward in Sterling, Virginia, a D.C. suburb. She had a doctorate from Rutgers University, had taught school in several Third World countries, and vehemently opposed the Church's active opposition to the Equal Rights Amendment.

Republican Senator Orrin Hatch of Utah, a devout Mormon, was on Bayh's committee and just as fervently opposed ERA. He hoped to demonstrate that Johnson represented a tiny minority within the Church. A clash at the hearing between Johnson and Hatch was almost a foregone conclusion. It included this exchange:

Hatch: Ms. Johnson, how many people do you represent in the

Mormons for ERA?

Johnson: I have no idea how many. We have not taken a poll...It is a steadily growing number of women. I think—I am sure there are more than we have any idea about. I think the numbers are growing.

Hatch: I think that you would have to admit that in the Mormon Church, almost 100 percent of the women are against the Equal Rights Amendment, right?

Johnson: Oh, my goodness. [Applause]...I do not have to admit that. It simply is not true.

Hatch: I think it is true...I would be surprised if the Mormon women who are for the ERA would comprise one-tenth of one percent. I think you would be surprised.

(After some banter between them they returned to the debate.)

Johnson: You may very well be wrong, as confident as you are...

Hatch: That is true and I am very confident...that I am right.

Johnson: And so am I.[5]

The tense exchange was widely reported in the media. Birch Bayh was painted as the hero and Orrin Hatch the villain. "It is true that some of Senator Hatch's words were not well-chosen," said Ellie. His debate with Johnson had the unfortunate effect of putting her tiny group on the map. The handful of Mormons for ERA got a publicity windfall that money couldn't buy. And Sonia was set up to play the public martyr in months to come.

"I was the first to greet Sonia" as she emerged from the hearing room, said Ellie. "Looking back, I don't believe Sonia had any idea how offensive her words were, how belittling of church leaders and of Mormon women who in good faith disagreed with her point of view."

Johnson, buoyed by a huge amount of publicity, grew more radical toward the Church. LDS leaders emphasized that open support of ERA by itself was not grounds for excommunication, but that "when those of its members publicly deride the church, demean its leaders, and openly encourage others to interfere with its mission, then it may exercise its right to disassociate itself from them."⁶ Johnson was excommunicated from the LDS Church in November 1979.

Ellie was sorry to see Johnson excommunicated, for her sake as well as the Church's, believing it "only poured gasoline on the fires of misunderstanding."

Ellie and Marilyn represented the Church in other forums. On a radio show they debated two women responsible for ERA in President Jimmy Carter's administration. The White House women slandered the Church. Just as time was about to expire, Marilyn charged them with falsehoods, and they had no time for a response. "I was so grateful for the timing," said Ellie.

The Senate vote on extending the ERA deadline came October 6, 1978. Ellie was there. She and her friend Marilyn stood in a crowded lobby off the Senate Chamber, when "a huffy woman behind me said, 'If these two Judases in front would move over, there would be room for more of us!'"⁷

Ellie turned to face the woman. With admirable control she replied, "Remember that in a political contest all wisdom and good motives and all good people are seldom found on only one side. If we're going to have to stand here all morning, let's at least be kind to each other."

The Senate passed the ERA extension 60-36; President Carter signed it into law, moving the ratification deadline forward to June 30, 1982. The basic unfairness of allowing states to ratify ERA but not rescind their prior votes during the three years dawned on the nation. Many news outlets and other powerful forces previously in favor of the extension turned against it. When June 30, 1982 arrived, pro-ERA forces had failed to persuade three more states, and ERA was dead.

On Christmas Eve a *Washington Post* editor phoned Ellie, explaining that Sonia Johnson had written a guest column the week before, and offered to publish one from Ellie as well. "Although this was the last thing I wanted to think about on Christmas," said Ellie, "I told them that if they would give me a few days to prepare, I would oblige."

On December 28, three days after Christmas, Sterling, always an early riser, went to their front porch to see if the daily *Post* had arrived. Indeed it had. He whipped it open to the editorial section. There, taking up a full third of a page, was Ellie's column, flanked by a photo of a pioneer-woman statue with a Mormon temple behind her.

Ellie's article noted that, in all the media coverage of Sonia Johnson, "nothing has been said as to the position of Mormon women who do not share her views." She wrote: "I know of no church that gives women the leadership responsibilities or opportunities to develop that the Mormon Church does. Almost every active Mormon woman is an officer or teacher in one of its organizations..."[8]

"Passage of the ERA has moral as well as political implications for us. Men and women are not the same. They differ physically, in life patterns, and in division of domestic responsibilities. We should have flexibility to enact laws that recognize 'rational differences.' The ERA would not permit such differences...Most of the important objectives of the women's movement can be and are being achieved through legislative and judicial processes..."

Ellie's most personal response to Johnson and other women who denigrated marriage in their support of ERA came in her *Dialogue* essay when she discussed Sterling, "who views our marriage as an equal partnership...I have felt from him a constant, loving support in all my responsibilities.

"He has pitched tents for girls' camp, blown up thousands of balloons, rolled out of bed in the middle of the night to rescue stranded youngsters, delivered endless loads of food and decorations all over the country, washed dishes and cleaned house when I have been ill...helped feed high school football teams, co-hosted dozens of slumber parties, and counseled our children with pride and wisdom."

Ellie ended her essay this way: "I am not blind to the imperfections and hypocrisies we struggle with. But I have witnessed and experienced great blessings because of the priesthood. I appreciate and respect the army of priesthood bearers who do their best to further the work of the Lord. I also love and appreciate the army of women engaged in this work. Together we are partners in building the Kingdom."[9]

During the five years she served as stake Relief Society president, Ellie innovated. She and her team held special leadership sessions to instruct new presidencies. At Christmas she and her co-workers started a tradition of preparing dinner for all missionaries in the D.C. North Mission. They held a special workshop for women in the stake on budgeting, taught by a noted LDS financial expert, Sid Jones.

In 1978 Ellie and seven other women in two cars drove to Nauvoo, Illinois, one-time headquarters of the Church, for the dedication of a new series of monuments dedicated to women. While there they saw an outdoor pageant called "Because of Elizabeth," about a courageous young Mormon pioneer woman. Returning to Washington, the stake leaders produced their own version of the play, with Sterling playing the part of Elizabeth's father.

Carolyn ably assisted her mother's efforts. "I helped Ellie and Carolyn in their preparation for the stake Relief Society leadership meeting," wrote Sterling. "They are both very talented and work hard on everything. The results reflect this. I am proud of both of them. It is interesting to see many of Ellie's characteristics in Carolyn, together with a little flair of her own. The meeting was a success."[10]

Stake leaders hosted "Roots and Wings," the first all-day LDS Stake Women's Conference in the East. A poetry book that included offerings from forty women was distributed; twenty-five women formed an orchestra, another thirty-five comprised a chorus. Andrew Kimball, President Spencer W. Kimball's son and biographer, gave a workshop.

Ellie's team also hosted a four-day multi-stake Area Conference at the Capital Centre, a basketball arena, attended by church leaders from Salt Lake and their spouses. As the conference proceeded inside, ERA protesters led by Sonia Johnson picketed outside.

Years later Marilyn Rolapp Brinton wrote a paper about Ellie. It recounted a surprise fiftieth birthday party Ellie and a dozen other friends threw for Marilyn at the Marriott Marquis Hotel in New York City. Ellie sat at a piano and played her "sixth-grade victory march" from 1942, the U.S. Marine Corps hymn, as the others marched and sang, tears of laughter rolling down their cheeks. Marilyn wrote, in part:

Eleanor Ricks Colton is another light in my life...She often quoted poetry to make a point...She was a magnificent leader who guided effortlessly and taught and demonstrated principles of stewardship...She exemplified unselfishness in leading. She shunned the spotlight and gave credit to everyone involved in any project...She took me with her to several ERA meetings and to interviews with the media. Even though she was the one with the wisdom and inspiration, she supported my utterances and gave me confidence in that arena populated by politically savvy and sometimes hostile women...I wanted to be just like her in all her wonderful ways. I still do. She is in her early 80s now and though she has slowed down a bit, she continues to entertain and she is and always will be 'amazing Ellie' to me.[11]

24

MARRIOTT SALES PASS $1 BILLION

The year 1977 was a special time for the Marriott Corporation, which was fifty years old. As noted earlier, in 1927, their first year of business, Hugh Colton and J.W. and Allie Marriott had sales of $16,000, mostly from nickel root beer. Now, a half-century later, Marriott for the first time surpassed $1 billion.

Marriott hotels continued to lead the lodging industry, with an overall occupancy rate above 80 percent. Sun Line Cruises returned to profitability, after weathering a downturn when war broke out on the Greek island of Cyprus, the heart of where its ships cruised. The two Great America Theme Parks in the San Francisco and Chicago areas did well, with annual attendance at each in the 2.5 million range.

As an important influence on Bill Marriott, Sterling could take justifiable pride in company growth during the decade he had been at Marriott. Sales had gone from less than $100 million in 1965 to the billion-dollar level. During the same period, the number of Marriott facilities grew from 127 to 843 nationwide and in many foreign countries.

But the year was not without challenge. Inflation inexorably was on the rise—from 5.8 percent in calendar year 1976 to 6.5 percent in 1977. And it was about to get much worse, at 11.3 percent in 1979 to 13.5 percent in 1980.

The coldest winter in the company's history cut into restaurant operations, along with government-mandated wage increases. Farrell's Ice Cream Parlours was unprofitable, a drag on the division, which ended lower than the previous year. Contract food services had difficulty obtaining price increases from airlines to cover the rise in wages and food.

Nonetheless, the Marriott Corporation explained in the Annual Report, "As we address our future we are truly enthusiastic about your company's prospects. And we have launched a thorough, realistic planning effort to guide us to continued profitable growth."

Among reasons for optimism was the fact that Marriott served growth businesses; advances in transportation were shrinking the world; and personal income was rising. The company's goal for the past decade was to grow by at least 15 percent annually in sales and earnings—a goal that had been met and exceeded.

A key clue to the company's direction was growing emphasis on managing rather than owning hotels. "With investor-partners, we can generate growth in hotel rooms and earnings, and improve our return on assets, yet minimize demands for costly new debt...Soon more than 50 percent of our hotel rooms are expected to be under management agreement," said the 1977 Annual Report.

In 1978 Marriott changed its fiscal year to the calendar year. Early the following year the company moved into spacious new international headquarters in Bethesda, Maryland, about a ten-minute drive from the Coltons. "The new facility," wrote Bill Marriott in the Annual Report, "brings together all our staff people who had been scattered in various locations as our growth accelerated in the 1970s."

The same Annual Report had a photo of the Management Committee, the policy-making body of the corporation, including president and CEO Bill Marriott and eight senior line and staff officers. The nine men—perhaps the most talented management team in the country—are on a staircase, with Bill closest to the camera. Sterling, senior vice president and general counsel, is on the next step up.

Following them are Clifford J. Ehrlich, senior vice president, human resources; James E. Durbin, president, Marriott Hotels; Thomas E. Burke, senior vice president, corporate affairs and assistant to the president; Gary L. Wilson, senior vice president, finance and development; Frederick V. Malek, executive vice president; Richard E.

Marriott, corporate group vice president, and Francis W. (Butch) Cash, senior vice president, corporate services.

Many of these men joined Marriott from other impressive organizations. Those who later left Marriott typically leveraged their leadership experience and Marriott's reputation to become successful entrepreneurs or to join other ambitious enterprises in some of the nation's most prominent companies.

By 1979 these executives directed the activities of 66,000 employees—compared with 12,500 when Sterling joined Marriott in 1966. Sterling had expanded the Law Department to keep ahead of the company's swift growth. Legal would grow from six attorneys when he joined Marriott in 1966, to fifty-three attorneys plus paralegals and secretarial staff by 1994, when he was about to retire from Marriott.

In 1978 forty company-owned hotels and resorts operated in thirty-three U.S. cities, Mexico, the Caribbean, Europe, and the Middle East.

As Sterling visited new hotels, Ellie sometimes accompanied him. One trip stood out above all the others. It was to Egypt for three weeks of enchantment as well as a camel ride that would always live fresh in Ellie's memory.

Tourist demand from the West was strong in Egypt, which was woefully unprepared for it. The 1973 Arab-Israeli War was in the past and Egypt under President Anwar Sadat had distanced itself from the Soviet Union and was leaning toward the West. In 1978 the Camp David Accords in the U.S. included a schedule for normalized relations between Israel and Egypt—the first peaceful recognition of Israel by an Arab country.

The Egypt-Israel treaty was signed the following March by Sadat for Egypt and Prime Minister Menachem Begin for Israel, and witnessed by President Jimmy Carter.

It was an extremely brave action by Sadat. He was condemned as a traitor by most of the Arab world. Sadat and Begin were awarded the 1978 Nobel Peace Prize.

By then, seven western hotel companies were building in Egypt, including Marriott, whose plans were the most intriguing of all. In 1869, to celebrate the opening of the Suez Canal, Egypt built a guest palace in Cairo especially for the Empress of France.

The palace was handed over to Marriott for management in the 1970s. The company was refurbishing the historic palace and flanking it with two towers of guest rooms overlooking acres of palace gardens and the Nile River. The ancient palace was becoming a lavish five-star hotel, and included fifteen restaurants and the Omar Khayyam Casino. The Cairo Marriott opened initially in 1983 with 680 guest rooms; when the towers were completed it boasted 1,087, set among a large reflecting pool and six acres of impeccable grounds.

Sterling hosted three Egyptians in Washington, where they reviewed plans and went over legal issues for the Cairo Marriott. One evening Ellie hosted a delicious dinner at their home for the Egyptian team. She obviously charmed General Ahmed Zaki, a former top Egyptian military leader and now head of tourism. He insisted that Sterling bring Ellie to Egypt with him.

There was one small hitch. Ellie was teaching the sixth through eighth grades at the private Christ Episcopal Day School, which Steve, their youngest child, had attended. She loved teaching these bright, eager youngsters in class sizes of just fifteen students. A church friend, Janet Thomas, agreed to substitute teach for Ellie during her trip.

In 1979 Ellie and Sterling left for Egypt. On the way over they stopped in Greece, the cradle of western civilization, which, for two avid readers, had fascinated them both for many years. "Sterling was my tour guide," said Ellie. "We sat on the steps of the Parthenon while we studied all the wonders of Ancient Greece on a beautiful blue-sky day."

They landed in Cairo, finding a lot of armed security guards at the airport, apparent evidence of the tumult then shaking the Arab world. The Coltons were taken to a hotel where a large flower arrangement, fresh fruit, and other gifts awaited them.

The government had assigned a pleasant young woman who had a degree in Egyptology to be Ellie's guide. Ellie told her that she wanted to ride a camel—and wanted it to gallop. Once the guide realized Ellie was serious, she made arrangements with a camel sheik. The sheik insisted he ride behind Ellie to be sure she didn't fall off. They mounted a camel and trotted past a pyramid into the desert.

"As soon as the camel started trotting, he put his arms around me and held onto my boobs!" said Ellie. "Once the camel started running, I assured him I could manage without his grasp! I actually liked the loping way the camel ran. I was also relieved that, when we returned, my camel driver realized I didn't need him to hold me."

Later that day, when she met up with Sterling, she told him of her adventure. "It wasn't exactly how I imagined galloping into the desert with my sheik." Sterling had a big laugh.

Her guide took Ellie to visit a man who made camel blankets. "He had two wives, one who spun the yarn and one who wove the blankets," said Ellie. He treated her to a glass of warm coca-cola. ("Yuck!" she told her journal.) She purchased a camel blanket and a colorful camel bridle. Ellie also went to where artisans turned papyrus—which began as reeds in the Nile River—into paper. She took samples at each stage of the process to show her students back in Maryland.

Sterling and Ellie traveled up and down the Nile; at each stop gifts of flowers or woven native clothing awaited them.

Ellie loved every day except the next to last one in Alexandria. It started out pleasantly, as she and Sterling were allowed to swim in the private swimming pool of King Farouk, who was overthrown in a 1952 military coup. Later that day, however, Ellie ate large Red Sea shrimp, and got a "ghastly" case of food poisoning.

When Ellie returned to school she turned heads at every traffic stop—dressed as Cleopatra. She wrote individual post cards from Egypt to each of her students, and returned with wonderful stories to tell them. "I accomplished my goal of having my school kids loving to learn how papyrus was used as writing and drawing paper."

Ellie taught at Christ Episcopal Day School for four years, the subjects ranging from social studies and American history to spelling and English. Ellie's creativeness kept her students' rapt attention. When the nation was celebrating the anniversary of winning World War II, Sterling's dad Hugh happened to be visiting. She took him to school where he held students spellbound in describing D-Day, the Allied invasion of Europe starting June 6, 1944, and his team's mission when they went ashore five days later.

Hugh explained his role in building bridges that enabled the Allies to chase the Nazis across western Europe, all the way to Berlin, where the war ended.

She took students on field trips to Annapolis, home of the Naval Academy, and to Dutch Pennsylvania, where many Amish live.

Ellie's close friend Angela (Bay) Buchanan, Treasurer of the United States, was the guest in another class. Ellie had each student bring a one-dollar bill, which Bay autographed next to her official signature on all U.S. paper currency. Another time a California member of Congress, Republican Chuck Wiggins, came to Ellie's classroom and explained how a bill becomes a law. Wiggins was her daughter-in-law Darla's stepfather.

To explain how stock markets work, Ellie consulted a stock-broker friend, Frank Johnson. They had students pick a company and pretend they were investing $1,000 in it, then routinely follow its price. At Sterling's suggestion, Ellie invested a real $1,000 in a stock. By the end of the year, she was the only one who had lost money.

Sterling joined her in the classroom to explain how the judiciary works. Then he conducted a mock trial. She also had five LDS converts from South America tell what it was like to immigrate to the United States and have to learn a new language. Ellie assigned students to talk to their parents and learn when their ancestors came to the U.S.

She also taught students how to make a quilt.

Ellie didn't teach for the money. She did it to transition from raising four children to having an empty nest, and for the pure joy of watching the faces of her students light up with delight as they learned one intriguing fact after another about their world.

On the fifteenth anniversary of joining Marriott, in August 1981, the other attorneys threw a surprise party for Sterling, presenting him a handsome leather briefcase. "It hardly seems possible that 15 years have passed," said Sterling. "They have been interesting, challenging, and very rewarding years."

Sterling with Frank Kimball, who preceded him as general counsel of Marriott.

Ellie and Sterling exploring Cuzco in the Peruvian Andes, once capital of the Inca Empire.

Ellie and Sterling on a trip to South America for Marriott In-Flite business.

Boy Scout Camp. (l-r) Brad, Steve, Sterling and Dave.

Goshen, VA 1970

Carolyn after high school graduation, with Brad, Ellie, Irish Setter mother Kelly and her 13 puppies.

Bethesda, MD 1974

Ellie with Maryland state football champions Steve and Brad.

Potomac, MD 1976

249

Kensington, MD 1976

Ellie leading 1976 Bicentennial Celebration in Washington, D.C. Stake.

Potomac, MD 1976

Family winter walk along canal. (l-r) Brad, Dave, Steve, Carolyn and Ellie.

Sterling in parking lot of original Marriott headquarters on River Road, just outside Washington, D.C.

CEO Bill Marriott and Sterling confer during a company meeting.

Marriott relocated to new quarters in Bethesda, MD in 1978.

Marriott senior executives, clockwise from bottom: CEO Bill Marriott, Sterling, Jim Durbin, Gary Wilson, Dick Marriott, Butch Cash, Fred Malek, Tom Burke and Cliff Ehrlich.

Sterling and Ellie, clean-up crew.

Bethesda, MD 1970s

Three Kings Sterling, Ralph Hardy and Brent Pratt at Potomac Ward Christmas party.

Potomac, MD 1970s

Stake Relief Society leaders, led by President Ellie Colton (center of middle row), welcome General Relief Society President Barbara Smith (left of Ellie).

Kensington, MD 1970s

253

Lake Powell, UT 1978

The Coltons with David and Carol Salisbury family.

Lake Powell, UT 1978

Sterling skippering houseboat on Lake Powell.

Flaming Gorge Dam, UT 1970s

Day trip on Green River at Flaming Gorge Dam with Phil and Maughan Colton cousins. (l-r) John (on ground), Shawn, Carolyn, Kelly, Nancy, Marci, Ellie and Bobby.

254

Cairo, Egypt 1979

Chevy Chase, MD 1979

LDS singles ward bishopric. (l-r) counselor Brian Johnson, Bishop Sterling Colton, counselor Greg Prince.

With Giza Pyramid in background, Ellie is about to ride off into the desert with her sheik.

Chevy Chase, MD 1980s

Ellie and Bishop Colton.

Sterling with close friend David Salisbury (l) at University of Utah Board of Visitors meeting.

Sterling at Marriott's test kitchen.

Sterling with Ralph Hardy.

Ellie with first grandchild, Daniel.

Ellie (l) getting facial with little Mauri, Carolyn, a friend and Darla.

Bethesda, MD 1982

Two familiar Pharaohs visiting from Egypt.

Bethesda, MD 1980s

Sterling and Ellie with Carolyn at the Western Wall, Jerusalem, on a trip to open Cairo Marriott.

Jerusalem 1983

With Sterling's parents, brothers, sisters-in-law and brother-in-law at Hugh and Marguerite's 60th wedding anniversary. (l-r) Phil and Bobby Colton, Bob Bradley, Marguerite and Hugh, Ellie and Sterling, Colleen and Maughan Colton.

Sterling and Hugh lead a Vernal parade.

258

Washington, D.C. 1980s

Ellie with Donna Marriott.

Washington, D.C. 1980s

Ellie with Nancy Reagan and Mary Foulger at White House Council on the Family.

259

Sterling with his father Hugh and (l-r) sons Dave, Steve and Brad and grandson Daniel at Steve's wedding.

Bethesda, MD 1985

Sterling and Ellie with (l-r) Steve, Melanie, baby Rebecca, Jeri and Brad.

Bermuda 1986

Christmas at the Colton home. (l-r top row) Steve, Dave, Darla, cousin Shawn, Brad and Sterling. (l-r bottom row) Jeri, Carolyn, Becca, Melanie, Jenna, Ellie, Mauri and Daniel.

Tickle time with Becca and Scott.

25

DAUGHTERS-IN-LAW JOIN THE FAMILY

The academic allegiance of the Colton family changed dramatically starting in about 1972. That year David, seventeen and the oldest of the four children, was elected treasurer of his high school class, worked construction in the summer, earned his Eagle Scout rank, and made plans to attend Brigham Young University.

Sterling and Ellie had attended the University of Utah, which in their time was stronger academically than BYU, forty miles to the south in Provo. Sterling talked up their alma mater to their children, but it was no use. Their minds were all fixed on BYU. They had grown up seeing posters and other literature from the "Y" routinely tacked on church bulletin boards across the globe. LDS speakers often touted the assets of BYU, and church literature was filled with inspiring stories about its athletes and teams.

Among reasons the Colton kids gave for their BYU preference: There were relatively few Mormons in their high school, and they wanted to find their identities where being a Mormon was not the main difference with their friends; the church school now offered a strong secular as well as spiritual education; for the rest of their lives in church circles, they would likely run into friends made at the Y.

In 1973 Dave graduated a semester early from Winston Churchill High School—as his father had done in college. He worked to save money for college and enrolled at the Y that fall. In 1974 he received his LDS patriarchal blessing, was ordained an elder in the Melchizedek Priesthood, and left for a two-year mission to Alberta, Canada.

Carolyn, sixteen in 1972, worked for Marriott accounts payable that summer, and accounts receivable the following summer. At Christmastime she was Santa's helper at Montgomery Mall. In 1974 she got her patriarchal blessing, graduated from Churchill High, and began college at BYU. The following summer she worked for the clothier Garfinkel's and in Marriott's tax department.

Brad, eighteen in 1976, earned his Eagle Scout rank and had a life-changing spiritual experience. Twenty-five colleges tried to recruit him for their football teams, forcing Brad to decide between football and a church mission. During Christmas break he decided to test a famous promise in the Book of Mormon:

> And when ye shall receive these things, I would exhort you that ye would ask God, the Eternal Father, in the name of Christ, if these things are not true; and if ye shall ask with a sincere heart, with real intent, having faith in Christ, he will manifest the truth of it unto you, by the power of the Holy Ghost. And by the power of the Holy Ghost ye may know the truth of all things. (Moroni 10:4-5)

"I decided during the Christmas break of my senior year that I would read the Book of Mormon," said Brad. "I had a hard time putting it down." He read the book of more than 500 pages in less than a week. "I got down on my knees and put the Prophet Moroni's promise to the test...as I was praying...I felt the power of the Holy Ghost confirm to me the truthfulness of this book and that Joseph Smith was a prophet of God...With this confirmation, the course of my life was set."

After his freshman year at BYU, Brad accepted a call to the California Anaheim Mission.

Steve, the youngest, turned eighteen in 1978 and also earned his Eagle Scout award. Years earlier he had attended Christ Episcopal School to get help for a speech impediment and dyslexia, a learning disorder. What he learned was put to good use: He was inducted into the National Honor Society before graduating from Churchill High.

At Churchill, Steve was a superb multi-sport athlete, in football and track. Like Brad, Steve also was recruited heavily to play college football. Instead he opted to go to BYU for one year, followed by a two-year mission to Mindanao, Philippines.

Darla Burnett was the first daughter-in-law to join the Colton family circle. Her family moved to Potomac, Maryland when she was eighteen, after her stepfather, California Congressman Chuck Wiggins, was elected to Congress. Darla attended nearby Montgomery College, a local two-year community college, and at the age of twenty worked for the Veterans Administration, got her patriarchal blessing, and enrolled at BYU.

The following year, 1976, Darla worked for a member of Congress and was called to serve an eighteen-month mission in Dallas, Texas. In the summer of 1978 Darla returned from Texas and gave her homecoming address in the Coltons' ward. "I was smitten," said David, who was home from college for the summer, "and invited her and others to come over to the house."

Dave and Darla started dating at the end of June, got engaged in August, and were married in the Washington D.C. Temple on December 28, 1978. They honeymooned in Barbados at a Marriott resort hotel, where Dave scuba dived for the first time, sparking a longtime interest in the sport.

In the summer of 1979, with finances tight, Dave got a well-paying job lined up by Sterling's brother Maughan, to help build the Red Fleet Reservoir near Vernal.

Early in 1978 Sterling's sister Nancy discovered a lump in her left breast. Doctors in Greenville, South Carolina, where the Bradleys lived at the time, operated and found it was malignant and had started to spread. They performed a mastectomy, followed by radiation and chemotherapy, which failed to stop the cancer. Nancy was courageous and outwardly upbeat as her condition worsened.

Visiting the Coltons in Bethesda in 1983, a three-year-old Colton grandchild, Daniel, was startled upon entering Nancy's bedroom. "Aunt Nancy, you don't have any hair!" She answered, "Yes I do, it's right over there!"—pointing to her wig. Pulling on his hair, Daniel said, "Mine won't come off!"

In Nancy's last letter to Ellie, she wrote "What a lot of joy and happiness you've brought into my life — for so many, many years — I feel so PRIVILEGED — how LUCKY to have you — Ellie! As my own sister-in-law. Look at me & weep all you envious ladies out there! I don't care to question whether I 'deserve' you or not —I just accept! With eternal gratitude."

Nancy added, "You have added such a rich dimension to my life — to have someone like you that loves me — that has been & is such a truly beautiful example of womanhood — from the inside out & up and down!...My heart truly runneth over...You all must know how absolutely essential you all were...the knowledge of your love for us sustains, supports & continually warms my heart."

Hospice came daily to the Bradley home during Nancy's last month. Ellie had promised Nancy she would be her caregiver "when things got rough." In November she flew to South Carolina for three weeks. "I tried very hard to bring her all the comfort I could, with warm facials and massages," said Ellie. "I prayed every day to have the strength to bless her in her last month."[1]

Near the end of the year 1983 it was clear that Nancy did not have long to live.

Ellie had prepared to speak to a group of LDS teenage girls in their stake, on a date that came at the same time she was in South Carolina caring for Nancy. Instead, she wrote out her talk in long-hand and had someone else deliver it. "You are young with great potential and opportunities before you," she said. "What can you do to prepare for a full, rich life? We are going to talk about being educated and cultured. Wow, what big lofty goals!"

"We never really arrive at being educated or cultured. There is always more to learn, another skill to develop, something to rearrange or create. Once the mind is stretched to a new idea, it never goes back to its original dimension...it means your world can stretch from a nutshell to infinite space.

"We all came into this world as screaming, little, insecure babies... As we start to grow we become more aware of the world around us...I don't believe the Lord gave us senses only for our protection, but to bring us joy. The Lord has created lovely things on this earth to make our lives more meaningful and joyful." She continued:

> Girls, discover what you love, then follow your loves, cultivate them, share them. Your loves are actually your talents, gifts from a loving Father. We have to explore many different areas often before we discover what it is we love to do...Learning is not all fun, it's hard work! It takes effort! It takes discipline. It means studying when you would rather be playing...

> The class I put more effort into than any other was a Shakespeare class my senior year. The professor required us to memorize 890 lines for a passing grade. I had Shakespeare lines pasted on the bathroom walls, on the mirrors, on the headboard of my bed... everywhere that I might pause a moment...The night before our final exam, my roommate and I stood on our heads to memorize the last thirty lines, hoping by this technique the words would stay in our brains long enough to write them out the next morning! An amazing thing happened with all that effort. We fell in love with Shakespeare!

> To be educated makes life more interesting. Besides, you never know when you can use a little Shakespeare. One time when a doctor was giving me an unpleasant examination, I burst forth with "Oh, that this too too solid flesh would melt, thaw, and resolve itself

into a dew, or that the Almighty had not fixed his canon 'gainst self-slaughter." [Hamlet: Act 1, scene 2] The doctor laughed and said 'You are the first patient that has ever been inspired to quote Shakespeare on the examining table!'

You need to be educated for other reasons than for personal pleasure. The Lord needs faithful women. Even more, He needs faithful, competent women...Being educated will help you be responsible, intelligent leaders in the church and in the community...Some of you will be required to help with the family income to provide for yourself and your family. You need to develop marketable skills... We live in exciting times when opportunities to improve our minds, strengthen our bodies, heighten our cultural awareness and increase our spirituality have never been greater. Discover what your loves are and cultivate them with enthusiasm.

Melanie Farrell was the next daughter-in-law to join the Colton family. She first met Elder Brad Colton in 1978 when she was just fifteen and living in Fullerton, California. As a missionary, Elder Colton and his companion would sometimes be invited to have dinner at the Farrells' home. (Years later Melanie wrote of meeting him, "No fireworks for either of us.")

Melanie started college at BYU in 1981. There, when Brad was a senior, they ran into each other again. "We talked about the Book of Isaiah," recalled Brad, for a class Melanie was taking from noted LDS scholar Victor Ludlow.

On January 14, 1983, Brad took Melanie to the BYU vs. El Paso, Texas basketball game. "After the game we had a great time," said Brad. "That night I wrote in my journal, 'This is the type of woman I want to marry.' This was the only time I wrote something like this in my journal."

They got engaged later that spring and were married December 27, 1983 in the Los Angeles Temple.

The following day, Nancy Colton Bradley died. "I felt sure she did not want to spoil the wedding, and held on until it was over," said Ellie. Her funeral was held that week in Vernal. The Coltons had already sent out invitations for an open house at their home for Brad and Melanie when they returned from their honeymoon. "We arrived home the night before the reception," said Ellie.

Early the next morning the doorbell rang at their home. "Three of my friends came to help me prepare for the open house," said Ellie—JaLynn Prince, Barbara Mecham, and Marilyn Rolapp Brinton. "I have never forgotten those angels and how much it helped me when I was feeling so sad and yet happy for Brad and Melanie."

Nancy had lived around the globe with her family. She prepared her children for each new move by showing them maps of where they were going, and learning together what made the new place exciting. And everywhere they lived she made warm and welcoming. But her last wish was to go home.

Nancy died on December 28, 1983. She was buried in Maeser, Utah, outside Vernal, in the family's cemetery plot.

Sterling and Ellie maintained close contact with Nancy and Bob's three children, Robin, Bobby, and Elizabeth, and with Uncle Bob. Bobby lived with the Coltons for his senior year at Churchill High. The summer before entering Stanford, Robin lived with Sterling and Ellie and their children. When Elizabeth and her husband Dan had their first baby, a boy named Griffin, in 1994, Ellie flew to New Mexico and acted as a surrogate mother, assisting Elizabeth for a week.

Bobby contracted AIDS, a relatively unknown disease at the time. When Sterling learned he was sick, he flew to New York and spent two hours trying to console Bobby. Two weeks later he wired him $700. Sterling and Ellie offered to have Bobby stay with them again. Instead, Bobby moved to San Francisco, to be near his sister Robin in Marin.

Bobby died at age thirty-three on October 4, 1991. He is buried near his mother and other family members in Maeser.

In 1983 Sterling, Ellie, and Carolyn took a trip of a lifetime to the Middle East, for the grand opening of the Cairo Marriott, stopping for five days in Israel. Sterling kept a highly detailed account of their venture. Their trip was a year after Brad and Steve's semester abroad with BYU in Jerusalem. The Colton parents flew from Salt Lake City on Sunday, April 3, 1983, meeting Carolyn at JFK Airport in New York and embarking for Israel. The plane was not full and Sterling was able to stretch out over five seats and sleep.

They arrived in Tel Aviv in the dark and took a taxi to Jerusalem, where they settled into a small apartment next to the Daniel Rona family. Rona, who was born in Palestine to a Jewish family, converted to Mormonism in the U.S. and returned to what is now Israel. He was the only LDS-licensed guide in Israel at the time.

The following morning they left with Rona in a ten-passenger van to begin their tour. They passed through Samaria, stopping at an old inn reputed to be near the site where the story of the Good Samaritan took place. Next was Qumran, where two Bedouin shepherds in 1947 accidentally came upon a clay jar in a cave that contained seven ancient parchment scrolls known as the Dead Sea Scrolls.

They drove to Masada, a flat mountain top above a steep rocky crag where, according the ancient historian Josephus, some 900 Jews withstood a nearly three-year siege by 10,000 Roman soldiers in 73 AD., finally committing mass suicide rather than surrender.

Sterling and Carolyn swam in the Dead Sea. Many other bathers had covered themselves with black mud as a beauty aid, wrote Sterling. "We passed." They returned to Jerusalem, changed clothes, and went to a hillside overlooking Bethlehem, outside Jerusalem. There, with the local LDS branch and BYU students studying abroad, they celebrated the birth of the Savior, which Mormons believe, through modern-day revelation, was on April 6 in the meridian of time. Wrote Sterling:

> The stars were out. It was clear and we could see for miles in the moonlight. The hills were green as a result of the rains. They were

covered with small, bright red flowers...also with olive trees, some of them hundreds of years old. There were shepherds taking their sheep and goats home. A number of Bedouin children joined us. The setting was perfect.

The Coltons read scripture telling of the birth of the Savior, and sang Christmas carols. "I'm sure it will make future Christmases much more meaningful for us," wrote Sterling. "We truly felt we were walking where Jesus walked. It was a night we will always remember."

They rose early the next morning and headed for Galilee, 75 miles away, stopping at a church about a day's walk from Jerusalem. It could have been about where Mary and Joseph discovered their son was missing, when he was in the temple in Jerusalem, "sitting in the midst of the doctors, both hearing them and asking them questions." (Luke 2:46) Samaria was the next stop, where Jesus sought water from Joseph's well and told the Samaritan woman that he possessed "a well of water springing up into everlasting life." (John 4:14)

Sterling noted, "We picked up some delicious hot pita bread." They drove through Nazareth, where Jewish rabbis thrust Jesus out of the city for blasphemy. It was heavily commercialized, and the group did not stop. On the drive from Nazareth to Galilee, the view from the hills to the sea was "spectacular," wrote Sterling. They had lunch at Tiberius, where he noted the "Peter's fish" was delicious.

Among other stops, they climbed a hill through fields of olive trees, wild flowers, and small flocks of sheep, where Jesus may have preached the Beatitudes. They found a spot away from other visitors and read the Sermon on the Mount. Ellie and Carolyn picked wildflowers to be pressed. The group returned along the River Jordan as it descends to the Dead Sea, stopping at a kibbutz that grew bananas.

Sterling noted the transformation from the lush greenery of Galilee to the stark desert of the Dead Sea. "The Israelis have done an amazing job in improving the productivity of the land." From there they returned to their apartment in Jerusalem. "After a big dinner we collapsed like a brick wall."

Weather the next day, unlike the previous two, began cold, rainy, and blustery; however, by the afternoon it was blue-sky again. The group visited the Western Wall, then the Temple Mount, which includes the Dome of the Rock, beneath which is the Foundation Stone, the holiest site in Judaism. According to their tradition, the stone is the site were Abraham prepared to sacrifice his son Isaac. It is also holy to Muslims, some of whose scholars believe it is where the Prophet Muhammad ascended to Heaven in 621 AD.

The Coltons visited places believed to be where the Savior spent his last days on earth, including Bethany and what is believed to be the tomb of Lazarus, whom Christ raised from the dead. They followed the route of Christ's triumphal entry into Jerusalem, to where it is believed the Last Supper took place.

Then to the garden at Gethsemane, where Christ suffered and atoned for the sins of all mankind. On a hillside the Coltons read the scriptural account in Matthew 26 and Luke 22. "It made me realize perhaps more than ever before the great sacrifice He made for us," wrote Sterling. "It made me want to be a better person and strive harder to live as He would have me live." They visited a garden tomb that may have been the one where Jesus was laid and from where he was resurrected.

Saturday is the Jewish Sabbath and the Coltons attended LDS services that day, then walked through old Jerusalem. The Church at the time was trying to acquire property in Jerusalem for a BYU satellite campus. It succeeded, leasing a five-acre parcel on the Mount of Olives and constructing an impressive white building that opened in 1989 as the Brigham Young University Jerusalem Center for Near Eastern Studies.

The following morning, Sunday, the Coltons took a taxi to Tel Aviv and flew Air Sinai to Cairo. Also descending on the Egyptian capital from across the globe were extended families of other Marriott employees, top executives of many airlines, banks, insurance and travel agencies. The Egyptian ambassador to the U.S. and other government officials also were there.

They were there for the grand opening of the Cairo Marriott. "The hotel is outstanding," wrote Sterling. "It is much better than I imagined it could be. The restoration work is beautiful. It is truly one of the great hotels of the world." As an aside he added that, "It was nice to get into a Marriott room after the rather cramped quarters next to the Ronas."

The official celebration and dinner were on April 12, 1983. The following morning they flew to Luxor, Egypt, exploring the Valley of the Kings, then back to Cairo. Unfortunately Sterling, who loved to eat, was suffering from the "Pharaoh's plague"—known as "Montezuma's revenge" in the western hemisphere.

Early the next morning they caught a flight to Athens. They took a cab to the new Athens Marriott, scheduled to officially open the following month. Ellie and Carolyn shopped at the flea market. In mid-afternoon they drove to Piraeus, a port city in the Athens area, where they joined other Marriott guests of the Cairo opening in boarding the *Stella Maris*, one of the three Marriott cruise ships. They sailed to the island of Rhodes, then to Santorini, where they rode donkeys to the top of a hill.

The ship returned to Piraeus, where they took a flight headed to the U.S. "It was a wonderful trip," wrote Sterling, who had a considerable pile of work awaiting him at the office. "We returned home tired, but with many wonderful memories."

About a month after their trip to the Middle East, Sterling fulfilled a lifelong dream of his father Hugh—to see the Kentucky Derby. In May 1983, Sterling took his father and son Steve to see the world-famous horse race.

Sterling also lined up stops at nearby farms to check out some of the world's finest Thoroughbreds. Hugh, who had a magic touch with horses, rhapsodized about the experience for the rest of his life.

Ellie and Sterling celebrated their thirtieth wedding anniversary on August 6, 1984. Sterling surprised Ellie for the occasion, arranging for them to participate in a cruise of the Mediterranean to Tangiers, Malta, Corsica, and ending up in Porto Fino, Italy. Prior to the cruise Sterling was on a business trip in Athens and met Ellie in Venice. "We woke up early the morning before the cruise and jogged around Venice as everyone was waking up," reported Ellie. "The cruise was great. We danced every night and saw historical and beautiful spots every day. We had an unusually fine time!"

26

MARRIOTT RESURRECTS TIMES SQUARE

In May 1982 Bill Marriott did something especially brave. He decided to build a half-billion-dollar hotel in New York City's seedy Times Square, just a few minutes walk from what *The New York Times* had labeled the "worst block in the city."[1]

It would be the company's largest hotel and, said Bill, was "the biggest financial decision of my career."[2] Complicating the deal was a neighborhood that long ago had lost its luster and was now characterized by crime, a sordid sex industry, and few legitimate businesses. Ed Koch, mayor of New York City, wanted to redevelop Times Square and persuaded other city fathers to grant tax incentives to do so.

The story of the building of the New York Marriott Marquis is an example of the complicated legal deals Sterling coordinated.

Sterling said, "We knew it was risky." In addition to the unsavory neighborhood, "New York is a strong union city, and we planned to build it non-union. A lot of people said it could not be done. But if we succeeded, it had the potential to be one of the great hotels of the world."

In 1984 alone, on the "worst block"—the outer edge of Times Square on 42nd street between Seventh and Eighth avenues—there was an astounding 2,300 crimes committed, nearly 460 of them serious felonies such as rape and murder.

"Walking on 42nd Street," said Marriott's chief financial officer, Gary Wilson, "I felt it was the most dangerous place I had ever been."[3]

Sterling's opinion carried weight with Bill and other company leaders. Cliff Ehrlich, head of human resources, remembered a key executive staff meeting when the Marriott Marquis was discussed. "We were going to be the anchor in that part of the city to be developed," he said. "But what if the rest did not get redeveloped? Sterling discussed the pros and cons, then he'd say, 'Here's where I come down.' Bill always had great respect for Sterling's judgment."[4]

To be recognized as a major hotel company, some observers considered it important to have a visual presence in the Big Apple. Marriott already owned the Essex House, acquired in 1969, but its outside signage did not carry the Marriott name and wasn't quite the same as having a major hotel with "Marriott" in lights.

Meanwhile, a celebrated architect, John Portman, Jr., based in Atlanta, approached Marriott with a set of plans he had drawn up years earlier for a hotel he hoped to see built in Times Square. Portman, known for his soaring hotel atriums, had designed the 1,674-room Atlanta Marriott Marquis, the South's largest hotel, which opened in 1985. The hotel in New York would have 1,949 rooms, making it Marriott's largest anywhere.

Portman had already tied up the land at Broadway and Seventh Avenue for a British developer. After that deal fell through he approached Bill Marriott. Bill turned to Sterling for advice, and Sterling and others helped Bill see through the forest of potential problems to find the trees that represented considerable potential benefits.

Sterling met with Portman and his top people in Atlanta, including two all-day sessions on January 8 and 9, 1981. "It is a very complex transaction," said Sterling. "We are making progress, but it is a slow process."

"Portman is talented but is a tough negotiator, difficult to deal with," said Sterling in an interview. On Marriott's side the deal was done almost entirely in-house. "It was a great team effort, a credit to Bill for the strong group he had put together. A lot of Marriott people contributed to the project, but there was no doubt Bill drove it. Without him none of this would have happened."

Bill and his team faced a tough set of circumstances. Would New York officials make good on promises to clean up Times Square's thirteen acres? They planned to drive out seedy, illicit enterprises, and offer tax breaks to other business leaders to relocate to the area. If this did not happen, Marriott could find itself an island of class and commerce in a cesspool of a lake for many years to come.

Labor unrest was also a concern. Marriott tried hard to avoid union entanglements. Marriott's general contractor tried but failed to get a no-strike clause included in the construction contract.

As with other hotels, a company team was formed to take the Marriott Marquis from concept to completion. Marriott had among its own people virtually all the qualified experts needed to do so—a strength probably unequaled elsewhere in the lodging industry. CFO Gary Wilson did a feasibility study. After he left the company he was replaced by Steve Bollenbach who, along with an assistant, Al Checchi, negotiated the original deal with Portman for both the Atlanta and Times Square Marquis hotels.

Jack Graves, head of architecture and construction, inherited Portman's finished design and faced the task of trying to make all the spaces conform to Marriott's specifications. The projected overall budget was $265 million. Marriott owned 89 percent of the project, Portman 11 percent.

John Bacanskas, head of Marriott real estate development, assembled the financial pieces of the complicated agreement. They totaled $60 million in three deals: $10 million in a first mortgage, borrowed from three sources; $30 million in a second, from a city tax abatement; and a $20 million federal UDAG grant from the Department of Housing and Urban Development to revitalize severely distressed urban areas.

Sterling had the crucial responsibility of ensuring that Marriott's interests were protected each step of the way in the very complicated deal. He tapped Steve McKenna, a group leader in the Legal Department, as day-to-day legal counsel on the Times Square hotel team. McKenna drafted the real estate contracts. "Sterling let me do everything, but I always reported to him on these big projects," said McKenna.

Sterling himself was active, usually behind the scenes, backstopping McKenna and others. His journal shows he worked on the Marriott Marquis on hundreds of days. Construction began in 1982.

On July 23 Sterling met at the Times Square site with attorneys regarding syndicating the hotel financing. "The hotel is moving forward with demolition about completed and excavation started," he wrote. "They hope to have the cement out of the ground by December."

As feared, some unions went out of their way to cause trouble. "There were a couple of big incidents," said Don McNamara, a vice president of finance who played a major role in the development. "When the hotel was pretty far up, someone put concrete down the toilet."[5] Agitators for one cause or another periodically stopped the project as well. Company observers believed unions were behind the stoppages.

A nonunion contractor from Houston tried to deliver steel beams to the site. Members of the New York City local teamsters union were waiting for the trucks on the New Jersey side of the New York line. The Texas trucks' cargo had to be offloaded in a New Jersey marshaling yard, then reloaded onto local teamster trucks for delivery to the hotel construction site.

Another Texas steel problem arose when Trinity Industries of Dallas sent steel that had to be refabricated. Both issues delayed construction, throwing schedules off for subcontractors and adding millions of dollars to hotel costs.

(A decade later Marriott sued Trinity to recoup the cost. Marriott attorney Steve McKenna told Trinity that Marriott would settle the lawsuit for $15 million. Trinity made a costly mistake by refusing the offer. In October 1997 the suit was settled in a higher court for $70 million, a great majority of it going to the Times Square hotel.)

Marriott also had various issues with architect John Portman as the project went forward, though they were resolved amicably. "Bill Marriott is a great diplomat," observed McNamara.

In the end everyone celebrated when the Marriott Marquis was completed and opened in November 1985. The elegant 49-story hotel with a 45-story atrium—tallest in the world at that time—was topped by a revolving restaurant. Some knowledgeable observers believe it is the most profitable hotel in the world.

It didn't come cheaply, however. The original $265 million budget doubled to $530 million by the time it was completed. Marriott subsequently sold Essex House to Japan Airlines for about $300 million, equaling the difference.

Taming the rest of Times Square did not happen overnight, but it did happen. After years of false starts, it began in earnest with Mayor Ed Koch. In 1980 he announced the coming resurgence of Times Square. Successive mayors were also supportive, including David Dinkins and Rudy Giuliani.

The Marriott Marquis, one of the first major pieces of the puzzle to restore Times Square, helped give other companies the courage to jump in.

Among those signing new leases were Viacom, the global entertainment company, in 1990; publishing giant Bertelsmann AG in 1992; and the Morgan Stanley investment firm in 1993. Good new restaurants also opened. Marriott leaders breathed a sigh of relief as Times Square began to fill with such blue-chip neighbors.

Early on the morning of October 10, 1985, Sterling, Ellie, and Carolyn flew to New York for the grand opening of the Marriott Marquis and a few days of R&R. They took a beautiful hospitality suite in the new hotel.

Mayor Koch, who called himself "a liberal with sanity," spoke. A former U.S. congressman, he had helped clear the roadblocks for building the Marquis. Other speakers included Bill Marriott, architect

John Portman, and former all-pro NFL linebacker Sam Huff. Since leaving football, Huff had worked for Marriott, selling over 600,000 room nights via a partnership between Marriott and the NFL that booked teams into Marriott hotels for away games.

Success of the Marquis led Marriott to repeatedly plant its flag across New York City. "…the hotelier has quietly set about turning New York into Marriott City," said *The New York Times*. Within a dozen years Marriott had eight hotels in the city, with 5,200 rooms—the most of any hotel chain.

27

GRANDCHILDREN ARRIVE

The next phase of Sterling and Ellie's life began on September 2, 1980 when Sterling Daniel Colton, their first grandchild, was born to Darla and David in Provo.

The eight-pound-eleven-ounce baby, noted Sterling, "has ten toes, ten fingers, two eyes and two ears. He is perfect." He and Ellie felt the same way about each succeeding grandchild, including Mauri Lyn Colton, Daniel's little sister, born July 9, 1981. Mauri also arrived in perfect health, said Sterling. "We rejoice and give thanks to the Lord."

During the previous year Darla attended BYU and Dave graduated from the Y in economics and enrolled at its J. Reuben Clark Law School. Dave was on the *Law Review* and in 1981 was elected president of the student chapter of the Cougar Club, BYU's athletic booster program. David graduated from law school in 1982 and started his career where Sterling's began—in Salt Lake City at Van Cott, Bagley, Cornwall & McCarthy.

He and Darla bought their first home in Taylorsville, Utah, and welcomed Ellie and Sterling's third grandchild, Jenna Arlene Colton, born August 11, 1984 in Cottonwood Hospital in Murray, a suburb of Salt Lake City.

Carolyn shined as a scholar, graduating from the Y in 1978 with high honors in psychology. She worked that summer for Utah Democratic Congressman Gunn McKay, and enrolled in the Y's law school in the fall as one of seventeen women in a class of 146. In 1981 she graduated from law school, passed the Washington, D.C. bar, and started as an associate in the Washington, D.C. office of the firm of Jones, Waldo, Holbrook & McDonough. After four and a half years with Jones Waldo, first in D.C. and then in Salt Lake City, Carolyn joined Marriott's Legal Department in 1985 and bought a home in Bethesda, Maryland.

Brad graduated from BYU in 1983 and married "the girl of my dreams," Melanie Farrell, near the end of that year. Their first child, Rebecca Anne Colton, was born May 20, 1985 in Salt Lake City. "Brad was able to be with Melanie the entire time," said Sterling. Starting in 1982, Brad was employed by Marriott in a series of positions at its full-service hotels, beginning in Salt Lake City.

In 1987 he earned a graduate degree at the University of Virginia's Darden School of Business. The Coltons then moved to Atlanta, Georgia, where their second child, Bradley Scott Colton, was born on May 19, 1987, the day after they landed. Jane Elizabeth Colton was born on January 11, 1991, and Thomas James Colton on January 15, 1994. Seven years after moving to Georgia they returned to the Washington area with Brad as general manager of area Marriott hotels.

Steve returned from his mission to the Philippines in 1981 and re-enrolled at BYU. In 1984 Steve was elected BYU's student body vice president.

Ellie had a direct hand in getting Steve and his wife Jeri Cash together. Jeri's father, Butch Cash, was also one of Marriott's top executives. After Steve and Jeri met at BYU, Jeri let Steve know that a roommate of hers was interested in dating him. Steve considered that a brush-off by Jeri. Later, Jeri's mother Judy and Ellie boarded the same plane to return from Salt Lake to Washington. As fate would have it, they were randomly assigned adjoining seats.

"While we were chatting," said Judy, "we got around to talking about Steve, Ellie's youngest, and Jeri, our oldest. Ellie said, 'Why do you think Jeri doesn't want to date Steve?' I said, 'No, she definitely *wants* to date him.'" That was communicated to both children, who began to court and fell in love. They were married in the Washington D.C. Temple on August 21, 1985. "Jeri was beautiful," said Sterling. "She and Steve are really a handsome couple."[1]

Sterling offered to help pay for the honeymoon. The evening of the reception he had two envelopes in his coat pocket. One held a small tip for the caterers and the other the honeymoon money. Near the end of the evening he gave Steve an envelope. Awhile later Steve approached his father. "Dad," he said, "I don't think this is going to work." Sterling had given him the wrong envelope.[2]

After graduating from BYU in 1986, Steve, like his brother Brad, earned a graduate degree at the University of Virginia's Darden School of Business. Jeri and Steve moved to Minneapolis, Minnesota, where their first child, Jared Cash Colton, was born on December 13, 1988. Jeri and Steve next moved to Newtown, Pennsylvania, where they welcomed their second and third children, Meredith Cash Colton on October 8, 1990 and Brandon Cash Colton on November 16, 1992. Jeri and Steve's fourth child, Sterling and Ellie's youngest grandchild, Kevin Cash Colton, joined the family on November 11, 1994 in Princeton, New Jersey.

As fellow in-laws of the new couple with Sterling and Ellie, Butch and Judy Cash had a lot of opportunities to observe the Coltons. Butch also knew Sterling from working together at Marriott for eighteen years.

Judy, a convert to the LDS Church, said, "Before the Coltons, we hadn't been around people who were role models. They were our role models. It was a blessing to our family just to watch what they did...I can attest to Ellie's strength of character. She is the kindest person you can find."

The foursome went to Thailand, meeting young married friends of the Coltons, Nancy and Mike Nebeker, who lived there. Mike took them on a hike up a steep hill. Crossing a creek, Ellie fell but didn't utter a word as they continued hiking. Later, large black bruises appeared on her hip and arm.

The Coltons and Cashes also rode elephants, one elephant per couple. Inspired by the lush foliage and blue-sky day, Sterling led in singing LDS hymns at the top of his lungs. Winding up a narrow path on a hillside, Sterling's hat blew off and flew partway down the mountain. With no room to turn around, one of the elephants backed down the precipitous path, reached the hat with its trunk, and gave it to Sterling.

On one hike they came across a series of cascading mountain ponds. The guide asked if they wanted to go swimming, but no one had a suit. It was a steamy hot day, and a cool pool was too good to pass up. They decided to skinny-dip. Butch and Judy picked one pool and Sterling and Ellie another. They disrobed and climbed in. Bill Marriott enjoyed teasing Ellie and Judy about it for years to come.

On March 29, 1980 Ellie gave Sterling a large black-and-brown account book, with 500 legal-size pages and this inscription on the cover page:

"Dearest Ster: Today is the first day of the rest of your life. BEGIN!! May these pages record a rich and rewarding life nourished by all of us who love, admire and appreciate the great dimension you have added to our lives. With much love, your posterity."

That same day, a Saturday, Sterling picked up a pen with black ink and wrote three and a half tightly spaced pages. He began, "I am Sterling Don Colton. I was born April 28, 1929 in Vernal, Uintah County, State of Utah." For the rest of his life Sterling rarely missed a single day of writing in such journals, well over 5,000 pages of his daily life and thoughts in remarkable detail. They included the names of family, friends, professionals with whom he interacted, and church members he helped.

As the journals witness, Sterling and Ellie lived extremely active lives. One cannot peruse his writings without wondering how they had the stamina to do all they did. It was not through extra sleep. Sterling's first entry noted, "I arose at 4:00 a.m. this morning" to prepare talks for a stake conference. Through the years Sterling not infrequently has risen around 4:30 a.m., sometimes wondering why he wasn't able to sleep longer.

One secret to the Coltons' stamina was regular exercise each morning, whether at home or traveling. They both loved tennis and played a lot of it, usually doubles. Or they jogged or walked. Ellie especially loved walking, perhaps a throwback to her youth in Idaho Falls when her family never had a car. In the winter they skied.

In thousands of his journal pages and the comparatively few written by Ellie, there is virtually no talk about the need to lose weight. In December 1980 Sterling described attending a surprise birthday party for Nancy Marriott. "It was based on a '50's theme," he wrote. "Ellie and I were able to wear the same clothes we wore to the U. of U. Junior Prom in 1951."[3]

Marriott encouraged its employees to get a physical exam each year. Sterling had gone three years without one when he went to his doctor in August 1980. "I have been blessed with excellent health," he wrote, "and haven't missed a day of work because of illness since I joined Marriott fifteen years ago."[4]

Back on January 27, 1955, when she was still in the States and he in Germany, Ellie wrote Sterling to say, among other things, "I went for the best walk this morning—all along the river…There was a big break in the ice and about twenty ducks were having a ball. It looked so strange—all of them were swimming together except one—and he was in front showing off by swimming backwards, sidewards, and making wave designs in the water. I wonder if he was chosen as the entertainer of the morning?"

Her letter the following week, on February 5, said, "Your accounts of the weather make me even more discontented…It has been an exceptionally cold winter. I can hardly wait for those walks!!" And in another letter around that time, she wrote, "I would have given anything to have you here today—it was so perfect for a walk…You do like to go for walks, don't you?"

Decades later, from their home in Bethesda, she recorded, "Sterling and I started walking the entire C&O Canal on Saturdays. We would drive two cars up 15 miles or so and then drive one car back to where we started. Each mile marker we would have a hug!"[5]

In July 1982 Sterling and Ellie drove to Rehoboth Beach, Delaware, on the Atlantic, a popular vacation spot for Washingtonians. Darla and the first two grandchildren, Dan and Mauri, were with them for the week, while Dave stayed behind in Utah, studying for the bar exams.

Sterling and Ellie jogged along the beach each day. On three successive days they jogged ten miles, fourteen miles, and another two hours and twenty minutes the third day. They swam in a pool, played tennis, and built sand castles with the grandchildren.

But Sterling was restless. "We had fun playing with Dan and Mauri," Sterling wrote in his journal on July 13. "We spent the day lying around. It is amazing how you can take so much time and do so little. Ellie keeps telling me it is important to unwind, but I cannot help feeling uneasy and a little bored." He called his office daily to check on the progress of a syndication deal.

The Coltons were drawn to adventure and excitement—as a couple and with friends. Tennis was a common interest. Sterling had liked tennis since high school days in Vernal. Uintah High School did not have a tennis coach, but he and some friends taught themselves the game and represented Uintah in matches with other small schools.

Sterling's dominant right hand was permanently disfigured after the accident with a glass door as a boy. It was an impediment to tightly gripping a tennis racket, though he was not known to use that as an excuse when playing.

In the spring of 1954, a few months before they were married, Ellie had written, "Oh—about my tennis—I've always been terrible—but I was really glad to hear that you've been playing—I've never played a game clear through, but I'll try to sharpen up my strokes." A few decades later she had improved to where she was beating Sterling on occasion.

Sterling played occasional pick-up tennis matches. Then, in the early 1980s, a friend, Merlon Richards, invited Sterling to play regularly, along with several other men. From then on, when not traveling, Sterling could be found on a court playing doubles two to three days a week from 6 to 8 a.m. They played on public courts, indoors in winter and outdoors the rest of the year.

Each day, Sterling began his journal entry by giving a brief weather report, followed by a description of the morning's exercise. If it was tennis, he always wrote the name of his doubles partner, who they played against, and the number of games or sets won by each team. Though good-natured, Sterling was seriously competitive in whatever he set out to do.

In the early 1980s Ellie organized a group of tennis-playing buddies, ten couples who played together in assorted combinations during the year. Annually for about seven years they took a tennis vacation together, each year staying at a Marriott hotel. Venues included Palm Springs, California; Hilton Head, South Carolina; Disney World in Orlando, Florida; and New Jersey.

Among those joining Sterling and Ellie were Butch and Judy Cash, Brad and Mary Jane Bryan, Jack and Renee Carlson, Jim and Ann Davis, Rusty and Janene Hall, Jeff and Sue Huguely, Dan and Linda Howells, Gordon and Lynne Mella, and Paul and Jan Yost. Wherever they went, there was always a lot of laughter, and not a hint of discord among the group.

"Since Sterling and Butch worked for Marriott," said Lynne Mella, "they could have gotten free rooms. But they gave up that option so we could all stay together. Otherwise some of us wouldn't have been able to afford it." The trips were usually in October. "Ellie organized everything," said Mella. "We called her 'Mother Superior.'"[6]

At most hotels two couples were assigned to a suite. Each year they rotated couple roommates. Mella, who played competitive tennis in a club, organized the matches, which included mixed-doubles—a man and a woman as partners playing another man and woman. They played tennis in the morning and afternoon, and were free to go their own way in the evening.

Sterling was generally a good sport and went along with what the others wanted to do. An exception was charades, a word game in which players try to guess a word or phrase whose words are acted out with physical rather than verbal clues. "The women played against the men," said Brad Bryan, "and the women always won. Sterling really disliked playing it."

During an outing to Hilton Head, recalled Judy Cash, "Ellie was a little quieter than usual. Then one day she broke into a great big smile." That's when the others learned that Ellie had been awaiting a call from her doctor on the result of a cancer biopsy. It was negative. She had not wanted to cast a cloud over their outing by expressing anxiety.

Though living in the East, Sterling and Ellie had a deep love for the Uintah Mountains. Echoing Sterling's father Hugh, his posterity still call them the "high and beautiful Uintas."

Located northwest of Vernal and a hundred miles from Salt Lake City, the Uintas, a sub-range of the Rocky Mountains, are the tallest mountains in the contiguous United States that lie east to west. They have more than 400 miles of streams and a thousand lakes and ponds.

Wildflowers, grasses, and shrubs are abundant in the Uintas, and the forests contain many types of trees including lodgepole pine, Douglas fir, Engelmann Spruce, and quaking aspen. Weather in these mountains can turn from lovely to ugly with scant warning.

Sterling's love of the Uintas was more than sentimental. Without the Uintas there would be a lot of thirsty people in the American Southwest. While much of the region is high desert and receives around ten inches of water from rain and snow each year, large portions of the Uintas get more than forty inches. Its highest peaks are snowcapped year-round except from late July through early September.

The Colorado River is the most important river in the region. Its major tributary is the Green River, which flows through the Uinta Basin. The Bear and Weber Rivers flow around the eastern side of the range and are the largest tributaries to the Great Salt Lake. The Provo River is born on the southern side of the range and is the largest tributary to Utah Lake.

Hugh Colton was one of a small handful of citizen activists in the 1950s who fought in Washington and won the rightful share of the Colorado River for Utah and three other upper-basin states—Colorado, Wyoming, and New Mexico.

The Colorado flows through three lower-basin states as well—California, Nevada, and Arizona. All seven states were apportioned shares of the river in the 1922 Colorado River Compact. The three lower-basin states proceeded to build infrastructure to capture their shares of water. When the four upper-basin states were slow to act, the three lower-basin states took their water as well.

The three lower-basin states understandably were reluctant to lose the extra water they had long enjoyed. It took a mighty struggle in

Washington, D.C.—with Hugh personally visiting the offices of more than thirty members of Congress—before the legislature passed and President Dwight Eisenhower in 1956 signed into law the legislation called the Colorado River Storage Project (CRSP). Hugh Colton then was a leader in getting new dams and reservoirs built in the Uintah Basin to collect Utah's share of water.

Sterling often has ventured into the breathtaking Uintas with friends and family, usually taking pack horses to carry food and gear. Two of those who went with him were former law partners at the Van Cott Bagley firm in Salt Lake City—David Salisbury and Howard Edwards. Salisbury went with Sterling about a dozen times, far more than anyone else.

Edwards went a single time, an outing that included a frighteningly close call. Also on that trip were Salisbury, Frank Richards, and Glenn Potter; the latter two living in Park City at the time. Most of the men rode small mustangs. Going up one mountain, the trail narrowed as they reached a half-mile stretch of sheer rock face.

The mountain was on their right; on their left was a steep drop-off of around 200 feet, followed by a sheer vertical precipice of probably another thousand feet into a canyon and river. As they crossed the rock wall, Edwards' horse suddenly lost its footing and stumbled. Its front legs buckled as Edwards flew over its head. He barely landed on the mountain side of the trail, saving his life. Edwards walked the rest of the way across the rock trail, leading his pony.[7]

Unfortunately the weather was awful that week. Said Potter, "We stayed in tents and it rained like crazy."[8]

On that particular trip Sterling had arranged for professional outdoorsmen to set up the tents ahead of their arrival and do the cooking for the week. Edwards and Richards fished, releasing most of their catch but keeping enough for dinner. The group also played cards to pass time. Despite the dangerous mishap and bad weather, "It was a wonderful experience," said Potter.

Sterling and Ellie periodically got together with these and other couples for dinner, the symphony, or other evenings out when staying at the Colton condo in Park City.

Ellie taught early-morning LDS Seminary during the 1984-85 school year. Many Mormon high school students meet each weekday starting at about 6:30 a.m. for religious instruction focused on the scriptures, including the Bible and the Church's three other standard works: the Book of Mormon, Doctrine and Covenants, and Pearl of Great Price.

As LDS seniors graduated from high school in the spring of 1985, those who had attended Seminary faithfully also graduated from that program. "Three battle-worn teachers and many weary-bodied students have reason to rejoice today," Ellie said in remarks to Seminary graduates and their families. "We endured to the end!"

She thanked eight other adult members who had substituted for her when she traveled with Sterling. Ellie, with her hearing impairment, had worried about not waking when the alarm went off. "I woke up at 4 and 4:30 to turn it off. It was the first time in thirty-one years of marriage that I awakened my husband. It has always been the reverse."

She and Sterling played musical beds all year. "We started out at night in our own bed. Then in the middle of the night I'd wake up and take the alarm clock with me to Carolyn's room, which would wake Sterling. He would go into Steve's room so I wouldn't wake him up when I came back to our room to get dressed at 5 a.m. It was very complicated!"

During the year, said Ellie, she had learned that humans "must learn capacities and skills, not just pick up information. When people are forced to be righteous, it interferes with the process that righteousness in a free environment is designed to produce.

"Righteous living causes something to happen to people. Just as we can never learn to play the piano, no matter how talented we are, unless we practice, learning how to love the Lord and to love and serve others requires participation in the process. Jesus said, 'If any man will do His will, he shall know of the doctrine, whether it be of God, or whether I speak of myself.'"(John 7:17)

28

Marriott Builds, Sells, Manages Hotels

The Marriott flower blossomed as never before in the 1980s. Sterling hired additional attorneys and his legal team was kept hopping as company units multiplied. Marriott's metamorphosis from a majority restaurant company to a majority lodging company was a fact from then on.

In 1985, when Times Square came on line, eight other full-service Marriott hotels opened as well. Marriott was the largest operator of hotel rooms in the United States; it would later become the largest hotel company in the world.

By then Marriott used a greater range of financing methods than any other major lodging company. Among them: private and public tax-exempt financing; savings and loan financing; public syndication of partnership interests; syndication of partnership interests through insurance companies; and tax-advantaged partnerships sold to European investors.

All the creative financing required complicated legal documentation, masterminded by Sterling.

About 40 percent of hotel revenue came from business guests, another 40 percent from all kinds of groups using its meeting space. The final 20 percent comprised people traveling for pleasure.

Marriott began developing specialized lodging products, ranging from all-suite hotels, mega convention hotels—including the two Marriott Marquis hotels—vacation ownership resorts, retirement communities, and moderate-priced lodging. Courtyard was the first offering in the last category. After five Courtyard hotels were tested successfully in Georgia in 1983 and 1984, the company went all-out with the brand.[1]

Marriott followed the success of Courtyard by creating two other moderately priced lodging groups, Residence Inn and Fairfield Inn. Residence Inn was started in 1975 as the nation's first extended-stay hotel. It was launched in Kansas by a man named Jack DeBoer and acquired by Marriott in 1987.[2]

Fairfield Inn, the lowest-priced company lodging at the time, was created by Marriott in the late 1980s to compete against such hotels as Days Inn and Hampton Inn.[3]

Marriott was well on its way to an eventual thirty brands of hotels, across all hotel segments.

"Bill Marriott's leadership was the key to the growth," emphasized Sterling. "He believes strongly in teamwork, and has valued each team member's contribution. He has gone out of his way to give credit all around."

It was an exciting time at Marriott, whose ranks included entrepreneurial leaders recognized at the top of their respective fields. Sterling was praised by his legal peers, reported Martindale-Hubbell, the national attorney ranking system. Anonymously, his peers gave him an "AV" rating. The two letters, A and V, measure different criteria. The first letter measures professional legal ability, with an "A," the highest mark, equivalent to a letter grade of A in academia. The second letter measures adherence to professional standards of conduct and ethics, with a "V" being Very high, the highest mark.[4]

From the time Sterling joined the company in 1966, its growth was steadily upward. In his first year, Marriott had about 10,000 employees, 150 separate restaurants and other facilities of all types, and 2,450 hotel rooms. Over the next decade, by 1976, those numbers grew to 51,000 employees, 825 units, and 14,510 rooms. By 1987 the numbers had turned explosive: nearly 210,000 employees, 4,000 units, and 100,000 rooms. Marriott was one of the largest real estate developers in the U.S.

Stockholders had long had a love affair with the company, for many good reasons. In 1984 Marriott's stock had grown at an amazing compound rate of 35 percent annually for the previous five years. Marriott sales and profits had doubled since 1980 and had increased tenfold since 1971.

Marriott was the nation's most profitable hotel company, occupancy rates continued well above the industry average, and Marriott received more Mobile and American Automobile Association awards than any other lodging chain.

"Yes, we 'sell' room nights, food and beverage, and time-shares," wrote Bill Marriott. "But what we're really selling is our *expertise in managing the processes that make those sales possible.* And that expertise rests firmly on our mastery of thousands of tiny operational details."[5]

Marriott's high-powered leaders made a pivotal decision in the 1970s, to capitalize on its unique management systems and considerable hotel experience. From 1980 to 1984, Marriott financed nearly $3 billion worth of hotels. A great majority of the amount came from Marriott's building and selling hotels to investors, and taking back management contracts, often for seventy-five years.

As lodging mushroomed, it steadily crowded out other Marriott segments. Early in 1982 Marriott sold Farrell's Ice Cream Parlour Restaurants, which had not performed well. Over the next several years other restaurant businesses were sold as well. Sterling and his attorney colleagues found that selling off Marriott businesses was not always easy. In 1983 the company decided to sell the two Marriott's Great America theme parks, which had been problematic from the start. They operated only about half the year, when students were out of school and available to fill jobs.

Both parks were put on the market in 1984. The one near Chicago sold relatively easily in 1984, but the one in Santa Clara, California gave Sterling and his colleagues fits. The California park was on some pricey real estate in Silicon Valley, home to some of the world's largest high-tech companies. The NFL's San Francisco 49ers later built a stadium at the site.

A Marriott attorney and real estate developer, Bob Droege, found a buyer, Caz Development Company. Marriott granted Caz an option agreement worth $36 million in August 1983. Sterling, however, advised by assistant general counsel Steve West, who had overall responsibility for the theme parks, believed the company could do better.

Santa Clara City made a bid for the park, offering $101 million—$65 million more than Caz. When Marriott decided to accept the city's offer, Caz sued. Marriott finally settled with Caz for $12 million and sold the park to the city for the $101 million, netting the company $53 million more than it otherwise would have received.

Marriott hung on with its Sun Line cruise ships—the *Stella Oceanis*, *Stella Maris*, and the 45-percent-Marriott-owned *Stella Solaris*—for fifteen years. "We started making some money, but it wasn't enough," said Fred Malek.[6]

Sterling, responsible for legal services during the acquisition, operation, and now disposition of the ships, commented, "We found that cruise ship operations are very sensitive to political turmoil and fuel costs. Also, that foreign partners and management often have different objectives and standards."

Sterling led the negotiations that finally sold off the ships in 1987.

"Not only were cruise ships more complicated than we realized," said Bill Marriott, "but we made the error of letting ourselves get into a partnership in which we didn't have the controlling interest.

Given our corporate culture based on systems and attention to detail, it drove us crazy to not be calling the shots."[7]

The year 1985 was one of milestones for the Coltons. Hugh and Marguerite, Sterling's parents, observed their sixtieth wedding anniversary on September 3. They had made enormous contributions to their country, community, and family. Sterling and Ellie and other family members celebrated the anniversary in July, when all but a few family members were able to attend.

On July 11 Hugh and Sterling rode horses in the Vernal rodeo parade. The anniversary party in Vernal was two days later. "Mother and Dad were in their glory," said Sterling. "It is a great family." About 250 family and friends attended the celebration.

A month later, on August 13, 1985, a number of the Marriotts were at their family compound at Lake Winnipesaukee, New Hampshire. After an evening cookout, J.W. walked inside and sat down. When others went to check on him, he was unresponsive. He had died from a heart attack at age eighty-four.

"He was a remarkable man," wrote Sterling. "He had lived a full life and had made many contributions. The world is a better place because of his life. He was a wonderful friend and we will miss him." Sterling spent a good part of that night answering media queries about Mr. Marriott.

Carolyn Colton witnessed a poignant scene with J.W. and Hugh a few months before J.W.'s death. "I spent a wonderful day chauffeuring Grandpa and Mr. Marriott down to and around the Marriott farm in Virginia," said Carolyn. "…They really didn't say much. I guess after sixty years you really don't need to. We sang old songs—well, Mr. Marriott and I sang while Grandpa listened and once in awhile joined in—and looked over the ranch, the haymaking, and the animals.

"The love and admiration each felt for the other was contagious. Even though they didn't say it when they shook hands goodbye, I felt

Grandpa was saying 'I love you and I don't think I'll see you again.'"

At the request of J.W.'s widow, Allie, Ellie arranged a veritable Garden of Eden floral display for the funeral. Sterling worked late into the night helping Ellie arrange the flowers. Hugh and Marguerite flew in from Utah for the funeral. Hugh had recently returned from a pack trip in the Uintas, which in the past he had sometimes shared with his dear friend. Approaching J.W.'s coffin at the viewing, Hugh softly wept.

The family prayer just before the funeral was offered by Dick Marriott. "It was very moving," wrote Sterling. "I wished I had taped it. It was a very spiritual experience."

J.W. had cut a wide swath. Speakers included former President Richard Nixon, Christian evangelist Billy Graham, and LDS general authorities including Ezra Taft Benson, Boyd K. Packer, and Gordon B. Hinckley.

J.W. Marriott passed away one week before Jeri and Steve's wedding on August 21, 1985. After the funeral, Ellie had access to the dozens and dozens of roses that had been on display, including roses from Ronald and Nancy Reagan. The petals from the roses were thrown as Jeri and Steve departed their wedding reception at Congressional Country Club.

Sixteen days after his father's death at Lake Winnipesaukee, Bill and other family members were there again. Bill was in a boathouse, fueling his motorboat to take his grandchildren and an adult guest for a ride. Unbeknownst to him, gasoline fumes had filled the fuel compartment of the boat. When he turned on the ignition switch a spark ignited an explosion, setting Bill, the boat, and the boathouse ablaze.

His pants and sweater on fire, Bill jumped or was blown into the lake. A helicopter transported him to Massachusetts General Hospital (MGH) in Boston.

Bill had third-degree burns on his hands and legs. He credits Dr. Jack Burke, chief of trauma at MGH and head of its burn unit, with saving his life. Dr. Burke treated Bill for sixteen days.

Once more Sterling was called into service as the spokesman for the Marriott family. "I spent most of the night coordinating and handling media calls, etc.," said Sterling. In the following days, as Bill recuperated, Sterling had to shoulder a greater share of the work at the company.

In 1982 Marriott had acquired Host International, which specialized in airport retail outlets including food and merchandise, and roadside restaurants along interstate highways. Three years later Marriott completed the acquisition of Howard Johnson. It had been the largest restaurant chain in the U.S. in the 1960s and '70s, but had become stale and outdated, ending up on the market.

Sterling had misgivings about acquiring HJ. "I don't think they are up to Marriott quality," he wrote several times, as he became weary of the transaction. Others came to agree with him. Marriott converted some Howard Johnson restaurants into Big Boys—the nation's second-largest chain of family restaurants. Then, with second thoughts, Marriott sold the 335 restaurants along with 130 hotels.

Marriott also made a strategic decision to sell all stand-alone restaurants. Roy Rogers went to Hardee's for $365 million; family restaurants would be sold over the next eighteen months. In addition, the company sold its pioneering airline-catering operation to a management-led group for $570 million.

Marriott saw a bright future for contract food services, however, which would produce a third of company profits in 1990, making Marriott the largest provider of institutional food service in North America, serving business, health care, and education organizations.

"Although restaurants and airline catering were profitable," explained Bill, "these operations did not offer the same long-term growth potential as our other major businesses." This meant that two of the three primary businesses in Sterling's early years at the company—restaurants and In-Flite—would soon be gone. Marriott's future depended on the success of its hotels.

29

Hugh Dies — The Torch is Passed

While fighting off legal and business alligators, Sterling's attention was also drawn to the Rocky Mountain West, where the health of his father Hugh was deteriorating. Hugh had had prostate cancer for years, which spread through his body. By the start of 1990 he could no longer enjoy outdoor activities with his horses, and often was in pain.[1]

Knowing his father's days were numbered, Sterling approached officials at the J. Reuben Clark Law School at BYU to establish a living memorial to honor Hugh. In October 1988, Hugh and Marguerite's three living children—their deceased daughter Nancy was represented by her widower husband Bob—and a number of grandchildren gathered at the law school in Provo. The occasion was the announcement of the Hugh W. Colton Professorship in Law.

The Law School explained in a brochure that "Hugh Colton attended law school at George Washington University. Except for the time he was in the military, he was actively engaged in the practice of law, including natural resources, livestock and public lands, water law, commercial litigation, and other aspects of private practice throughout Utah and Colorado."

Speakers noted his life's work was marked by humanity, productivity, and heroism. The last trait was demonstrated repeatedly in World War II. A war correspondent had called Colonel Colton and his band of Army combat engineers "the bravest of the brave" as they cleared the path and bridged the rivers from Normandy to Berlin. In part because of his leadership, thousands of Allied soldiers in the Greatest Generation lived to return home, take up their careers, marry, and father the next generation.

A classic country lawyer, Hugh was known for never turning down a case because a client could not pay. "His greatest mark," said Sterling, "was that he served the people of the Uintah Basin to see that justice was done…To my knowledge, no one who came to Dad for help was turned down because they couldn't pay. Sometimes he'd take a pickup truck or a saddle. We had those all over the ranch."

Law School Dean Bruce Hafen, in remarks that would become a permanent fixture to the professorship, said, "The writer Bellamy Partridge concluded some years ago that 'the country lawyer, as he existed between the days of Abraham Lincoln and Calvin Coolidge is no more.'

"But in the life of Hugh W. Colton, we find embodied the same independence, versatility, and boundless sense of public service that have long characterized the legal profession: the country lawyer. This endowment will help keep that valuable heritage alive in the minds of our law students…"[2]

Sterling represented the Colton family in speaking of his parents: "I can't speak of Dad without speaking of Mother. In my mind they are one…Our parents have given us a great heritage. They taught us to love God, family, and our country…They taught us by example that we had great blessings and had a responsibility to serve others and serve our community."

Hugh, with "all humility and with a great deal of thanks to many, many people," expressed gratitude to school officials and guests. He noted that he represented hundreds of Utah lawyers in rural areas of the state.

Dick Marriott represented his family, which contributed resources to help fund the professorship. "Hugh used to put me on his knee and tell me the corniest stories," said Dick. "You were really a member of our family. My father would sometimes drive my mom, my brother and me crazy. At about that time he would go out West into the Uintas and drive *Hugh* crazy! I think those trips helped preserve my dad's life for as long as they did."

Dallin H. Oaks, a former BYU president and current member of the Church's Quorum of the Twelve Apostles, was the last speaker. "Someone said that history is the length and shadow of great people," said Oaks. "It's apparent that Hugh Colton and his wonderful companion Marguerite have cast a very long shadow. Everyone here has stood in that shadow…and the shadow will go on and on into the generations to come."

The prestige of the Hugh W. Colton Professorship is obvious from those who have held it. They include James R. Rasband, dean of the law school from 2009 to 2016, and Kevin J. Worthen, president of BYU at this writing.

Early in 1990 Sterling and Ellie were in Utah when Hugh saw his oncologist in Salt Lake for the last time. Sterling was at the wheel of a van as they returned to Vernal, with Marguerite riding shotgun. Hugh was lying down in back with Ellie next to him. "Hugh could not see out of the window," said Ellie, "so he asked me to describe what we were passing. I tried to describe in detail the beauty of the trip he had taken so often and loved so much."

Sterling returned to Washington and Ellie remained behind to help care for his parents. For many years that responsibility had belonged to Sterling's brother Maughan, who long since had also taken the primary role of running the ranch.

Sterling's other brother, Phil, who lived in suburban Maryland with his wife Bobby and family, played a crucially important role in comforting Hugh in his last days. A bedroom at Hugh and Marguerite's home had been converted to a hospital room, and nurses tended to Hugh around the clock. Phil asked Hugh repeatedly if he wanted him to set up a television, with Hugh always saying no, he just wanted to sleep.

One morning Phil took his camera and began videotaping the ranch animals, including the cattle and two mares about to foal. Twenty calves were born that morning. He also went to the rodeo grounds where two of Hugh's horses were being trained to race. A trainer had two jockeys put the horses through their paces around a quarter-mile track. Phil filmed it all.

Phil returned to the house and told his father that he had just videotaped the ranch and its animals. Hugh, reaching for his glasses, suddenly became animated. "Set up the TV!" said Hugh. His attention was glued to the monitor showing the VCR tape of his beloved ranch. Each time he was conscious after that, Hugh asked to see the video again.

Hugh died on April 14, 1990, the Saturday before Easter. A filly was born the night Hugh died, and the next morning began with rain. Ellie told Sterling that "Hugh was already talking with the Lord to obtain water for the valley and a colt for the grandchildren." The morning clouds changed to a spectacular rainbow and the weather was beautiful the rest of the day.

Sterling spoke at the funeral, following a country-western ballad, "Land Beyond the Sun," sung by a mixed ensemble, accompanied by two guitars. Many in the audience dissolved in tears, including Sterling, who had trouble getting through his talk.

Obituary news articles appeared in many newspapers, including *The Washington Post* and *The Washington Times*, *The New York Times* and *Los Angeles Times*, and was carried nationwide on the AP newswire. Radio commentator Paul Harvey summarized Hugh's story in a nationwide broadcast, noting he co-founded Marriott International and was a hero in World War II.

About a year later, Sterling and Ellie, his mother Marguerite, Bill and Donna Marriott, and Butch and Judy Cash flew to Buffalo, New York for the dedication of the Hugh W. Colton Administration Building. It was a 50,000-square-foot facility to house computers, accounting and other administrative services. A large bronze plaque said:

> *Hugh W. Colton*
> *Building*
> Dedicated May 22, 1991
> *Marriott*

Hugh W. Colton, co-founder of what was to become Marriott Corporation, was a constant example to others of high character, commitment to ideals, dedication, perseverance and achievement.

In 1993 Ellie was called by LDS leaders as the first chair of the Women's International Committee. It was formed in the capital area to assist the Church's worldwide effort to build relationships with people in the public sphere whose influence and actions are relevant to the Church's mission. Ellie worked under the guidance of Beverly Campbell, Director of International Affairs for the Church.

That summer Ellie helped organize one activity that was highly popular among diplomatic families—a western family picnic, where ambassadors and embassy staffs shed their suits and ties and, with their families, donned cowboy hats and bandanas for a real-life experience of the American West. It was held at the Marriott Fairfield Farm in rural Hume, Virginia.

As usual, Sterling was at Ellie's side, helping in every way possible. Ellie arrived at the farm in the afternoon, driving a new red Jeep Cherokee, filled with flowers and other items. Sterling left after work and was caught in rush-hour traffic, arriving that evening.

They stayed in the manor house and ate a dinner Ellie had packed for them. Then they put tiny cowboy hats on hundreds of lollypops. Afterward Sterling went to bed. Ellie had too much nervous energy to sleep, and wandered the house, puttering. "She is like a child on Christmas Eve," wrote Sterling.

The next day, in a happy atmosphere and perfect weather, there were pony rides, hay rides, clog dancing, blue-grass music, and a lot of food. Welcoming everyone was Elder M. Russell Ballard of the Church's governing Quorum of the Twelve Apostles. Sterling and

Ellie had special responsibility to host the ambassadors and their families from India and Greece, and the diplomatic representatives from Romania and Indonesia.

Nearly twenty ambassadors and about 180 other members of the diplomatic corps and their families attended.

Word got around, and a year later, in 1994, ambassadors and embassy officials from forty nations attended the picnic. Their numbers, including spouses and children, nearly doubled those of the year before. "The deputy ambassador of the Czech Republic," wrote reporter Alysa Hatch, "arrived with his two children tugging at his arms to get to the play area. 'They were up before the sun this morning wanting to know when we could go to the ranch,'" he said.[3]

Elder Ballard, on hand again, welcomed the activity as a way to thank diplomats for the hospitality shown by their respective nations to members of the Church who lived in their countries. "Events such as this are mutually supportive," he said, "and are joyous ways of extending hands of friendship, and offer positive opportunities to develop and expand relationships with ambassadors and embassies."

Hatch wrote, "One ambassador commented that with the busy schedules of ambassadors in the nation's capital, this is one of the few places they can come to know other ambassadors and their families and make new friends outside the diplomatic community."

Each dignitary and his or her family was given a memento of the hosts' pioneer heritage and history. It was a small replica of a buffalo skull with the insignia "All is Well." Chairing the event under Ellie's guidance was Joy Korologos, whose husband Tom was a well-known Republican lobbyist and former White House liaison to Congress.

Dick and Nancy Marriott thanked guests for coming. Nancy said, "I am sure there's nothing that father (J.W.) Marriott would enjoy more than having this farm used for this purpose. In fact, I think he must have arranged this magnificent weather."

Another favorite tradition among diplomats and the greater D.C. community is the annual Christmas season Festival of Lights at the

Mormon Temple Visitors Center. An annual tradition since 1976, the temple grounds glow with more than a half-million outdoor lights all through December, while inside the center a different musical group from the community performs each evening. Ellie's Women's Committee assisted with the Festival of Lights.

Among good friends Ellie made during this time was Verona Croitoru, whose husband worked at the Romanian Embassy. Ellie learned that Verona's daughter-in-law, Anca, at home in Bucharest, was pregnant and had a rare blood disease. If she were to bleed, it could be difficult to stop the flow. Both families, including Anca's husband, were worried. Romania's medical system was not well advanced, a legacy from Communism. Hospitals did not even feed patients.

Sterling and Ellie invited Anca to come to America to have her baby. "I came over in May of 1992," said Anca. "The Coltons took me into their home and made me feel so welcome." She was given a bedroom on the upstairs level of their home. Anca added, "The first time I went into a grocery store here, I actually cried. I thought of the last food line in Romania I was in. I stood in line six hours for three bananas."[4]

"Ellie was so cute. She was always cooking and introducing me to new foods. When I said I had never tasted peanut butter and jelly sandwiches, her eyes lit up. She tried to find everything I needed, anything she could do to make me comfortable. Ellie held a baby shower for me, something I had never heard of. A number of her friends came."

Anca's family was considered upper-middle class in Romania. Like many other Romanians, however, they had suffered under the dictatorship of Nicolae Ceausescu, a Communist who ruled the country with an iron fist from 1965 to 1989, when he and his wife Elena were executed by a hastily assembled firing squad. Anca herself had gone to medical school in Romania and had nearly finished a residency in pediatrics when she came to the U.S. Her husband was an engineer.

The Coltons arranged for Anca's medical needs. A young ob/gyn doctor, Theressa (Tia) James Nowitzky, a friend of the family, offered Anca free medical care. During the days leading up to the birth, Ellie walked with Anca in their neighborhood. On June 21, 1992, with Ellie at her side, Anca checked into Georgetown University Hospital, where doctors induced labor. Given her blood condition, Anca could not have an injection to ease the pain.

"It was long and painful," Anca remembered. "Ellie never left my side for a minute. She was such a relief." Ellie held her hand as the contractions began and got harder, and at the moment of birth that night. Anca was rewarded with a beautiful baby girl they named Carina. Anca and Carina lived with the Coltons another two months until Anca's husband Cristian arrived from Romania. "Ellie took me to get a new dress so I'd look pretty when he came. She thought of everything."

The Croitorus returned to Romania. Three years later they emigrated to the U.S. Cristian earned an MBA at Harvard and Anca did a residency at Mt. Sinai Hospital in New York City. She spent another year learning to treat diseases of the skin. Today she lives in Ellicott City, Maryland, and works at a private clinic, midway between Baltimore and Bethesda. Carina studied psychology at a small liberal arts college.

The Coltons remain often in touch with the Croitorus.

30

STERLING LEADS THE SPLIT THAT SAVES MARRIOTT

Sterling's finest hour at Marriott came in the early 1990s, when the future of the proud six-decade-old company was on the line. Marriott had evolved primarily into a manager rather than owner of hotels. Throughout the affluent 1980s it perfected a seemingly fail-safe formula to continue flying high—build a hotel, sell it to someone else, keep a lucrative long-term management contract.

In 1989 alone the company added sixteen full-service hotels to its inventory. That gave Marriott 539 hotels and 134,000 rooms, the largest number of hotel rooms in the world. "Through development and acquisition," said Bill Marriott in the 1989 Annual Report, "we plan to double the number of our hotels by the mid-1990s. One-third of the new hotels are already in the pipeline."

That bullish outlook was about to be mauled by a bear. Bill's annual report to shareholders just one year later told a quite different story: 1990 became "a year of substantial difficulty, in Marriott's external business environment and one of significant change for our company."

A major federal tax change made real estate investing less attractive; the economy was in recession; a third of savings and loan institutions were failing; real estate values were down; there was a worldwide credit crunch; and an oversupply in the lodging industry. Finally, the U.S. was at war with Iraq in the Persian Gulf.

Marriott was nearly dead in the water. It had sold more than $6 billion in lodging in the 1980s, but now had $1 billion worth of hotels it couldn't sell, part of $3.4 billion in debt built up to finance all the construction. A final blow came when a Japanese company reneged on an agreement to purchase a Marriott hotel in San Francisco for $190 million, leaving Marriott to find the money in its own wallet.

"The late Mr. Marriott's words kept ringing in my ears," said Sterling. "He warned us over and over about the dangers of debt." As their precarious position dawned in the fall of 1990, Marriott leaders scrambled to preserve cash in a tense atmosphere. They stopped virtually all new construction, sharply cut capital spending and administrative costs, and ordered departments to reduce payrolls. About 2,000 employees were laid off.

Morale took a hit as individual employees wondered if their company would survive the crisis. "I was very worried personally," said Bill Kafes, one of Sterling's legal group leaders. "…you hate to see your net worth go down to nothing. A lot of it was only disappointment, thinking that a company in which you had invested so much of yourself could get in that kind of trouble."

Sterling already had his hands full, negotiating with the U.S. General Services Administration (GSA) over an unrelated accusation of company overcharging. Now he worried about the "adverse publicity regarding our debt." Good or bad news is quickly felt in a publicly traded company, as individuals and institutions decide where to invest.

In his journal Sterling listed seventeen hotels in "serious financial trouble…we continue to have a large number of layoffs. The people costs are substantial. It is the most difficult time I have had with Marriott."[1]

Amidst the chaos and uncertain days ahead at Marriott, Sterling believed the company's strong legal team was needed now more than ever. He made that case quietly to Bill Marriott. Given the high level of trust Bill had in Sterling's judgment, the scores of attorneys and other employees in the Legal Department were spared, as other divisions lost workers in 1991.

Despite the trauma inside Marriott, outsiders continued to have high regard for the company. In 1990 *The Wall Street Journal* cited an independent survey of business leaders across the U.S. who were asked: "What company do you believe sets the standard for service in America?" Marriott was ranked ninth, the only lodging and service company named. In 1991 a *Fortune* magazine survey ranked Marriott as the second most-admired diversified service company. No lodging competitor made the list.[2]

Such plaudits were gratifying but did not address how the company could begin the process of shifting into higher gear. That answer would come down the road, Marriott leaders hoped, through a plan being quietly developed. Its code name was "Chariot"—which rhymes with Marriott.

In January 1992 Steve Bollenbach returned for a second tour of duty at Marriott, after straightening up future President Donald Trump's finances. Bollenbach, a consummate deal-maker, came up with a radical plan to split Marriott into two publicly traded companies. One company would take hotel properties and the debt; the other company would manage them. It would be the biggest change at Marriott since its founding.

Marriott shareholders—those who owned the original company—obviously would benefit from having the debt reassigned to a newly created company. But bondholders—those who lent money to the original company—would be disadvantaged by having a new and unproven company assume all the debt. Not all Marriott leaders were onboard. Thomas Piper, a Harvard Business School professor and one of Marriott's directors, quit in protest over the issue.

Numerous Chariot meetings were held behind closed doors in subsequent months. The plan evolving would be complicated, raising a host of legal issues.

It became increasingly clear that the success or failure of Chariot hinged on Sterling himself. "Steve is a great idea man," said Bill Kafes, "but he does not do the detail work...The job of getting the deal done basically developed with Sterling Colton to a very large degree.

"People recognized, as the deal progressed, that even though it came out of Treasury, Sterling had a very low-key way of dealing with people, and the whole situation. In the end, people recognized the premier role that he played."[3]

Bill Marriott said, "Sterling did all the legal work in the split. We had a major lawsuit, the value of bonds went down, people said we had abused investors. Sterling handled all of it."[4]

There was no instruction manual telling how to engineer the first major corporate split of its kind. Sterling's innate sense of fairness was the best hope for all parties. On October 5, 1992, Marriott publicly announced Chariot in a news release. Two companies would be created: Marriott International Inc. and Host Marriott Corp.

Marriott International would be led by Bill as chairman and CEO. It would include all hotels, motels and timeshare properties managed by Marriott, along with food and facilities management businesses and retirement communities. Those activities in 1991 totaled $7.4 billion in sales.

Host Marriott Corp. would be led by Dick Marriott as chairman and Bollenbach as CEO. It would include 141 hotels and other real estate owned by Marriott, along with Host airport and travel plaza turnpike restaurants and gift shop businesses. It would have 23,000 employees and nearly $3 billion worth of debt. Its sales in 1991 totaled $1.7 billion.

Shareholders would have to approve the plan. Wall Street liked what it saw, quickly bidding Marriott stock up by more than 10 percent. But Marriott bond prices fell by as much as 30 percent, and bondholders screamed that they were being cheated.

From then on, for nearly a year, scarcely a workday passed in which Sterling did not do something to fend off critics and advance

Chariot. Early reaction to the news ensured a rocky road ahead. Moody's Investors Service Inc., which rates bonds, downgraded most of the company's $2.9 billion long-term debt. Other rating services threatened to do the same.

"Host Marriott will represent most of the bad things that Marriott Corporation now has in its portfolio," said Bruce Thorpe, an analyst with PNC Financial Corporation. "There is a very uneven split."[5]

By the end of October three lawsuits had been filed against Marriott by bond investor groups. Eight more would follow. Host Marriott, they charged, far smaller than Marriott International, would be burdened with all the Marriott debt. Host faced the real possibility of defaulting. The cruelest blow was an accusation of fraud. Marriott had issued bonds the previous April and May, without disclosing the potentially damaging fact that the company was about to be split in two.

"The issue is a simple one," said F. John Stark III, general counsel of PPM America, an investment advisor for Jackson National Life Insurance Co., a Marriott bondholder. The restructuring plan "had to be in the works for many, many months," he added, noting that it even had a code name, Project Chariot.[6]

Stark was wrong, however. As Bill Marriott testified in court, he knew of the division plan as early as May 7, 1992, but "I had made no decision" and was "wrestling with trying to understand" the proposal right up until a few days before the announcement in October. Steve Bollenbach said he had not thought of the final plan until about a week after selling $400 million in bonds that spring. Both acknowledged that the plan as rolled out was not favorable to bondholders.[7]

As the issue played out in the court of public opinion as well as the court of law, Sterling was burning the midnight oil. His duty: Make the split more fair and acceptable to bondholders. On Tuesday, February 9, 1993, Sterling met with representatives of bondholders until 1:30 a.m. "It is frustrating and exhausting," he told his journal.

"We are making progress — but it is slow."

After four hours of sleep, he met with them again the following day from 7 a.m. until 7:30 p.m. Also that day, he worked on six other major Marriott projects ranging from a hotel in Kuala Lumpur, Malaysia, to an expansion of the San Francisco Marriott Marquis adjacent to the Moscone Convention Center.

On Friday, February 11, "We had all-day negotiations with the bondholders, but ended with what I hope will become an agreement in principle that will enable us to move forward. I feel that it is to the best interest of the company and the shareholders."

Sterling prepared a memo-of-understanding news release. Marriott had reached a settlement with four large institutional investors holding about $400 million of its bonds, and with plaintiffs in eight class-action suits consolidated in U.S. District Court in Baltimore. Those accepting the plan would get new bonds with an interest rate one percentage point higher, which would take four more years to mature. Sterling also worked on three other Marriott projects that day.

Negotiations continued with other bondholders. On March 11 Sterling wrote: "I have been working around the clock on the bondholder negotiations, exchange offer warrants, proxy material," and related steps, as well as four other Marriott projects.

Sterling maintained his stamina by playing two hours of doubles tennis almost every morning, as he had done for years. He sacrificed sleep on many days, but had done so routinely for decades while enjoying excellent health. In a routine physical exam in February 1990, Sterling's blood pressure was 110/80, even better than what doctors consider ideal—120/80.

Chariot had yet to survive the federal bureaucracy. Two agencies with the potential to curtail or seriously damage it were the Securities and Exchange Commission (SEC), which rules on fairness and adherence to law, and the IRS. "I worked on Chariot," wrote Sterling on May 24, 1993. "We are not making any headway with the SEC."

Finally, on June 18, Sterling had some good news. "We had a good day in the Baltimore court. The judge conditionally approved the bondholder settlement despite the opposition of the PPM bondholders. We started mailing the proxy materials to shareholders."

A month later, on July 19, Marriott's executive committee met and "spent most of the time reviewing the Chariot transition and related matters," wrote Sterling. "Last Monday the judge in the preferred shareholders portion of Chariot denied the plaintiff's motion for reconsideration. We started mailings of the exchange offer and consent solicitation. It is going to be a difficult job locating all of the bondholders."

Two days later, Sterling reported, "It looks like we have a settlement of the preferred shareholders litigation…They will dismiss their claims and convert their stock. If we are able to finalize it, it will be an excellent result."

Meanwhile, Bill Marriott and his company were taking it on the chin in the media. "Bill Jr. must be able to withstand a hurricane by now," said *The Washington Post*, adding that he "has endured gale-force contempt. Lawsuits against him and his Bethesda company have come whistling in like Scud missiles…The verbal abuse has been nearly constant. 'Someone called me the scuzz of the earth,' Marriott recalled last week."[8]

By July 1993, nine months after the split was publicly announced, Marriott's stock had risen by more than 60 percent. In that heady atmosphere, shareholders gathered for their annual meeting on July 23 at the stately J.W. Marriott Hotel adjacent to the National Press Building in downtown Washington. Eighty-five percent of attendees in the jam-packed ballroom voted in favor of the plan.

Shareholders, under a special dividend, would receive a share of Marriott International, one of the two new companies, for every common share they held in the Marriott Corporation, which was renamed Host Marriott.

In a crucially important development, Bill also was able to tell shareholders that a group of banks, led by Citibank, had agreed to provide more than $1 billion in revolving credit to Marriott International. Finally, capping an electrifying annual meeting, Bill announced plans to add 400 hotels with some 50,000 rooms over the next five years.

Meanwhile, twenty-year bonds had plunged nearly 30 percent after Chariot was announced in October 1992. Within a year, however, bonds had recovered to their face value.

Nonetheless, PPM America, representing its group of holdout bondholders, vowed to continue pressing its lawsuit against the company. The tide had turned strongly against the dissenters, however. Sterling's office scheduled a series of open meetings across the country, where Marriott attorneys met with regional groups of bondholders. "The bond exchange road shows are going better than we had anticipated," he wrote.

With Chariot very likely heading for a successful conclusion, Sterling turned attention to the internal machinery of the two new companies, Marriott International and Host Marriott. Company divisions and individuals had been jockeying for position for nearly a year.

It was now time to decide definitively what individuals and services would end up in which company. Each new company would occupy current Marriott headquarters, but would be on separate floors and have its own staff and board of directors and otherwise operate separately.

"We called Sterling 'the Judge,'" said Steve Bollenbach. "When the split happened, different people wanted to have certain assets, divisions, and services in their company." A schedule was drawn up and "the parties would sit down with the Judge. They had two minutes to state their cases. Sterling would then take about a minute to decide, and would say to one of them 'Ok, you win.'"[9]

"Sterling facilitated the internal process of dividing the companies into two pieces. He is such a good guy—smart and fair—that his decisions usually were the final word."

On one typical day of this phase, Sterling wrote, "I spent the day on Chariot. It is an extremely complex project but we are getting there. I worked on the intercompany exchange, intercompany agreement and staffing."[10]

Sterling's Law Department was among those divided. On its new organizational chart, Marriott International listed Sterling as vice chairman and senior vice president.

The favorable IRS ruling arrived September 28; Chariot closed October 8. As the end neared, Sterling typically went out of his way to praise the role of others, while Bill Marriott and Bollenbach singled him out as the conspicuous hero.

"We closed on Chariot in the morning," wrote Sterling on October 8. "This was one of the most complex and legally challenging transactions in corporate annals...It is a relief and great personal satisfaction to have it successfully concluded. We couldn't have accomplished what we did without everyone fulfilling their responsibilities. It has been a great team effort."

The Law Department ended work early on October 18, and its members and spouses gathered at Smokey Glen Farm, a barbecue restaurant in a Maryland suburb. After family activities and eating, the attorneys had a program. The lead attorney from each department spoke. Together they had helped guide Marriott to new heights and helped pull it back from the brink of potential insolvency with the split.

Now they were separating into two new companies, and this presumably was the last time they would all be together. "It was very emotional," recalled Sterling. His colleagues presented Sterling with a book of pictures and letters from Law Department associates and former associates.

"I can't think of a gift I'd appreciate more," wrote Sterling. "I have had a great job and have been able to associate with many wonderful people. I have been greatly blessed."

On October 21, thirteen days after Chariot closed, many of those who played key roles gathered at the J.W. Marriott Hotel in downtown Washington to celebrate. Joining Sterling and Ellie and other company figures were investment bankers, consulting attorneys, appraisers, accountants and others whose efforts contributed to the outcome.

A gourmet dinner was followed by a clever program patterned on the Academy Awards. Winners were introduced by famous film clips. "Best Director" went to Sterling, and the clip was Moses—Charlton Heston—parting the Red Sea.

31

"Ellie Has Made All the Difference"

Sterling's successes, as he was the first to acknowledge, also belonged to Ellie. They loved each other completely and shared everything. Ellie gave Sterling a lighter heart, total loyalty, and his own cheering section. He was unfailingly tender with her. In March 1990, he flew back to Washington after a visit with his parents in Utah, arriving late at night. He had not asked Ellie where their car was parked, and he didn't want to call and wake her. Instead, with two inches of new snow covering most cars, he walked the parking lot searching for theirs. Finally giving up, he called her to learn where the car was.

He often said and wrote that she was the greatest blessing in his life. In thousands of pages of his personal journal, Sterling almost never criticized another person, least of all Ellie. On their thirtieth wedding anniversary, he wrote, "It has been a wonderful thirty years. I have been blessed to have Ellie as a companion. She is wonderful!" Among traits he noted were "her love of life, creativity, sense of humor, care for others…The thought of spending eternities with her is nice."

Seven years later he wrote, "It has been a wonderful 37 years. We have been greatly blessed. Ellie is really a rare jewel. I am so grateful to have been able to spend my life with her. It has made all the difference."

When Ellie was in her sixtieth year in 1990, they went to a symphony ball with friends. "It was a wonderful evening," wrote

Sterling. "...Ellie seems to be getting more beautiful each year."

Occasionally they gave each other course corrections. Once when Ellie got frustrated she wrote Sterling a letter, saying all she was to him was a "mistress, a cook, and a maid."[1]

Sterling said, "I rose early one morning and had a long talk with Ellie—When I get under pressure I tend to hunker down and close everything out including her. I will repent! She means more to me than anything else and I must be more considerate of her."[2]

One way Sterling and Ellie kept their love fresh was by enjoying many leisure-time activities together and with friends. They played tennis, walked the C&O Canal—sometimes as much as fourteen miles at a time—or the beaches when traveling, and enjoyed the same kind of movies, books, television series, and plays.

Among movies they saw were "Amadeus," "Out of Africa," "Mutiny on the Bounty," "Stand By Me," "Driving Miss Daisy," "Return of the Jedi," "To Kill a Mockingbird," "A River Runs Through it," "The Natural," "The Untouchables," and "Sleepless in Seattle."

On television they watched Cecil B. DeMille's masterpiece, "The Ten Commandments." They also saw a five-part television series, "The Winds of War," based on Herman Wouk's book on World War II; and a second series based on another Wouk book, *War and Remembrance*. They listened to books on tape including *Tom Sawyer*, Joseph Conrad's *Out of Darkness*, and *Lord of the Rings*.

Stage productions they saw included "Les Miserables," "Phantom of the Opera," the Bolshoi Ballet, "Swan Lake" performed by the Royal Ballet; "Sheer Madness," a spoof murder mystery; "Into the Woods," and Shakespeare's "A Comedy of Errors."

Books read by Sterling included *The Brethren: Inside the Supreme Court*, by Bob Woodward and Scott Armstrong; *The Last Lion*, a biography of Winston Churchill by William Manchester; *Red Storm Rising*, a novel about World War III by Tom Clancy; and *The Russia House*, a spy novel by John le Carre.

For Christmas in 1986, Sterling gave Ellie a small box in a stocking. Peering inside, she found it contained a miniature red Mercedes convertible and this note: "If you would still like a red Mercedes convertible, this is your year! Love, Santa."

She first wanted one thirty-one years earlier, in 1955, when they lived in Germany, where Sterling was stationed with the Seventh Army. Ellie, who grew up in a family with no car, dreamed of returning to the States in a red Mercedes convertible. She had planned to teach school in Germany to earn the money. The births of two children in Germany, David and Carolyn, ended her savings plan.

Ellie, now fifty-five, replied that "I think I'm too old," but their children protested together: "No Mom, go for it!"

The following Valentine's Day, in 1987, Ellie was working in the house when Sterling came in. "Come on, Ellie, let's go look at convertibles." At the dealership a salesman was explaining the features of a Mercedes, when a second salesman handed him some keys, which he in turn gave to Ellie. "They fit that red convertible waiting for you," said the first salesman.

Ellie was too nervous to drive it home. Sterling drove it and she followed in their family car. Many years later, in a note to their first grandson, Sterling Daniel Colton, Ellie explained, "I have many happy memories of driving with Grandpa on Skyline Drive (in Virginia's Shenandoah National Park) and listening to opera and other great music and feeling like the luckiest woman in the world!"

In the spring of 2014, Ellie made Daniel feel like the luckiest grandson in the world. Ellie had promised him the car, and made good on the promise, sending it to him on a car-carrier truck. At this writing Daniel lives in Arizona, tooling around in a classic red convertible in perfect condition, with only 71,000 miles lovingly driven by his Grandma Colton.

In March 1988 Elder Marvin Ashton, a member of the LDS Church's Quorum of the Twelve Apostles, phoned Sterling, calling him to be a member of the board of the Polynesian Cultural Center

(PCC). It meant that twice a year he and Ellie would be going to Hawaii to help guide the center.

The Coltons talked it through, then quickly got in touch with their children, inviting them to an exciting vacation in Hawaii. They would all go, ahead of his PCC meetings, and make it a family memory as well as a duty for Sterling.

The PCC is a Polynesia-themed park and living museum located in Laie, on the north shore of Oahu. The center, about thirty-five miles from Honolulu, reflects the long history of the Church in the South Pacific. Missionaries worked among the Polynesians in Tahiti and surrounding islands as early as 1844. By 1865 the Church had purchased the 6,000-acre Hawaiian plantation that includes all of Laie.

The swift growth of the Church in the Pacific led to the building and dedication of a temple in Laie in 1919—the first LDS temple built outside the continental U.S. In 1955 a church college, now called BYU-Hawaii, was founded nearby. Today it is a four-year accredited university with about 3,000 students.

The PCC addressed two issues: Most BYU-Hawaii students were from families of very modest means, and the native cultures of Polynesia were being lost as more outsiders moved to the islands. The PCC opened in 1963 on just twelve acres to address both issues. Today the center covers forty-two acres and about two-thirds of the students at the university work there. The arts and crafts and peoples of seven cultures are on display: Hawaii, Samoa, New Zealand, Fiji, Tahiti, Tonga, and the Marquesas Islands.

The PCC is one of Hawaii's most popular tourist attractions. In addition to the villages there is an IMAX theater, a 2,800-seat amphitheater, and a lagoon where visitors can paddle canoes.

On Saturday, July 2, 1988, Sterling and Ellie and the Colton children and their spouses left for Hawaii. They visited Maui first, where they checked into the beautiful Maui Marriott, staying in five rooms in a row overlooking the pool area. They all walked on the beach.

Next morning the parents were up before sunrise and, typically, walked the beach again before returning to the hotel. The family attended an LDS fast and testimony meeting, in a nice chapel overlooking the Pacific, where they could see and hear waves breaking on the rocky shore. Then the nine were off in a crowded station wagon to see the Seven Sacred Pools at Hana.

On the long and winding road to Hana, they sang many songs, including, repeatedly, the theme from the late TV show, "Gilligan's Island."

Sterling called the setting "one of the most beautiful I have ever seen." It rained on them at the pools, a frequent occurrence in the lush tropics. Later they rode in a helicopter over old lava fields and the crater of an active volcano. That evening, the day before the Fourth of July, they saw a patriotic program and concert.

Adventure was on tap the next couple of days. Dave, Darla and Steve scuba dived while the others snorkeled. Ellie had a fear of water but lost it long enough to thoroughly enjoy snorkeling in a lagoon with a great variety of fish. That evening was an Independence Day celebration with fireworks on a golf course.

On July 5 Sterling, Ellie and Steve played tennis in the morning. In the afternoon everyone except Ellie went paragliding. One at a time, they mounted a platform, were harnessed beneath a brightly-colored parachute-like wing, and a boat pulled them about 200 feet into the air. Then another hike in a densely forested area, where Carolyn and Ellie unfortunately picked up poison ivy.

The following day they flew to Honolulu on the island of Oahu, and were met by PCC personnel who placed a traditional flower lei around each of their necks. They split up into a sedan and eight-passenger van for the hour-and-a-half drive to Laie.

On July 7 Sterling rose early to work on his talk for the board meeting. Most of the family attended an endowment session at the Hawaii Temple.

Sterling met with other board members for the first time, learning that Marvin J. Ashton was stepping down as chairman for health reasons. His place was being taken by another member of the Twelve, Dallin H. Oaks, an old friend of Sterling's from their days growing up in Vernal. Thomas S. Monson, Second Counselor in the Church's First Presidency, would arrive the following day to make the change. Another member of the Twelve, Joseph B. Wirthlin, Sterling and Ellie's former bishop when they lived in Salt Lake, also was added to the board.

Over the next four days PCC board members conducted business, feasted in the villages, and toured facilities at the site. They dedicated a new Tongan village. They also held a motivational meeting for members and their families, during which each board member spoke. Sterling termed his talk, "Love God With All Your Heart." Although he undoubtedly delivered a thoughtful message, he wrote privately that "I felt that I was out of my league."

Sterling and Ellie continued to travel to Hawaii twice a year, in January and July, for the board meetings, until 1995 when Sterling stepped down from the board and left to serve a mission. During the semi-annual PCC meetings they played tennis with Elder Wirthlin and his wife Elisa, and Ellie also played with June Oaks, wife of Elder Dallin Oaks.

The Coltons were part of a continuing miracle in Hawaii. When ground was broken for the college in 1955, LDS President David O. McKay prayed, "We dedicate our actions in this service unto thee and unto thy glory...that this college, and the temple, and the town of Laie may become a missionary factor, influencing not thousands, not tens of thousands, but millions of people who will come seeking to know what this town and its significance are."[3]

That was a very tall order, a vision that only a prophet could discern. Laie is more than thirty miles from the capital, Honolulu, and there was no reason anyone would travel to that tiny corner of the island, let alone "millions of people."

Several years later, however, church building missionaries arrived to design lagoons and construct thatched huts that began the development of the Polynesian Cultural Center, whose doors opened just eight years after President McKay's prophetic prayer. In the early years students would stand at the side of the highway and flag down cars, inviting their occupants to visit the PCC.

By 1977 more than a million people had visited the center. And by 1994, when Sterling was on the board, the PCC had hosted more than twenty million visitors from across the globe, and six million annually.

Travel also took the Coltons to the other non-contiguous U.S. state, Alaska. In June 1994 Sterling took David, Brad and Steve, and oldest grandson Daniel on an experience of a lifetime—fishing in Alaska. Also along were Sterling's close friend Dave Salisbury and Dave's son-in-law Thayne Larson and Thayne's son Ben Larson.

The timing of the trip was not convenient for all the families. Brad and Melanie had moved back to Maryland just one day before the men departed for Alaska. Melanie was left with their four-month-old baby, Thomas, and many full boxes. "Ellie came over all week to offer unpacking, prepare meals, and help with the kids," said Melanie. "Many times, while the Colton boys were salmon fishing, she reminded me that payback was coming in the form of a girls' trip the next spring."[4]

In Alaska, the men's guide was Dennis Harms, who owned Alaska Trophy Safaris and had been helping fishermen and women fill their freezers with fish for fifteen years. Harms had a small lodge on the Ayakulik River, a premier river for fly-fishing for chrome-bright kings, sockeye, and coho salmon, as well as steelhead, char, and pink salmon.[5]

Sterling, who shared a lodge bedroom with Dave Salisbury—"the snorers," he explained—saw a lot of wildlife, including a moose, Kodiak bear, herd of seals, four sea otters near the lodge, fifteen bald eagles, deer and fox, and salmon swimming up the river.

The group flew in two small seaplanes to the fishing grounds. "The kings are magnificent fish," noted Sterling; "they were running 20 to 40 lbs, and are great fighters. We caught them with salmon eggs and some lures. The sockeye run 6 to 8 pounds. We fished for them with fly rods and flies." There was a limit of two kings a day and they could not keep the steelheads. Walking along the river they saw the skeleton of a large whale that had washed ashore five years earlier.

The first day they fished until 10 p.m., still daylight in Alaska. The fishing was slow on the second day. The kings and sockeye were heading up river and, noted Sterling, "they were not stopping." The weather was turbulent. Sterling fell into the water twice. Unfortunately his camera got wet and did not work well the rest of the trip.

Two men served as guides and fish processors; as fish were caught they took them back to camp and cleaned and froze them. They also packed lunches for everyone. The fishermen's days quickly fell into a pattern: sleep, eat, fish, relax. Daniel caught what turned out to be the biggest fish—forty-two inches long and thirty-four pounds.

By the sixth day they had caught and frozen all the fish each of them could take home in forty-eight-quart coolers. Some then fished for fun, while others hiked to the top of a nearby mountain and spied a Kodiak sow with three cubs. They followed the bears at a discreet distance and watched the cubs frolic for a couple of hours.

The last fishing expedition was in a saltwater safari seeking halibut. Fifteen people piled into a boat, which motored for two and a half hours in the Pacific to reach fishing grounds. Each was allowed to keep two halibut; again members of the Colton party all caught their limit.

On the tenth day of their trip, they headed home, Sterling flying United Airlines through Chicago to Dulles Airport. He loved the experience but was glad to get home.

For their fortieth anniversary in August 1994, Sterling and Ellie traveled to western Canada—a region already special to them for a number of reasons. It was where they honeymooned four decades earlier; not far from where their son David served his mission; and the Canadian Rockies reminded them of the high and beautiful Uintas near where Sterling grew up.

They flew into Vancouver, British Columbia, and traveled by rental car from there to Banff, overnighting in Kamloops. The scenery was breathtaking. "We hiked to every waterfall, staying at Moraine Lake Lodge," wrote Ellie, "which had an incredible view of mountains and lake from our window. We had a fabulous time."

North of Banff, in Jasper, they rented horses and had an exhilarating ride. On the way out of Jasper they saw five bull elk sparring with each other alongside the road. "We stopped and were so mesmerized that we accidentally delayed our trip to Edmonton where we were to catch a plane," said Ellie.

"We barely made it in time. As Sterling got out to get our luggage from the trunk, I got out to change into the driver's side to return the rental car." The engine was still running, however, and the doors locked automatically. The Hertz dealership was a half-hour away, so the writing was on the wall. They missed their flight and got to spend the day in the Edmonton Mall.

Sterling flew all night to get back in time for a meeting at Marriott, while Ellie flew to Salt Lake City.

Bird-watching was a favorite pastime of the Coltons. Over a half-century they identified fifty different kinds in their forested backyard in Bethesda.

"We have a great variety of birds coming for food this spring," Ellie wrote to a grandson on a mission. "Grandpa is diligent in providing them with a nice variety. I take care of the sugar water for the humming birds and they provide us with constant delight from our kitchen dining table watching their pecking order, caution, and competition.

"We have a pileated woodpecker couple who are regulars to the suet feeder. Every once in a while they sharpen their beak by pecking another hole in the deck. We will probably replace the deck next summer as it is showing signs of wear and tear and woodpecker, squirrel, and raccoon attacks."

Evidences of keen interest in birds are inside their home as well. On a shelf in the living room is a large, lifelike porcelain red-shouldered hawk that Sterling gave Ellie, created by Edward Boehm (1913-1969), the most noted sculptor of porcelain birds. On the floor in the dining room stands the bird Ellie gave Sterling—a metal, brightly colored, loony-looking bird, over two-feet tall. She explained it was to remind him of the rare bird he married.

Their interest in birds—and even bigger interest in adventure—took them halfway around the world to New Zealand, a bird-watcher's paradise, early in 1995. They were on a tour group with about twenty others, including Suzanne and Jay Glassman, newlyweds who were the Coltons' backyard across-the-creek neighbors. An adventure tour company, Butterfield and Robinson, organized the hiking and biking tour of New Zealand's breathtaking south island.

"We rode bikes about twenty-seven to forty kilometers a day (seventeen to twenty-five miles)," said Ellie. "We also helicoptered up to the St. Joseph Glacier and flew in a small plane to the Milford Track," a well-known tramping route amid mountains and temperate rain forest in Fiordland National Park.

One day they exited their tour bus near Kawarau Gorge, the world's first commercial bungee-jump. Over breakfast the next morning, Jay—who was undefeated as a boxer in the Navy—said "I've got to go back and bungee-jump."

"We'll come watch," said Sterling. The four walked to the suspension bridge 145 feet above the raging Kawarau River. Jay and Suzanne signed waivers and headed out onto the bridge. Sterling surprised Ellie by also signing. As for Ellie, "I was not even tempted!" Sterling was jumping at the age of sixty-six, Jay at seventy, Suzanne at fifty-two.

An instructor secured a stretchable bungee cord to Jay's lower legs. When the instructor said "Go," Jay jumped. Unfortunately his shirt flew over his head so he couldn't see where he was going.

Sterling was next. Although he had known it for a long time, as he stepped off the platform into thin air, Ellie screamed, "Sterling, I love you!" The video of the jump has been shared by many family and friends, to everyone's delight.

32

Family Motto: "We Will Serve the Lord"

Mormons teach that no other success can compensate for failure in the home. Whatever other challenges and pressures they felt through the years, Sterling and Ellie never lost sight of their most important task—rearing children of character, who are doing the same for their own children.

How does a family achieve this goal? It begins with parents who love each other completely and who are on the same wavelength on issues that matter. The Colton children grew up feeling secure, in a home without rancor. If Sterling and Ellie had significant differences of opinion, they were usually talked out in private.

By every measure they have succeeded in their efforts. "Look at Sterling and Ellie's workmanship," said Ralph Hardy, an LDS leader in Washington and close friend of the Coltons. "The four Colton children are excellent in every way. Whether in church or at Marriott, Sterling had a great compass. It always pointed True North. And Ellie is one of the choice Latter-day Saints I have known."[1]

A key to the Colton children's many successes was the example set by Sterling and Ellie, notably old-fashioned hard work. Their family motto was taken from the Old Testament, when Joshua said to the people of Israel, "...choose you this day whom ye will serve;...but as for me and my house, we will serve the Lord." (Joshua 24:15)

"Our parents did a wonderful job providing financial, spiritual, physical and all of our other needs, as well as our wants," said Brad. "I have said that it is easy for me to know that I have a Heavenly Father, as He is just a little bit better than my earthly father. My dad is one of the most Christ-like men that I know. He has been very generous with his wealth in giving to those in need.

"...Some of the phrases that my parents stressed to us and our children include 'Keep the commandments,' 'Remember who you are and what you can become,' 'Work hard and work smart,' 'If a job is worth doing at all then it is worth doing right,' 'Do your best,' 'We are all children of God,' 'Love God and love your fellowman.'"

Sterling and Ellie played a significant role in the lives of their grandchildren, wherever the grandchildren lived—Pennsylvania, New Jersey, Georgia, Utah, Arizona, Maryland, California, Nevada, New York, Connecticut, Virginia, Minnesota, Oregon, Colorado, Texas, Washington, D.C., Germany, Brazil, Japan, Argentina, Chile, Russia, Spain.

With the new grandchild generation, Sterling and Ellie repeated lessons they had found helpful in teaching values to their own four children. Those lessons were largely internalized by their children and were being passed along successfully to grandchildren.

At the top of the value chart for Sterling and Ellie were education, mission and temple marriage.

Dave and his former wife Darla Burnett Colton had three children together: Daniel, Mauri, and Jenna. Several years after they divorced, Dave married Julie Claire Haycock Jensen. She brought six children to their union: Ben, Trevor, David, Niels, Sarah, and Elizabeth (Lizzie), for a family total of nine children.

Six of Dave and Julie's children and six children-in-law served missions. (In 2017 Dave and Julie completed a two-year special diplomatic mission to the United Nations.) All nine children married in the temple; all but the two oldest—plus Dave and Julie—were married and sealed by Sterling.

Daniel served a mission to Argentina and earned three degrees—

a bachelor's in geography at BYU, a law degree and an MBA from Arizona State University. Dan's wife Holly received a bachelor's degree in classical civilizations from BYU.

Mauri earned a bachelor's in English from Utah Valley University. Her husband Nathan served a mission to the Dominican Republic and earned a bachelor's in construction management from UVU.

Jenna earned a bachelor's in education from Arizona State University and a master's in reading education from Grand Canyon University. Her husband Jared served a mission to the Dominican Republic and earned an associate's degree in auto mechanics from Utah Valley University.

Ben served a mission to Pennsylvania, earned a bachelor's in marketing communication from BYU, and an MBA and a master's in real estate development from the University of Southern California. His wife Sara served a mission to Sweden and received a bachelor's in geography from BYU and an MBA from USC.

Trevor served a mission to Mexico, earned a bachelor's in psychology from BYU, and attended dental school at the University of North Carolina. His residency in pediatric dentistry was at Primary Children's Hospital in Salt Lake City. His wife Brooke earned a bachelor's in family science - marriage and human development - from BYU.

Dave served a mission to Uruguay and earned two degrees at BYU, a bachelor's in international relations and an MBA. His wife Liz served a mission to Croatia, earned a bachelor's in family science - marriage and human development - from BYU and a law degree from Fordham University.

Niels served a mission to Argentina, earned a bachelor's in psychology at BYU, and attended dental school at the University of Nevada, Las Vegas. His residency in periodontics was at Georgia Regents University. His wife Susie earned a bachelor's degree in communications at BYU.

Sarah is working on a bachelor's in art and visual communications at Utah Valley University. Her husband Ryan served a mission to

Iowa, earned a bachelor's in housing and community development from Arizona State University and an MBA from BYU.

Lizzie served a mission to Chile and earned a bachelor's in family studies, with an emphasis on human development, from BYU. Her husband Abe served a mission to Australia and earned a bachelor's in mechanical engineering from Arizona State University.

Brad and Melanie have four children: Rebecca (Becca), Scott, Jane, and Thomas.

Becca has a BS degree in human biology from Stanford and a master's degree in special education through Teach for America. Becca's husband Matt Alleman graduated from BYU with a degree in Russian, went on to dental school at the University of Nevada, Las Vegas, followed by oral surgery residence at Yale. Matt served a mission in Russia. Sterling performed the temple marriage for Becca and Matt.

Scott served a mission in Chile and, after graduating from BYU with a degree in physiology and developmental biology, he went on to earn a medical degree at Georgetown University. He is currently doing his residency in internal medicine. His wife Brittany served a Spanish-speaking mission in Arizona and, also after graduating from BYU with a degree in secondary education, earned a master's degree in social work from the University of Utah. Sterling performed the temple marriage for Scott and Brittany.

Jane and her husband Ethan Black both graduated from Brigham Young University with degrees in business strategy. Ethan served his mission in Brazil. Jane and Ethan were married in the temple.

Thomas served a mission in Russia and is an undergraduate at BYU at this writing, majoring in economics.

Steve and Jeri have four children: Jared, Meredith, Brandon, and Kevin. Jared served a mission in Brazil and married Eden Jensen in the temple, with Sterling officiating. Jared earned bachelor's and master's degrees at BYU in accounting. In 2016 he started an MBA program at the University of Virginia's Darden School. Eden has three degrees from BYU—a bachelor's in bioinformatics and a second bachelor's in accountancy, and a master's in accountancy.

Meredith married Trent Hazy in the temple, with Sterling officiating. Trent served his mission in Hungary. Meredith and Trent both graduated from Stanford, Meredith with a degree in English and Trent with a degree in product design. As of this writing they are both headed for MBAs at Stanford's Graduate School of Business in the fall of 2017.

Brandon served a Spanish-speaking mission to Salt Lake City, and currently is working on a bachelor's and master's degree in information systems at BYU.

Kevin completed two years at the United States Military Academy at West Point, followed by a mission in Japan. He returned to West Point in the fall of 2017.

For many years the Coltons had an annual tradition of choosing a family-oriented topic for each member to write about. Their articles became Christmas gifts to be exchanged and cherished.

In 1994 the family compiled a "Colton Family List of Virtues." It included things each person thinks he or she does well, and a list of things other family members believe about that person. Together they help draw a portrait of what the Coltons have valued and the traits they considered worth passing along to other generations.

Sterling listed about himself—lawyer, bishop, organizer, meeting people, business executive. Others added an additional sixty-plus traits, including: makes you feel important, always nice to people, a good listener, always happy to help, a fun grandpa, good at telling me birds' names, reminding grandma, giving sage advice, living a Christ-like life, calling every Sunday, hugging.

Also: has a sympathetic heart, is generous, an excellent conversationalist, a fun dancer, a ham, a good storyteller, hiker, tennis player, writing inspiring letters, giving gifts, keeping confidential issues, taking Thomas during sacrament meeting, keeping us up to date on appropriate news articles, singing in shower, letting us know he loves us, teaching us family history, caring about people, helping Grandma.

Ellie listed about herself—making cinnamon rolls, arranging flowers, playing games with children, sympathizing with others, reading stories. Others added another fifty or so traits, including: loves a party, she makes me feel good, always happy & positive, always thinking of others, interested in the world around her, a good storyteller, hiker, gourmet cook, cheerleader, making us laugh, listening, keeping cookie jar filled, playing with children, hugging.

Also: loves her family, has good style of clothes, has fun ideas, she gives presents to me, sympathetic, a perfect wife for Dad, energetic, physically fit, tennis player, encouraging you to do your best, being cool under fire, being fair to all her grandchildren, making people happy, spending time with grandchildren, decorating her house, helping others, great mother-in-law.

Communication and accountability are additional traits Sterling and Ellie have always valued. When the children were out late on a date in high school, they were required to "report in" to their parents as they returned, even though Sterling often was snoring too loud to hear them and Ellie was temporarily deaf after removing her hearing aid for the night.

Phone calls were frequent after the four children went away to college. "They'd always ask two questions," recalled Brad. "Dad would ask, 'How are your grades?' and Mom would ask, 'How is your social life?'"

On early Saturday mornings from afar, Sterling could no longer turn on the vacuum cleaner outside the kids' doors to get them moving, but he did the next best thing.

"After late nights and tough classes, my dorm roommates and I would be sound asleep," said Steve, "and every Saturday about 6:30 in the morning, our phone would ring." They always knew who it was. Without having to answer it, "One of the guys would yell, 'Colton, your dad's calling!'" Dave reported the same calls when he was in college.

Sterling and Ellie have also made it a lifelong habit every Sunday to call each of their children and grandchildren after they left home—along with their own parents when they were alive.

Sterling gave the children career advice. "When I was in high school I really enjoyed the outdoors," said Dave, "I had a passion for it." He explained to Sterling that he wanted to be a forest ranger. "He didn't tell me to go into law; he just said, 'Dave, you've got to decide whether you want to raise your family in a double wide.'"

His father calmly explained that as a forester, David would be traveling to different sites and likely living in accommodations furnished by the government, typically trailer houses. Sterling suggested there may be other ways for Dave to experience the great outdoors without relying on it to provide a living.

Dave took his father's advice to heart. After graduating from BYU he remained there and earned a law degree. Dave then joined the same Salt Lake firm where Sterling's career began—Van Cott, Bagley, Cornwall and McCarthy, whose specialties included natural resources. Six years later, just after becoming a partner, Dave accepted a job as exploration counsel at Phelps Dodge Corporation in Phoenix. It was a mining company that explored and acquired minerals across the globe.

Sterling talked with the other three as well about their career aspirations. Carolyn, after graduating from BYU with a degree in psychology, also followed her father into the law, graduating from BYU Law School. She spent most of her career at Marriott, retiring after twenty years as a vice president in the Law Department.

Brad and Steve both graduated from BYU with degrees in business finance. Both brothers went on to earn MBAs from the University of Virginia's Darden School. Brad became a manager of Marriott properties, and Steve eventually launched a residential and commercial carpet-cleaning business based in Atlanta.

Charity is another strong Colton trait. Sterling's journal through the years documented the numerous times he and Ellie invited people over for dinner. They always worked as a team. Sterling—helped by the children when they were home—cleared furniture out of the living room and set up tables and chairs. Ellie prepared a delicious meal, and Sterling and kids cleaned up and did the dishes. Frequently their dinner guests included individuals going through tough times.

Sterling and Ellie visited the homes of neighbors and others, especially those who were lonely, shut in, or experiencing difficulty. Often Ellie brought along baked treats or an armful of flowers. Even more compelling were the times they took someone into their home for an extended time.

In the summer of 1979 a young woman from South America came to their attention. A twenty-six-year-old Mormon living in the Washington area, Claudia was single, pregnant, and scared. "One day my bishop said a family named Colton wanted to help me," explained Claudia. She moved into their home on Greentree Road in July. "They were very kind," said Claudia, whose son Alex was born in February 1980.[2]

Claudia continued to live with the Coltons until her mother came to the U.S. in April, about two months after Alex was born. Her bishop arranged an apartment for the three of them to live in. Claudia subsequently married, moved to Salt Lake City, and had three more children.

When her second child, Melissa, reached college age, Claudia wrote the Coltons to ask if they knew of any scholarship that might help Melissa attend Brigham Young University. "To my surprise, Sterling called and said he'd be glad to help. He paid for Melissa to go to BYU." She got a degree in history there, then earned a master's in public policy management at elite Johns Hopkins University in Maryland.

"Ellie has been like a mother to me," said Claudia. "One time I said to her, 'What can I ever do to repay you?' Ellie said, 'Pass it along to someone else.'"

Having fun was also important to the Coltons, and almost any occasion, Ellie believed, could have an element of fun. Long car rides

FAMILY MOTTO: "WE WILL SERVE THE LORD" 333

from Washington across the plains to the Rockies went faster by singing and playing games.

There was the license plate game: Who could find the most states and countries on license plates? The billboard game: Find all the letters of the alphabet, in order, on billboards. The nursery rhyme game: Each person sings a different nursery rhyme, until the next person cannot.

For Christmas 1991, the topic for the family memory book was "My Favorite Vacation." The five oldest grandchildren were among those who weighed in, sharing memories from some of the many Colton family vacations:

Daniel, age eleven—"Trails End Ranch...the family was there and there were lots of things to do. We could go fishing and horseback riding. The ranch also had a boat that you could paddle in the pond... We slept in log cabins. The fish you caught you could give to the cook and she would cook them for breakfast. (But GGma cooks fish a lot better!)"

Mauri, ten—"Disneyworld 1988...I liked it because the whole family was together...There were frogs on the grass and all over. Scott (then one year old) almost ate one...we fed ducks at the pond and there were fish in the water. Disneyland was fun because we had our own tour guides...My favorite ride was seeing Captain Eo with our three D glasses with Grandpa."

Jenna, seven—"Hawaii 1990...because I liked to play on the beach. There was a fun dog who liked to dig for crabs...Mauri, Daniel and I were buried in the sand...Grandpa, Grandma and Gran were there... There was a funny person who climbed up trees...I went snorkeling for the first time with my dad. I saw some little fish...At the end of the trip I was able to fly with Grandma and Grandpa."

Rebecca, six—"New Hampshire because I got to play with my cousins...I liked to swim in the big lake out to the green thing. It was fun to sleep with Jenna, and play with Jared. It was funny that a bat came in our house."

Scott, four—"New Hampshire. I could play with Daniel, and Jared, and Jenna. I had to go to the hospital and they had to put stitches in my head. I liked going on a boat ride."

Sterling's work with Marriott rendered the family financially secure. He and Ellie could be very generous with their children, and in fact were. "They provided the financial support to make sure that we siblings, and our posterity, gathered together regularly," said David. "That made us a very close family."

33

MISSION TRUMPS MARRIOTT

In the fall of 1994 Dallin Oaks, a friend and member of the Quorum of the Twelve, telephoned Sterling. Elder Oaks asked if he and Ellie would be receptive to a call to preside over a church mission.

Sterling and Ellie readily said yes. They would serve full-time for three years at their own expense, he as mission president and Ellie as his strong right arm, informally known as the "mission mom."

President and Sister Colton would be responsible for the physical and spiritual well-being and productivity of up to 200 missionaries at a time, mostly young men but also some young women and a dozen or so older couples.

On February 10, 1995, Sterling and Ellie received a letter from church headquarters in Salt Lake City, informing them that they would be called to an English-speaking mission. It was signed by the Church's governing First Presidency—President Howard W. Hunter, Gordon B. Hinckley, First Counselor, and Thomas S. Monson, Second Counselor.

Another letter from the First Presidency followed the first one by less than two weeks. The February 23 letter thanked the Coltons for their willingness to serve, and informed them that they would preside over the Canada Vancouver Mission in British Columbia. (The Church customarily names its missions by the country first and major city second.) Canada Vancouver was one of more than 300 church missions.

They were delighted. It was a region they loved, and a place they had visited just months earlier when celebrating their fortieth wedding anniversary.

At the same time, that mission had special challenges. Mormon missionaries in British Columbia (BC) typically did not find people as receptive to the gospel as in many other missions.

There had been a dramatic drop in religious observance across Canada. Over the previous half-century, the percentage of Canadian adults attending religious services had decreased from 67 percent in 1946 to 22 percent in 1998. Between 1988 and 1998, attendance at religious services at least once a month fell from 41 percent to 34 percent among citizens aged fifteen and over.[1]

In addition, Vancouver was one of the most ethnically and linguistically diverse cities in Canada. More than half its residents had a first language other than English.[2]

Building and maintaining the enthusiasm and confidence of BC missionaries would be a challenge. But Sterling and Ellie were well prepared for any challenges the mission would present because they lived as they believed and taught.

Their physical fitness for the calling was confirmed when they walked all 184 miles of the C&O Canal, in approximately ten- to twelve-mile daily segments during the months preceding their mission.

New mission presidents begin their service around July 1 of the year they are called. Those going to English-speaking missions spend a shorter time in the Missionary Training Center in Provo, Utah than those who will be speaking a foreign language; hence there is a practical reason for knowing the primary language of your mission.

Following Sterling's formal calling as a mission president, written and electronic mission training materials began to arrive at the Coltons'. Sterling typically buried himself in memorizing the materials, often arising at 4:30 a.m. to do so.

His journal records a new personal emphasis on re-reading the Book of Mormon. Latter-day Saints consider this sacred text a book of scripture, along with the Bible, and a second witness of Jesus Christ. Among its 500-plus pages is a description of Christ's visit to the Americas following his death and resurrection in the Eastern Hemisphere.

Sterling and Ellie were serving at the Washington D.C. Temple at the time of their mission call. Sterling was a "sealer," performing sacred ordinances meant to bind couples and families together for eternity. As a sealer, Sterling performed marriages and sealings for living individuals as well as vicarious sealings for the dead, with living persons being proxies for the deceased.

Although Sterling was nearly sixty-six when called as a mission president, he had had no imminent plans to retire from Marriott. Bill Marriott congratulated Sterling and Ellie, while acknowledging that he would greatly miss having Sterling by his side. They were best friends as well as a highly successful business team.

The Coltons' impending departure from Marriott and their home in Bethesda set off a round of farewell events. The company's retirement party for Sterling was April 25, 1995 at the Gaithersburg Marriott in Maryland. It included a video of Sterling's activities at Marriott and remarks by several colleagues, including Bill and Dick Marriott.

"Sterling is known for his tremendous judgment, compassion, and insight," said Dick. "He is a person of penetrating analytical ability and extraordinary judgment. With all his success and what he has been able to do with Marriott Corporation, Sterling is still humble. I have never known him to brag about himself or to push himself forward, and that's a rare quality in today's environment."[3]

Bill said Sterling's contributions at Marriott were "absolutely invaluable. Over the years I've valued his wonderful guidance and counsel. He has been a terrific friend and highly effective member of our team…Sterling, you're an inspiration to all of us. We thank you for sharing with us your enduring commitment to excellence."

Dick had both Sterling and Ellie come to the podium, noting that Ellie was "such a great part of this team." Bill presented Sterling a special J. Willard Marriott Award of Excellence. Ellie remarked that her husband is an adventurer at heart, "basically a Daniel Boone. Whenever we go someplace he never likes to go back the same way, and we have had a lot of adventures in the backwoods. If there's not a road, he's often made his own."

Ellie added, "I have been in awe with the extent of his compassion for people…to me that's been one of the most impressive things I've seen living with him, his kindness to other people."

Former Utah Senator Jake Garn also spoke: "Law schools can teach ethics and other schools can do the same thing, but if the student doesn't have those basic traits of honesty, trustworthiness and loyalty by the time they reach school, it's going to be very difficult to change them and teach them those things.

"If all the attorneys were like Sterling Colton, with the honesty and integrity, you wouldn't be able to tell all the attorney stories about them. You can't tell attorney stories about Sterling Colton."

Guests gave the Coltons many gifts, including a porcelain Boehm Canadian goose and Maryland cardinal; a Stetson hat; and an art book with photos of western sculptures and paintings by Charles M. Russell. After the formal events of the evening, a band played music for dancing. Nearly all attendees left at that point. Those who stayed to dance included Dick and Nancy Marriott, Brad and Melanie Colton, and Sterling and Ellie.

A few days later, following a black-tie dinner to raise funds for an art collection, Bill and Donna gave the Coltons a Toshiba laptop computer and Hewlett Packard laser printer, both of which would prove helpful during their mission.

Dinners or parties in their honor were also sponsored by Dick and Nancy Marriott; by Ralph and Barbara Mecham; and by neighbors in Bethesda. They received more thoughtful gifts, including a large British Columbia flag.

While strongly focused on preparing for their mission, Sterling monitored his posterity's achievements. Many of their grandchildren were standout athletes, including their oldest grandchild Daniel, son of Dave and Darla. In March 1995 Dan's middle school basketball team in Phoenix played in a championship game. Sterling left a meeting at headquarters early and caught a cross-country flight to Phoenix. Rain delayed a connecting flight from San Francisco to Phoenix, however, and he arrived after the game had ended.

"Daniel's team lost by 3 points in overtime," wrote Sterling. "Daniel scored over 20 points even though he was in foul trouble and had to sit down part of the fourth quarter and fouled out in overtime." Dan was also on the track team. The following month he phoned Sterling and Ellie to report that he was the new middle school high jump champ for Arizona, having just soared cleanly over a bar five-feet-eight-inches off the ground. He also earned his Eagle Scout award that year.

As Sterling and Ellie prepared for their mission, Ellie made good on her promise of a girls' big trip, with Carolyn, Darla, Melanie, and Jeri. Destination: France. They had a grand time, how could they not with Ellie leading the way? Their husbands watched the children while their wives were gone—including David, who had just returned from a business trip to the Philippines, where he caught dysentery and lost fifteen pounds.

The women flew to Paris on Thursday, May 4. Jeri's sister Lori and her family lived there, and oriented them on what to see. The following day, they walked to the Eiffel Tower, where they posed for silly pictures. They got ice cream cones, $72 for five—a timely reminder that Paris was expensive.

Other famous sites they visited in the City of Light included Notre Dame Cathedral, Sainte-Chappelle, and Musee d'Orsay. They had dinner at the home of Lori and her then-husband, Mark Richards. Three of the women slept there, while Ellie and Darla bedded down for the night at a nearby hotel.

The next day they took the subway to Porte de Clignancourt, a famous flea market, then visited the palace and gardens at Versailles, the magnificent palace of Louis XIV. They went to the Louvre, the world's largest museum, stopping to see, among other world-class art, Da Vinci's Mona Lisa and the ancient, armless Greek statue Venus de Milo.

The Colton women visited the magnificent Monet's Garden in Giverny—a particular treat for Carolyn and Ellie with their love of flowers. Then they rented a van and headed south, stopping at the breathtaking medieval cathedral at Chartres, and the Loire Valley with its many castles. They took an hour-and-a-half balloon ride over the

Loire Valley, called the Garden of France for its fruit orchards, vineyards and vegetable fields, all of which they saw from the air. They landed in a field where a picnic lunch awaited them.

They continued to drive south in the rented van, Carolyn doing most of the driving. They especially enjoyed driving through medieval towns on streets barely wider than the van. Finally they headed over mountain roads to Saint Siffret, a pretty little village in the south, where Bob Bradley and his second wife, Patricia Segal Bradley, were converting a 300-year-old French building into a home. The third household member was Champ, a young boxer that often sat in Bob's lap. The Colton women shopped and visited Roman ruins in the region.

On May 13, 1995 Sterling joined them, landing at Charles De Gaulle Airport and taking a commuter flight to Avignon. He rented a car and drove to Saint Siffret. The Bradleys' house, still under construction, was an adventure. Ellie's room, directly below the other women, had large cracks in the walls and a space heater she didn't know how to light. The girls on the next floor up discovered a peep hole in the floor above Ellie's bathroom in the form of an unfinished drain. One time when Ellie entered her bathroom, a shout of "Boo!" through the peep hole above startled her.

Pat was creative, and Sterling surmised the house-to-be would be lovely when finished—which indeed it was.

The evening of Sterling's arrival they had an excellent dinner at a restaurant. When they returned to their hosts', Sterling got the heater working in their bedroom. The following morning the younger women left for Paris and a flight to the United States. Bob, Pat and Champ took Sterling and Ellie for a drive in the countryside.

For the next several days Sterling and Ellie traveled on the Austrada, a highway system, through mountainous northern Italy and into Austria, rhapsodizing over the towering, rugged Alps on one side and, part of the way, the Mediterranean Sea on the other. Periodically they stopped to hike. They were fortunate to find accommodations at small hotels each evening, including one in Austria where they had a particularly good meal—garlic soup, asparagus, and fresh fish, washed down with johannisbeersaft, a local non-alcoholic drink made from red currants.

On May 17 they took a delightful walk through Austrian woods and meadows full of brilliant wildflowers, then drove to a house tucked in the Alpine forest high above Lake Trounsee, with what Sterling called an "incredible view" of the Alps. His youngest brother Phil, who lived in Vienna, had reserved rooms at the house, and Phil, his wife Bobby, and their daughter Nancy met Sterling and Ellie there. Bobby prepared a lunch of rolls, ham and cheese. Also with them was Nancy's one-year-old daughter Jeannie Marie.

Unlike Sterling and Ellie, Phil's purpose in Austria was anything but casual. He had served his mission in Germany and later spent a good part of his career in that region, helping to stop the proliferation of nuclear weapons around the world. Of all the types of weapons with the potential to cause the most damage to humans and property, nuclear is generally considered the worst.

Phil was a senior scientist in the State Department's U.S. Arms Control and Disarmament Agency (ACDA). He shared responsibility for the transfer of U.S. nuclear technologies to countries that had signed a treaty agreeing to use them for peaceful purposes only. He also helped evaluate and train foreign nuclear scientists studying in the U.S. to use nuclear power for such purposes as medicine and agriculture.

Phil was now serving abroad for the second time as a senior diplomat with the International Atomic Energy Agency (IAEA), based in Vienna. He led the IAEA's transition into the use of computers and system automation. He and his staff also arranged the nuclear-power training of thousands of leaders of key industries from about 140 countries.

A decade later, in 2005, the Nobel Peace Prize was jointly awarded to the IAEA's Director General, Mohamed El-Baradei, from Egypt, and the current and former IAEA staff, including Phil. The Norwegian Nobel committee said the award was "for their efforts to prevent nuclear energy from being used for military purposes and to ensure that nuclear energy for peaceful purposes is used in the safest possible way."

Sterling, Ellie, Phil, and Bobby enjoyed the beauty of their surroundings and, wrote Sterling, "some wonderful fattening bakery products." Driving the Autobahn, they visited a pottery factory, castles, ancient ruins, several of Beethoven's homes, and other sites. That evening, Sterling and Phil went to a concert at the LDS meetinghouse, while Ellie stayed behind, relaxing in a hot soaking bath.

The next day Sterling and Ellie took a brief side trip to Romania. They flew from Vienna to Bucharest, for a reunion with Anca and Cristian Croitoru and their family. Anca, the young doctor who stayed with the Coltons when having her baby, met them at the airport with a large car and driver and took them to the Intercontinental Hotel. The hotel, noted Sterling with his practiced eye, was old but in an excellent location.

"Bucharest is a rather depressing city," wrote Sterling. "It is dirty and most of the people do not look happy. Many are hard-looking." Romanians had suffered a lot. For three decades they had been ruled by Nicolai Ceausecu, who enforced his will through secret-police terror. He was overthrown and executed in the violent Romanian Revolution of December 1989, just six years earlier, as European Communism crumbled.

Anca took the Coltons to their apartment, where her husband Cristian and daughter Carina waited. Anca had prepared a wonderful meal. After dinner the Coltons walked back to their hotel. The next morning the Croitorus took them sightseeing around Bucharest.

Late that afternoon they caught a flight back to Vienna. The following morning, on May 22, 1995, they flew Austrian Airlines to Paris, leaving there at about noon on United Airlines to Dulles Airport and home. "It was a wonderful trip," wrote Sterling, "but it was good to arrive home."

One of Sterling's first concerns back in Maryland was Kresimir Cosic and his young family. The Coltons had befriended Cosic, a six-foot-eleven gentle giant who hailed from the same global neighborhood as Romania.

Cosic was a phenomenal basketball player from Croatia, one of five states that later emerged independent with the breakup of Yugoslavia in the early 1990s. He played for his hometown team, KK Zadar, and made Yugoslavia's national team at the age of seventeen. That team won three Olympic medals, including gold in 1980. In 1969 Cosic moved to the U.S. to play basketball for BYU.

He led BYU to the WAC championship twice, and was named an All-American by United Press International—the first non-American so honored. In 1972 he was picked by the Portland Trail Blazers of the NBA, but elected to stay at the Y. The following year he was drafted by the Los Angeles Lakers, but again opted to stay at the Y. Upon graduation, for the third time, he rejected several professional offers to return to his hometown team in Zadar.

While at BYU, Cosic converted to the LDS Church, an action that could have had serious consequences back home in Communist-dominated eastern Europe. His proven loyalty to his country, however, instead was rewarded, and he became deputy ambassador of Croatia to the United States, stationed in Washington, D.C. Cosic also was a leading Mormon figure for his home region in Europe and did much to open the way for missionary work there.

Ellie was deeply involved, on behalf of the Church, in befriending the diplomatic community, and Cosic was a natural ally. The Coltons came to know and love Cosic and his wife Ljerka and their three children. They saw Cosic as a good father and husband as well as athlete. Tragically, while a young man, he became ill with non-Hodgkin's lymphoma, a type of blood cancer, and his health was deteriorating rapidly when the Coltons returned from Europe.

Two days after returning, Sterling drove to Baltimore, where Cosic was in Johns Hopkins Hospital. His body was shutting down. Sterling picked up Ljerka there and drove her home. Cosic died four days later, on May 28, 1995, at the age of forty-six.

For Cosic's funeral, Sterling offered the prayer for the family prior to the service, and was an honorary pall bearer. The following year Cosic was inducted into the U.S. Basketball Hall of Fame.

344

Family vacation to Disney World. (l-r) Sterling, Ellie, Dave, Darla, Carolyn, Scott, Brad, Melanie, Steve, Jeri, Mauri and Becca.

Orlando, FL 1988

Tennis group annual outing. Sterling and Ellie are at top center.

Hilton Head, SC 1980s

Coltons' annual backyard Easter Egg hunt.

Bethesda, MD 1980s

Sterling with grandchildren at surprise 60th birthday party at Marriott farm. (l-r) Daniel, Sterling, Mauri, Becca, Scott and Jenna.

Ellie and Sterling riding elephants in Thailand.

Sterling and Ellie with Butch and Judy Cash in Thailand.

Sterling pumpkin picking with Jared and Steve.

Sterling with Marguerite at the dedication of Marriott's Hugh W. Colton Building.

Ellie and Sterling in New Hampshire with grandkids. (l-r top row) Jenna, Mauri, Daniel. (l-r bottom row) Meredith, Jared, Scott, Jane and Becca.

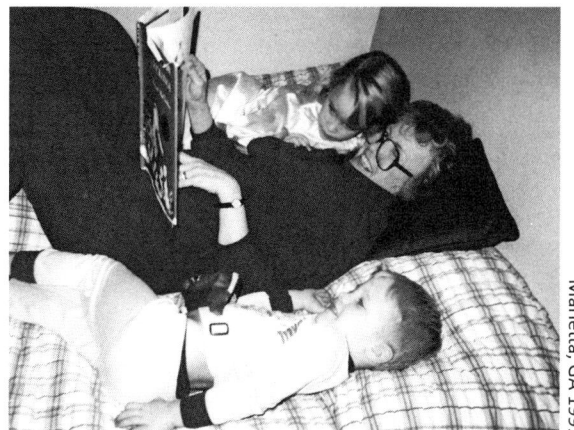

Grandma time with Rebecca and Scott.

Ellie and Sterling with young violin virtuoso Jenny Oaks (Baker).

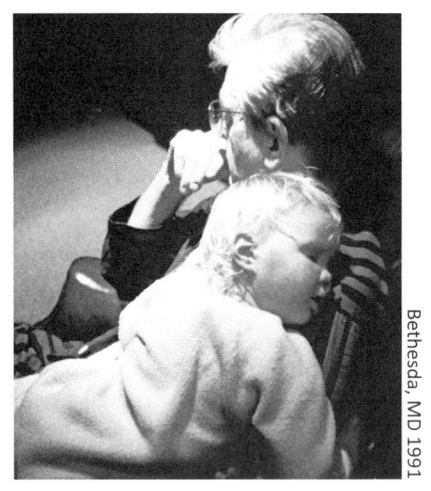

Late night with granddaughter Meredith.

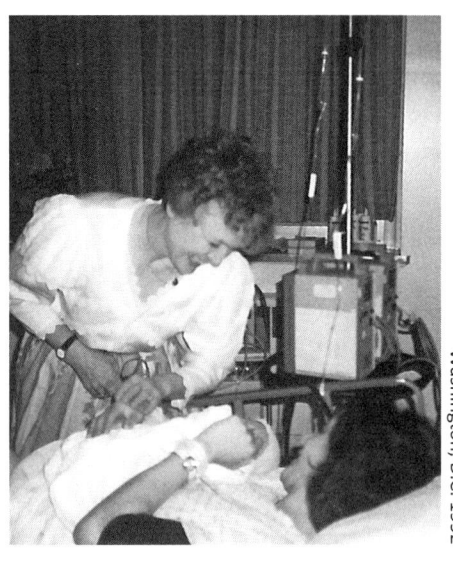

Bethesda, MD 1991

Ellie with newborn baby Carina and mother Anca Croitoru.

Washington, D.C. 1992

Utah horseback adventure with Dorotha (l) and Charles (r) Smart. Ellie is in the middle.

"High and Beautiful Uintas" 1990s

Marriott human resources head Cliff Ehrlich, along with Sterling and Bill Marriott, at the Marriott farm in Virginia.

Hume, VA 1990s

Hugh and Marguerite Colton family reunion, whitewater rafting on the Green River.

Sterling and Scott in waterfall on Green River trip.

Christmas Eve pageant. (l-r top row) Sterling, Daniel, Steve and Carolyn. (l-r bottom row) Mauri, Jenna, Jared, Dave and Meredith.

Polynesian Cultural Center Board. Howard W. Hunter, middle front row, was President of the Church at the time. Sterling is top row, second from right.

Sterling and Ellie snorkeling in Hawaii.

351

Ellie with former sorority sister Norma Warenski Matheson. *Salt Lake City, UT 1990s*

Sterling bungee jumping in New Zealand. *Kawarau Gorge, New Zealand 1995*

Sterling fishing in Alaska with (l-r) Steve, Brad, grandson Daniel and Dave. *Alaska 1994*

352

New York City 1994

Mauri and Ellie in New York City. Note Twin Towers in background.

Bethesda, MD 1995

Easter bonnets. Ellie with (l-r) Jane, Rebecca and Meredith.

France 1995

Ellie with (l-r) Jeri, Carolyn, Melanie and Bob Bradley on girls' trip to France.

353

Loire Valley, France 1995

Landing after a hot-air balloon ride on girls' trip to France. (l-r) Carolyn, Ellie, Melanie, Jeri and Darla.

Switzerland 1995

Sterling and Ellie hiking in Switzerland.

Bethesda, MD 1995

Family gathers on the weekend of Sterling and Ellie's mission farewell.

Sterling at his retirement party with several direct reports. (l-r) Fred Vogel, Myron Walker, Sharon Hermon, Ed Bednarz, Steve West and Steve McKenna.

Ellie and Sterling at retirement party.

Ellie and Sterling dancing at retirement party.

34

PAYBACK TIME

On Saturday, June 10, 1995 the extended family gathered at the Colton home in Bethesda, for their last get-together before Sterling and Ellie left for their mission.

At midday they went to a chapel for the baptism of eight-year-old Scott Colton, Brad and Melanie's son. Melanie gave the opening prayer and was the pianist; Carolyn conducted the music; Sterling conducted the meeting; Brad baptized Scott; Rebecca, Scott's sister, played "Jesus Once Was a Little Child"; Ellie gave a talk on the Holy Ghost. Sterling laid hands on Scott's head, confirming him a member of the Church and giving him the gift of the Holy Ghost.

Sterling's brother Maughan and his wife Colleen joined them from Vernal. Also Butch and Judy Cash and several other friends joined them as well. Following the baptism, family and friends gathered at the Colton home for dinner, after which the group watched a video Melanie had created on Sterling and Ellie.

The following morning members and guests packed the Bethesda Ward chapel for sacrament meeting, filling every pew and the entire cultural hall, for the Coltons' missionary farewell. Sterling and Ellie had influenced a wide circle of friends and associates, who had come to wish them well—showing up at 8:30 on a Sunday morning.

Again it was a Colton affair. Jeri offered the opening prayer; Carolyn, Steve, Brad, David and Darla all gave short talks. The grandchildren sang a favorite Mormon hymn, "I am a Child of God."

Ellie then spoke. In part, she said:

> We will have the privilege of working with some of the finest and best men and women of the rising generation. Our responsibility will be to help them help others realize the importance of the gospel of Jesus Christ. We have lived long enough to see the powerful influence that the gospel can have in one's life. We have seen marriages strengthened, tragedies overcome, families drawn closer and more loving to one another, and more forgiving, loving attitudes developed.
>
> Jesus likened a man who lived by His teaching unto a house built upon a rock. And a man who did not live His teachings to a house built upon the sand. The rain descended, the winds blew, and the floods came and beat upon both houses…the one based on faith held up in troubles. Believing and following Jesus does not enable us to escape all tribulations. But it does fortify our spirits so we can accept and face them when they come.
>
> I have a testimony that the Book of Mormon is another testament of Jesus Christ…when I read it I learn…how we can love God and our fellow human beings. It helps me know…how to overcome evil with good…I am grateful for the courage and faith of the Prophet Joseph Smith…and to have a living prophet today, President Gordon B. Hinckley…Through our parents and grandparents we were shown that service, not self-interest, holds our family, our church, and our community together…Someone penned the lines: 'Hold high the torch! You did not light its glow. 'Twas given you by other hands, you know.'…We hope to hold high the torch.[1]

Then it was Sterling's turn. He began by noting the opening hymn was called "Because I Have Been Given Much." The first verse:

Payback Time

Because I have been given much, I too must give;
Because of thy great bounty, Lord, each day I live.
I shall divide my gifts from thee
With ev'ry brother that I see
Who has the need of help from me.

"It's payback time for Ellie and me," Sterling began. "We have been given much and we're grateful for it. We have also felt your sadness, your pain and despair. And we've counseled and prayed together... We've shared lonely nighttime vigils with you at the bedsides of loved ones, suffering from illness and the infirmities of old age."

Sterling thanked the diverse congregation, saying, "There are with us today those of many faiths—Jewish, Christian, Muslim, Buddhist. We respect your beliefs, and take great comfort in knowing that we share common values: love of God, family, friends, and country.

We are grateful for seven children (including three daughters-in-law) and eleven grandchildren. We are proud of them...Ellie tells me that I shouldn't brag, but even a grandpa hippopotamus thinks his grandbabies are beautiful. So do I.

Joshua, that great prophet of the Old Testament, said "Choose you this day whom ye will serve...but as for me and my house, we will serve the Lord." (Joshua 24:15)...We welcome the opportunity to serve the Lord and our fellow men and women, for the next three years in the British Columbia mission. We ask for your prayers that we might do the will of our Father in Heaven while we are there.

The message we take with us and leave with you is simple and yet profound: God lives; He is our eternal Father...He loves us, He cares for each of us. He wants us to be happy. He wants us to return to Him. He wants us to help each other do this...We were sent here to prove ourselves, given our free agency, the ability to choose between good and evil. Our memory of the past was removed, so we could live by faith. God our eternal Father sent his only begotten son, Jesus Christ, to be our Savior and our Redeemer. He suffered in Gethsemane and on the cross at Calvary, so we could be free of physical death and know that we will live again. He suffered that we might be forgiven of our sins, those sins that would make us unworthy to return to our Father in Heaven.

His first commandment was to love the Lord our God with all of our heart, mind and strength. And the second commandment was like unto it, to love our neighbors as ourselves. It is His gospel... restored in its fullness through modern-day prophets, that we will take to the people of British Columbia. Christ said 'Go ye therefore, and teach all nations, baptizing them in the name of the Father, and of the Son, and of the Holy Ghost: Teaching them to observe all things whatsoever I have commanded you.' (Matthew 28:19-20)

In many ways Ellie and I do not feel prepared and do not feel worthy to do this. But...we go to do that which the Lord has commanded, knowing that He gives no commandment but for which he provides a way for it to be performed...Life is fragile, none of us knows what tomorrow will bring.

We should live each day as though it may be our last, prepared to meet our Maker at that judgment bar with a clear conscience, ready to report that we have fought a good fight, and that the world is a better place to live because of our lives. We pray that we may do this, and we ask that God will bless you and yours until we meet again.

In priesthood meeting that day, Sterling described the "pillars of my faith." The courage of his ancestors in migrating to America, crossing the plains, and building a new life in the rugged Rocky Mountain

West was one pillar. Their honesty and hard work were other pillars. "I learned how to work, working on a farm...as a boy of fourteen or fifteen, oftentimes I would walk five miles up to the farm and spend ten to twelve hours working in the hay or grain fields."

Friendship was another pillar. "Friends impact your life substantially... They strengthen your testimony, they're there when you have hardships, and you can share your joys and sorrows with them. My father taught me the importance of friends."

The pillar of prayer was taught to Sterling by his mother. "She taught me of God, taught me how to pray. She taught me the importance of doing things right...There's a right place to put the fork and spoon on the table, and we did it and we didn't sit down unless the spoons and forks were in the right place. She also taught me how to organize."

Service was a particularly strong pillar for Sterling. "I learned of service from my dad. He spent his lifetime helping people when they needed help—building dams, building hospitals that benefitted the people in the Uintah Basin."

Sterling spoke candidly about why he didn't serve a mission as a young man. "I was not born with a firm testimony," he told the congregation. "Some people are. Some people are blessed to have faith. I was not born that way. I have a questioning mind and I have had doubts. I have had to struggle at times with my testimony."[2]

He added: "...I could have gone but I didn't know that I should go out because I didn't know that I knew that God lived and that this gospel is His...A pillar of my faith is the importance of service. The importance of serving and accepting callings. Don't wait until you have a testimony fully until you do that, but accept the calling and serve, and as you serve that testimony will come."

"...as I have served I found that my testimony has grown and grown and grown, and I bear witness to you...that God lives; we are His children; that Jesus Christ has prepared the way for us to return to our Father in Heaven, and this is His church. We are here to serve one another and we need to help one another to return to our Father in Heaven."

After church Sterling and Ellie greeted friends, then headed home for lunch. Joining the Coltons were the Cashes and two longtime friends from Utah days, Des and Marilyn Barker. That evening Bill and Donna had an open house for them at their home. A large crowd of about 300 were there. The Marriotts gave the Coltons an exquisite Boehm porcelain statue of two hummingbirds—a bird species that had given them many hours of viewing pleasure out their back window for decades.

Over the next few days Sterling tied up loose ends at the office. He gave away to friends and colleagues fifty copies of a church DVD, "Man's Search for Happiness." It explains the LDS belief that all people lived as spirits in a pre-mortal existence, and came to earth to gain a body and, by following God's commandments, prove worthy to return to Him after death.

Sterling had been missionary-minded through the years. Quentin L. Cook was also a Stanford Law School alum and one of the Church's Twelve Apostles. Brad and Melanie ran into Cook at an event in New York City. "He eagerly told us how he appreciated Sterling's news updates to the Stanford Alumni Magazine," said Melanie, "and the emphasis he places on church service in those updates...Elder Cook remarked that it is touching to see the value Sterling places on church service."[3]

One such Stanford alumni update was in the fall of 1995. The article said, "In July, Sterling Colton '53 became president of the Mormon mission in Vancouver, British Columbia, where he oversees 150 young missionaries throughout the province. 'It is quite a dramatic change from what I was doing,' says Colton, who retired May 1 as Marriott International's senior vice president and vice chairman of the Board of Directors.

"'I am responsible for training and motivating them, and for serving as a surrogate parent when they are homesick or lovesick,' Colton says. 'The volunteers, some only 19, learn self-discipline, how to work, and how to express themselves. You have an opportunity to really have an impact.'...While a Stanford Law student, he received scholarship aid.

Now he has pledged $250,000 to establish the Sterling D. and Eleanor R. Colton Scholarship Fund. University matching funds will bring the total to $332,500."

A moving van arrived at their home to transport some furnishings to the mission home in Canada. The Coltons gave Steve and Jeri their Jeep, Brad and Melanie their Cadillac, and left their Mercedes in the garage. A family rented their home while they were in Canada.

On the Friday after their farewell, Sterling and Ellie flew to Salt Lake City. They drove to their condo in Park City, then to Vernal the next morning. Meeting with his mother Marguerite was a bittersweet experience. She looked healthy but her memory was almost completely gone.

They took Marguerite and Maughan for a drive in the area. At one point Sterling and Maughan got out of the car to look at a fence line. Marguerite asked Ellie, "Who are those two boys?" "It was a poignant time for me," wrote Sterling. "I realized that I may not see her alive again during this lifetime. I love her so much." He and Ellie tried to explain that they would be gone for three years, but Marguerite had trouble taking it in.

On Monday, June 19, they drove to Bountiful, north of Salt Lake City, where Maughan and Colleen and their family hosted an open house for Sterling and Ellie. Many relatives attended. They stayed in their condo in Park City that night. The following morning, as usual, they played tennis.

Their mission formally began that afternoon, June 20, when they drove to Provo and registered at the Missionary Training Center (MTC) at 4 p.m. "They are well organized," noted Sterling. Eighty-nine other mission president couples from fourteen nations also signed in, with a number of familiar faces. Couples they knew from back in Maryland included their close friends Steve and Martha West, headed for San Antonio, Texas, and Bob and Luanna Rowe, for Leeds, England.

They slept in an MTC bedroom that night, and the next morning rose early for breakfast in the cafeteria. Sterling's journal is a measure of how packed their first full day in the MTC was. He wrote four full legal-size pages, perhaps the most of any day in his journals. Repeatedly through the day he jotted down variations of the sentiment, "I have never felt the Spirit so strongly."

A new First Presidency was formed three months earlier, upon the death of Church President Howard W. Hunter. Gordon B. Hinckley was the new President; Thomas S. Monson was First Counselor and James E. Faust was Second Counselor.

The 303 missions around the world were divided into twenty-two geographical areas, with a presidency over each. British Columbia was part of the North America Northwest area. Spencer J. Condie was president; his counselors were Glenn L. Pace and C. Scott Grow.

President Monson spoke at the first training meeting of the new mission presidents and their wives on June 21. "The world hungers for our message," said Elder Monson, including the Book of Mormon; the true nature of the Godhead; the Church, built on a foundation of Apostles and prophets, with Jesus Christ as the chief cornerstone; a living prophet, the plan of salvation, and the First Vision when God the Father and his son Jesus Christ appeared to the boy-prophet Joseph Smith in 1820.

Sterling recorded that President Monson spoke of the five M's of missionary work: the message, missionary, mission, member, and the mission president. He asked each president and his missionaries to work closely with members. "Each member district is a future stake," he said, emphasizing the importance of referrals and open-house events. "Members and missionaries are on the same team." Presidents and their wives also are a team and should be worthy models to follow.

As the seminar continued with another trainer, wrote Sterling, "We had been instructed to follow President Monson after he left the podium, to be set apart." President Monson was to return to Salt Lake, and, continued Sterling, "We thought it would be rather perfunctory." It was anything but perfunctory, Sterling and Ellie learned, as President

Monson instructed them for thirty minutes.

Ellie tearfully shared with President Monson her concern that she might not hear well enough to be fully effective. President Monson set Sterling apart first, blessing him that he would be an influence for good among the members and the missionaries in British Columbia. "I have never felt the Spirit stronger than I did at that moment," said Sterling.

The two men, along with a member of the Seventy, Rex D. Pinegar, then set Ellie apart and gave her a beautiful blessing. "President Monson blessed her that she would be sensitive to the needs of the missionaries and that she would be able to inspire and motivate them," said Sterling. "Further, that her hearing would not be a hindrance, but that she would be able to hear all she needs to know. He also blessed her that our family would be protected while we served the Lord, and that they would be blessed because of our mission."

Presidents and their wives were then divided into fourteen smaller training groups. The Coltons' group included the first couple to be baptized in the Soviet Union, who had been called to preside over a new mission being formed in Siberia. "You really receive a vision of how the Church is spreading across the world," said Sterling.

That evening the ninety mission couples had a devotional dinner at which Boyd K. Packer, Acting President of the Quorum of the Twelve Apostles, spoke. "The purpose of missionary work," said Elder Packer, "is to help our brothers and sisters to return to our Father."

Missionaries represent the Lord and should dress, act and teach accordingly, said Elder Packer. To be successful, missionaries should study two hours a day and have the Spirit. He quoted from the Book of Mormon: "...For when a man speaketh by the power of the Holy Ghost the power of the Holy Ghost carrieth it unto the hearts of the children of men." (2 Nephi 33:1)

That evening Sterling and Ellie took a pleasant walk up Rock Canyon, a trail about five miles long, and had a nice visit with Brad, who was in town for a BYU Management Advisory Council meeting. Sterling learned that he was not the oldest new mission president—he was the second-oldest at sixty-six years and three weeks. The oldest was a Danish president who was three weeks older than Sterling.

The next morning Sterling and Ellie were up early again for breakfast with the MTC missionaries, then convened for the next training session at 8 a.m.—a routine followed each day.

Conducting the second morning was the oldest apostle, David B. Haight, eighty-eight. He and his wife Ruby had welcomed Sterling and other LDS students into their home in Palo Alto, California when Sterling was in law school at Stanford four decades earlier.

Elder Richard G. Scott of the Quorum of the Twelve Apostles was the first presenter. The Coltons knew him personally from when he lived in the Washington area, where he was a highly regarded nuclear engineer. After forty-two years of marriage, his wife Jeanene Watkins Scott had died of cancer just the previous month. The Scotts were very close and, said Sterling, "it was obvious he was suffering."

Elder Scott began by noting that music sets a good tone for any meeting. He counseled mission presidents to have quality time with spouses; to write down impressions when the Spirit speaks; to study the life of the Savior; to teach pure doctrine and not get bogged down in detail; and to balance their efforts among conversion, retention, and activation of new members. Other speakers included L. Aldin Porter of the Seventy, a friend of Ellie's from high school.

President James E. Faust, Second Counselor in the First Presidency, spoke first the next morning. He told presidents that missionaries should be "so in tune with the guidance of the Holy Spirit that every one of them can speak in the name of God as they witness and testify of the Savior."

Four things Elder Faust would like his own sons and grandsons to learn on their missions included how to acquire a testimony of the Savior and understand the blessings of the Atonement; how to be honest in all relationships; how to have courage to teach eternal principles; and how to be obedient. The best missionaries, he said, are not always the smartest, but they are the most obedient. "Mission presidents nurture obedience by loving their missionaries."

Sterling's notes from Elder Faust's talk also included: "Obedience is critical. Importance of scripture study. Importance of fiscal responsibility; church funds are sacred. Goal setting is important. Teach eternal principles."

That evening the Coltons had dinner with Spencer J. Condie, area president for the region that includes British Columbia. Then they met with two young missionaries headed for their mission. Both were in language training at the MTC, learning Cantonese and Mandarin Chinese. The province had a very diverse population, including a large number of Chinese.

The Coltons ended the day with another walk up Rock Canyon, Sterling writing that the sunset and wild roses were "spectacular."

Elder Henry B. Eyring, First Counselor in the First Presidency, was the lead-off speaker on the final day. "Sound with a clear trumpet," Sterling said he told them, "make clear to the missionaries what is expected...The Spirit will not dwell in an unclean temple." Teach the Plan of Happiness, that all people lived as spirits in a pre-mortal existence, that we are on earth to be tested, and that how we think and act while here will determine our eternal destiny.

Church President Gordon B. Hinckley, who had just returned from being the first LDS President to speak to members in Alaska, said, "I never get over the fact that what we're doing is in very deed a remarkable miracle: to send out young men and women into a world that is unfriendly, generally, to their message, and to teach that world, and to have one here and there listen and give attention."

"We are among the 'weak and simple,'" he added. "We are not very professional, most of us, in this work. We're ordinary people with ordinary capacities, who have been given an extraordinary assignment—to teach the gospel to the world, which will save the world, if people of the world will hearken unto the message we have to give."

President Hinckley pronounced a collective blessing on the

presidents and their wives—health, safety, strength and vitality, prudence, leadership, wisdom, understanding, and humility before the Lord. "Be thou humble; and the Lord thy God shall lead thee by the hand, and give thee answer to thy prayers." (Doctrine and Covenants 112: 10)

Other blessings he added included patience, testimony, the spirit of love and trust, a sound mind, faith and courage, revelation and discernment, "to be able to listen to the whisperings of the Spirit in the middle of the night, the ability to speak with power, to teach simply and boldly…"

At lunch and dinner that day there were hugs and tears of joy as presidents and their wives prepared to depart for missions across the globe. The Coltons headed for their condo in Park City. "We drove Provo Canyon feeling the Spirit and counting our blessings," wrote Sterling. "Our experience at the MTC has been the spiritual highlight of our lives."

35

Welcome to British Columbia

British Columbia is Canada's westernmost province, defined by a 17,000-mile Pacific coastline and soaring mountain ranges. Sterling and Ellie faced daunting distances in the mission, which would require almost constant travel—by car, ferry, and airplane to the many small airports in the vast region.

The Coltons would be traveling from mission headquarters in Richmond, a suburb of Vancouver, in the far southwest, to Prince Rupert, near the Alaska border on the northwest. That distance is as great as Richmond is from church headquarters in Salt Lake City.

The BC province is larger than France and Britain combined—or equal to the total area of California, Oregon, and Washington together. What British Columbia lacks is the population density of those three states. Today those states have about 50 million people—ten times more than BC's 5 million. About half of BC's people are in the far south, including Vancouver Island, thinning out the vast area even more.

British Columbia has a great variety of topography, as described by Ellie: "Forested slopes, rocky summits, gleaming glaciers, alpine meadows, sagebrush deserts, rain forests, ranch lands, orchards laden with fruit." Also: "island-studded coastlines where mountain cliffs plunge into fjords overlooked by snowy peaks, northern prairie wheat fields, rivers, lakes, sleeping volcanoes, hot springs, gorgeous gardens, and magnificent sunsets."

The province likewise has a range of climates. Winters are usually severe in the northern interior, but the ocean drift current and the blocking presence of successive mountain ranges help keep the south relatively mild. Heavy rainfall dominates the coast in winter.[1]

BC is also home to Whistler Blackcomb, a world-class ski resort, which hosted the 2010 Winter Olympics.

Canada had long been a fruitful field for the Mormons, but the growth was largely elsewhere, especially next door to the east in the province of Alberta, rather than in British Columbia. The first members of the Church arrived in Alberta in the early 1880s as contract workers on a rail line. A few years later other LDS settlers began arriving and farming what is present-day Cardston.

The Church grew rapidly in Alberta. The first stake of the Church was established in 1895, followed by the first LDS temple outside the U.S. in 1923. Alberta got a second temple, in Edmonton, in 1999, and a third one, in Calgary, in 2012.

The saints in British Columbia longed for the day when they too would be blessed with a temple of their own. During three years of consecrated service in BC, Sterling and Ellie and hundreds of missionaries would bring that day closer.

Near the end of 1995 Andrew (Drew) Shirley of Rexburg, Idaho received his mission call to British Columbia. His father was a vice president at local Ricks College. When Ricks' president, Steve Bennion, learned where Drew was going, he told Drew's dad that, if he could choose any mission president in the world for his own son to serve under, he would choose Sterling, who was Bennion's cousin.

"I was just a normal nineteen-year-old kid," said Drew. "I didn't know much about where I was going or what to expect. But immediately I felt lucky. When I met President Colton, he reminded me of a gentle giant. He had military bearing, and big eyes you can see love in. My impression was that he was obviously strong and capable of leading, but also loving."[2]

Sterling's role was to train missionaries to find, teach, and baptize converts into the church; inspire members to assist the effort and welcome and befriend newcomers; and encourage less-active members to return to full fellowship. Sterling was also determined to strengthen the testimony of each missionary. He recalled his own testimony at their age, which was not strong enough to impel him to serve a mission at that time.

Ellie, as always, would be his irreplaceable other half. As the "mission mom," she would be a loving, sympathetic presence wherever they went. Her warmth and humor would have a profound effect on missionaries. At the same time, recalled those who served under them, Ellie could be stern and forthright when she saw something amiss.

Ellie's role was outlined by the First Presidency. "You will be responsible for sharing the gospel and assisting your husband in teaching and giving leadership to the missionaries," they wrote. "They will look to you for guidance, encouragement, and motivation to put forth their best efforts. They will need and deserve your understanding and sympathetic counsel."[3]

On June 29, 1995, the Coltons flew to Vancouver, via Portland. They were met at the airport by Heber and Ardeth Kapp, whose place they were taking, along with two young male APs—assistants to the president—Elders Cristian Bell and Tyler Harris. They took the Coltons to the mission office, a model of organization, then to dinner at a nearby restaurant, the Prow.

"Then the Kapps dropped us off at the mission home and said, 'Goodbye!' recalled Ellie. "We said 'Don't leave us!' They replied 'God bless you!' and left."

The mission office was attached to the local chapel. Its kitchen was kept busy feeding elders and sisters as they arrived in the mission, transferred to new areas, and departed the mission when their service ended.

"Fortunately, we had some very good people in the office," said Ellie. One of them was Jay Burnett, Darla Burnett Colton's uncle. His wife, Yvonne Burnett, was office manager and a "saint," wrote Sterling. Another office couple was Walter and Anne Perry. They had the critically important responsibility of managing the motor vehicle fleet, and carried it out expertly. Given the great distances involved, unlike most missions, nearly all BC missionaries had access to cars.

The Burnetts and Perrys left the mission in August, replaced by another excellent office couple, Elden and LaDawn Jackman. They in turn would leave midway through the Coltons' tenure, replaced by Don and Sid Oakes.

Each Monday morning the Coltons, the APs, and the office staff met together in a devotional and planning meeting. Someone said a prayer, a spiritual message was delivered, and the upcoming schedule and any special concerns were considered.

During their first day the Coltons became acquainted with the staff and facilities. Mormon missionaries travel two-by-two, and are virtually never to be alone. Sometimes the closeness leads to personality problems. During the Coltons' first twenty-four hours, Sterling—now President Colton—had to discipline two young elders who had broken mission rules. He transferred both to new areas.

Missions are challenging and can be discouraging. Most missionaries receive far more rejection than acceptance—notably in missions like British Columbia, where membership grew very slowly. "The Vancouver mission has struggled for years to increase the number of people who join the Church," noted the Church's *Ensign* magazine.

"Collin Van Horne, president of the Nanaimo British Columbia Stake, explains that in British Columbia 'there is an unspoken understanding that religion is not a topic for discussion. In Canada, the phrase is 'I'm all right, Jack.' For a long time that culture left missionary work to the full-time missionaries, who spent most of their time tracting.'"[4]

The number of missionaries at any given time in their mission ranged from about 150 to more than 200. During their three years, the Coltons would watch nearly 600 missionaries come and go, including a number of retired couples; single sisters typically in their early twenties and several older sisters; and—the bulk of the mission force—young male elders, averaging about twenty years of age. Couples and elders typically served for two years, sister missionaries for eighteen months.

The Church was well organized in BC. There were six stakes, each of which had six to eight wards, and two districts, which would grow into stakes when they gained enough priesthood members. Mission organization reflected local church organization. The mission was divided into eight zones, one for each stake and district. Missionaries were instructed to work closely with local leaders to help find and fellowship potential converts.

In addition to the two APs, who worked closely with Sterling, missionary leadership included two zone leaders over each of the eight zones, and district leaders within each zone. In addition, there was a zone for non-English-speaking missionaries. It usually included eight who spoke Spanish, six Mandarin Chinese, and two Vietnamese. Sterling's first action was to schedule eight zone conferences throughout the mission, something repeated monthly. Sterling would begin each conference by greeting missionaries and sharing a message. Then he would retire to another room and privately interview each missionary as Ellie and the two APs addressed the others.

This meant that every missionary was interviewed at least once a month. "It was probably the most valuable thing I did," said Sterling. In addition, each missionary was interviewed as he or she entered the mission and prepared to go home.

While President Colton conducted one-on-one zone conference interviews, Ellie and other mission leaders trained the other missionaries. The APs shared monthly progress in the number of baptisms and other metrics, and discussed effective ways to proselyte. Ellie focused on staying close to the Spirit and on practical day-by-day routines for missionaries, some of whom were living away from home for the first time.

Ellie warmed their stomachs as well as their hearts, always bringing something good to eat—typically her signature cinnamon rolls or fresh-baked cookies, often accompanied by apples or another fruit and a drink. Missionaries were to bring their own sack lunch.

Zone conferences sometimes unearthed interesting situations. One missionary asked if they could teach and baptize a man on parole from prison; another asked about baptizing a Muslim. (Muslims who convert to another religion often face punishment, including imprisonment and even execution if they relocate to some Muslim-dominated countries.)

In another case, the husband of a new convert, who had run over his former wife's father in his car, now threatened to kill a missionary who taught her. Sterling quickly transferred him to another area.

One of the BC missionaries, Elder Cannon Neslen, had been introduced at a general conference to the entire Church nine years earlier. Elder David B. Haight, a member of the Twelve Apostles, spoke of Cannon in his October 1986 talk.

One summer, Clarence Neslen, Jr., Cannon's father, took his family to Jasper National Park in nearby Alberta. While exploring the Columbia Icefields, family members were jumping over crevasses. "It was an exciting experience until eleven-year-old Cannon…missed and fell into the deep chasm," said Elder Haight. He was wedged thirty feet deep between frozen walls. Beneath the crevasse could be seen a river of icy water.

Time was short and hypothermia was setting in. Cannon's shirt had been pushed up as he fell, and his bare skin was pressed against the walls of ice. His father shouted encouragement to keep Cannon conscious, urging him to wiggle his fingers and toes and sing his favorite songs. "I am a child of God," Cannon sang over and over, from a favorite Mormon hymn, his voice growing dim.

Two park rangers were located by radio and rushed to the scene. The rangers drove spikes into the ice and one roped up and descended toward Cannon. However, the walls were too narrow and he had to abandon the effort. Their only chance was to lower a strong rope and pray that Cannon was alert enough to grasp it and hold on as they tried to pull him out. If he lost his grip he could continue falling into the river below.

His family prayed hard, including his father who pled for his son's life. "A feeling of assurance and calm came over me," he said, "and I knew that he would be saved."

Cannon's icy fingers caught the rope and he was pulled up, inch by inch. "When he was finally to the surface," said Elder Haight, "he was unconscious. His fingers had miraculously frozen around the rope and had to be pried loose.

"He was immediately wrapped in blankets and rushed to a waiting ambulance, but there was not enough warmth to raise his body temperature sufficiently. A paramedic undressed Cannon, then took off his own coat and shirt and held Cannon against his bare chest so that his body heat would radiate to the boy." Cannon slowly responded. His life was spared.

As Sterling introduced an emotional Elder Neslen to the other missionaries at Elder Neslen's first transfer meeting, he later wrote, "there wasn't a dry eye in the room…While in the crevasse, he later told his father, he felt a comforting assurance that he would be saved. He knows God loves him and that he was spared for a purpose…that he has a special mission to perform in this life." Now he was on that mission in British Columbia.

The most hectic time of the month was transfer day, often involving dozens of elders and sisters who passed through Richmond on the way to their newly assigned areas and companions.

Each month, to prepare for transfers, Sterling and his two assistants—who served typically for five or six months and rotated back into the field as other elders took their places—sat around a board with photos of all the missionaries. "We were thinking of where to put missionaries to help them grow," said Elder Tom Hawes, an AP. "On several occasions we put those who were struggling into leadership roles.

"President Colton spent time with them, letting them know they had wonderful potential, not just on the mission but after they went home. He reminded them of their personal strengths, especially the strengths of those who were struggling. He wanted to raise their vision of who they could be. He'd say, for instance, that 'You would be good working with people.'"[5]

Another AP, Elder Troy Thurgood, said, "One time we had two elders who were trouble-makers. President Colton suggested we make them companions and send them to Burns Lake, about as remote as you can get." My companion and I both said it was risky to put them together. President just said, 'I have a feeling about this.'"[6]

The two elders were shipped off to Burns Lake. Within about a month the trajectory of their missions had changed from down to up. They worked faithfully and completed honorable missions. "One of those elders has since been a bishop," said Thurgood.

Each month a group of new elders and sisters would arrive in the mission and another group would head home. Ellie said, "We would get back to Richmond from the zone conferences just in time to plan the welcome dinner and goodbye breakfast and interviews before we started north again for another eight zone conferences."

The Coltons were fortunate to have several local "kitchen angels" who prepared group meals at the meetinghouse in Richmond for missionaries who were transferring as well as entering or leaving the mission. They were led by a hard-working member named Marie. Ellie coordinated the meals and often baked treats—tripling or quadrupling the recipes. On occasion she also prepared whole meals at the mission home.

Unlike some missions across the world which have sleeping quarters attached to the mission home, the Coltons' mission home was a modest three-bedroom structure without additional sleeping areas. Instead, most missionaries staying overnight in Richmond did so at a hotel.

Missionaries loved Ellie for far more than her cooking. She spread sunshine wherever she went, greeting them with her million-kilowatt smile, and helping them see a silver lining in the darkest clouds.

An elder wrote of his first day in the mission. "One of the other new elders pointed out that President Colton seemed to show special respect for his wife," said Elder Clay Jones. "That night at dinner I watched for this and by the way President Colton looked at his wife, I knew it was true. I remember during that first meal how Sister Colton took extra care learning each of our names and engaging each one of us in conversation."[7]

One of Ellie's goals was to help improve the manners of their missionaries. In a series of zone conferences, she donned an apron and chef's hat and sat at one end of a dining table; Sterling or an elder was at the other end. The table had bowls of fake food. Ellie picked up a dinner roll and threw it at Sterling. He threw one back at her. Then they both dug into grapes and other foods, chucking them at each other. Meanwhile, the silverware had been set all wrong. Ellie, in her typically playful way, successfully taught missionaries the value of good manners and proper etiquette.

During another series of zone conferences, Ellie played the role of BC Tel, the local phone company. Some missionaries had figured out how to make free calls on the system. They would tell the operator to place a collect call. When the other party answered, before the operator could finish asking if they would pay for it, the first party would blurt out a five-second message and hang up. If it lasted longer than five seconds the mission would be charged. The Coltons strongly discouraged such calls.

"I could always count on Sister Colton to liven up zone conference with some fun activity, a colorful handout or poster, or one of your incredible costumes," wrote Elder Aaron Kashiwagi, in a letter to the Coltons. "It's something I constantly have looked forward to." He mentioned a conference in Kamloops. "You were giving a training session on stress, I think, and you had gone through a pamphlet and several scriptures in it.

"With a huge finale, you finished off your training by breaking out in singing with a song about accenting the positive and downplaying the negative. I have to smile just thinking about it. We need variety and change so much as missionaries and you have been perfect for giving us that. It's amazing how much energy and enthusiasm that you bring along with you."[8]

Regarding President Colton, Kashiwagi wrote that "you have taught us of the Savior and His Atonement. Always your words are accompanied by the Spirit." Another favorite memory, he wrote, was the times President Colton "told us that you love us and that you care for us...It is a wonderful feeling to know that you are loved by someone else. To know by the Spirit that this love is real."

Though fun-loving, Ellie by no means was light-minded. She had keen judgment when an issue could be treated lightly and when it called for serious consideration or action. "She could be sharp with us when she needed to be," said one assistant to the president.

On one occasion, four sisters from a faraway zone drove to Richmond for a special sisters conference. There was a strict mission rule against driving outside prescribed boundaries, and the sisters were told which route to take.

"One sister, who had been in the mission longer, was driving," recalled Sister Annette Adams (Esplin), a new arrival. "We went out of the boundaries." They stayed at the mission home that evening, and when they arrived Ellie confronted them "the way a mother would do."[9] Ellie did not mince words as she told them what they had done wrong.

"Then she gently chastised us," as all of them, including Ellie, shed tears. "It was clear that her love and concern was for us. The rest of the time she was so loving. She made you feel important, made you feel like gold, that you were one of a kind." After Ellie talked with the sisters, Sterling met with them.

"Sister Colton had a lot of spunk, a lot of energy," said Elder David Williams. "If she felt you were out of place, she would diplomatically put you in your place quickly." Williams recalled saying to Sterling, "I've heard that the golden years are filled with lead." Sterling's response: "Not if you are married to Sister Colton!"[10]

Sterling and Ellie spent a lot of time on the road, sometimes traveling ten hours or more a day. On occasion the incessant travel got to both of them. One time Ellie was driving and she missed a sign to turn. When Sterling's reaction hurt her feelings, Ellie asked him to "pull the car over, because I'm going to walk!"[11]

Sister Kristi Hollingshead said in a letter to the Coltons she could "write pages on you two!!! Two of my favorite memories are when Sister Colton told us all to do our 'damnedest' and when we shared favorite sonnets with each other...I loved the time you took with the sisters. I thank you for everything and you've made a huge dent in my heart!!!!!"... And just to let you know, I took notes on your marriage and I plan to review them when the time comes!"[12]

36

CARE AND FEEDING OF 200 MISSIONARIES

"I promise you that the time you spend in the mission field, if those years are spent in dedicated service, will yield a greater return on your investment than any other two years of your lives!"[1]

President Gordon B. Hinckley, leader of The Church of Jesus Christ of Latter-day Saints, made that promise to missionaries worldwide in 2002. This same sentiment was voiced often by Sterling and Ellie during their three years in British Columbia.

The Coltons took every opportunity to train and inspire missionaries with the importance of their service. One tool they used was the *Mountain Top Messenger*, a monthly newsletter distributed to each missionary. Their first *Messenger* was issued during their first month in BC, July 1995. Part of its message read:

> The Gospel of Jesus Christ is a Gospel of love and service. It has been restored in its fullness through modern-day prophets. The Book of Mormon is another witness of Christ. Jesus Christ is at the head of the Church. It is His Church. We accept, honor and love Him as our Lord and Master.

> Each of us has been called by the Lord to serve as His representative to the people of British Columbia. The Holy Ghost assists us in

this ministry. We bring a priceless gift, the Gospel of Jesus Christ, to all who will receive it. This Gospel provides the principles and ordinances required to return to the Father and obtain eternal salvation. We are engaged in saving souls and bringing joy and happiness to all who will accept and follow Christ.

The Coltons emphasized that, while missionaries spread the good news of the gospel and teach investigators its principles, only the witness of the Spirit converts. Each *Messenger* listed the number of baptisms during the previous month and which missionaries did the teaching. There were 31 convert baptisms in June, with four missionaries being acknowledged for the most baptisms.

Missionaries were encouraged to memorize key passages in the Bible and the Church's unique three books of scripture—the Book of Mormon, Doctrine and Covenants, and Pearl of Great Price. They also had about a half-dozen suggested discussions to be followed sequentially in introducing someone to the gospel.

Discussions included the nature of Heavenly Father and His Son Jesus Christ; the establishment of Christ's church when He was on the earth; the apostasy, or falling away of the true church after the death of Christ and the early apostles; and the restoration of Christ's true church starting with the appearance of the Father and Son to the boy-prophet Joseph Smith in 1820 in upstate New York.

The most common LDS proselyting method in British Columbia was to tract—go door to door—seeking those willing to listen to a message about the Savior and His restored gospel. President Colton required his missionaries to tract at least fifteen hours each week. He also emphasized the need to not just baptize new converts but to work with wards and branches to ensure that new converts remained active in the Church.

The Book of Mormon played a central role in missionary work in BC, as it does in missions all over the world. The Book of Mormon is a second witness, along with the Bible, of the divinity of Jesus Christ.

Investigators are encouraged to read the Book of Mormon and pray to know of its truthfulness.

Although tracting typically consumed the most proselyting time of most missionaries, usually it was not the most effective way to find interested individuals. So when moving to a new area, BC missionaries were instructed to obtain a copy of the ward or branch membership list, meet with key local leaders to review the lists and, within four weeks, meet with every part-member family.

Ellie had a unique way of preparing missionaries for transfers. "The true 'Celestial' transfer," she explained in one *Mountain Top Messenger*, "is finding your way successfully, stress-free, greeted by a smiling companion at the door of an immaculate, uninfected apartment, and seeing a hot, gourmet dinner awaiting your arrival, just before going to the baptism of a family of eight that evening.

"Since we have yet to have a 'Celestial' transfer day, my best advice is on a small plaque on our refrigerator. It provides: 'So this is not Home Sweet Home. Adjust!'"

President and Sister Colton stressed the importance of a missionary being bold. Potential investigators are everywhere a missionary goes, and can be found by simply asking a stranger what are traditionally known as the "Golden Questions," or "GQs": How much do you know about the Mormon Church? Would you like to know more? "When the Spirit is present, people are not offended when you share your feelings about the gospel," President Colton told the missionaries.

Elder Jeffrey Rawlins and his companion were the top baptizers one month and as a reward the Coltons took them to dinner. "I remember how President Colton expressed his love for his wife by always making sure that she was okay," said Elder Rawlins. "Then President Colton, without fear, GQ'd the waitress."[2]

During the Coltons' first few months in British Columbia, these are some of the tips they passed along to missionaries via the *Messenger*:

"Use the study guides and suggestions you have received. Teach a discussion every day...Whom the Lord calls, the Lord qualifies... Never be ashamed of the gospel of Jesus Christ...Never feel inadequate and unsettled because you cannot explain sacred doctrines to the satisfaction of all...if you will explain what you know and testify of what you feel, you may plant a seed that will one day grow and blossom into a testimony of the gospel of Jesus Christ..."

Senior missionary couples were assigned to inspect missionary apartments every three months for cleanliness and orderliness. Sterling and Ellie also called every missionary on his or her birthday, to sing a duet of "Happy Birthday."

Sterling's singing produced a chuckle at a Christmas zone conference. "We were singing a certain hymn," recalled Elder Jared Mortensen. "The entire group sang the first verses, and then the third verse was to be a solo by a particular sister missionary. But because of his continual willingness to assist, President Colton continued to sing, making it a very powerful duet, which was followed by healthy but reverent laughter."[3]

Sterling and Ellie continued to rise early and walk. Now their walks typically were in the neighborhood or along a river trail called the Richmond Dike. Sterling had always risen early in the morning and put in long days at Marriott, rarely mentioning how tired he was. Now, with the temporal as well as spiritual lives of hundreds of missionaries in his hands, he and Ellie often fell into bed, both saying they were "exhausted."

As with most parents, the Coltons, in rearing their own children, could not sleep soundly at night until they were confident the children were safe and accounted for. They had the same concern in the mission—except now, instead of their four children, they in essence had to be sure 200 or so young people were tucked safely into bed every night.

One night at 10:25 an elder called Sterling to report that his companion had been missing for nearly a half-hour. Sterling also learned that the missionary's girlfriend had been in Vancouver for several weeks. The missing elder was discouraged and talked of going home. Sterling and a number of missionaries began calling and checking places where he might have gone.

The missing missionary phoned his companion the following afternoon, asking to meet him at a park and take him back to their apartment. Instead, Sterling directed the companion to bring him to the mission office.

"I had some idea how the father of the Prodigal Son felt," said Sterling. "I wanted to hug him and at the same time I wanted to give him a kick in the pants." He had a long talk with the elder, who said he felt inadequate. Sterling also talked with the elder's father and brother back home.

"I think I have him recommitted," wrote Sterling. "His girlfriend is to return home to Salt Lake City on Monday." The elder was transferred to another mission, which he completed successfully.

Another night the phone rang again at about 10:30. It was a young elder, saying he and his companion had lost track of time and missed the ferry taking them south to Victoria. "I got dressed and drove to the ferry crossing," said Sterling. "Needless to say I was not in the best of humor." The elders spent the night at the mission home.

Another after-hours call was far more serious. It came at 2 a.m. from an elder whose companion felt excruciating pain in his groin area. Sterling instructed the first elder to drive his ailing companion to a nearby medical clinic.

A doctor diagnosed a testicular torsion. If treated promptly the testicle can often be saved. Otherwise the condition can lead to infertility. Unfortunately, the nearest major medical center was nearly 500 miles away in Prince George. The missionary was given pain killers and taken there by ambulance, a nine-hour trip.

Sterling spent a good part of the day informing and securing permission for surgery—from the missionary's parents, his bishop and stake president, and a doctor at Church headquarters. Sterling also alerted a member of the Church in Prince George who was a nurse. A Dr. Hassan performed the surgery, which was successful.

More difficult to accept were the actions of a tiny number of missionaries who flaunted mission rules. Whenever possible, if a missionary broke the rules, Sterling went far out of his way to help him or her repent and remain in the mission. Serious moral offenses, however, could take the issue out of Sterling's hands and mean immediate release from the mission.

Sterling was innately kind, and only as a very last resort would he send a missionary home early.

One day he received a disturbing videotape apparently shot by one of four elders who lived together in a Vancouver suburb. "It causes me great concern," wrote Sterling. "I was so agitated that I couldn't get to sleep...I am going to have to take some decisive action."

Along with whatever else was on the tape, it showed one elder who had dyed his hair, grown sideburns, and was wearing earrings. Sterling summoned the four elders to his office and interviewed them. One of the four was humble and penitent. "He is a good elder who was led astray," Sterling concluded. A second elder also apologized. The other two were recalcitrant and wanted to go home.

"I have not been able to get him motivated," said Sterling of one of the latter two, who at least agreed to stop wearing earrings. His interview with the second rebellious missionary produced similar results. "I have not been able to create a desire to do missionary work. He just wants to go home."

For the moment, Sterling assigned each of the four to new companions in new districts. One of the rebellious elders had left some of his clothing at their apartment. Sterling drove him there to retrieve it. "The apartment was in deplorable condition," said Sterling. "I can't imagine how they lived in it."

He took the elder to the mission home to sleep that night. Next morning Sterling rose at five and rousted the elder out of bed. At 6:30 they left for the apartment, where they worked for several hours to put it back together.

It was now December and holiday preparations in the mission field further cut into Sterling's time. But he refused to toss in the towel on the two elders, even though that would have relieved him of a big headache. Sterling continued to phone their families, ecclesiastical leaders, and even other BC missionaries who might have a positive influence on them.

"I think I am making some headway but it is slow," wrote Sterling. "The final outcome is much in doubt. But I will not give up on them."

One of these two elders remained in the mission, but nothing could dissuade the other elder. Finally, nine days before Christmas, Sterling escorted him to a Delta flight heading to Salt Lake City. Such an outcome was rare and heartbreaking for President Colton.

At the opposite end of the devotion scale was Muffy Evans, a young woman from the Coltons' ward in Maryland, discussed in an earlier chapter. She had been in pain since the age of three as rheumatoid arthritis attacked her joints, destroying cartilage and leaving bone rubbing against bone. She had had multiple joint replacements and related operations. She also had diabetes, for which she gave herself a daily shot.

Muffy had a burning desire to serve a mission. Church officials doubted whether Muffy's health would permit such a rigorous experience. Sterling had been close to the Evans family as their home teacher and bishop in Maryland. When the issue came to his attention, he asked the missionary department to grant her wish to serve, and to send her to his mission.

"I put my papers in at the end of July in 1995," said Muffy. Receiving and opening the letter from the First Presidency assigning a prospective missionary to one of the more than 300 missions is an exciting, time-honored ritual for LDS families. Muffy's case was different. In mid-August, before the official letter arrived, Sterling telephoned her with the news. "He was so excited!" said Muffy.[4]

Muffy—Sister Evans—arrived in BC in September. Sterling assigned one of his best sister missionaries as her companion, and arranged for them to live and proselyte close to the mission home. "During my eighteen months he was a father figure to me. Very protective," said Muffy. "We would meet at zone conferences and every couple of months he called to see how I was doing and if I needed a break."

Her faith and uncomplaining courage produced miracles. "I was serving in north Vancouver, and one day was out tracting (going door to door) with my companion," said Muffy. "It had been raining and the pavement was a little slick. I had this terrible pain in my leg. In that area, most houses were up stairs. The next house we came to had about ten steps. I prayed to take away the pain. The pain left and a rainbow came out."

Winter days occasionally got down to eighteen below zero. On one cold day, Muffy and a local member were tracting. They returned to the member's Toyota to find the keys locked inside. "That was not good," said Muffy, "because we had to be back to the church soon to give the last discussion so a person could be baptized." They hurriedly approached a couple of people in the neighborhood for help, but no one knew how to get inside the car.

"I had the impression that I should try to see if my Chevrolet key would open the Toyota," said Muffy. "I dismissed that idea, then had it again…I tried it, and it worked!" They quickly went to the church, about a ten-minute drive, for the lesson and baptism. "When we got there, I tried my Chevy key in the Toyota door, and it wouldn't go in."

About every three months Muffy had to cross the U.S. border and meet with a doctor, a rheumatologist, in Bellingham, Washington. Ellie usually drove Muffy and her companion there. "After the appointment, Sister Colton would take us to lunch, then we'd go shopping. We were still in our mission clothes. She always made it a fun day."

In October 1996 Sterling drove Muffy and her companion, Sister Brimley, to Bellingham. "We had lunch at the Red Robin," said Sterling, before taking Muffy to see her doctor. "She needs some cortisone shots for her elbows, but will have to wait until next month to obtain clearance from her insurance company. She is a courageous young woman."

Two months before her eighteen-month mission was complete, Sterling phoned Muffy to ask if she would like to go home early. "I said 'Let me pray about it, and I will let you know.' I did pray, and had the impression that I should serve out my full time." During the two months, Muffy and her companion taught an older couple. Just before the end of her mission in March 1997, the couple was baptized. "Definitely worth waiting for," she observed.

Muffy Evans returned home after serving her full eighteen months. "Sister Evans has been unbelievable," wrote Sterling as she left. "I don't know how she has done it. She has been in pain throughout her mission."

A decade later, while serving as a volunteer in the Mount Timpanogos Utah Temple in 2007, Muffy met Kevin Cook, a young mental-health therapist from California. Fourteen months later they were married. They have two children. The first is a daughter, Kira. The second is a son. They named him Colton.[5]

As they traversed the mission each month, Sterling and Ellie made a special point of meeting local leaders and other faithful members who worked hand-in-glove with the missionaries to harvest souls for the kingdom. The Coltons made many new friends for the Church and its missionary efforts.

"Today," wrote a noted historian in Canada, "the influence of the Church is felt in every province and territory in this vast dominion, from the rugged eastern coasts of Newfoundland to the western shores of Vancouver Island, and from the Alberta wheat fields in the south to the Arctic Ocean on the north.⁶

"Although the Church has not grown here as spectacularly as in some regions of the world, it has nevertheless done so consistently year after year, one faithful life upon another."

Sterling's brothers Maughan and Phil asked what they could do to assist him and Ellie. Sterling suggested they check in their hometown of Vernal to see if some older LDS couples might want to join them. That proved fruitful. Three Vernal couples journeyed north to the mission. Garth and Marita Batty served in the office; Larry and Luanne Searle served in a branch; Gene and Lynell Anfinson also served in a branch.

The Anfinsons drove a large pickup truck filled with various supplies northwest from Vernal for twenty hours to Vancouver. They stopped at mission headquarters long enough to get running orders from Sterling, then drove another eleven hours north to a remote outpost named Bella Coola, famous in wartime lore as a haunt for American draft-dodgers. Nearly half of the approximately 1,800 residents in the valley were native Canadians of the Nuxalk Nation. Most worked in the logging or fishing industries.

"The Anfinsons demonstrated the great good a couple can accomplish by showing Christ-like love to everyone," said Sterling. "They endeared themselves to members and other townspeople. Before long Elder Anfinson was coaching the native basketball team, and raised money to take them to the all-native tournament at Prince Rupert. Sister Anfinson taught an art class at the church twice a week and had twenty-five students.

"She gave gospel messages indirectly while they painted. Her students adored her as she helped them develop talents they didn't know they had."

When the Anfinsons arrived at the start of the Coltons' mission, only about a dozen members regularly attended church in Bella Coola, struggling to keep the branch going. The Anfinsons dug in and visited inactive members, while helping out every way they could in the community. As a result there was a resurgence in the branch, with more members attending than ever before.

In June 1997 the Coltons traveled to Bella Coola by way of an all-day ferry, to help honor the Anfinsons as they completed their one-year mission.

"They softened many hearts," said Sterling. "Over a hundred people came to the farewell dinner on Saturday at the church, and the next morning there were more members at church than had ever attended the branch. Some of them hadn't been to church for many years."

In October 1997 a new stake was organized in Nanaimo, giving British Columbia its seventh stake. General Authorities assisting with the organization were Elder D. Todd Christofferson of the First Quorum of the Seventy (later a member of the Quorum of the Twelve Apostles) and Steven H. Pond of the Fifth Quorum of the Seventy. The new Nanaimo Stake included five wards and four branches.

Back home in Vernal, Sterling's mother Marguerite had been suffering from serious dementia for a half-dozen years, and Sterling and his siblings knew she could pass away at any time. On November 17, 1995 Marguerite and a care-giver walked down the lane to the post box. When they returned Marguerite said she was a little tired and laid down on her bed for a nap. She never woke up. Maughan, who had run the ranch and borne the heaviest load in caring for their parents, telephoned Sterling with the news.

After the initial shock, wrote Sterling, "Ellie and I were both filled with a deep sense of gratitude...for her life and her great love and many sacrifices for Dad, her children, and grandchildren. We are grateful that she was able to stay in her own home where she was cared for by those who loved her, and that she was in no pain...We will be eternally grateful to Maughan for all he did for Mother."

Marguerite was ninety-three when she died. Her funeral was on November 24. Ellie attended. As was required for mission presidents with their enormous responsibilities, Sterling remained in BC and did not attend.

37

Last Months in Mission Field

In a sacrament meeting one Sunday in British Columbia, Ellie shared her faith with other members of the congregation, noting that "On my next birthday I will have reached the speed limit!"

"That is long enough to have known doubt, sin, tragedy, and failure. It is also long enough to have experienced faith, happiness and even ecstasy. I have felt the great joy of bringing babies into the world, and the agony of watching loved ones die. Through all of life's experiences the gospel of Jesus Christ has given me purpose, hope, and comfort."

As a young girl, said Ellie, "the pillars of my faith were people, who by love and example gave me the emotional security to determine my testimony on the building blocks of faith, principles, and affirmation of the Spirit."

Her first pillar, said Ellie, "was my mother, who, despite great difficulties and great loss, rejoiced in her blessings." But the untimely deaths in her family, including those of her father and three sisters—the last one, Vie, leaving two small boys and a newborn girl—shook Ellie's testimony.

"I went back to college at the University of Utah disillusioned, and registered for some philosophy classes. I became converted to whatever philosopher we were studying at the time, and was not the least bit shy in sharing my profound knowledge with my mother. Instead of tearing at her hair and despairing at her daughter gone adrift, she would say,

'All I ask is that before you give up the Church, you understand what you are giving up.'"

Ellie said, "I accepted that challenge and am still learning and trying to understand what the gospel is. What I have discovered is that the more you learn, the more there is to learn. We learn precept upon precept, and when we understand and try to live one precept, we are able to understand another. That, I suppose, is what eternal progression is all about."

Sterling was another pillar of her faith. "His genuine concern and love for others has been a great example to me. I have been blessed to share my life with a fine, decent person. His love for the Lord and me has been strong and steady.

"Our children have also been pillars for me…The satisfaction of watching our children grow into caring, loving people has been both amazing and gratifying. I now benefit from their testimonies." She also said:

> Prayer is an important aspect of my faith. I have experienced healing of both body and soul through prayer. I feel the power of prayer saved my life and the life of our eldest son in a traumatic, risky birth. We almost lost another son when he was three weeks old. My husband and I pled with the Lord for his life, and have never stopped feeling grateful for having him as part of our family…
>
> I partially lost my hearing with the birth of our fourth child, but with a series of operations can hear 40 percent in only one ear. A doctor told me I needed to face the fact that I might be deaf over half my life. That was twenty-five years ago and I'm holding steady at 40 percent. You would be amazed at how much one can hear at 40 percent…
>
> To understand God, we need to understand one another. When we are open to the promptings of the Spirit, we are made aware of the

needs of our friends and neighbors and family...I believe our biggest and most important challenge is to be creative in the area of human relations. We must treat others with courtesy, with encouragement, with sisterly and brotherly love in ways that help and motivate them to be their finest selves...I believe the best way to strengthen the pillars of my faith is to strive for personal integrity, to work hard at sincerity, humility, honesty, moral courage, and self-control.

While in Canada, the Coltons stayed close to their children and grandchildren by phoning each one they could reach each Sunday, as they had done for many years. After a round of phone calls in September, Sterling said, "The grandchildren are all back in school, doing very well." The family in turn sent Sterling and Ellie cards, letters, and videotapes.

Sterling and Ellie often participated in inspiring events, including the baptism of new converts. When missionaries prayerfully believed someone they were teaching was ready for baptism, Sterling or another presiding authority interviewed the individual. In the process Sterling learned how the gospel was changing and improving the lives of hundreds of converts and their families.

"We took Meredith to a wonderful baptism," wrote Sterling of his granddaughter, Steve and Jeri's daughter, who was visiting at the time. "One father was baptized, received the Aaronic Priesthood, then baptized his daughter."

While a handful of missionaries with special challenges periodically required an inordinate amount of their time, Sterling and Ellie overall were awed by the caliber of their missionaries. "We love these elders," wrote Sterling, after a special training conference for zone leaders. "They will be the leaders of the Kingdom. They are outstanding."

Sterling almost always tried to convince missionaries to serve out their full allotted time in the mission. One of his two assistants, Elder Andrew Shirley, was frustrated one time by a struggling missionary who was trying to find his girlfriend. He asked President Colton,

"Why don't we send him home?" President Colton "taught me a great lesson. He said, 'That would mean he has given up.' President Colton's goal was to save the souls of missionaries as well as the souls of people living in our mission."[1]

Sister Muffy Evans was at the mission home one day when an elder who had broken mission rules was leaving with Sterling for the airport and a flight home. "The President had tried to help him choose the right things," she said. "President Colton started crying, tears of love and tears of sadness."

Sister Mary Jones, a widow and single-senior missionary who spent months at the mission office, witnessed a similar scene. "There was a missionary from Alaska," she said. "President Colton loved him so much, but he got in some problems and the President had to send him home. I remember President Colton sitting in his car with tears in his eyes as he was about to take him" to the airport.[2]

While never sanguine about any missionary going home before the scheduled time, eventually Sterling seemed to have accepted, however reluctantly, that some missionaries were bent that way and, in the end, he could do little about it. In the case of one elder, he wrote, "It is hard to reason with a love-sick missionary."

Around that same time, Sterling wrote about a sister missionary who was depressed and heading home prematurely. "I surely hope they will be able to help her overcome her depression. She is a wonderful sister."

Occasionally missionaries had medical emergencies that required specialized care. One elder developed Crohn's disease, a type of painful inflammatory bowel ailment that attacked his lower and upper intestines. It progressed so far that he was not able to walk.

Another time two elders were driving their mission car, a blue Chevy Cavalier compact, when a red pickup truck broadsided it. They were transported by ambulance to two different hospitals. Elder Steven Peterson was treated and released, but Elder Gregory Johnson had serious head injuries. Sterling and an elder rushed to the Royal

Columbia Hospital, where Elder Johnson was on a board, his neck in a rigid brace and his arms and legs buckled down to keep him immobilized.

They had sedated him with morphine, and he was on a ventilator and monitor. "His head was bloody and swollen," said Sterling. He was unconscious and the emergency room doctor did not know the seriousness or extent of his injuries. Someone from the mission office picked up Elder Peterson and took him to his companion. He and Sterling blessed Elder Johnson, with Elder Peterson anointing his head with a few drops of consecrated oil and Sterling pronouncing the blessing.

"He was unconscious and couldn't hear what we said," recalled Sterling. "But I had a sweet feeling come over me and received an assurance that he would be okay. I was very grateful for the power of the priesthood."

Sterling and Elder Peterson spent the day by Elder Johnson's side. Elder Peterson was physically huge, but was very tender with his companion. At about 4 p.m. the nurses cut Johnson's clothing off and put a hospital gown on him. That roused Elder Johnson a bit. Sterling recalled that "He looked up and said 'Hi President!' To me, those two words sounded like the 'Hallelujah Chorus.' It meant that he could see and remember." Johnson fell right back to sleep.

Meanwhile another elder slipped on ice while tracting that same day and slashed open his head, requiring nine stitches. "That was not a good day," Sterling drily recorded in his journal.

Sterling had been on the phone throughout that day, talking to Johnson's parents, the missionary department in Salt Lake City, and others. He left the hospital at about five o'clock to interview a woman who was about to be baptized, then returned to the hospital. Johnson's swelling was reduced considerably, but one eye was discolored and swollen shut. Satisfied that his missionary was in capable hands, Sterling at last went home.

For the time being, Sterling and Ellie decided that Elder Johnson and Elder Peterson would stay with them at the mission home while

Elder Johnson gained strength. "They are being fed well by Sister Colton," noted Sterling. When Elder Johnson's stitches were removed, the doctor discovered that the cheekbone beneath his right eye was fractured. A plastic surgeon recommended surgery as soon as possible, before the bones had knit together out of alignment.

Elder Johnson was sent home for the surgery and would not be returning. Sterling reasoned that this made sense, since Elder Johnson's two years would end in just one more month. A surgeon performed the successful three-hour operation in Provo.

Christmas can be a lonely time away from home for missionaries. Recognizing this, Ellie did a lot to try to cheer up missionaries for the holidays. For their first Christmas in BC, she and the office staff prepared packets for each missionary, containing letters and pictures from parents, stake presidents, bishops, and others.

Packets were distributed during the eight zone conferences in December. Missionaries were given forty-five minutes in the chapel alone with their letters and thoughts, as Christmas hymns played. Then they were ushered into the cultural hall for a Christmas dinner prepared by the local ward. After dinner they returned to the chapel for a program produced by Ellie and presented by the missionaries.

Carolyn joined her parents for Christmas, and was a great help to Ellie in the preparations. Carolyn and her siblings sent their parents a Christmas tree decorated with little red hearts with the names of the children and grandchildren on them. They also each sent Sterling and Ellie a letter expressing their testimonies—presented to them as a surprise at a zone conference. On Christmas day the Coltons had an open house at the mission home, beautifully decorated by Ellie and Carolyn.

In what little spare time he had, Sterling finished reading the sixth volume of a nine-volume series by Gerald Lund, *The Work and the Glory*. It includes actual and fictional events in the history of the LDS Church, starting from the time of Joseph Smith's first vision of the Father and Son in a grove of trees in 1820.

Sterling and Ellie walked on many mornings, but seldom more than an hour. They also rode the mission's new bikes. When the weather turned ugly they sometimes used a treadmill. Tennis was a measure of how busy they were. Prior to BC, Sterling usually played several mornings a week. They were on their mission almost exactly one year before they played their first set in Canada.

Nearly all of Sterling and Ellie's children and grandchildren visited twice, in mid-summer of 1996 and mid-summer the following year. In the first summer most arrived on a Saturday in July and stayed the first night in the mission home. That meant wall-to-wall bodies on the floor of the three-bedroom home.

The next morning, noted Sterling, the large group taxed the house's hot-water heater for baths and showers. They ate in shifts. Then they all went to church in the Richmond Ward, where they filled two rows. "There was perpetual motion," wrote Sterling. "The little boys are a handful…I have great respect for our daughters-in-law. They are wonderful mothers."

After lunch the family convoyed to Stanley Park, Vancouver's largest urban park, almost entirely surrounded by Vancouver Harbor and English Bay. A special attraction in the park is Canada's largest aquarium.

From there they headed north to Whistler, about eighty miles from Vancouver. Whistler is a forested resort town in the southern Pacific ranges of the Coast Mountains. During the Vancouver 2010 Winter Olympics, Whistler Blackcomb—the largest ski resort in North America—hosted most of the alpine, Nordic, luge, skeleton, and bobsled events.

Whistler has a Residence Inn by Marriott, a lovely hotel with spacious guest suites, indoor-outdoor connecting pool, multiple hot tubs, and fitness center. The Coltons had four adjacent suites. The hotel sits at the base of the Whistler Blackcomb mountains, close to the vibrant village of Whistler, which, at this writing, has been named *Ski Magazine's* No. 1 winter resort in North America, three years running.

The family rode three different chair lifts to get to the top of Blackcomb Mountain. The high region was still snow-covered, with skiers and snowboarders. Rather than ride the lifts all the way down, Sterling and Ellie and eight other family members hiked partway, over mountain meadows and through a forested area. Throughout the day the Coltons saw a variety of animals, including deer, marmots, and several black bears with cubs.

That evening they held a short family home evening, singing "I Am a Child of God," and discussing the importance of families.

Sterling and Ellie returned to Richmond, a drive of about two hours, leaving the others in Whistler. Ellie had a responsibility to prepare dinner and breakfast for a large transfer group of forty-eight missionaries. At midday Thursday she returned to Whistler, followed by Sterling that evening.

During that week the family visited Butchart Gardens, world-class flower gardens on Vancouver Island and, just a short distance from Butchart, the Butterfly Gardens, an indoor kaleidoscope of color created by seventy-five varieties of butterflies.

On Saturday the Coltons split up, some playing tennis and others golf. Family members then headed home.

While Sterling's time and attention as mission president was almost all consumed with missionary work, his pre-mission life periodically required his attention. During the week after the one spent with family, he hosted Kathi Ann Brown, a writer from Virginia who was helping Bill Marriott write a book. At Bill's suggestion, she was interviewing individuals who had the biggest impact on the company.

"I spent six hours in interviews regarding Marriott history," wrote Sterling. "Kathi is a delightful person." The book written by Bill and Kathi was *The Spirit to Serve: Marriott's Way*, published by the company in 1997.

The Colton clan returned to British Columbia a year later, in the summer of 1997. On this trip Sterling and Ellie shared with family members a favorite pastime—bird-watching. With the possible exception of their own backyard in Bethesda, there was no better place to bird watch than at the Reifel Migratory Bird Sanctuary, less than a one-hour drive from Vancouver. Millions of birds find safety and sustenance at the 850-acre wetlands refuge as they migrate south in the winter and north in the summer.

The Coltons also visited Squamish, a valley comprised largely of native people who live on Indian reserves. The community had a tiny LDS branch; eight local members and two missionaries attended. The Coltons added eighteen members—more than double local attendees—and presented the sacrament program. They also taught most of the lessons in other meetings.

Then it was on to Whistler, staying in four adjoining suites at the Residence Inn again. Sterling and Ellie rose early and took a long hike on a beautiful morning. The family ate breakfast together at the hotel, then walked down to the Blackcomb chair lift. Riding to the top of the second lift, they elected to walk rather than ride to the base of the third lift. They rode the third lift to the top of the mountain, for a spectacular view of the valley.

They stopped for lunch at the mid-mountain lodge, seven of them deciding to walk rather than ride the distance of the last lift down. It proved very hard, especially for Ellie, who had already taken a long walk with Sterling that morning, and a second walk from the second to the third lift.

"It was much longer and more difficult than we thought," noted Sterling. "Ellie's knees gave out on her and David and I had to help her down. We were exhausted when we got down."

While Ellie rested her knees at the hotel, the others left to keep a date with some canoes. Jenna, thirteen, and Rebecca, twelve, were Sterling's paddlers, with him seated on the bottom of the middle—where he sat in water much of the way. "We ended up going backward for a good part of the trip," said Sterling, "and hit the bank and bushes many times." By the end of the ride they were paddling straight.

Sterling was stiff and cold by the time they finished. "Next time I will be one of the paddlers," he decided. "I like to be more in control of my own destiny."

On Monday they had a "heritage night" for family home evening. Ellie told the story of her great-grandfather Thomas E. Ricks, who led the colonization of eastern Idaho, including Rexburg, where he founded the educational institution that carried his name for generations—Ricks College—and today is Brigham Young University–Idaho.

Sterling told of his great-grandparents Polly and Philander Colton, expressing thanks he was named after his grandfather and not his great-grandfather. Philander was one of the first volunteers in the U.S. Army's Mormon Battalion, which made one of the longest military marches in history before he and Polly settled in Utah.

Sterling returned to Vancouver while Ellie stayed in Whistler with the family. They had a more restful day on Tuesday, wrote Sterling. On Wednesday family members hiked to a waterfall, then flew through the air on a trapeze—an actual outdoor flying trapeze, connected to a safety harness with a net below. Sterling's last journal entry that day: "I do not like to be without Ellie!"

On Thursday the Coltons in Whistler took a whitewater rafting trip. Sterling rejoined his family in Whistler late Thursday evening, bringing with him one other family member, their grandson Daniel, who he picked up at the Vancouver airport that afternoon.

Friday was for family photos—"a major undertaking," said Sterling. Then he returned to the mission office for an exit interview with Elder Cannon Neslen, the elder who had been trapped in the ice chasm and who was enrolling the following week at the Naval Academy in Annapolis, Maryland.

Saturday afternoon the entire family had yet another outdoor thrill, at Capilano Suspension Bridge Park. Set in a cedar-scented rainforest, the 450-foot-long bridge soars 230 feet above the Capilano River, just minutes from the bustle of downtown Vancouver. That evening, back at the mission home, the family sacked out back-to-back on the floor and slept soundly. Most family members left for home the next day.

Later that summer Sterling and Ellie organized two innovative missionary conferences, one for single sister missionaries and the other for senior couples. Although members of each cohort had a lot in common, they hadn't had an opportunity to get acquainted with each other. Both conferences were very successful.

Sterling and Ellie took a long hike to Blue Lake in the Cascade Range. Sterling stopped for a bit as Ellie went ahead. When he followed, Sterling found she was out of shouting range. "It was getting dark and I was concerned because she didn't seem to hear my calls." Soon they were together again and everything was okay.

Sterling helped introduce another missionary innovation—BC's first member-missionary coordinating council meeting. Presiding was Elder Stephen Pond, an Area Authority Seventy. Also participating were three stake presidents in person and three others by teleconference. They discussed ways to encourage more member involvement in missionary work, for more convert baptisms as well as new-member retention.

At the beginning of the Nanaimo zone conference in November, a young man came to the chapel and said he wanted to learn more about the Church. Sterling invited him to join them. Twenty years earlier, missionaries in Ontario had met his family and left a Book of Mormon. He had read it, along with other LDS scriptures—the Doctrine and Covenants and Pearl of Great Price—and believed they were true.

Sterling learned he was a helicopter pilot and a single parent with a seven-year-old son living with him. At the first break in the conference, a sister missionary obtained a commitment from him to be baptized the following month.

The Coltons' last Christmas celebration in BC began December 5 with a zone conference bringing together three zones—fifty-four missionaries—meeting in the Vancouver Stake. Five elders who would finish their missions before the next zone conference shared their testimonies. Sterling and Ellie gave all of them letters from home, which they read in the chapel as Christmas music played. The Coltons then gifted—from their personal resources—each missionary a T-shirt with "Mountain Top Mission" printed on it.

Carolyn arrived on Christmas Eve, always to her parents' delight. Sterling and Ellie received an enormous number of gifts. Sterling filled a full legal-size page jotting down each giver and gift.

"I love Christmas," said Sterling. "I am grateful for the opportunity to celebrate the Savior's birth and remember all he did for us. It is also a time to remember the birth of Joseph Smith (December 23, 1805)."

As 1998 began, Sterling and Ellie were just a half-year from the end of their mission. For Mother's Day some missionary leaders paid special tribute to Ellie as well as their own mothers in the *Mountain Top Messenger*:

> *To our special Mission Mother. To the Mothers of our birth.*
> *Your constant love and teaching bless our time upon the earth.*
> *Thank you for your fervent prayers. May they never cease.*
> *May knowledge of our grateful hearts bring you daily peace.*
> *'OUR mothers knew it' too. With faith you guide our feet.*
> *Our commission is to Witness. We are Warriors of the Street.*
> *Canada Vancouver Missionaries*

On February 25 the Coltons received a letter from the First Presidency, saying they would be officially released July 1. Replacing them would be Kenneth Young Knight and his wife Nancy, of Salt Lake City.

The new year brought more evidence of Sterling's guilelessness. Criticizing others simply was not in his nature. In March a missionary was "driving too fast...and hit a slick spot, lost control of the car, and ran into a tree," wrote Sterling. "It sounds like the car is totaled, but fortunately neither elder was seriously injured...We are now two cars short in a fleet that is already inadequate." Not a word of condemnation.

Later, Sterling returned from a mission conference to the Vancouver airport. "I found that the back trunk of the Pontiac was damaged. It was a day of mixed blessings," was all he said.

Soon afterward, he began adding a scripture each day to begin his journal entry. The first one was on charity, from Moroni 7:45 in the Book of Mormon, followed the next day by a similar one from the Bible, I Corinthians 13:4, 8: "Charity suffereth long, and is kind; charity envieth not; charity vaunteth not itself, is not puffed up,... Charity never faileth."

Sterling and Ellie spoke at a series of stake conferences, continuing to urge members to assist missionaries in increasing the number of convert baptisms and help ensure that new members felt welcome and remained active.

In preparing to leave Canada, the Coltons purchased a 1997 Cadillac Seville with about 1,000 kilometers (600 miles) on it. They bought it in Richmond for about half what it would have cost in the U.S., and had to get it to Bremerton, Washington to have it shipped home.

Sterling drove a mission car and Ellie the Cadillac to Bremerton. On the way Ellie passed Sterling, whose car quickly became a distant dot in her rear-view mirror. When she got to the U.S. border, Ellie wondered what was taking Sterling so long.

When he pulled up he was sputtering, in a most un-Sterling-like manner. She didn't know that he had the speedometer changed from kilometers to miles. Ellie had been driving 120 miles an hour.

The Coltons had hoped to reach a level of fifty convert baptisms a month. They fell a little short, but were on a strong upswing in their final months. From January through May of 1998 there were 218 convert baptisms—45 percent more than during the same period the previous year.[3]

The mission had excellent success in retaining new converts. "We had the highest retention rate (82%) of the nine missions in the North America Northwest Area for the first quarter of 1998," Sterling reported.

"We have tried to have each missionary develop a strong personal relationship with the Savior by meaningful daily individual and companionship prayers; daily individual and companionship scripture study; striving to develop Christ-like attributes by following His example in serving others; and always being worthy to have the companionship of the Spirit and learning how to hear and heed His promptings."

Sterling also wrote that "Our mission has been a great blessing for our family. As Sister Colton and I have worked together in the service of the Lord our relationship has grown deeper and more meaningful than ever before. She has been a great support and strength to me."

As the Coltons prepared to return to the U.S., missionaries in one zone presented Ellie with a bouquet of roses. Missionaries also gave them a scrapbook with photos of elders and sisters along with farewell letters. It explained that "we put together this book to let you know just how much your examples have touched our lives…You will never be forgotten!! We love you!!"

Years later, a former LDS colleague of Sterling's at Marriott, Steve West, who also became a mission president, was traveling in British Columbia. "I would say to church members, 'Did you ever know Sterling Colton?'" recalled West. "They'd say 'Oh yes, I knew Sterling.' There was a lot of respect for Sterling that I got to hear."[4]

Sterling prepared a thorough briefing book for the Knights, and Ellie filled the mission home with beautiful flower arrangements. The Coltons stayed their last night in a new Marriott hotel in Richmond. "It was an emotional time," said Sterling, "particularly saying goodbye to our missionaries." This was Sterling's final journal entry in British Columbia, on June 30, 1998:

> We had dinner at the Prow. It was a glorious evening and the food was good. We had the Knights drop us off at the Richmond Marriott. We had very mixed emotions as we gave them the keys and said goodbye. We will miss the missionaries and the work. There is nothing like it. But there was also the feeling of satisfaction that we had done our very best and that to a large extent we had accomplished what we were sent forth to do. It was definitely a high point in our lives…I could never have done it without Ellie. We will never be the same.

38

HOME SWEET HOME

On July 1, 1998 the Coltons rose at 4:30 a.m. and took a shuttle bus from the Richmond Marriott to the airport. The flight home seemed "surreal" to Sterling after three years of being immersed in missionary work, during which he never left the environs of British Columbia.

A joyous greeting awaited them at the airport in Washington, D.C. There with signs and hugs were Carolyn, Brad, Melanie, Rebecca, Scott, Jane, and Thomas. They caravanned home to Bethesda, finding that their family and neighbors on Greentree Road had hung "Welcome Home" signs all over the house. Brad, Melanie, and Carolyn had mowed the lawn and set flowers all around.

Within a few days of arriving home, Sterling accompanied his three sons to a 6 a.m. session in the Washington D.C. Temple. They had to arrive in time to change into all-white clothing for the two-hour ceremony.

"It was very good to be with the three of them in the Lord's house," said Sterling. "They are good men. I am very proud of them."

Eleven days after arriving home, they reported their mission to their congregation in Potomac South Ward. As at their mission farewell three years earlier, Coltons again filled two rows of pews.

"Quite a few years ago," said Ellie, "I was asked to give a talk on Mother's Day about my mother. On the way to church I said to my family that I hope I don't cry, and Carolyn said, 'Is the sky blue?'"

"You know you never really leave a place you love, you take part of it with you and you leave part of it behind," said Ellie. "And we felt your love and your prayers for the three years, and want to thank you for your love and your support…while we were away, and for making us feel so welcome to be back."

She thanked their children and grandchildren "for their prayers and for their letters, their phone calls, their flowers, their visits, and for all the wonderful drawings and photos that kept our refrigerator well-decorated for every season."

Ellie also thanked teachers, scout leaders, and other LDS leaders of children and youth for preparing the kind of young missionaries they grew to love in British Columbia. "You are doing a superb job. We were just amazed as these young people came into the mission field…with their knowledge of the scriptures and their dedication to serve a mission. We had many missionaries who sacrificed a great deal to earn money for their missions."

Ellie said one elder "worked a year in a very dangerous job in a mine that almost ruined his lungs to pay his own way on his mission. Another worked high on an offshore oil rig in Texas to pay for his mission. And why? Because he had a great desire to share with everyone who was willing to hear of the great gift of the atonement of Jesus Christ, that the gospel has been restored, and that there is a prophet on the earth today.

"We saw and heard monthly miracles as we watched. Many of our missionaries come in timid and insecure and two years later leave confident of themselves and of their teaching skills. They learned about their Savior's love not only for them but for all His children, and we all marveled together at new converts who totally changed their way of life, grateful for the blessings of the gospel, and we saw and watched them become happier and better people." She continued:

> In our mission we all felt close to our Savior because we were trying so hard to serve Him. And He was in our thoughts, and in our hearts. And we came to know Him better. Our scriptures became very precious to us because they gave an affirmation of the divinity of our Heavenly Father and His Son Jesus Christ…if I were to choose some of the most profound lessons I learned personally, one would be that I learned to appreciate and discern the presence of

the Holy Ghost and the promptings of the Spirit in testifying of divine truth...

Jesus said I am the light and life of the world...hold up your light that it may shine unto the world. Behold I am the light which ye shall hold up...We hold up that light when we witness to the truthfulness of the gospel. We hold up that light with our acts of service and thoughtful behavior...

And I thank the Lord for the great privilege of serving this mission with my eternal companion. I love watching him in his straightforward, loving way inspire those that he was in charge of. I loved hearing him share his testimony many times a month, and I loved our long, beautiful drives over high mountain passes, past lakes, along great rivers, and marveling at the beautiful world God has created for us. I thank my Heavenly Father and His son Jesus Christ for the health and safety of our family...and for friends who lift, inspire, give us comfort and courage, to have a good laugh with and to love and be loved.....I am thankful for life itself.

Sterling said, "We're so grateful for the opportunity that we've had...as representatives of the Lord Jesus Christ, to bear His name over our hearts, to be able to testify of Him daily. As we have done so our relationship with the Savior has become deeper and more meaningful than it ever has been before. He's answered our prayers and we have felt His presence and love as we've strived in our feeble way to walk in the steps of our Savior and to assist Him and our Father in their great work...

"I know that God lives. He is our Father. We're made in His image. We are His children and He knows us. He wants us to come home and has given us a plan that will enable us to return. Jesus is the Christ, our Savior and Redeemer. He loves us and at great personal sacrifice through the Atonement made it possible for us to overcome the bonds of physical death and sin, returning to our Father in Heaven."

Sterling also spoke directly to non-LDS friends in the congregation.

"I hope that you feel the Spirit that is here, and you'll open your hearts to the message that these wonderful sisters and elders have to offer. There's nothing of greater worth...Everyone will be resurrected and freed from the bonds of physical death that prevent us from returning to our Heavenly Father.

"He also gave us the opportunity for eternal life, the opportunity to return and live in the presence of our Father in Heaven...This gift too is universal but yet conditional...Available only to those who respond to the Savior's invitation to come follow me."

Sterling added that "Knowledge alone cannot save us...In addition we must develop the virtues of love, mercy, meekness, and patience, which were so well exemplified by the Savior...Discipleship requires translation of doctrines, covenants, ordinances, and teachings into improved personal behavior."

Speaking of their mission experience, Sterling said, "We love our missionaries. We feel that our family has been extended by over 600 young men and women, senior couples and senior sisters. They have touched our lives and will always have a place in our hearts."

Two returned BC missionaries who had been assistants to Sterling were in the congregation—Cannon Neslen and Tom Hawes. Sterling asked them to stand.

"Elder Hawes' hair has grown a little bit since...I think it's those barbers up in Connecticut. Elder, we're going to have to take you down and introduce you to Elder Neslen's barber in Annapolis.

"You know it's easy to be a mission president. All you have to do is pick the right companion, call the right assistants, and then sit back and watch the work happen. These two great young men, they are the Lord's elect. They've been saved for this time when the gospel is spreading across the face of the earth. They've been refined and trained in the mission field. They are ready for leadership in the Kingdom...The Kingdom is in good hands."

On March 5, 1999, eight months after their return, the Coltons were asked to speak on the campus of Snow College, a public two-year institution in Ephraim, Utah, where they addressed a large audience of mostly LDS students.

In her remarks, Ellie encouraged the students to discover their God-given gifts and develop them. "The value of what you have to contribute will come through the expression of your own personality, and that particular spark of the divine that makes you unique, setting you off from every other living creature…The mark you leave on the world, on the hearts and minds of others, is just as distinct as your thumbprint or your DNA."

"We are here to experience joy," said Ellie. "God created us in His image, and said that His greatest work was to bring to pass the immortality and eternal life of man. He created each one of us with multiple talents, and we are here to discover ourselves, to discover the richness that God created in us. We can do this by taking time to get to know others, what they're thinking."

Ellie had seen much of the world with Sterling, and valued what she learned. "Develop relationships not only with people but with places and ideas. It's so wonderful, we never stop growing…Even when you get to be an old gray-haired lady you keep learning new things. The world is more interesting the more we understand and know of others and places."

She referenced a report on happiness by two psychologists, based on a decade of scientific study involving hundreds of thousands of people around the world.

"They discovered that many myths people have about what makes us happy just don't hold up. The idea that being rich, famous and beautiful, for example, turns out to be wrong…What makes people happy? These researchers say it boils down to faith, hope, attitude, friends, and family."

The chief limitations to happiness, said Ellie, "are not age or sex or race or money. They are laziness, shortsightedness, and lack of self-esteem. Self-esteem and spirituality are the temporal expressions of our eternal capacity to love all things, including ourselves, for love is the highest level of human functioning."

"We cannot change our past," noted Ellie, "we cannot change the fact that people will act in a certain way. We cannot change the inevitable; the only thing we can do is to play on the one string we have, and that's our attitude. So I say to you, face your problems. Don't run from them. Everybody has problems...but as you face them and trust the Lord to help you, He will."

Sterling followed, beginning with what he often had said to their children: "Isn't she wonderful?! If there's any advice I can give you elders here today, it is to pick the right companion. It makes all the difference. I'm glad that she wasn't very picky, and she married the first boy she met when she went to college, even though he was just a farm boy from Vernal. She's made all the difference in my life."

"As a mission president you grow to love your missionaries. They become part of your family." Sterling introduced four elders and two sisters who served with him in British Columbia.

"You elders, I want you to stand up. You sisters, I want you to look at these elders. Now they're available! When they left the mission field I told them that the most important thing for them to do was to find that eternal companion—to not rush into it...but they need to get after it, so identify who they are and you go up and say hello to them after this meeting. A year from now I don't want to see them here alone."

That, however, should be their second priority, said Sterling. Their first priority should be gaining and strengthening a testimony of God the Father and His son Jesus Christ. "If you've got that relationship with your Father in Heaven and your Savior, you can overcome everything that the world might throw at you."

Heavenly Father "knows each one of you. He knows you by name, just as He called Joseph Smith by name, just as He called Paul on the road to Damascus by name, He knows each one of you. He loves you, He wants you to come home. That's His work and His glory, that each of you may return home.

"Jesus is the Christ. He's real. I know Him. I love Him. He's been at my side when I've needed Him—when our children were born, when I served as a bishop or elders quorum president, when I worked as a sealer in the temple and performed those ordinances which bring salvation doing His work. As I labored in the mission field with these wonderful elders and sisters, He was there."

"The Savior loves you and we love you," said Sterling.

Missionaries who served under Sterling and Ellie loved them back, and the Coltons' influence continued to be reflected in their lives. Sister Sid Oakes, who served in the mission office with her husband Don, wrote several small notes to Ellie after the Coltons left the mission. "Our memories of you are so precious," she wrote in one note. "We constantly use those things we learned from the two of you.

"Sister Colton, many times I see the Elders and Sisters do things regarding their manners that you taught them. It is so gratifying…You are always loved and remembered. I hear the echo and whisper of your days here daily through the Elders and Sisters."[1]

The Coltons' powerful impact on the elders and sisters was still evident decades later. On Ellie's personal Facebook page are warm greetings through the years from scores of former missionaries.

A sampling:

"Happy early Birthday to an amazing lady! We love you. XO."

"You are a wonderful soul."

"Happy Birthday!!!! I'm so glad you were born before me because you have been a great role model for me."

"Sister President!! Happy Happy Joy Joy missssses you! I'm happy we can keep in touch on facebook…Love ya both!"

"And I thought my mother was the only great-grandmother on Facebook."

"I recently saw the Pixar movie UP. If you haven't seen it its about an adventurous older couple and the wife was named Ellie. The movie reminded me of you."

The missionaries revered Sterling; they laughed with and loved Ellie. "President Colton was Cool, but Sister Colton was cooler," wrote Kenney Higley, one of the elders in the Language Zone. "I always remember the way she would teach proper manners to us. We had some good laughs. They were good sports about it too, realizing every culture is different and Vancouver, Canada was nothing less than a lot of culture."[2]

A former sister missionary who sent Ellie birthday greetings also benefitted from her manners lessons, adding this note: "I'm still eating with my mouth closed!"

Sister Mary Jones served in the BC mission after the death of her husband. "I was called as a proselyting missionary but worked in the mission office more than six months," she said. Mary sorted referrals—names, usually from members, of non-Mormons who may be receptive to meeting with missionaries—and inspected missionary cars and apartments. She also helped Ellie prepare meals.[3]

"When I think of Ellie, I think of how much fun she was. We were the party girls, always putting on dinners for missionaries."

Krista Smith (later Worth) wondered, "What would we have done without Sister Colton? Our mission mom always had a kind word or a needed hug. She was a mom to us all but had a special way of helping the elders as they learned about mission life and life itself. I will always be grateful I had the blessing of being under their wings."[4]

"I came into the mission with some background trials," said Annette Esplin. "My bishop called and talked to President Colton. He took me under his wing the minute I got there...He was like a dad, would check on me constantly. He represented the Savior's life to a T, someone who loves and cares for his kids. Stalwart.

"Not only a father, a leader true to the gospel. You could see in his eyes he had a testimony of the Savior. He had a lot of compassion in his voice when he talked to you. I admired him for the love he showed missionaries who struggled...You come across bishops, stake presidents sometimes who touch you. I had a bishop who taught me a lot. President Colton was another one of those men I truly say I loved. When people mention him, I get that really good feeling that I knew them."

Krista Smith said, "I was just reading through my mission journal the other day and an interview I had with President Colton. I was wondering like most missionaries: Am I really making a difference? He said 'Sister Smith, you do not realize the difference you made. We have given you some special assignments because we knew you would do well.' That made all the difference to me as I sat across from that gentle man. It seemed time and time again like I was speaking to my Savior."

Tom Hawes, one of Sterling's two assistants for six months, said, "President Colton was so eager to serve his missionaries. He was tender-hearted, and loved each of us. I saw him pray for hours over a good number of missionaries struggling with various things. He really desired that everyone feel included and loved, and leave the mission field with a strong testimony of the Savior and a deep understanding of the atonement."[5]

The BC mission had an incentive program called Mountain Top Missionary. It was a program encouraging missionaries to memorize scriptures and discussions used for teaching. Such efforts helped prepare Tom for life after the mission. "I learned to be diligent, focused, and committed to something—also to plan and set goals, and to be accountable for all the time in my schedule."

Sterling's exit interviews were upbeat and practical. "He always asked what he could do better as a mission president," said Annette Esplin. "He talked to me about coming home and marrying, like a conversation with my dad. President Colton said that, when I looked for my soul mate, 'You'd better be in love mentally, physically, and spiritually. If not, don't marry him.'"

There were two other standard themes in Sterling's exit interviews: Find something you enjoy doing, and become the best at it. Don't make your homecoming talk a travelogue.

The Coltons continued to stay in touch with their missionaries after leaving British Columbia. In March 1999 they hosted thirty of their young returned sister missionaries for dinner at their condo in Park City. Sterling had a long private talk with one sister who was suffering from depression.

Tom Hawes has earned multiple degrees, and Sterling wrote letters of recommendation as part of his applications. Sterling also married and sealed Tom and his wife Andrea in the Washington D.C. Temple in August 1999, and later sealed Andrea's parents.

Andrew Shirley served an internship in Washington, D.C. after his mission. "After landing the internship, I called the Coltons to ask their advice on where I should stay back there. Sterling said 'Why don't you stay with us.'" Andrew lived with them for four months.

Andrew was slated to be the starting safety on the Ricks College football team. In August 1999 the Coltons went to Rexburg, Idaho and watched a scrimmage.

David Williams also served an internship in Washington. During his time in the capital he also visited the Coltons.

Cannon Neslen repeatedly interacted with the Coltons. In December 1998 the Coltons drove to Annapolis, with Carolyn and granddaughter Rebecca, for a Messiah concert featuring the Naval Academy Chorus. Neslen provided the tickets.

Neslen came to dinner at the Coltons' in January, and stayed overnight. The following month, he returned, and Sterling took him to Bill and Donna Marriotts' house to see Bill's stunning collection of twenty or so Ferraris and other exotic cars. Neslen dropped by with friends on occasion as well, and the Coltons attended his graduation from the Naval Academy.

The day after Christmas in 2009 Sterling and Ellie sent this message to their missionaries on the mission Facebook page: "Happy New Year to all you wonderful Canada Vancouver missionaries. How exciting that the Vancouver Temple will be dedicated this year! We love all of our happy memories of you all! Keep the commandments and remember who you are and what you can become!"

Marvin Gregory Miller, also writing on the mission Facebook page, recalled when the Coltons had all the BC missionaries read chapter five of Alma in the Book of Mormon, which includes what Ellie called the "spiritual inventory checklist."

Miller wrote, "How in tune with the Spirit President Colton was in helping Missionaries in their own spiritual life, along with helping investigators. What a glorious thing it was to serve a Mission and what a blessing it was to have President and Sister Colton as our Leaders!"

39

SAFARI IN SOUTHERN AFRICA

The America Sterling and Ellie returned to was more troubled than the one they left. Global terrorism was on the rise. On August 7, 1998 the U.S. Embassies in Dar es Salaam, Tanzania, and Nairobi, Kenya were bombed, killing 224 people and injuring more than 4,500.

Thirteen days later the Pentagon launched cruise missiles against alleged al-Qaeda camps in Afghanistan and a suspected chemical plant in Sudan, destroying the plant. Sterling wrote: "I agree wholeheartedly that we cannot tolerate terrorism. I only hope they correctly targeted the responsible parties."

During the months since returning from British Columbia, Sterling and Ellie volunteered time to the Potomac South Ward, Sterling teaching a group of teenagers. He also "split" with Mormon missionaries in their area, meaning he met with potential converts with one full-time missionary while another lay member proselyted with the missionary's companion.

Sterling was sixty-nine; Ellie sixty-seven in 1998. They resumed playing tennis, Sterling on the court several times a week at 6 a.m. He almost always played doubles, less strenuous than singles because a player has only half as much court to cover. When he wasn't playing doubles, sometimes he and Ellie played each other. Occasionally he also played what he called "Canadian doubles," in which one player competes against two players, and the players rotate positions following each set.

The Coltons had a new couple they were playing tennis with, Jim and Dolly Pickerell; Ellie especially played often with Dolly. Although the Coltons walked as well, they felt a need for more rigorous exercise to fight the onslaught of old age. Doing so in a gym, however, would have taken more time than they wanted to give it.

Fred Daniels provided the solution. His mobile thirty-two-foot trailer, filled with custom exercise equipment, was at the service of individuals in the Washington area. At 9 a.m. on October 30, 1998, Daniels' Ford F-450 pickup pulled the trailer to the curb outside 8005 Greentree Road.

Sterling and Ellie emerged, dressed in sweats, for the first session in what they would come to call the "torture chamber." For most of the next two decades Daniels led the Coltons in physical fitness sessions twice a week, from 9 to 10 a.m.

"They just went for it," said Daniels. "I don't think they have another speed." His equipment offered aerobics as well as weight-training. It included bikes, rowers, a Stairmaster, a stretch cage, cross-trainer, free weights, and a rotary torso machine.[1]

The Coltons continued to enjoy working in their yard, and now had more time to do so. Sterling was his usual benevolent self. Their backyard was dedicated to birds, yet pesky squirrels kept showing up and eating the bird seed. The simple solution would have been to shoot the squirrels with a BB or pellet gun. Instead, Sterling trapped and relocated them. Wrote Sterling, "We continue to trap and relocate squirrels. I moved another 5 today. I believe that is 14 over the past few days." The Coltons also oversaw construction of a major renovation to their home, updating the master bedroom and bathroom.

In the summer of 1998, "Mulan," an animated musical-action-comedy-drama by Disney, became the first film they had seen in three years. They flew to London in August and saw a live performance of "Miss Saigon." Sterling's assessment: "I wouldn't recommend it for missionaries, but after the first half-hour it did have a powerful message."

Sterling also watched football and basketball games on television, especially if a team was from one of his alma maters, the University of Utah or Stanford, or from BYU. Otherwise fairly consistent about his bedtime, he was known to stay up late for a good game.

In March 1999 Sterling and Ellie were called and set apart to assist with sacred ordinances in the Washington D.C. Temple. Sterling was also reinstated as a sealer, a position he held prior to their mission.

On May 27, 1999 Sterling and Ellie left for an adventure in Africa with their good friends Frank and Sally Johnson. It was an ideal pairing. Frank was an astute thinker and writer on global politics, and Sally was as gracious as Ellie.

The foursome flew through Britain to Zimbabwe in southern Africa. They spent the first night at the Wild Game Lodge, a delightful facility with just twenty-two beds, on the outskirts of the capital, Harare. Each guest room overlooked the beautiful rolling hills of a private game preserve. On a nearby pond were Egyptian geese.

There are more than 1,000 species of mammals in Africa and over 2,500 species of birds. The "big five" animals are the lion, elephant, Cape buffalo, leopard, and rhinoceros. The two couples saw all of the big five repeatedly, along with many other animals and birds. They would stay at a variety of camps in the heart of African game country and go on frequent safaris during the three weeks.

In mid-morning of their first full day, they flew an hour, from Harare to spectacular Victoria Falls. The Falls, twice as high as Niagara and half again as wide, are on the Zambezi River at the border of Zimbabwe and Zambia. A second flight in a six-passenger Cessna ended at a landing strip where a van transported them to Makalolo Plains Camp in Hwange National Park, Zimbabwe's largest game park.

Accommodations were self-contained tents, two comfortable beds to a tent, which was also equipped with a toilet and solar-heated water for showers.

From the camp, nestled in a tree line between the forest and a waterhole, they watched a Noah's Ark parade of animals come to drink: elephants, Cape buffalo, giraffes, zebras, wildebeest, lions, cheetahs, and sable antelope. Later, among others, they also saw baboons, eland, hippopotamuses, hyenas, impalas, jackals, warthogs, and wildcats.

The daily agenda: wake-up call at 6 a.m., light breakfast 6:30, game rides or walks 7 - 10:30, large brunch 10:30 - 11:30, game walks or rides 12 - 1:30 (especially for those who chose not to awaken early), tea and snacks 2:30, game rides 3 - 7:30 (usually with spotlights). Back to camp for a fabulous dinner around 8 p.m., then visiting around the campfire until bedtime.

On May 30 they arrived at Mahalo Plains Tented Camp in South Africa's Kruger National Park. "Sunset was magnificent," wrote Sterling, "with a herd of elephants and numbers of giraffes silhouetted against a bright red sky, highlighted with palm, mahogany, and acacia trees. What a day!" They also found the daytime sky bluer than they had experienced and, in the night sky, with little light to obscure, the stars were brilliant and constellations distinct.

But sleep was difficult that night. A herd of elephants, harassed by hyenas, was trumpeting, and baboons in the trees above their tents made a racket all night long. Lions roared in the distance. Ellie unfortunately had a sore throat and laryngitis as well.

"We flew from camp to camp," wrote Ellie in a journal. "At one camp we watched a mother cheetah and three grown siblings try to catch a warthog, which was using a thorn tree to protect itself. After dark we were especially amused by the hippos. When the searchlight would focus on them, they would turn around and 'moon' us.

"In another camp we were on an early morning ride and stopped on what we didn't realize was near a warthog hole. We watched as a leopard sat very still right by us. When the warthogs came rushing out of their hole the leopard immediately grabbed one by the neck and instantly killed it. He then dragged it into some bushes, had his breakfast, then came out with a bloody mouth and looked at us as if to say, 'Okay, now you have seen how it is done. Move on!'"

On another day, wrote Ellie, "we came upon wild dogs and spent about three hours, fascinated by their behavior. The Alpha male rules, while the Alpha female is protected by guard dogs at all times. Only one female produces the young, the rest search with the males for food."

A van transported them into Botswana and the Chobe Game Reserve. Their quarters were a beautiful Mediterranean villa-style lodge overlooking the Chobe River. Boat-riding that evening, they saw numerous elephants at bath and play, along with hippos and crocodiles.

They were up at 5:30 the next morning and went by Land Rover to find game, seeing their first lion pride, eight to ten adults with cubs, resting after stuffing themselves with a nighttime kill. White-backed hooded vultures were now picking apart the remaining scraps on the carcass. Returning to the lodge, they ate a big breakfast, shared with a baboon that darted into the dining room, grabbed a roll, and scampered out.

One morning they tracked a pride of seven lions as the lions stalked a herd of Cape buffalo. "The lions had great respect for the buffalo," said Sterling. "The old bulls would get the females and young ones together, then the bulls would face the lions. The pride made one run at the herd and soon we saw lions chasing buffalo and buffalo chasing lions. The lions had an old bull isolated, but they were not willing to take him down."

They watched a similar chase by two male cheetahs—the fastest land animal, which has been clocked at 75 mph. "They had an impala isolated," recalled Sterling. "The impala ran directly at a thorn thicket and at the last moment turned sharply. The cheetahs didn't turn and ran into the thicket, while the impala got away."

The group crossed from Botswana back into Zimbabwe, ending up at the Victoria Falls Hotel. Sterling, who had seen hundreds if not thousands of hotels as general counsel at Marriott, had special praise for this one, built in the early 1900s.

"It would be impossible to duplicate it and its setting today," wrote Sterling. "The colonial architecture, elegance, spacious terrace, and gardens overlooking Victoria Falls and bridge are impressive." The hotel had 139 rooms, a swimming pool, and tennis court. They dined on wild game including ostrich, eland, and—the tastiest—warthog.

The next morning Sterling and Ellie rode a helicopter over Victoria Falls, one of the seven natural wonders of the world. Then they rode elephants for two hours. Sterling's was named Jumbo and Ellie's fittingly was Miss Ellie.

They flew to the Matusadona Game Reserve near the southern shore of Lake Kariba, the world's largest man-made lake and reservoir. At the lodge each couple had their own floating houseboat and canoe. Guests could paddle over or take a houseboat to the dining and lounge areas. There were an estimated one million crocodiles in or around the lake. After an evening boat ride to see animals, they returned to a dinner of roast pork.

"The gentle rocking of our room," said Sterling, "accompanied by bird calls and the snorting and grunting of the hippos, enabled us to have a very restful evening."

Next they went to a camp called Chikwanga on the Zambezi River. Ellie discovered feathers from a guinea fowl that had been some animal's dinner or breakfast, and arranged them artistically on her hat.

Ellie described a heart-stopping few minutes. One night while watching the sunset on the banks of the Zambezi River, "a large male elephant charged us." The tusker was at least twice as heavy as their Land Rover.

"Our guide James started banging on the side of the Land Rover to send him away. Then James made the mistake of getting out of the van for a picture and the elephant turned around and charged again, to about fifteen feet from us. After the third attempt to charge us, he stomped into the river and crossed to the other side."

A special bonus on this trip for the Coltons was identifying more than 180 different kinds of birds.

After three weeks in Africa, the Coltons and the Johnsons departed for the U.S., landing at Dulles Airport outside Washington and arriving home in the early evening of June 18, 1999.

On July 2 Sterling received a phone call from Gordon B. Hinckley, President of the LDS Church. The Prophet asked if Sterling felt rested since completing his three-year assignment as president of the Canada Vancouver Mission a year earlier, and if he was in good health.

Sterling answered yes to both questions. President Hinckley then asked if Sterling would serve as president of the Washington D.C. Temple. "I told him that I felt very inadequate, but would do my best at whatever President Hinckley asked of me."

Serving as a temple president—like a mission president—also depended on the acceptance of a calling by the president's wife, who in this case would become temple matron. Ellie was at a luncheon when President Hinckley called, and not at home to speak with him. President

Hinckley said he had a busy schedule in the following days, and asked Sterling to have Ellie call him on July 13.

Soon after President Hinckley's initial call, the Coltons left for an extended vacation and Ricks Family reunion with their children and grandchildren, in southeastern Idaho and the Jackson Hole, Wyoming region.

As Ellie waited for July 13 to arrive, the family enjoyed all kinds of outdoor adventure. One morning Sterling and Ellie, along with their children and grandchildren, filled two large rafts for a float on the Snake River. That afternoon the family drove to Jenny Lake in Grand Teton National Park, had a picnic, then took a boat across the lake where they hiked Hidden Falls Trail.

On July 13, in Coulter Bay, Wyoming, Sterling and Ellie left the group briefly to telephone President Hinckley from an outside pay phone. He officially extended calls as temple president and matron. "President Hinckley called me to be the matron of the temple," wrote Ellie in a journal. "I explained to him that I had a severe hearing loss which might be a problem. He replied, 'Do you wear a hearing aid?' When I said I did, he said, 'Well, can't you turn it up?'" She agreed she could.

That evening the family stayed in Jackson Lake Lodge. Early the next morning, July 14, they went to the stables and mounted horses for a ride through the scenic countryside. The next day they caravanned through Yellowstone National Park, seeing elk, bison, deer, and a coyote. They watched Old Faithful erupt, as it had done for ages, spewing thousands of gallons of boiling water more than a hundred feet into the air.

On July 17 the Colton family rose early, headed for Rexburg and the Ricks Family reunion. Sterling, as he was wont to do, took a "shortcut" over a dirt road. They got lost on the way, arriving forty-five minutes later than if they had remained on the highway.

The Ricks Family reunion was an all-day affair. The descendents of Orson and Margaret Archibald Ricks, Ellie's grandparents, gathered first at the Rexburg cemetery to find and photograph grave markers. Then they drove to the Ricks College pavilion for a family gathering and lunch, organized by Ellie's brother Lloyd. Ellie saw cousins she hadn't seen in years. Afterward, some families, including Sterling and Ellie's, drove to nearby Heise Hot Springs and swam.

Sterling and Ellie had invited their older grandchildren to join them for more adventure following the reunion. Along with Daniel, Mauri, Rebecca, Scott, and Michael Falater, a friend of the family, Sterling and Ellie drove to Stanley, Idaho for a whitewater expedition.

The Middle Fork of the Salmon River is legendary among whitewater rivers of the world. Its clear, pure water free-flows for a hundred miles, dropping 3,000 feet through the River of No Return Wilderness. Rafting the river is a major enterprise in the region. It was a beehive of activity while the Coltons were there.

A guide service called River Rats transported the Coltons to Salmon, Idaho, the put-in point on the river, about an hour and a half drive from Stanley. Two couples from Michigan were added to the Colton party for the journey down the river, which took place in three large and one small rubber rafts. They all took turns paddling. Four guides from River Rats went with them, one in each raft. They had a fun time along the way, playfully splashing those in the other rafts.

The Coltons were on the river five days, stopping at scenic spots for lunch and other breaks. The guides cooked all the meals. The rafting party slept in tents which they assembled each evening and took down each morning. Sterling called the whitewater excursion "the trip of a lifetime."

On Saturday morning, July 25, 1999, they were up early and off to Park City, Utah, via Ellie's home town of Idaho Falls.

40

President, Matron of Washington D.C. Temple

Since its opening in 1974, the Washington D.C. Temple had become a familiar landmark in the capital area. Radio traffic reports routinely referenced the temple in describing traffic patterns on that portion of I-495, the Capital Beltway. Approaching the temple driving west on the beltway, one cannot help but be stirred by the tall white edifice suddenly looming straight ahead above the tree line.

It is the Church's tallest temple, with a spire rising 288 feet, and has the third-largest floor space at 160,000 square feet. Nearby is a well-appointed visitors' center. The temple, encased in white Alabama marble, was dedicated in 1974 and closed to the general public after an open house period that attracted more than 750,000 visitors.

To be admitted to an LDS temple, a Latter-day Saint must be living the commandments, as verified by a bishop or branch president, plus a stake or district president. A recommend is issued, signed by ecclesiastical leaders.

Sterling's first major responsibility as temple president was to select two counselors. After prayerful reflection he recommended two men he didn't know personally but who were highly regarded by other church leaders.

Ed Scholz, a native of Germany who retired from the U.S. Air Force as a full colonel and who had a consulting business, was named First Counselor. Charles (Chuck) Eckery, a retired businessman who had served as a temple missionary, was named Second Counselor. Their wives, Lois Scholz and Marlene Eckery, were called as assistant matrons to Ellie.

In October Sterling and Ellie traveled to Church headquarters for several days of training with other new temple presidents and matrons. On the twelfth of that month, President Hinckley invited the Coltons into his office, where he set them apart for their new callings. "We were able to spend a half hour with him," said Sterling. "It was a very sacred and spiritual experience. To have the hands of a prophet of God upon your head and set you apart to do the Lord's work is very very special."

President Hinckley, assisted by Sterling, then set Ellie apart as matron. "He gave Ellie a special blessing that her hearing will be adequate to enable her to perform her responsibilities. After, he took both of us in his arms. It was a very emotional and spiritual experience for both of us."

On November 1, 1999 Sterling and Ellie began three years of full-time service as temple president and matron. They met with the Executive Committee that day in what would be a weekly meeting. Sterling set apart Richard Wildrick as acting First Counselor until Ed Scholz's prior commitments would enable him to join them; and Chuck Eckery as Second Counselor.

Then Elder Wildrick set apart his wife Ruth Wildrick as acting assistant matron, and Elder Eckery did the same for his wife Marlene. Others on the Executive Committee were David Wright, temple recorder; John Lang, assistant recorder; and Luis Alvarez, temple engineer.

A special bonus for the Coltons was that their dear friends Dave and Carol Salisbury had been called to direct the Temple Visitors' Center. The two couples would collaborate and enjoy each other's company.

The Washington D.C. Temple was the first LDS temple built in the United States east of the Mississippi River since 1846. At the time of completion in 1974 the temple was designated to serve members in an enormous geographic district: 31 states and the District of Columbia, seven Canadian provinces, Cuba, Haiti, Puerto Rico, the Bahamas, and the Dominican Republic.

The temple was the 18th constructed and 16th operating temple when it was completed. The Church later embarked on a massive temple-building program, building many smaller, less-expensive temples. By 2017 there were 155 operating temples and 27 others under construction or announced. When Sterling and Ellie served as president and matron, the Washington D.C. Temple district included sixty-eight stakes from Maine to Virginia.

Mormons believe the most important covenants—promises—between men and women and God are made in temples. Faithful members go to the temple the first time to make covenants with God for themselves. Afterward, each time they go to the temple it is to make vicarious covenants with God for a deceased individual. Such individuals, in the spirit world, have a choice of whether or not to accept the covenants made in their name.

A primary responsibility of church members is to learn who their ancestors were on earth and to participate in covenant-making ordinances in the temple on behalf of their ancestors. A temple has sacred spaces designated for these ordinances.

On the lowest level is a baptistry. Faithful members as young as twelve may participate in the ordinance of baptism and be baptized by immersion on behalf of deceased ancestors.

Another temple ordinance is the "endowment." As part of this ordinance, individuals are taught about the purpose of life, the mission and atonement of Jesus Christ, and Heavenly Father's plan for his children. In the peaceful, uplifting atmosphere of the temple, individuals gain a glimpse of what it will be like to live in the presence of our Heavenly Father.

The highest ordinance, essential for living as couples and families in God's presence, is the "sealing" ordinance. Husbands and wives are sealed or married to each other for eternity. In addition, children are sealed for eternity to their parents. By being sealed, families have the assurance of being together eternally if they faithfully keep the covenants they've made in the temple.

The Washington D.C. Temple has more of these sacred ordinance rooms than most temples. It has a baptistry, six rooms for endowments and fourteen rooms for sealing. Each sealing room has an altar, around which individuals kneel as a specially authorized priesthood-holder performs the sealing ceremony.

Sterling and Ellie worked twelve-hour temple shifts, from Tuesday to Saturday. On their assigned days, the Coltons typically arrived at the temple by 5:45 a.m. At 6:30 they gathered with the first shift of temple workers for a prayer meeting. At 12:30 they gathered with the second shift of temple workers for their prayer meeting.

Staffing the temple was an ongoing challenge. Several thousand men and women volunteered their time. They ranged from a solid corps of temple missionaries, who were formally called to serve in the temple for a period of eighteen months, to members living in the temple district who volunteered their time on a weekly basis. Many of the temple missionaries lived in one of forty-three Brookside Apartments about a mile from the temple.

Sterling and Ellie made a good impression on temple colleagues. "Sterling was a great leader," said Ed Scholz. "There never was an issue among us about anything. We all recognized what had to be done, and we worked all together to do it."[1]

Chuck Eckery said, "Sterling was very accepting of people. We talked about things that could be done better. I don't think he ever criticized anyone. He was a true leader who wanted to do everything properly." Sterling standardized all procedures by creating a new handbook. "He wanted to be very specific, to make it more comfortable for patrons and so ordinance workers could do their best. I'd write up certain things and he would change it where necessary."[2]

Sterling continued to hold weekly Executive Committee meetings, as Ellie held matron meetings in her office, usually on Wednesdays. "We talked about staffing and any special training that was needed," said Marlene Eckery. Ellie divided the work among herself and the two assistant matrons. Lois Scholz helped those coming to the temple for the first time for their own endowment; Marlene, among other duties, arranged music for prayer meetings.[3]

"Ellie was a good, positive leader," said Sister Eckery. "There was a special atmosphere all the time. In our meetings there was always a bit of humor. We knew the Lord was with us. Both of the Coltons were strong, faithful, and positive."

Addressing her fellow temple workers, Ellie shared her thoughts about the temple and temple work. "In every shift we are blessed by competent angelic coordinators, directors, and workers who serve with distinction...

What a privilege it is to be here with you. Along with Isaiah we invite each of you: 'Come ye, and let us go up to the mountain of the Lord...and He will teach us of His ways, and we will walk in his paths...'" (Isaiah 2:3)

Ellie discussed her first endowment session, in the Idaho Falls Temple when she and Sterling were married. "I felt the spiritual presence of my father, who died when I was six years old, and my grandfather, who passed away a year later. I felt the spirit of my older sister, Vie, who had been my mom's chief helper in trying to civilize me, and who had died three years earlier. I was weeping steadily.

"My mother squeezed my hand and I knew she was aware of them also. I looked down the row at my darling grandmother Ricks and felt deep gratitude for her love and caring...I thought of my great-grandparents who worked anxiously to complete the Nauvoo Temple so they could receive their endowments before being driven from their homes...I remember thinking: 'This must be what is meant by the Spirit of Elijah, of turning the hearts of the children to their parents.'

"Here was my mom sitting next to me, who took from her paycheck faithfully 10 percent for tithing and 1 percent to pay her English genealogical researcher, Molly, who never found much. I often teased her about her Spirit of Elijah and her boring relatives. I could never get too excited about genealogy."

Ellie's attitude changed some time later, after her mother's death. "We had a young man join the Church in the Potomac Ward. At his baptism I met his father, not a member of the Church, whose lifetime hobby was genealogy. To my amazement his line was the same as my mother's. There in his big book was the missing link my mom had searched in vain for which extended her family back to the twelfth century!"

"What a pleasure it is to look out at all you beautiful people dressed in white," said Ellie. "Our Savior desires to make the feeblest of us into kings and queens, priests and priestesses...radiant eternal creatures to rule and reign in the House of Israel forever."

She noted that President Hinckley said, "The altars of the temple are places of offering and sacrifice. There we offer our Father in Heaven our hearts and our lives. There we are taught how to come unto Christ and offer our whole souls as an offering unto him, but we also offer him the greatest selfless act of Christian service that we can perform in mortal life, that of work for the dead."

President Hinckley, she added, has also said, "Every temple is an expression of our testimony that life beyond the grave is as real and certain as is mortality. There would be no need for temples if the human spirit and soul were not eternal. Every ordinance performed in these sacred houses is everlasting in its consequences."

In January 2000 Ellie had a serious accident. On a very cold day she was walking through the woods behind their home. Going down a hill she tripped and fell hard, flat on her face, her chin striking a rock and taking most of the impact. The fall drove her lower teeth through her lower lip, cutting through two muscles.

Sterling rushed her to a doctor who closed the wounded lip with about twenty stitches. "Ellie was a sight to behold," wrote Sterling. "When she does anything she does it right!" Her face was swollen, her chin black and blue, and a knee was scraped as well, swelling to twice its normal size. But she took it well, missing the next two days at the temple but attending for several hours the third day.

In June, two months before her sixty-ninth birthday, Sterling recorded that "Ellie went to the spa today to have a facial. She continues to be very beautiful."

Along with their tireless work at the temple, Sterling and Ellie offered other church service. Sterling continued occasionally to go on proselyting splits with full-time missionaries. He and Ellie made monthly home teaching and visiting teaching visits to several assigned families in their ward.

Sterling and Ellie continued to be very generous. Among many other quiet actions, they bought a used car and gave it to a sister in their ward. They gave funds to a man to start a business. They "loaned" a family thousands of dollars to save their home from bankruptcy. "I do not expect to get it back," wrote Sterling. They consistently donated 10 percent of their income as tithing to the Church, and contributed to a variety of other non-profit organizations.

41

ANGELS IN WHITE

Given their various leadership roles, on occasion Sterling and Ellie were the Church's voices to the public in the capital area. While they were directing the Washington D.C. Temple in 2001, *The Washington Post*—one of the nation's leading newspapers—ran a large feature article on the Mormons.

The underlying purpose of the temple, Sterling told the *Post*, is to fulfill "our Heavenly Father's plan by which we are able to return to Him." The reporter quoted Ellie about sacrifices made by women members, especially older missionaries serving in the temple. "So many of these women have large families," said Ellie. "Many have grandchildren, but they are willing to leave home for eighteen months and serve in the temple."[1]

The article strikingly lacked the criticism or stereotyping of Mormons that was often found in the mainstream media. The Church was a well-established fact in the capital area.

"We have an obligation to share with others the Gospel of Jesus Christ," Ellie said in the article. "I think this is the best calling that I have had. It is a very sweet and tender experience this time in our life to be co-workers. We don't worry about the fact that time is ticking away and we are getting older."

As president and matron of the Washington D.C. Temple, the Coltons often spoke to church groups in the greater capital area. Some common themes from Ellie's temple talks:

The temple is a place where we can feel God's love. It's a place to heal our hurts and inadequacies. In the temple we are taught by the Spirit. The Holy Ghost bears witness of Jesus Christ and teaches us eternal truths. He teaches us with symbols and through our feelings as we become spiritually mature enough to understand according to our needs and in response to our prayers.

In the temple we are taught eternal truths. We are shown the way back home. We are taught there the purposes of life and death, of good and evil, our world of opposites. It is there we learn where we came from, how we got into the present situation we are in, and what it will take to get us back into the presence of our Father in Heaven…Everything in the temple is designed to bring about a transformation of our hearts. For most people that takes many visits, and a desire to know and understand.

The temple has been called "The Lord's University." Some truths matter more than others. It is valuable to know the laws of gravity, but it is vital to know of the reality of a Redeemer. It is helpful to know math and know how to manage your money. It is essential to know how to repent and call upon God, in the name of His Son, for forgiveness.

We live in perilous times. Bad influences seem to be all around us. Television, the Internet, and newspapers report a troubled world with wars and rumors of wars. The Lord counsels us to "stand in holy places, and be not moved." He also counsels: "Let not your hearts be troubled, neither let them be afraid." You face challenges in rearing your children that are greater than in any other generation…We all receive adversity in one form or another that we didn't expect…The temple offers us a place where we come to know God and Jesus Christ. We have the opportunity there to see our lives in an eternal perspective.

In 2001 temple leaders organized a Christmas devotional for temple workers. More than 600 workers, all dressed in white, attended. President Ed Scholz conducted and President Chuck Eckery gave the opening prayer. Remarks were given by Elder Sheldon F. Child, area authority for the Washington, D.C. region, and by Sterling and Ellie.

"God sent angelic messengers to the earth to prepare minds and hearts for the birth of His only begotten Son," said Ellie. "...Will he not prepare a people to receive His Son at His second coming?

"The past two years we have been touched by many earthly angels as we have served in this holy temple. I have watched earth angels ministering to the needs of those who have come to reverence the Lord in His House. I have seen a white-haired angel cradling a sleeping baby on the sixth floor, waiting to take the baby into a sealing room to be sealed to her parents.

"I have observed a host of angels in white hovering over a family of eight handicapped children coming to witness the sealing of another brother. I have been touched by watching angels attend a dear sister, severely handicapped, coming to the temple for her own endowment, with only months to live, and seeing the sparkle of gratitude and love in her eyes for the considerations shown her."

Ellie added, "We have heard the prayers of our worker angels petitioning the Lord to help us make His holy house truly a house of prayer, a house of faith, a house of learning, a house of glory, and a house of order. We have felt the hushed reverence in the baptistry as sacred baptisms for the dead have been performed.

"We have experienced reverence and manifestations of the Spirit in the initiatory. We have felt the wonder and blessings of the atonement as endowment covenants are made. We have rejoiced witnessing families being sealed for time and all eternity."

Ellie said, "If we do not understand all we see and hear in the temple, we must not be apathetic. We must go home, ponder, pray, prepare, and then return...Pondering spiritual things the scriptures teach us is an invitation to receive spiritual revelation...

"The temple is a house of prayer where you can take your anxieties and the deepest desires of your heart. In the peaceful and holy atmosphere of the celestial room in silent prayer, share them with the Lord. When I do this, the Spirit seems to whisper, 'Be still and know that I am God.' I leave with the reassurance that God knows my problems and will bless me to face them."

Sterling and Ellie's last day at the temple was October 31, 2002. "We had very mixed emotions," wrote Sterling. "Our tenure at the temple has been a spiritual highlight of our lives…We love temple co-workers dearly and will always value their friendship."

Ellie told a group of college-age members how the temple had affected her personally. "I have gone to the temple seeking comfort for the loss of loved ones, and have received assurance of the great atonement of our Savior. I have gone in fear of physical problems and operations that faced me and received peace that the Lord would bless me to cope with the pain and frustration and the healing. I have gone to pray for my children and for friends, seeking inspiration on how I could help them.

"I am an old lady now. As I look back on my life I am very grateful for the spiritual equilibrium the temple has given me. I have been prompted when pride, anger, vanity or selfishness have become stumbling blocks, to 'cool it' and repent—and keep trying to do better."

Fellow temple workers and the temple employees had a farewell party for Sterling and Ellie, presenting them with a scrapbook of pictures and letters of thanks.

The following day Sterling wrote, "It was our first day without responsibility for the temple. We missed being in the temple but it also felt good to be relieved of the responsibility."

On Monday, November 4, Fred Daniels drove his "torture chamber" to the curb outside their home on Greentree Road, and gave each of them a vigorous workout. The following day they threw their suitcases in the car and hit the road like two youngsters eloping. With no reservations and only a rough idea of where they were going, they headed through a heavy rainstorm to Kirtland, Ohio, a place important in LDS history.

For at least one week they were not scheduled to be anywhere, see anyone, or do anything. Sterling and Ellie had each other, and for the moment that was enough.

42

FAITH OF A PATRIARCH

By 2003, Sterling and Ellie had cycled through many positions in the Church, serving as teachers and leaders of priesthood and auxiliary organizations, as leaders of their wards and stakes, and as leaders of a mission and a temple.

They were now more free than at any previous time in their lives together to experience the world in ways that only sufficient time and resources afforded. Their first priority, as it had always been, was being present for important events in the lives of their children, grandchildren, and increasing number of great-grandchildren. Sterling and Ellie attended numerous church, academic, music, and sports events which involved their posterity, wherever their posterity lived.

They walked or played tennis most days of the week, and surrendered themselves to Fred Daniels' torture chamber for a rigorous hour of exercise once or twice a week.

They spent a lot more time at their condo in Park City, Utah, especially in winter, inviting their children and grandchildren at every opportunity to join them for their ski outings.

Ellie would usually make oatmeal and hot chocolate for the skiers before they headed out in the mornings to ski, and would often make chili stack ups, a Colton family favorite, for dinner for the skiers after a long and tiring day on the mountain.

There were signs, however, that age was starting to creep up on them. During a ski trip in 2003, family members hit the Park City slopes on a bitterly cold, blustery day. Ellie was an experienced skier. On this day, however, coming down a trail called Claim Jumper, she fell hard on her face and chest two times. Sterling and Steve helped her into a ski hut at mid-mountain. Ellie was disoriented and couldn't remember the falls or how she got into the hut. The ski patrol took her off the mountain on a snow mobile, and a doctor at the base took X-rays and said she had a slight concussion.

Three days later, a Sunday, Sterling developed a severe pain in his lower back, sharper than any physical pain he could remember. Though it turned out to be nothing serious, it took Sterling several days to fully recover.

About a month later, Sterling decided to take up scuba diving. He bought $500 worth of equipment and registered for certification class, which included two day-long sessions. Each session included four hours in a classroom and four hours in a pool. After the first session, Sterling said, "It was hard work. I found that I really don't feel comfortable under water. I was exhausted."

The second class was the next day. He did well on a written test but once more had difficulty after four hours in the pool. "Again I didn't feel comfortable and my ears bothered me...I decided not to do the open water dives required for a certificate."

Sterling was now seventy-four and Ellie seventy-two. They had a lot of living yet to do, but were learning that some compromises with Father Time were now called for. Cruising the Seven Seas and birding would become more important.

Their first foreign trip in 2003 was relatively close to home. In January they flew to Cabo San Lucas, Mexico, with Africa-safari friends Frank and Sally Johnson and two other couples—Ken and

Sharlene Bentley and Charles and Dorotha Smart. The temperature in Bethesda was far below freezing when they left; when they arrived in Cabo it was in the seventies.

Cabo is at the southern tip of the Baja California Peninsula, one of Mexico's top tourist destinations and arguably its nicest. Cabo is known for its beaches, sport fishing, scuba diving, and other water sports. Overall it is serene and scenic, with handsome high-rises as well as individual seaside condos.

The four couples stayed in two condos, Spanish-style with whitewashed exteriors, tile floors and red-tile roofs. Sterling and Ellie, the first ones up each morning, were on the beach before sunrise, where they walked several miles, studying an assortment of seabirds, including pelicans which, said Sterling, "amazed us with their kamikaze fishing skills." After a glorious sunrise, they returned for breakfast with the others.

The Coltons played mixed-doubles tennis daily against one of the other couples, the Bentleys, who beat them every day except one. They all lunched together and relaxed the rest of the day, the women usually shopping and the men reading. Then they went out together to dinner.

They motored into the Gulf of California on a catamaran—a watercraft with two parallel hulls—scouting for whales. In the winter, whale pods arrive from Alaska and Siberia, 6,000 miles away, to bear calves in the warm waters of the Gulf of California. The couples got up close to one whale and watched for an hour as it breeched repeatedly, rolled, and flapped its tail at them.

The Coltons' next trip was more exotic—to Southeast Asia, a corner of the world not as familiar to them as many other regions. Arrangements were made by Sterling's law school alma mater, Stanford University, which facilitated travel, accommodations, and expert guide service to Cambodia, Vietnam, and Laos. Sterling and

Ellie left home in February 2003, flying the longest leg on Cathay Pacific, the flag carrier of Hong Kong.

In Vietnam, Sterling noted many signs of economic activity. "Saigon is a bustling city," he said. "The streets are full of cycles and mopeds. There was much construction going on for roads and other infrastructure. There are over 80,000,000 people in Vietnam. They seem to be hardworking and ambitious. We didn't experience any animosity." Some 58,000 U.S. service personnel were killed in the Vietnam War, which ended in April 1975 with defeat for America and its allies in the West, and victory for North Vietnam and its Communist allies. Today Vietnam is one country.

They visited Danang, a major port city in central Vietnam and, during the Vietnam War, home to the busiest airport in the world. As always, Sterling and Ellie rose early and took a long walk each day. They saw others exercising, and many fishing boats in the bay.

The Coltons were taken with the numerous Buddhist temples in Southeast Asia, starting with the most famous, the Temple of Angkor Wat in Cambodia, the center of the Khmer Empire, from the ninth to the fifteenth century. "It is but one of over 30 temples in a vast complex" covering nearly 10,000 acres, wrote Sterling.

After three weeks the Coltons were greeted by familiar faces—Sterling's brother Phil and his wife Bobby. For more than two years Phil had been serving as president of the LDS Cambodia Phnom Penh mission, representing the Church's activities in four countries: Cambodia, Vietnam, Laos, and Myanmar (Burma).

"Our stay with Phil and Bobby was very special," wrote Sterling. "It was wonderful to be back in a mission field." The mission had about seventy proselyting missionaries—half of the elders were Cambodian—and they were having tremendous success, baptizing the equivalent of a stake a year. There were seven church buildings in use and a large stake center under construction.

While the Coltons were visiting Phil and Bobby, the Ministry of Culture and Religion in Cambodia issued an edict prohibiting door-to-door proselyting and other religious activities. The order appeared to be aimed directly at the LDS Church and one of its most important methods of finding investigators.

Challenges to religious freedom such as these provided the background for establishment of the International Center for Law and Religion Studies in BYU's J. Reuben Clark Law School. The founder of the Center, longtime law professor Cole Durham, is a second cousin to Sterling—his grandmother Zora was a sister to Sterling's father Hugh.

"Sterling was one of the people I consulted with a lot before the Center was established in 2000," said Durham. "Because of his breadth of experience, I'd go to Washington and sit down with Sterling, who gave us valuable guidance."[1]

Durham has made a life crusade on behalf of religious freedom and is considered by some observers to be the world's leading expert in the field. Each year the Center brings together scholars and government officials from throughout the world to discuss the state of religious freedom and address issues threatening it. The conferences have been held annually at BYU for twenty-three years at this writing, attended by nearly 1,000 scholars from over 120 countries.

"In any given year," said Durham, "ten to twenty countries will tinker with legislation in the area of religion." The Center tries to anticipate the changes to law and regulations that could compromise religious freedom. "We can't always stop a law, but sometimes we can offer a draft that will improve it. We have worked on laws in more than fifty countries." They also offer to help with friend-of-the-court briefs in court cases.

In 2008 the Center established the Sterling and Eleanor Colton Chair in Law and Religion. The Chair provides between a third and a fourth of the center's resources, said Durham. The Chair was funded initially by the Colton family and a generous gift from the Marriott Foundation. Dave Colton, a major contributor to the chair, is now vice chair of the Center's board.

On March 12, 2005, Sterling's brother Hugh Maughan Colton passed away in Utah. He had suffered a stroke in 2002, ending his ranching career. He died from complications of cancer. Maughan was four years younger than Sterling and had lived a full life—as a fine athlete, an Army intelligence officer, longtime manager of the family ranch, and husband and father of three children.

Maughan's funeral, on March 17, brought Sterling and Ellie and many other family members to Vernal. Among other participants, Brad gave the family prayer, Sterling spoke, and Carolyn gave the benediction. Maughan was buried in the family plot at the Maeser Cemetery near Vernal.

On February 4, 2007, Washington, D.C. Stake President Nolan Archibald, with Ellie sitting nearby, placed his hands on Sterling's head and ordained him to be a patriarch for the stake. The office of patriarch is a unique calling in the LDS Church. Individuals in other callings solicit the Lord's blessings; a patriarch is privileged to pronounce blessings, as moved upon by the Holy Spirit. There is usually just one patriarch per stake.

"Patriarchs are often among the most humble and faithful of our brethren," said the late James E. Faust, a member of the Quorum of the Twelve and the First Presidency. "These chosen men live lives that entitle them to the inspiration of heaven...They are entitled to speak authoritatively for the Lord.

"The patriarchal office is one of blessing, not of administration, nor of counseling. It is a sacred, spiritual calling...Our patriarchs give total devotion to their callings and do all they can to live in faith and worthiness so that each blessing is inspired."

Members may receive a patriarchal blessing when they are old enough to understand its nature and are living gospel standards. They are encouraged to periodically re-read their blessings, as a reminder of promises to come if they are faithful.

The blessing given by a patriarch is similar to a road map. It suggests paths that an individual may travel and destinations they may reach if the member stays faithful. The patriarch blesses the recipient with spiritual gifts and he makes promises, gives advice, and issues admonition and warning tailored specifically for each recipient. In essence, the patriarch's blessing is prophetic.

The patriarch also may make an inspired declaration of the recipient's lineage, relating to Abraham of the Old Testament, through whose posterity the Lord promised that every nation would be blessed.

Sterling was fortunate to have someone at hand who would be of great help in his new calling—Phyllis Hester, who had been executive assistant to Bill Marriott for more than twenty-five years. Phyllis, also a Mormon and in the same ward as the Coltons, had transcribed blessings given by two previous patriarchs, one of whom, John Baker, continued to do a small number of blessings as Sterling did most of them.

Sterling recorded his blessings on a small cassette tape, then took the recording to Phyllis. She typed a draft copy using a transcriber, then, usually the next day, Sterling picked up the draft from her. He would make any corrections, then return the draft to Phyllis for her to make a final copy.

On Sunday, March 18, 2007, Sterling gave his first patriarchal blessing, to a young man whose parents accompanied him. "It was a very humbling experience," wrote Sterling. "I pray that the blessing was acceptable to the Lord."

Years later, one of the last patriarchal blessings Sterling gave was to the oldest grandchild of a close friend, Ralph Hardy. "It was a revelatory experience," said Ralph. "Out of his mouth was the voice of the Lord."[2]

Sterling gave patriarchal blessings for seven years; the last one was on February 21, 2014. By then he had given several hundred blessings, including blessings for his four youngest grandchildren, Jane, Brandon, Thomas and Kevin.

43

Traveling the World

The makeup of the Colton family changed during the first decade of the new millennium. David and Darla divorced, in a sad experience for all the Coltons. "Mom and Dad were a constant support during this time," said Dave.

Two years later Dave began to date again. He met Julie Haycock Jensen, who lived in Las Vegas, Nevada, and their friendship grew into love. They were married in the Bountiful Utah Temple on December 27, 2005, with Sterling conducting the sealing. Julie brought six wonderful children to their union—Ben, Trevor, David, Niels, Sarah, and Lizzie. Sterling and Ellie welcomed Julie and her children to the Colton family as warmly as they had welcomed all of their daughters-in-law and grandchildren.

"Sterling has had a profound impact on my life and the lives of my children," said Julie. "He has shown a precious example of kindness, generosity, a strong work ethic, faith, complete non-judgment of other people, quiet goodness and compassion, and unconditional love."[1]

The Coltons' Golden Wedding Anniversary was August 6, 2004, and they celebrated all year long. They visited Norway, where the mayor of Oslo, a Stanford University graduate, showed them his city. They saw "gorgeous fjords, waterfalls, and mountains," said Ellie, and attended a piano concert in the home of Romantic era composer and pianist Edvard Grieg.

In March they took a National Geographic cruise with their children and spouses through the Panama Canal and into Costa Rica, where they saw "amazing birds" and rode a series of zip lines eleven-miles long. In June they rendezvoused with four couples from early-married days in Salt Lake City and took a cruise from Boston to Halifax, Nova Scotia.

For their actual fiftieth anniversary on August 6, Sterling and Ellie returned once more to southwestern Canada. They visited Banff and Lake Louise in Alberta, and traversed British Columbia, where they had spent three years leading that LDS mission.

One day they hiked nine miles among the wild flowers at the tops of the mountain in Sunshine Meadows, near Lake Louise, where they had spent their honeymoon, and were surprised to locate the same small honeymoon cabin.

"We have been greatly blessed," said Sterling. "Ellie is the best thing that ever happened to me. She is the love of my life."

They spent time with friends and relatives in five states; while in Utah Sterling led another pack trip into the high and beautiful Uintas. They skied in Park City, Ellie reporting that "our bodies aren't quite as daring as we used to be...our ski days are numbered!"

A repeated travel highlight for Sterling and Ellie through the years was sailing on the cruise ship *Sea Cloud* in the Mediterranean. A cruise ship guide called *Sea Cloud* "the most romantic sailing ship afloat."[2] It was built in Germany and, when launched in 1931, was the largest private yacht in the world. It subsequently served the U.S. Coast Guard and other government agencies before returning to private hands.

The Coltons first sailed on the *Sea Cloud* as guests of Bill and Donna when the Marriotts celebrated their fiftieth wedding anniversary in 2005. The *Sea Cloud*, with a capacity for sixty-four passengers and a crew of sixty, took the Coltons and other close friends from Istanbul around the islands of the Aegean Sea.

In 2012 Sterling and Ellie again boarded the *Sea Cloud* as guests of the Marriotts, this time sailing from Athens and assigned to the same lovely state room as before. They visited ports of call at a half-dozen sites in Italy, ending in Rome.

In March 2006 Sterling and Ellie traveled to New Guinea with a group of alumni from Stanford University. "I would not have believed there could be such a culture still active in the world," said Ellie. The Huli warriors wore nose bones and hair wigs decorated with rare bird feathers, and they put war paint all over their bodies and faces, reported Ellie. "It was definitely a man's world. The children were naked until they reached puberty. I felt great sympathy for the women."

On the way back home Sterling and Ellie stopped in Australia to catch their international flight to the U.S. Ellie forgot that she had put two apples in her backpack to eat for breakfast. When a customs official asked if they had any food products, she unthinkingly said no. Checking their luggage, the agent found the apples and told Ellie she had a choice of paying a $220 fine or going to court. Ellie was furious and refused to pay.

"She said she would go to court," recalled Sterling, "I said we'd pay." He calmed her down and paid, as Ellie swore she would never again visit Australia.

In September they cruised the remote northern British Isles with Carolyn. The following February, 2007, they took a National Geographic tour of Antarctica. They embarked on a ship, the *Endeavor*, from Ushuaia, Argentina—the southernmost city in the world—to the Antarctica Peninsula, alive with penguins, soaring sea birds, and seals. On the return voyage a twenty-foot wave hit *Endeavor* while they were at a table eating. The ship suddenly lurched, spilling food onto those sitting on one side of the table—luckily not their side.

In April 2008, with Carolyn, they toured China for two weeks, as part of a group that included two Stanford professors steeped in Chinese history. They walked on the Great Wall, visited the storied terra cotta warriors and underground museum, ending up in Shanghai with its flashy modern skyscrapers.

That September, with Carolyn, David, Julie and Julie's youngest daughter Lizzie, they were back in Africa, this time in Tanzania. While on the Serengeti plains the annual migratory march of more than a million wildebeest thundered through. They stayed in moveable camps with surprisingly good chefs.

As they traveled the plains, they sang every hymn, Primary song, and high school and college song they knew, much to the delight of their driver Mohammed, who insisted they start each day with a prayer once he realized they were people of faith. The songs were led by the three younger women as Sterling, Ellie, and David gamely tried to stay in tune.

In 2009, Brad and Melanie delighted Brad's parents when they moved into a house right next door to them. They have been helpful to Sterling and Ellie, and the reverse is also true. "We gave them a key and first thing in the morning they took our dog Hannah for a walk," said Brad. He and Melanie often are invited to share Ellie's meals. "And," said Brad, "it's also fun when you come home from work to have my mom waving and smiling as I pull into the driveway."

In 2009 Sterling and Ellie went to Hawaii with David and Julie. Dave and Julie hiked a difficult trail, which his parents had hiked in the past. "That was when we were younger," explained Ellie. "Now we were content to just walk along the beach."

While there, Ellie's sister Doretha passed away in California. Sterling and Ellie rerouted their return flight to San Francisco, then drove to Santa Rosa for the funeral. Three years later Ellie's brother Lloyd, her last living sibling, died in Idaho Falls.

Also in 2009 Sterling and Ellie flew to Chile with Brad and Melanie, where they visited Torres del Paine National Park. They hiked rugged trails, rode horses on the pampas—sweeping, flat, grass-covered plains—and ate lamb roasted on a huge fireplace.

They then flew to Santiago and drove a rented van to Viña del Mar where they had a joyous reunion with Elder Scott Colton, Brad and Melanie's oldest son, serving a mission there.

In April, joined by their children and three daughters-in-law, Sterling and Ellie celebrated Sterling's eightieth birthday at the Enchanted Inn in Sedona, Arizona. Near the end of that year they welcomed home Elder Jared Colton, Steve and Jeri's oldest son, from his mission in São Paulo, Brazil.

"We loved hearing Jared's homecoming talk and the open house his parents hosted afterward," said Ellie. "We are so grateful for our family and the devotion they have to the Gospel of Jesus Christ. Our greatest joy!"

The year 2010 found Sterling and Ellie again in Europe and the Mediterranean. They met up with family, including Dave and Julie in Frankfurt, where Dave was Area Legal Counsel for the LDS Church, and with Robin Sitar, her husband Nick, and their twin sons Cole and Ryan, in Greece. The Sitars were spending a sabbatical year from Nick teaching at UC-Berkeley.

In 2006 Sterling was diagnosed with Parkinson's disease, a long-term disorder of the central nervous system that mainly affects motor movement. Sterling has had the common symptoms of shaking, rigidity, slowness of movement, and difficulty walking. The last symptom has robbed the Coltons of their longstanding love of walking long distances together.

By the dawn of 2016 it became evident that Parkinson's had taken a toll on Sterling. A man of action throughout his life, he moved at a slower pace and it was difficult for him to travel.

For as long as they could, Sterling and Ellie continued to work out with Fred Daniels in his exercise van. In the summer of 2015 Daniels said, "I tell him he didn't get the memo that Parkinson's is degenerative. He's actually gotten stronger, through sheer willpower. Sterling still presses the same amount of weight. Physical training has helped keep them young."

"I take more care of him than I do of her. Ellie repeats the same exercises, doing the Stairmaster, bike trainer, chest press, stretching, and abdominal. He does Stairmaster, leg presses, and curls. He rolls from his back to his stomach. What he does I have to do with him."

Daniels created a number of exercises especially for Sterling. One was beating on a drum with a drumstick. Another was a specialty exercise with a ball. Daniels would take a ball with bulges and drop it from the second level of the trailer to the first level. However it bounced, Sterling was to catch it.

Parkinson's patients often slur their words, though Sterling has not done so. Daniels created tongue-twisters which helped Sterling continue to speak clearly. One was:

The skunk sat on a stump.
The skunk thunk the stump stunk.
The stump thunk the skunk stunk.

"I think God has given me the ideas of things to help him," said Daniels. "He is walking slower but is still just as strong. How can you not love them? What's cute is that they will walk past each other in the trailer, and hug each time they do. They are the perfect example of two together being greater than two separately. She gives him life; he adores her."

"Ellie once told me, 'I am honored to be married to Sterling,'" said Ron Harrison, a friend who knew the Coltons well both professionally and personally. "'The time I have now to take care of him in his declining health is a privilege and an honor for me…For the love and attention he has given me all of our lives.'"[3]

Suzanne Glassman Cooper, the Colton's neighbor across their backyard canal, has been close friends with the Coltons for decades. Ever since the untimely death of her husband years earlier, Sterling and Ellie have provided tender watchcare for Suzanne and her three children.

On one occasion Suzanne was having difficulty with her teenage son Andrew. When he leaned over the banister and hurled a word she didn't like, Suzanne called Sterling for advice. "I'll come over and take him for a ride," Sterling offered. Suzanne wondered if Andrew would even consent to a ride, but he did.

"They came back in about fifteen minutes," she recalled. Years later she told Andrew she was surprised he went with Sterling that day.

"You can't disrespect Sterling," Andrew's brother Peter Royal cut in. "He and Sister Colton are on a bullet train to Heaven."

Sterling and Ellie, above all else that they could do or say, would like their testimony to be passed on to their posterity, to whom this book is dedicated:

We testify that God lives! He is the Father of our spirits. We are His children, made in His image. He loves us. If we keep His commandments we will inherit all He has and help Him administer the worlds without number He has created.

Jesus, our elder brother, is the Christ, our Savior and Redeemer. Through His atoning sacrifice we have been saved from physical death and been given the opportunity to be cleansed from sin to enable us to return to our Heavenly Father.

The Gospel of Jesus Christ has been restored in its fullness as set forth in the Bible, Book of Mormon, Pearl of Great Price, Doctrine and Covenants, and words of modern-day prophets.

It is our prayer that each member of our family will live so we can return to be with our Heavenly Father as an eternal family.

President and Sister Colton at new mission presidents' training with Steve and Martha West and Bob and Luanna Rowe.

Mission home in Richmond, outside Vancouver.

President and Sister Colton welcoming new missionaries to Canada Vancouver Mission.

448

President Colton teaching missionaries the gospel.

Sister Colton teaching missionaries manners.

Sister Colton (second from right) with kitchen angels in mission home making Christmas treats for missionaries.

President and Sister Colton.

Vancouver snow.

Apostle Neal A. Maxwell and Sister Colleen Maxwell visiting the mission.

President Colton and two assistants planning missionary transfers.

Grandkids Meredith, Kevin, Brandon and Jane visiting President and Sister Colton.

Canada Vancouver missionaries.

451

Grandchildren Becca, Scott and Jane welcoming President and Sister Colton home from their mission.

President and Sister Colton gather with family upon returning from their mission. (Ellie took photo.)

452

To get back in shape after their mission, the Coltons hired this "torture chamber," which came to their home twice a week loaded with exercise equipment and a personal trainer, Fred Daniels.

Bethesda, MD 1998

Grandchildren ready to explore the woods at night with Grandma. (bottom to top, l-r) Kevin, Thomas, Meredith, Brandon, Jane, Scott, Jared and Becca.

Bethesda, MD 1999

Ellie with good friends Barbara and Ralph Mecham.

Bethesda, MD 1990s

453

Sterling and Ellie on safari in southern Africa with Frank and Sally Johnson.

Sterling and Ellie, Washington D.C. Temple president and matron.

Sterling and Ellie on ski lift at Park City, where they had a second home.

Ellie and Sterling skiing Park City.

Ellie and Sterling skiing.

Sterling with grandson Eagle Scouts (l-r) Daniel, Jared and Scott at Jared's Eagle Court of Honor.

Sterling with sons and grandsons fishing in Alaska. (l-r) Nathan, Dave, Scott, Sterling, Steve, Brad, Jared, Dan, guide and little boys Brandon, Kevin and Thomas.

Ellie with Colton girls in Nova Scotia. (l-r) Melanie, Jeri, Becca, Meredith, Ellie, Mauri, Jane, Jenna and Carolyn.

Ellie biking with granddaughters (front to back) Meredith, Jane, Becca and Jenna.

Prince Edward Island, Canada 2003

Sterling and Ellie delivering Christmas gifts.

Bethesda, MD 2000s

Sterling and Ellie celebrating their 50th wedding anniversary on trip to Panama Canal and Costa Rica.

Costa Rica 2004

Dave, Sterling and Ellie bird watching in Costa Rica.

Costa Rica 2004

Sterling (back row, sixth from right) and Ellie (second row, far left) on a sailing cruise aboard the *Sea Cloud* with friends and family of Donna and Bill Marriott, who were celebrating their 50th wedding anniversary.

Ellie and Sterling exploring Papua New Guinea, one of the world's most culturally diverse countries.

Ellie and Sterling in Antarctica.

Sterling and Ellie exploring the Forbidden City in Beijing, China with Carolyn.

Sterling and Ellie exploring Tanzania with (l-r) Julie, Dave, Carolyn and Lizzie Jensen (Langston).

Sterling and Ellie with Brad and Melanie at the Explora Lodge in Torres del Paine Mountains.

Patagonia, Chile 2009

Ellie with daughter Carolyn and daughters-in-law Melanie, Julie and Jeri, celebrating Ellie's 80th birthday.

Wintergreen, VA 2011

Luncheon celebrating Ellie's 80th birthday and the many hats she's worn. (l-r) Melanie, Ellie, Carolyn, Julie and Jeri.

Bethesda, MD 2011

Sterling and Ellie with grandson Kevin at West Point.

Ellie and Sterling dancing at the wedding of granddaughter Meredith and her husband Trent Hazy.

Sterling dancing with granddaughters Mauri, Jenna, Becca and Brittany at the wedding of granddaughter Meredith and her husband Trent Hazy.

Celebrating Jeri's 50th birthday. (l-r) Carolyn, Melanie, Ellie, Julie and Jeri.

Abdul and Sophia Walele family visiting Sterling and Ellie. The younger daughter is Imani; the older daughter is Zanita.

Dancing to Eternity.

Epilogue

On May 2, 2010 the Vancouver British Columbia Temple was dedicated by LDS President Thomas S. Monson—fulfilling a dream shared by BC saints and by Sterling and Ellie Colton, among many others. It was the eighth temple in Canada and the first in British Columbia.

Sterling and Ellie were in attendance and were honored by being seated in the celestial room among a number of general authorities as President Monson delivered the dedicatory prayer. "It was a thrill to be there and feel the joy of the saints in that area," said Ellie.

Nearly 40,000 people toured the temple during the public open house, held in the weeks prior to the temple dedication. The temple serves members in British Columbia and northern Washington, USA.

Marriott International, which Sterling helped lead at a pivotal time in its history, continued to flourish after the wholesale restructuring conceived by Steve Bollenbach and engineered by Sterling. They split the company to save it from possible financial ruin, with Sterling structuring the highly complicated deal. By every measure the restructuring, which closed in 1993, has been a boon.

In 1992 Marriott had $7.8 billion in sales. By 2015 the company, under a new name, Marriott International, had nearly doubled that amount, to $14.5 billion. Meanwhile, Host Hotels & Resorts—the other company created by the split and also under a new name—in 2014 had $5.4 billion in sales, for a combined total of $20 billion. In September 2016 Marriott completed the acquisition of Starwood Hotels and Resorts, creating the world's largest hotel company with over 5,700 properties.

Appendix

Grandchildren of Sterling and Ellie Colton: "Lessons We Have Learned From Our Grandparents"

Sterling and Ellie's greatest treasure is their eternal family, including four children, three daughters-in-law, seventeen grandchildren, fourteen grandchildren-in-law, and thirty-six great-grandchildren at this writing. Each grandchild has written a special tribute to their grandparents.

STERLING DANIEL COLTON
Spouse: Holly Christine Colton
Children: Joshua Sterling, Marguerite (Maggie) May, Bradley David, Adam James

The affect Grandma and Grandpa Colton's example has had on my life is best summarized by Grandpa Colton's oft-used phrase, "Remember who you are and what you can become." This phrase teaches me two important lessons: first, it motivates me to reflect on and live up to my own divine nature and eternal potential; and second, it helps me realize that those around me have the same nature and potential, and that I should help as many as I can to understand and live up to it.

They not only teach of divine nature and eternal potential, they personify it. They know who they are and who they can become because of the faith-filled life they have lived, wearing themselves out, hand in hand, in the service of God. My grandparents know all of Heavenly Father's children are endowed with that same divine nature and eternal potential because of the countless lives they have touched. Grandma and Grandpa have truly shown that they love God and their neighbor.

By demonstrating this enduring love for our Heavenly Father and His children, Grandma and Grandpa's lives exemplify the charge given by Paul to Timothy when he said, "Fight the good fight of faith, lay hold on eternal life, whereunto thou art also called, and has professed a good profession before many witnesses." The good fight my grandparents have fought throughout their lives has not only allowed them to lay hold on eternal life, but has also provided an example of faithfulness to their posterity.

I am grateful to know that while I strive to remember who I am and what I can become, I can look to Grandma and Grandpa Colton as examples of how to fight my own good fight along the path back to my Heavenly Home. Because I have known Grandma and Grandpa Colton, I want to live my life in such a way that I can pass their legacy of faith on to my children, grandchildren, and all with whom I come in contact.

Grandma and Grandpa have instilled within me the desire to want to help others reach their own divine potential. To me, this ability to influence another person in such a profound way is the true power of my grandparents' example, and I will be eternally grateful to them for the way they have influenced me.

MAURI LYN COLTON BREWER
Spouse: Nathanael (Nathan) Warren Brewer
Children: Katelyn Makay, Eleanor (Elli) Elizabeth, Wesley Paul, Darla Jane, Annie Arlene

There is so much that I have learned from my grandma and grandpa, from creating memories that last, encouraging family relationships, service, getting to know those around you (especially their last name and genealogy) and dedication to the Lord and church callings.

But the one that brings a smile to my face and a warmth to my heart is the devotion and love they show to each other. I can only hope that Nathan and I can show that same love to each other continuously, as grandma and grandpa have, for as long as I can remember and increasingly more now. They have truly been an example of placing their relationship with each other equal in importance to their relationship with Christ. It is a love you can see and feel in all their actions.

JENNA ARLENE COLTON JARVIS
Spouse: Jared Vernon Jarvis
Children: Jacob Earl, Abigail (Abbie) Arlene

"Remember who you are and what you can become." Finding my words next to those of my cousins is an honor; trying to write my words as eloquently as they have is impossible. My words are simple and few, but my sincere love and appreciation for my grandparents is deep. They have been my foundation for integrity, honesty, loyalty, respectfulness, testimony, responsibility, humility, compassion, fairness, forgiveness, generosity, kindness, reliability, self-discipline, and needing to be able to laugh at yourself.

Grandpa often says, "Remember who you are and what you can become." Through their words, examples, and encouragement, I have an eternal perspective and want to be the best that I can be. I am a better person because of Grandma and Grandpa and I hope their legacy will always be found in all of their descendants. They have always taught me in a loving way to work to be better. Another favorite Grandpa phrase is, "Work hard and work smart." I am forever grateful to my Heavenly Father for allowing me to be in their family.

REBECCA (BECCA) ANNE COLTON ALLEMAN
Spouse: Matthew Kurt Alleman
Children: John Sterling, Eliza Marie, Adam Matthew

Grandpa and Grandma's examples have affected my life in numerous profound ways, in particular through their beautiful example of Christ-like love. Their Christ-like kindness includes proactively developing meaningful relationships, from Sunday phone calls to family to regularly welcoming others into their home for Sunday dinners. Both traditions have enriched our lives immensely as Matt and I have moved all over the country.

Grandpa and Grandma are remarkable in how sincerely and thoughtfully they connect with individuals. I learned early in my youth the power of remembering someone's name and their story. During the summer of 2007, Matt and I lived with Grandma and Grandpa while completing internships. In a conversation about his Grandma Lewis, who passed when he was seven, Matt mentioned Danish desserts as one of the few memories of his grandma. Later that week, Grandma surprised us with a peach pie with raspberry Danish dessert, and Matt will never forget the loving, knowing look as she handed him that dish. This is just one example of countless thoughtful, touching gestures that shows that they value and love individuals.

I will also be forever grateful for how they taught me to look for the best in others. When I was sixteen, an experience with Grandpa in church significantly shaped my motivation to appreciate the best in everyone. A peer of mine was bearing her testimony. This young woman had some cognitive and emotional challenges, and I was consistently friendly to her truthfully for the sake of being consistently kind.

During her tangential words, my thoughts drifted to less Christ-like observations. Then as she closed, Grandpa turned to me, with tears in his eyes, and declared, "Isn't she wonderful?" I was struck to my core by the significance of valuing each individual as a beloved child of God. Grandpa, with that one comment and congruent example, taught me to view through his lens of Christ-like love, looking for the positive attributes in the people in my life and cherishing them for those attributes.

I believe we are here on earth to learn, love, and become more like Christ. I can't imagine a better legacy. Matt and I hope to teach and show our children how to be proactive, be thoughtful, remember names, and really love God's children. How blessed we are from the example set by Grandpa and Grandma!

BRADLEY SCOTT COLTON
Spouse: Brittany Pierce Colton
Children: Pierce Bradley, Amelia Jane, Theodore (Theo) Sterling

Words cannot adequately describe the impact and influence my grandfather, Sterling D. Colton, has had on my life and the lives of my family. In every area in my life I can clearly point out where my grandfather has helped me become a better person.

As a saint, he taught me how to develop perfect obedience, faith, and discipleship.

As a patriarch, he demonstrated how to exercise righteous dominion and raise my family in the gospel.

As a priesthood holder and laborer in the Lord's vineyard, he showed me how to be worthy for and seek out every calling, role, and task the Lord might have for me.

As a child of God, he illustrated how to view everyone as brothers and sisters and to treat them all equally with love and respect despite what they look like, where they come from, what they believe, their level of education, or financial or social status.

As a scholar, he taught me how to love and treasure learning and maximize the development of professional training.

As a worker, he demonstrated how to "thrust in your sickle" and "put your shoulder to the wheel" without complaint but with joy and satisfaction in the labor.

As a leader, he showed me how to lead with love and by example.

As a businessman, he taught me how to be successful in my trade.

As a provider, he illustrated how to meet family needs while still keeping a clear perspective as to what is truly important in life, and that financial means are simply a tool to accomplish righteous needs, goals, and desires. His generosity made it possible for me to pursue my medical degree and start my family without fear of financial restraints.

As a grandfather, he was the perfect example of strong, ever-present love and support. He demonstrated the value of a warm smile, an open ear, a rock-steady example, a strong cattle-call cheering you on from the bleachers, and sage advice to always remember who you are, what you can become, to work hard and smart, and to always remember that I love you.

The legacy of this man will live on forever through the thousands he influenced by who he was as a person and how he lived his life.

My grandmother, Eleanor Ricks Colton, is the most perfect grandmother you could ever ask for. She is the epitome of Christ-like charity. She teaches by example how to love your neighbor as yourself and to view and treat everyone as equals with respect, kindness, and generosity. She has held many impressive responsibilities, met with important authorities, and traveled to exotic places, yet she is always your number one cheerleader, supporter, and advocate, and makes everyone feel like the most important person in the room. Her cheery, caring nature always brings a warm feeling to your chest and a smile to your face. Her empathy can lift you out of any slump, then her wise words will help point you in the direction to make right of any situation. Her stories, songs, and quoted Shakespeare soliloquies are captivating and can turn any encounter into an adventure. Her cooking can appease the most delicate and picky of palettes yet also fill the ravenous teenage boy appetite. Her creative ideas, talented craftsmanship, and generosity mixed with determination resulted in innumerable priceless, joyous memories. I love my grandmother and am incredibly grateful to have her in my life.

JANE ELIZABETH COLTON BLACK
Spouse: Ethan Wallace Black

Sterling and Eleanor Colton are wonderfully inspiring and uplifting people. They display true devotion, graciousness, charity, love, and all-around kindness to those in their lives, from friends and family, to strangers on the street.

Throughout my childhood my grandparents invited concourses of people to share home-made Sunday dinners with them and their family. These guests had all, at some point, crossed paths with my grandparents, who graciously helped them at difficult times in their lives. Growing up, these dinners were among the first memories I had of recognizing my grandparents' love for others.

Later, in high school, they demonstrated their love for me by supporting me in everything I did. Grandma and Grandpa attended hundreds of my events, from athletic competitions, choir concerts, and graduations, to weekly phone calls for life updates. My favorite memories of playing lacrosse and field hockey were the times when I sprinted down the field, cradling the ball, and immediately recognized Grandpa's unmistakable cattle call coming from somewhere in the stands.

Another occasion that profoundly impacted my life was receiving my patriarchal blessing from my Grandpa, who had been called as a Stake Patriarch the same summer my family moved to Arizona. I will always cherish the experience of flying back to D.C. and being solely in the company of the grandparents I adored; my grandfather bestowing heavenly blessings upon me, and my Grandmother listening alongside.

I attribute all my success to the values my grandparents taught my father and me. More importantly, my father and grandfather set the standard to which I compared every man I dated. It's a high standard! I wanted a man like Brad and Sterling, who would treat me the same way my dad treats my mom and my grandpa treats my grandma. Ethan reached that bar, and we look forward to leading a life in which we hope to be like my grandparents.

THOMAS JAMES COLTON

The rock of love. Grandpa and Grandma have actively been involved in every aspect of my life since I was born. I've been blessed to spend over fifteen years of my life either a ten-minute drive or ten-step walk away from this dear couple. The impact they have had on my life and on my friends is incalculable and will continue to be felt as long as there is a Colton relative or friend on this earth.

Growing up, I looked to Sterling and Ellie as examples of *perfection*. Every Sunday I remember sitting with my family and grandparents and looking at their behavior. Dad sat on the stand as the bishop, my brother passed and blessed the sacrament, and grandpa sang monotone, bass hymns and voiced loud, confident "amens" to the talks given.

As years passed by and my life became more complex I began to look past the surface and seek for guidance. After becoming a deacon, grandpa would look intently at me when I passed the sacrament and nod approvingly while grandma would check to see if I was distracting by chewing gum. As a priest, I remember practicing the wording of the prayers at first to make my grandparents proud. Ellie would tell me how much she loved my bass voice every Sunday.

At age nineteen I prepared to leave for my mission and more than ever looked to Sterling and Ellie. Grandpa taught me discipline, perfect obedience, dedication, and faith. Ellie taught me to laugh, love, and enjoy every day. A memory that will never fade is that of returning home at midnight on a summer's day in 2015. Despite the taxing nature of staying up that late in their eighties and declining health, I was surprised and overwhelmed with emotion as I ran to two of my biggest fans awaiting me with proud tears and smiles on their faces. In everything they did, Grandpa and Grandma demonstrated an absolute dedication to God, family, and friends.

Innumerable sacrifices, righteous daily living, and unbounded love. That is what these two larger-than-life role models I've been blessed to call Grandma and Grandpa represent to me.

JARED CASH COLTON
Spouse: Eden Jensen Colton
Children: Sterling Joseph Colton

As my wife and I were deciding on a name for our first son, the name we immediately chose was Grandpa's name—Sterling. This is because Grandpa and Grandma exemplify who we aspire to be and whose legacy we hope that our children will follow.

We hope our children remember that everything Grandpa and Grandma did had one purpose: to raise an eternal family and return to live with our Heavenly Father together. These role models lived this goal daily by embracing three key attributes: optimism, hard work, and service.

First, optimism. I have never heard a complaint pass by Grandpa or Grandma's lips, despite the challenges both have endured. Instead, they chose optimism, focusing on the positives in life. I want my children to always embrace the good in life for it is always there. Second, hard work. I want my children to remember that the most important things in life do not come easily but take hard work. By working hard and smart, Grandpa and Grandma accomplished more and touched more people than I will ever know. They worked hard to educate themselves, to provide for their family, and to serve their neighbors.

This leads me to the third trait I want my children to remember—tireless service in the community, in a career, and in the church. Grandpa and Grandma always centered their efforts on the people with whom they interacted, and sacrificed much to lift those around them. I hope that my children will remember this legacy of Grandpa and Grandma Colton every time they see their own last name—Colton.

MEREDITH CASH COLTON UDVAR-HAZY
Spouse: Trenton (Trent) Scott Udvar-Hazy

 I could write an entire book on my admiration for my grandparents. Here are just a few of the many values I have learned from them.
 Loving unconditionally: My grandparents have had a tradition of calling all their kids every Sunday to check-in with how they were doing. When I went to college and moved away from home, I assumed this meant I wouldn't be part of the weekly call. But I should have known better! I started getting weekly calls from my grandparents—just to me. Through this I learned just how much they valued our personal relationship and I saw how they unconditionally and actively love everyone in their family.
 Enjoying life: I remember one particular call, when at the end, my grandpa was sharing his signature words of advice: "Remember who you are, and what you can became," "Work hard and work smart," "Know that we love you." Between each statement, my grandma was piping in, with her usual cheerful tone: "And have fun! And have fun! And have fun!" I love that my grandparents have always found ways to make fun happen in between life responsibilities.
 Valuing education: On our calls, when I explain something going in my life at work or school, my grandpa always follows up with, "So, are you learning anything?" My grandparents both value learning in any stage of life, and I love that my grandpa is always reminding me through questions like that to learn throughout life. I will be forever grateful that they made my Stanford education possible, but even more importantly, that they have instilled in me a love of learning.
 Welcoming others: When my husband, Trent, and I were dating, my grandparents welcomed him into their home and into their lives. From the start, they took the time to learn about his family and remembered everything. As we got more serious, on our Sunday calls, they wanted to hear all about how his life was going. When we got married, it was such a privilege to have my grandpa perform our marriage in the LDS Atlanta Temple. This love has only continued;

they treat Trent like he is their own grandson.

I hope that I can follow my grandparents' example of loving unconditionally, enjoying life, valuing education, and welcoming others. There are so many important lessons I have learned from them, and Trent and I both hope to build on their legacy in our own family.

BRANDON CASH COLTON

Grandma and Grandpa know love. They are beloved by all who know them, and they demonstrate their love for others in all they do.

On my mission, a senior couple invited my companion and me to their home for dinner. After a few minutes of discussion, they asked if I was related to any Coltons in Washington, D.C. Upon learning that Sterling and Ellie were my grandparents, they spent the next ten minutes telling me all the wonderful experiences they had with my grandparents while serving in the Washington D.C. Temple. Stories like that are common in our family. Everyone who knows Grandma and Grandpa loves them.

At perhaps the lowest point in my teenage years, my parents sent me to Washington for a weekend with Grandma and Grandpa. Prior to that point—in typical teenage fashion—I had rebuffed every attempt from my parents and youth leaders to navigate me through a few difficult months. Those four days with Grandma and Grandpa changed my life.

Grandma made dozens of her famous ginger snap cookies, including an extra two dozen to take back to Georgia (with specific instructions that sharing with my family was optional). Grandpa took me to all the places in Washington he felt I would enjoy.

Grandma and Grandpa show their love in different yet compatible ways. At the end of every phone call they repeat the same adages. Grandpa says, "Remember who you are and what you can become," "Work hard and work smart," "Keep the commandments," and "Remember that we love you." Between each of those phrases, Grandma simply repeats "Have fun."

In 2015 I happened to be in Washington on Grandma's 84th birthday. A mix of first, second, third, and fourth generationers gathered around a table to share one thing we loved about Grandma. Grandpa spoke last. With tears streaming down his face, he simply said, "I love that she is the love of my life." Grandma and Grandpa know how to love, and they especially know how to love each other. That is a lesson I will never forget.

KEVIN CASH COLTON

Love. While I could write books about what I have learned from Grandma and Grandpa, the main lesson I have learned from every interaction with them is love, especially love for our Savior, Jesus Christ, love for family, and love for others.

Their love of Jesus Christ has created a foundation of faith for the generations that have followed. Receiving my patriarchal blessing from Grandpa was an opportunity that I will always treasure. Grandma and Grandpa's faith show in everything they do, including sharing their testimony of Jesus Christ in every letter they have written to me so far on my mission (in Fukuoka, Japan).

Their love of family has instilled in my immediate family the notion that "family comes first." Despite their success in the business world, they have always said their greatest success has been family. The often-said Colton phrase "No empty chairs" has carried me time and time again in my pursuit in the gospel.

Their love for others has set the example for me to give unconditional love for all. All of my high school friends seem to know and remember Grandma and Grandpa, despite only meeting them once or twice! Everyone they meet can feel their immediate love for them.

Thus, if I could pass on one trait from Grandma and Grandpa to my children, it would be their unconditional, Christ-like love.

BENJAMIN GREG JENSEN
Spouse: Sara Toolson Jensen
Children: Hugh Benjamin Jensen

Two of the greatest qualities we admire in Ster and Ellie are their love and service for their family. We have not only witnessed this first-hand, but we have also experienced it through their children and grandchildren. It is because of their example that we have received one of the greatest gifts of our lives.

Two years ago their granddaughter, Jenna, offered to be our surrogate after learning we had been struggling for years trying to have a baby. At first we didn't believe it could be true—we told her she had no clue what that would entail, and if she did she would never offer. Jenna insisted, saying that family is the most important and this is what you do for family. After several tests, surgeries, and three attempts later, we were thrilled when Hugh Benjamin was born on May 23, 2017—just in time for our fifteen-year wedding anniversary. There is no greater gift of love and service.

While Jenna is the one selflessly giving us this gift, we know who she learned these qualities from. Throughout this process Sara and Jenna have become close and often discussed people and things that are meaningful to them. Jenna knows how much Sara admires her grandfather, and Jenna has often discussed Ster and Ellie's deep impact on her life. We learned of their many selfless acts of service—providing means for people who weren't able to provide it for themselves. Their legacy lives on through their amazing granddaughter and great-grandson. We will forever be grateful for their example.

TREVOR MICHAEL JENSEN
Spouse: Brooke Anne Jensen
Children: Caden Michael, Hailey Mae, Tyler Don, Gavin Trevor

I have been so very blessed to know Sterling and Ellie ever since my Mom married Dave. I was completely amazed at how they welcomed my mom into their family, and how they made me feel like I was as important to them as the grandchildren they have lived with and helped raise for years. I suppose that is what I admire most about them, their ability to meet someone and instantly – but very sincerely – make them feel loved.

They have been very successful throughout their lives, which would make some people feel elevated or entitled to admiration, yet from the very first moments I met them I felt none of this. I felt that they were entirely more interested in caring about others and making them feel loved and important than in receiving any praise or admiration.

When my wife and I stayed with them the first time, which was actually a few months before my mom and Dave were married, they were so kind to us. Sterling and Ellie spent time getting to know me and asking me about what I had done during my life. For the rest of the few days we spent there, every time they introduced me to someone else, Sterling would mention something that he had learned about me to that new individual. He highlighted the positive things he had learned.

This was a small and simple thing, but it drew me to them and made me desire to learn more about them. I hope my children will learn this lesson – to be selfless and generous with compliments to others. To care more about the feelings and interests of others than about receiving praise themselves.

DAVID CANNON JENSEN
Spouse: Elizabeth (Lizzy) Ann Jensen
Children: Tillie Rose, Jane Elizabeth, Clara Mae, Ezekiel Cannon

Sterling and Ellie represent so many good things to me. When I think of them I think of two loving, happy people who love to serve. I'll always remember the first time I met them in Wyoming at my Aunt Marie's place. Sometime during the day I met them, some music came on in the living room and Sterling reached over and grabbed Ellie's hand to stand up and dance together! It was a really special memory.

They both love to serve. In addition to the many formal service assignments they've completed over the years you don't want to mess with Sterling when there are dishes to be done; he is a serious dish washer and may just box you out!

I and so many people I love revere them and have been strengthened by their faith and examples. They always seem to find the positive in things and care as much or more about their family and faith than anyone I know. I'm confident the David and Lizzy Jensen family will be passing down stories of Sterling and Ellie's happiness, faith, and service to our kids!

NIELS CHRISTIAN JENSEN
Spouse: Susan (Susie) Margaret Jensen
Children: Claire Marie, Noelle Margaret, Mae Rebecca

Sterling and Ellie came into my life when I was in my mid-twenties and my mother married their son, Dave Colton. They immediately welcomed us with open arms into their family. It was amazing to feel of their acceptance and love right from the start. Since then, I have been immensely grateful to witness their example of faith, charity, and selfless service.

There is no one experience that I can pinpoint, but what is truly amazing is the way they interact together and with others. Sterling is constantly looking for ways he can help those around him—doing dishes, tidying up, or fixing a door.

Theirs is an example of how a marriage should be. They are so kind and sweet in all their interactions with each other. They are always the life of the party, and have danced at all their grandchildren's weddings, even into their eighties. They constantly have a pulse on what is going on in the lives of their children and grandchildren, and want to know if they can help in any way.

While we were in residency, our daughter Claire was diagnosed with autism. Soon after the diagnosis, we were struggling to get the finances together for the many therapies that Claire needed. We were poor students living on student loans, and the therapy bills were much more than we could afford, with no insurance that covered autism therapy.

When Sterling and Ellie learned of our situation, they selflessly contributed to help us continue Claire's therapy. We had no intention of asking, and were prepared to pursue other avenues, but they knew of our situation because they loved us, and they helped. I have strived to follow their example.

SARAH MARIE JENSEN TERRY
Spouse: David Ryan Terry
Children: Finn Leroy, Leo David, June Elizabeth

Sterling and Ellie have been an example of many things my husband and I aspire to be like. From exemplifying a wonderful marriage to raising incredible children, they have shown how a life full of hard work can and does pay off.

The wonderful results we see now are an output of their lifelong living of righteous lives and working hard to instill values in their children. They always have the happiest, most positive and upbeat demeanor. It is something that draws everyone to them.

I have always loved how, even though they are such impressive individuals, they are not above being silly. I have loved watching them interact with my own children and nieces and nephews. They speak the same language as little children, which makes them even more endearing. I love watching them dance. It will always be a favorite memory of mine. We love them dearly.

ELIZABETH (LIZZIE) JENSEN LANGSTON
Spouse: Abram (Abe) Clinton Langston
Children: Jensen Thomas, Roslyn Claire, Amos Cannon

Sterling and Ellie have been an example of celestial marriage to me, ever since my mother married into their family. When our family moved across town after living in my mother and Dave's guest house for two years, the one thing I took was a picture of Sterling and Ellie. I placed it in my bathroom and look at it in the morning when I'm getting ready for the day. I think of how they treat each other, and whenever I feel frustrated toward my spouse, I try to think of what Sterling and Ellie have done to be this much in love at their age.

They have treated each other with respect and kindness, with the grace that the Savior gives each of us. Their legacy of service is one that will remain with me and with my children throughout our lives. I feel extremely blessed to have been able to associate so closely with them and call them family.

One of my favorite memories is being in their home. It is such a special place, a haven from the world. I love to smell the sweet aromas of Ellie cooking in the kitchen, and I love to hear Sterling's deep booming voice laughing and chatting from his office. I feel their connections to the people they have tenderly loved as they have traveled and served in the Lord's name, and as they have worked to make a great living for their family.

Another cherished memory is the trip I was able to take to Africa on a safari with Sterling and Ellie, Aunt Carolyn, Dave, and my mother. I will never forget the many happy songs that we sang—even with Sterling's less-than-pitch-perfect voice. The happiness he and Ellie exuded throughout our travels was contagious and remains with me.

The support they show by attending family activities including games, graduations, celebratory showers of honor, weddings, and blessings, shows their dedication and love to their family and the gospel of Jesus Christ. Sterling and Ellie have given me a strong desire to leave such a legacy for my posterity. I love them and thank Heavenly Father for intertwining them in my life.

Sources

Sterling and Ellie Colton furnished the most important sources for this book. Of particular note are a dozen legal-size bound journals of approximately 500 pages each, for a total of about 6,000 single-spaced pages.

Ellie gave her husband the first journal on March 29, 1980. "May these pages record a rich and rewarding life," she inscribed on the flyleaf. From then for the rest of his life, Sterling almost never missed a single day of recording in the journal. He usually did so in black ink, chronicling each twenty-four hours of his life in remarkable detail.

Prior to 1980 Sterling used a three-ring binder to record "memories."

Ellie's written memoirs—which do not approach her husband's in volume—are found in a number of places, including a white three-ring binder and a number of folders and large envelopes. She gave various talks in church and elsewhere through the years, and furnished the author copies of many of them.

Both Coltons furnished copies of their school yearbooks. At a high school in the heart of Idaho potato country, Ellie's yearbook was called *The Spud;* Sterling's in northeastern Utah was the *Uintahn*. The thick yearbook published annually at the University of Utah was called the *Utonian*.

Midway through researching for this book, some Colton kids went up into their parents' attic in Bethesda, Maryland, and came down with gold: scores of letters between Sterling and Ellie, tucked away in his old Army footlocker. The letters cover in colorful and often humorous detail their relationship during college, courting, and new marriage, plus—especially captivating—their correspondence while separated by an ocean for months as Ellie carried within her their first child.

Sterling's first position after Stanford Law School and the Army was at Utah's oldest firm, Van Cott, Bagley, Cornwall & McCarthy. He joined the firm in 1957 and became a partner. In 1974 S.N. Cornwall wrote a 160-page history called *The Van Cott Firm: First Century*, which helped to set in context Sterling's service there.

Sterling left Van Cott and joined the Legal Department of Marriott International in 1966. Marriott's annual reports traced the company's evolution during the three decades Sterling was employed. Corporate archivist Beth Schuster shared other Marriott literature, including monthly employee newsletters. Katie Dishman, who replaced Schuster, and Kristen McGregor, senior manager of Cultural Affairs, also furnished helpful materials.

Kathi Ann Brown, a freelance writer, has helped Bill Marriott author two books: *The Spirit to Serve: Marriott's Way* and *Without Reservations: How a Family Root Beer Stand Grew into a Global Hotel Company*. In interviewing key Marriott executives for the first book, Brown journeyed north to Vancouver, Canada in July 1996 and spent six hours with Sterling, then a mission president. That in-depth interview and those two books were helpful for this one.

The Coltons led the LDS Vancouver mission for three years, producing a wealth of insightful information, including missionary eyewitnesses to leadership and character traits of Sterling and Ellie. The Coltons produced a monthly missionary newsletter called the *Mountain Top Messenger*, which detailed mission progress, including baptisms, and encouraged and instructed missionaries.

Years after the Coltons' three-year mission ended in June 1998, those who had served under them established a Facebook page, where returned missionaries (RMs) from 1995 - 98 described experiences in Canada and what they had done with their lives since then. Ellie established a personal Facebook page, on which scores of their RMs paid tribute to the Coltons.

The views of many other family members, personal friends, professional colleagues, and fellow volunteers contributed to an engaging double portrait of Sterling and Ellie.

The *Vernal Express* newspaper in Sterling's hometown was a useful source of information, as was the Idaho Falls *Post Register*. The Idaho Falls Public Library, and the Museum of Idaho within it, likewise were helpful sources.

Introduction
xiii "*billion-dollar ideas…*" Interview with Ron Harrison, February 4, 2016.

Chapter 1   Colton Pioneer Heritage
1 "'*Quartermaster' George Colton…*" For more on Colton ancestors, especially Sterling's parents, see the author's book, *Bridge Builder: Hugh Colton, From Country Lawyer to Combat Hero* (Los Angeles: Probitas Press, 2010).
2 "*to eat head, heels, hide…*" Henry Bigler diary cited at a Colton family reunion in about 1953 by Charles H. Colton, a grandson of Philander and Polly's. Copy in Colton family files.
3 "*Without any hesitancy he replied,…*" From the most complete source on the Coltons, *An Historical and Biographical Record of the Sterling Driggs Colton Family, Descendents and Related Families*, published by the S.D. Colton Family Organization, edited by Miriam C. Perry, 1977.
4 "*They brought flour in fifty-gallon barrels…*" Transcript of a lecture by Clara Colton Hall, a niece, in October 1984.
5 "*Sterling drew and fired…*" Ray Haueter, "Early Law Enforcement: Sterling Driggs Colton, First Sheriff of Uintah County, Utah," in a newsletter of the Utah Peace Officers Association, date unknown.
6 "*…this thing has impressed me…*" Letter from Hugh to Bill, dated February 9, 1927 in family files.
7 "*My prayer was answered…*" Transcript of a dinner announcing the establishment of the Hugh W. Colton Professorship in Law, Brigham Young University, October 29, 1988, 14.

Chapter 2   Like Father, Like Son
1   *"of course he is the finest child…"* Hugh Colton letter to his parents, dated May 2, 1929.
2   *"arrival of a bonny baby boy…"* Vernal Express, May 2, 1929.
    "he has a will of his own…" Hugh's letter dated October 14, 1929.
3   *"Peeking through a cracked-open door…"* Clara Hall, speaking at the dedication of the Vernal City pavilion named in Marguerite's honor, July 7, 1985.
4   *"Such a man understands the structure of society…"* Robert H. Jackson, "The County-Seat Lawyer," 36 *ABA Journal*, 1950, 487.
5   *"'that's quite a bit of money'…"* Interview with Kenneth Anderton, November 29, 2007.
6   *"Uintah Basin people were depressed…"* Builders of Uintah (Uintah County: Daughters of the Utah Pioneers, 1947), 307.
7   *"he has had much public experience…"* Vernal Express, June 13, 1929.
8   *"The first assistance given to the public…"* Builders of Uintah, 522.
9   *"They were allowed to sleep…"* From a paper written in December 1991 by Sterling, called "A Pre-High School Vacation."
10 *"the empty fork jumped…"* See Morgan Family Pioneer Heritage online.

Chapter 3   Man of the House at Twelve
1   *"Hugh W. Colton, [temporary] captain…"* Vernal Express, March 30, 1939.
2   *"We certainly wish we could bring our daddy…"* Letter to Marsale Siddoway, February 19, 1942, copy in family files.
3   *"traditionally considered the elite…"* Schwarzkopf, *It Doesn't Take a Hero* (New York: Bantam Books, 1992), 69.
4   *"I can't tell you where I am…"* Letter dated December 16, 1943 in family files.
5   *"continue your straight A record…"* Handwritten letter from Hugh to Sterling, dated February 28, 1944.
6   *"…Bring your marks back UP…"* Hugh's handwritten letter to Sterling, March 28, 1944.
7   *"perhaps the best and most heroic job…"* AP reporter Hal Boyle, Alton (Illinois) Evening Telegraph, July 21, 1944.
8   *"the highest honor a soldier can receive."* Stephen Ambrose, *Citizen Soldiers: The U.S. Army from the Normandy Beaches to the Bulge to the Surrender of Germany* (New York: Simon & Schuster, 1997), 375.
9   *"Although wounded in the face…"* Colonel H.S. Miller, report dated May 18, 1945.
10 *"decisions made by Colonel Colton…"* Colonel H.S. Miller, Ibid.
11 *"'the bravest men on the western front'…"* Article by a columnist for the *New York Herald Tribune* in April 1945. Exact date of article unknown.

SOURCES

Chapter 4 A Rich Ricks Heritage

1 "*The accident stunted growth…*" Wanda Ricks Wyler, *Thomas E. Ricks: Colonizer and Founder* (M.C. Printing, 1988).

2 "*A week later the potatoes…*" James W. Davis, *Aristocrat in Burlap: A History of the Potato in Idaho* (Idaho Potato Commission, 1992).

3 *"Many of our brethren and sisters…" Deseret News*, October 15, 1856.

4 "*Thomas immediately responded…*" "Founders of the Snake River Valley," compiled by the Daughters of the Utah Pioneers in the Upper Snake River Valley; digitized and available in the BYU - Idaho library.

5 "'*Put your hands up, Jim!*'" "Rexburg 7th Ward Area," a publication in the Library Digital Collection, Brigham Young University–Idaho.

6 "*The dying bandit, George Munn"* One source for this true story is the same as for the previous outlaw anecdote, the Rexburg 7th Ward. For the fate of the other two outlaws see Gary A. Wilson, *Outlaw Tales of Montana: True Stories of the Treasure State's Most Infamous Crooks, Culprits, and Cutthroats* (Kearney, Nebraska: Morris Book Publishing, 2003) 9 - 11.

7 "'*My means have been used up'…*" *Ensign* (official LDS periodical), October 2001.

8 *"It may be a long time…" Ensign,* October 2001.

9 "*Orson was the first person…*" "Pioneer Memories: History of Hibbard Ward to 1904," Sunday School genealogy class, Hibbard Ward, 1963.

10 "*As a young man Emerson…*" From a paper written by his son, E. Lloyd Ricks, "Life History of Thomas Emerson Ricks," available online at FamilySearch.org.

11 "*before the LDS Manifesto…*" See Doctrine and Covenants "Official Declaration — 1," proposed by LDS President Wilford Woodruff and approved unanimously by vote of members attending general conference, October 6, 1890.

12 "*William's service in Southern Utah…*" Some of this information about William Willard Hutchings is from a four-page life sketch by a daughter, Vie Lettie Hutchings, in family files.

13 "*Emerson and Annie were strongly attracted…*" From E. Lloyd Ricks' paper on Thomas Emerson Ricks.

Chapter 5 Ricks Family Tragedies

1 "*A dryland farmer plants and prays,*" Molly Messick of National Public Radio, quoting retired farmer Stan Gortsema, NPR, August 11, 2012.

2 *"his condition was not regarded as critical…"* Idaho Falls *Post Register*, September 30, 1937.

3 "*One of the temple rites is baptism for the dead…*" The Bible has a reference to

this rite, suggesting it was not unknown in the primitive Christian church. Paul, in his first epistle to the Corinthians, said "Else what shall they do which are baptized for the dead, if the dead rise not all? Why are they then baptized for the dead?" (I Corinthians 15:29)

4   *"The opening song at Marie's funeral…"* Idaho Falls *Post Register*, July 16, 1940.

Chapter 6   The Education of Ellie

1   *"always tried her own way…"* Interview with Marilyn Pond Bengston, October 2, 2015.
2   *"Ellie and I both came from parts…"* Interview with Paula Stanger Stanley, October 5, 2015.
3   *"She had a great sense of quality…"* Interview with Shirley Stanger Berrett, July 25, 2015.
4   *"a series of amusing incidents…"* Idaho Falls *Post Register*, February 9, 1945.
5   *"a Harvard faculty committee chose four…"* *Harvard Crimson*, May 30, 1962.

Chapter 7   All-American Adolescent

1   "*Marguerite was something else…*" Lowell Caldwell, interview with author and Phil Colton, November 28, 2007.
2   *"the brains of that ranch for five years…"* Ralph Siddoway at the dedication of the Marguerite Maughan Colton pavilion in Vernal City, July 7, 1985.
3   "*When we got sick he would tell us…*" Interview with Phil Colton, November 29, 2007.
4   "*Sterling picked up various awards…*" *The Salt Lake Tribune*, April 8, 1945 and March 23, 1946.
5   "*Sterling was a favorite student…*" Dallin H. Oaks, transcript of a taped interview in Colton family files.

Chapter 8   Ellie Bonds with the Coltons

1   *"were doing a tango when…"* Wanda Beitel, *The Salt Lake Tribune*, February 11, 1950.
2   *"Combined Operations Prom."* *The Salt Lake Tribune*, April 15, 1950.
3   *"heaviest primary balloting…"* *The Salt Lake Tribune*, May 6, 1950.
4   "*Ellie was wonderful, effusive…*" Interview with Norma Warenski Matheson, June 26, 2015.
5   "*Occasionally they got together…*" Interview with Joan Douglas Earl, January 30, 2016.
6   "*She ran home so fast…*" This incident was recalled several years later by Ellie in a letter to Sterling, dated January 21, 1955.
7   "*Nanny and grandpa will be heart broken…*" Hand-written letter from Annie Hutchings Jaques to Ellie, date unknown.

Sources   489

    8   *"the first Marriott Hot Shoppes…"* Full-page ads in Salt Lake newspapers announced "the grand opening of the Hot Shoppes drive-in restaurant." *The Salt Lake Tribune*, April 1, 1951.

Chapter 9 From Oilfields to Stanford Law School
    1   *"If the best minds in the world had set out …"* Secretary of Defense Leon Panetta, speech on the commemoration of the Korean War Armistice, July 27, 2012.
    2   *"Exploratory drilling began as early as 1900…"* Red Wash Field—U.S.A. Uintah Basin, Utah, report by J.M. Kelly, Chevron U.S.A. Inc. and J.W. Castle, Cabot Oil and Gas Corporation. AAPGDatapages/archives.
    3   *"Honestly, these men live only…"* Letter to Ellie, July 29, 1950.
    4   *"about half the students were veterans…"* David Lempert, *After Five Decades: Stanford Law School's Class of 1952,* HeinOnline, 27 Legal Studies, F. 265, 2003, 267.
    5   *"The intensity nearly killed me…"* The Church and Matheson quotes are also from "After Five Decades," 274.
    6   *"he lived up to his name Sterling."* Interview with Nancy Peery Marriott, February 8, 2016.
    7   *"It was twenty degrees below zero…"* Interview with Bill Marriott, November 24, 2015.
    8   *"Are you ashamed to let other people know…"* Letter from Ellie to Sterling, November 26, 1951.
    9   *"I have no wonder that I left you…"* Letter from Sterling, December 1, 1951.
    10   *"it wasn't or isn't due to your selfishness…"* Letter from Ellie, December 4, 1951.
    11   *"she had decided to marry for money…"* Letter to Sterling, January 13, 1952.

Chapter 10 Love Story for the Ages
    1   *"beaming smile and cultured diplomacy."* *Utonian*, (Salt Lake City, Utah: University of Utah, 1953) 329.
    2   *"was recently chosen president…"* Idaho Falls *Post-Register*, February 24, 1952.
    3   *"Learn to like what doesn't cost much."* Quoted in many publications, including Eugene England, ed., The Best of Lowell L. Bennion: Selected Writings, 1928-1988 (Salt Lake City: Deseret Book Company, 1988) xxiii.
    4   *"Someone thinks you're wonderful…"* Letter from Ellie, February 16, 1952.
    5   *"Golly,"—a youthful term…"* Letter from Sterling, December 4, 1952.
    6   *"I still think you're an okay kid!!"* Letter from Ellie, December 9, 1952.
    7   *"…much of what I am…"* Letter from Sterling, January 26, 1953.
    8   *"I kept my shoes on…"* Letter from Ellie, February 1, 1953.

9   *"I love you for the happy memories…"* Letter from Ellie, January 10, 1953.
10   *"All at once it occurs to me…"* Letter from Ellie, March 21, 1953.
11   *"I was really a physical wreck."* Letter from Sterling, March 30, 1953.
12   *"…for three days…"* Ibid.
13   *"forward observers overwhelmingly suffered…"* John K. Rieth, *Patton's Forward Observers: History of the 7th Field Artillery Observation Battalion, XX Corps, Third Army* (Richmond, Va.: Brandylane Publishers).
14   *"Even your faults…"* Letter from Ellie, January 27, 1954.
15   *"Eleanor Ricks to Marry Utah Man…"* Idaho Falls *Post-Register*, June 6, 1954.
16   *"examining items in a 'hope chest.'"* Idaho Falls *Post-Register*, June 27, 1954.
17   *"I gave the customers bigger frosties…"* Letter from Ellie, exact date unknown.

Chapter 11   Temple Marriage, Long-Distance Love
1   *"The bride was lovely in a summer gown…"Vernal Express*, August 26, 1954.
2   *"The day we were married in the temple…"* From a transcript of a talk by Ellie, date unknown.
3   *"Oh what lucky people we are…"* Nancy Colton Bradley letter to Ellie Colton, date unknown.
4   *"fundamental honesty…"* Letter from Ellie, early 1954.
5   *"I asked for something non-alcoholic…"* Letter from Sterling, January 9, 1955.

Chapter 13   Exploring Europe
1   *"Nancy and Faye Knudson 'left early'…" Vernal Express*, June 24, 1954.
2   *"the problem of not having a temple marriage…"* Letter from Nancy Colton to Sterling Colton, winter of 1955.
3   *"Bob and Nancy have a gorgeous apartment…"* Marguerite letter in family files.
4   *"Welcomed back to Salt Lake City…" The Salt Lake Tribune*, June 13, 1957.

Chapter 14   First Home
1   *"looked for top academic credentials…"* Gregory Williams, "Cover Story, Van Cott, Bagley, Cornwall & McCarthy, *Attorney at Law* magazine, 2016.
2   *"Salisbury, said lawyer-historian…"* S.N. Cornwall, *The Van Cott Firm, First Century* (Self-published by law firm, 1974), 93.
3   *"Sterling was just extremely likable…"* Interview with David Salisbury, September 9, 2015.
4   *"how much clothing he had on…"* Interview with George and Joan Douglas Earl, February 4, 2016.

Chapter 15   Taming Ellie's "Herd"
1   *"chairman of the Tax Section…" The Salt Lake Tribune*, June 22, 1965.

Sources 491

2   *"Where my father was perhaps the rock…"* David Colton, oral history transcript, Aspen Grove Family Camp and Conference Center, Provo Canyon, 2007.
3   *"They have a sign of three taps…"* Carolyn Colton, Aspen Grove, 2007.
4   *"Of Sterling, Brad said…"* Brad Colton, Aspen Grove, 2007.
5   *"They just had great expectations…"* Steve Colton, Aspen Grove, 2007.

Chapter 16   Recruited to Marriott

1   *"Allie was the first to suggest…"* Interview with J.W. (Bill) Marriott, Jr., November 24, 2015.
2   *"were cooking more steaks…"* John de Ferrari, D.C. History Network Blog.
3   *"Heavens, no!"* J.W. Marriott, Jr. and Kathi Ann Brown, *The Spirit to Serve: Marriott's Way* (Snowball Publishing, 1997), vi.
4   *"Had I had my way," said Bill* Ibid, 81.
5   *"he grimaced, I borrowed."* Ibid. 70.
6   *"Sterling was the rock of common sense…"* Interview with Gary Wilson, March 22, 2016.

Chapter 17   Marriott Soars

1   *"Sterling has always had a dear place…"* Interview with Nancy Marriott, March 9, 2016.
2   *"He was just terrific."* Transcript of interview of Bill Marriott by Kathi Ann Brown, July 10, 1996.
3   *"many corporate law departments…"* Saundra Torry, *The Washington Post*, July 10, 1995. The recruiter quoted in the article was Beth Green Olesky of Russell Reynolds Associates.
4   *"She is one of my very closest friends…"* Interview with Barbara Mecham, June 26, 2015.
5   *"That's when I asked Sterling…"* Interview with Ralph Mecham, June 26, 2015.

Chapter 18   Sterling Named General Counsel

1   *"Very smart, very honest…"* Interview with Stephen Bollenbach, April 19, 2016.
2   *"Sterling is the best business lawyer…"* Interview with Francis (Butch) Cash, September 10, 2015.
3   *"…good management is important…"* Joint report of J.W. and Bill Marriott, 1968 Annual Report, 4.

Chapter 19   Sterling Builds Superb Legal Team

1   *"They considered him a father figure…"* Interview with Ron Harrison, February 4, 2016.

2   *"Sterling was a great leader…"* Interview with Ward Cooper, July 20, 2016.
    "Sterling was closely involved in the three…" Interview with Brad Bryan, April 13, 2016.
3   *"What an impressive guy Sterling was…"* Interview with Michael Jarrard, July 21, 2016.
4   *"Sterling's prudence in keeping…"* Interview with Myron Walker, July 20, 2016.
5   *"wished that he had gone off…"* Interview with Brad Bryan, April 13, 2016.
6   *"Sterling is a gentleman…"* Interview with Stephen McKenna, August 2, 2016.
7   *"Sterling is the finest man…"* Interview of Bill Kafes by Wesley and Marian Johnson, December 8, 1995.
8   *"We've had a story to tell…"* Bill Marriott, "What About This Business of Social Responsibility?" Marriott Corporation Annual Report 1973, 20.
9   *"Sterling is one of the finest…"* Interview with Joan McGlockton, August 8, 2016.

Chapter 20   Marriott Sails Into Troubled Waters

1   *"Dad didn't tell us we had to work…"* David Colton, transcript of an interview at Aspen Grove family camp, December 2007.
2   *"You get your job done…"* Dave Colton, transcript of oral history interview at Aspen Grove family encampment, December 2007.
3   *"the best human relations guy in the world…"* Interview with Clifford J. Ehrlich, May 21, 2016.
4   *"Marriott lost important money…"* Forbes, May 15, 1978.

Chapter 21   Charity Begins at Home

1   *"I wouldn't be where I am today…"* Interview with Angela Marie (Bay) Buchanan, August 14, 2015.
2   *"Ellie often spiced her talks…"* From a sheet of humorous wisdom in her Young Women's file.

Chapter 22   Coltons Lead Football Team to the Top

1   *"except when it came to his kids…"* Interview with Francis (Butch) Cash, September 10, 2015.
2   *"The coach, Fred Shepherd…"* The Gazette, Montgomery County newspaper, June 25, 2008.
3   *"We are cheering from this end…"* Letter to the Sterling Coltons from Hugh Colton, October 30, 1976.
4   *"we can do a lot of things better…"* Interview with Clayton Foulger, January 22, 2016.
5   *"Sterling is loyal, helpful…"* Interview with Ralph Hardy, September 8, 2015.
6   *"I visited Muffy Evans."* Sterling's journal, November 19, 1990.

SOURCES   493

7   *"Elder Oaks gave Muffy Evans…"* Sterling's journal, March 1, 1992.
8   *"After Sterling was released…"* Interview with Ron and Debbie Harrison, February 4, 2016.
9   *"When Dennis died…"* Interview with Suzanne Glassman, July 27, 2015.
10 *"Ellie, the flowers for the service…"* Note card from Suzanne Garff to the Coltons, July 8, 1985.

Chapter 23   Ellie vs. Equal Right Amendment
1   *"Brother Ladd," said Ellie…"* "My Personal Rubicon," in *Dialogue: A Journal of Mormon Thought*, winter 1981.
2   *"the Church's First Presidency…"* publicly issued in December 1976.
3   *"I am for women's rights…"* Eleanor Ricks Colton, "A Mormon Woman Looks at the ERA," *The Washington Post*, November 21, 1977.
4   *"They stepped aside,…"* *Dialogue*, 103.
5   *"Ms. Johnson, how many people do you represent…"* For more complete coverage of Congress and the ERA, see the author's book, *Leading the Charge: Orrin Hatch and 20 Years of America* (Carson City, Nevada, Gold Leaf Press, 1994) Chapters 8 and 15.
6   *"open support of the ERA by itself …"* "The Church and the Proposed Equal Rights Amendment," *Ensign* magazine, February 1980, 17.
7   *"a huffy woman behind me…"* *Dialogue*, 103.
8   *"I know of no church that gives women…"* Eleanor Ricks Colton, "Mormons and ERA: The Other Side," *The Washington Post*, December 28, 1979.
9   *"Together we are partners…"* *Dialogue*, 106, 108.
10 *"I helped Ellie and Carolyn…"* Sterling, journal entry on June 14, 1980.
11 *"Eleanor Ricks Colton is another light in my life…"* A paper written by Marilyn (Rolapp) Brinton, October 2013.

Chapter 25   Daughters-in-law Join the Family
1   *"What a lot of joy and happiness you've brought…"* Letter from Nancy Colton Bradley to Ellie Colton, late in 1983.

Chapter 26   Marriott Resurrects Times Square
1   *"worst block in the city."* Milton Bracker, "Life on W. 42nd Street: a Study in Decay," *The New York Times*, March 14, 1960.
2   *"the biggest financial decision…"* Bill Marriott, *The Spirit to Serve* (Snowball Publishing, 1997) 73.
3   *"the most dangerous place…"* Interview with Gary Wilson, July 4, 2016.
4   *"We were going to be the anchor…"* Interview with Clifford J. Ehrlich, May 21, 2016.
5   *"…concrete down the toilet."* Interview with Donald McNamara, July 5, 2016.

Chapter 27 Grandchildren Arrive

1. *"Steve, Ellie's youngest, and Jeri, our oldest."* Interview with Judy Cash, September 10, 2015.
2. *"One held a small tip…"* Interview with Butch Cash, September 10, 2015.
3. *"able to wear the same clothes…"* Sterling's journal, December 12, 1980.
4. *"haven't missed a day of work…"* Sterling's journal, August 29, 1980.
5. *"Sterling and I started walking…"* Ellie's hand-written note in a three-ring binder.
6. *"We called her 'Mother Superior.'"* Interview with Lynne Mella, July 21, 2016.
7. *"Edwards flew over its head…"* Interview with Howard Edwards, July 18, 2016.
8. *"…it rained like crazy."* Interview with Glenn Potter, July 10, 2016.

Chapter 28 Marriott Builds, Sells, Manages Hotels

1. *"After five Courtyard hotels…"* In mid-2016, Courtyard had 1,047 hotels with another 285 in the pipeline.
2. *"Residence was started…"* In mid-2016, Residence Inn had 702 hotels, with another 217 in the pipeline.
3. *"Fairfield Inn, the lowest-cost company lodging…"* In mid-2016 Fairfield Inn had 779 hotels, with another 332 in the pipeline.
4. *"gave him an 'AV' rating…"* Martindale-Hubbell, "The Martindale-Hubbell Peer Review Ratings," 1993.
5. *"Yes, we 'sell' room nights…"* Bill Marriott, *The Spirit to Serve*, 83.
6. *"We started making some money…"* Interview with Fred Malek, June 11, 2016.
7. *"Not only were [cruise ships] more complicated…"* Bill Marriott, *The Spirit to Serve*, 83.

Chapter 29 Hugh Dies — The Torch is Passed

1. *"Hugh had prostate cancer…"* For a more complete description of Hugh and Marguerite's last days, see the author's book, *Bridge Builder, Hugh Colton: From Country Lawyer to Combat Hero*, Probitas Press, Chapter 48.
2. *"Law School Dean Bruce Hafen…"* Hafen's description was in a booklet distributed to guests at the professorship dinner.
3. *"The deputy ambassador of the Czech Republic…"* Alysa Hatch, *The Church News*, October 15, 1994.
4. *"The Coltons took me into their home…"* Interview with Anca Croitoru, October 8, 2016.

Chapter 30 Sterling Leads the Split that Saves Marriott

1. *"the most difficult time I have had…"* Sterling's journal, November 1, 1990.
2. *"Marriott was ranked ninth…"* Marriott Corporation 1990 Annual Report.

Sources

3   *"Sterling had a very low-key..."* Interview with Bill Kafes by Wesley and Marian Johnson, December 8, 1995.
4   *"Sterling did all the legal work..."* Interview with Bill Marriott, November 24, 2015.
5   *"There is a very uneven split."* The New York Times, October 6, 1992.
6   *"The issue is a simple one..."* The Baltimore Sun, October 30, 1992.
7   *"Bill Marriott testified in court..."* The Baltimore Sun, October 5, 1994.
8   *"...the scuzz of the earth..."* The Washington Post, July 19, 1993.
9   *"We called Sterling 'the Judge.'"* Interview of Stephen Bollenbach, April 19, 2016.
10   *"Sterling wrote, I spent the day..."* Sterling's journal, August 14, 1993.

Chapter 31   "Ellie Has Made All the Difference"

1   *"mistress, a cook, and a maid."* Ellie recounted the incident in speaking to missionaries in British Columbia, as recorded by Elder Aaron Kashiwagi in a scrapbook compiled by the missionaries and given to the Coltons in June 1998.
2   *"I had a long talk with Ellie..."* Sterling's journal, December 5, 1981.
3   *"We dedicate our actions..."* Reuben D. Law, *The Founding and Early Development of the Church College of Hawaii* (St. George, Utah: Dixie College Press, 1972) 67.
4   *"Ellie came over all week..."* Email from Melanie, September 18, 2016.
5   *"...fly-fishing for chrome bright..."* Dennis Harms at http://www.alaskatrophysafaris.com/history.html.

Chapter 32   Family Motto: "We Will Serve the Lord"

1   *"Sterling had a great compass..."* Interview with Ralph Hardy, September 8, 2015.
2   *"They were very kind,"* Interview with Claudia, July 10, 2016.

Chapter 33   Mission Trumps Marriott

1   *"...a dramatic drop in religious observance..."* "Patterns of Religious Attendance," an annual survey by Canada's General Social Survey, conducted by the Gallup poll.
2   *"...a first language other than English..."* 2011 Canada census.
3   *"Sterling is still humble..."* Transcript of tape-recorded marks from the April 25, 1995 retirement dinner.

Chapter 34   Payback Time

1   *"We hope to hold high the torch..."* Transcript of a tape recording of the sacrament service.

2   "*I was not born that way...*" Talk on "Pillars of my Faith," spring 1995 to the Potomac South Ward, Potomac, Maryland, prior to departing to preside over the Canada Vancouver Mission. Transcript of an audio tape.

3   "*Sterling's news updates to the Stanford...*" Email from Melanie Colton, May 8, 2015.

Chapter 35   Welcome to British Columbia

1   "*Winters are usually severe...*" One of the coldest readings recorded anywhere in North America was in British Columbia's Smith River, at -74 degrees.

2   "*When I met President Colton...*" Interview with Andrew Shirley, October 3, 2016.

3   "*Ellie's role was outlined...*" Letter to Ellie from the First Presidency, Howard W. Hunter, Gordon B. Hinckley, and Thomas S. Monson, February 10, 1995.

4   "*I'm all right, Jack.*" R. Val Johnson, *Ensign*, August 2007.

5   "*...reminded them of their personal strengths...*" Interview with Tom Hawes, October 18, 2016.

6   "*...elders who were trouble-makers...*" Interview with Troy Thurgood, November 11, 2016.

7   "*President Colton seemed to show special respect...*" Elder Clay Jones, in a missionary scrapbook prepared and given to the Coltons in June 1998.

8   "*...by breaking out in singing...*" Elder Aaron Kashiwagi, missionary scrapbook.

9   "*We went out of the boundaries...*" Interview with Annette Adams Esplin, October 14, 2016.

10   "*Sister Colton had a lot of spunk...*" Interview with David Williams, October 18, 2016.

11   "*pull the car over...*" Ellie described the incident to a friend, Sue Huguely, who related it to the author in an interview on August 8, 2015.

12   "*...you've made a huge dent...*" Sister Kristi Hollingshead, missionary scrapbook.

Chapter 36   Care and Feeding of 200 Missionaries

1   "*...will yield a greater return...*" President Gordon B. Hinckley, LDS General Conference, October 2002.

2   "*...without fear, GQ'd the waitress...*" Jeffrey Rawlins, missionary scrapbook.

3   "*President Colton continued to sing...*" Elder Jared Mortensen, missionary scrapbook.

4   "*I put my papers in...*" Interview with Marianne (Muffy) Evans Cook, June 15, 2016.

5   "*Muffy met Kevin Cook...*" Marianne "Muffy" Evans Cook returned to her

Sources

Father in Heaven as well as her deceased earthly father on May 29, 2017, following a series of strokes in St. George, Utah.
6   "...*the Church is felt in every province...*" Richard E. Bennett, "Canada: From Struggling Seed, the Church Has Risen to Branching Maple," *Ensign*, September 1988.

Chapter 37   Last Months in Mission Field
1   *"Why don't we send him home?"* Interview with Andrew Shirley, October 3, 2016.
2   *"President Colton loved him so much..."* Interview with Mary Jones, October 5, 2016.
3   "*45 percent more than the same period...*" "Returning Mission President's Report to the Area Presidency."
4   "*There was a lot of respect for Sterling...*" Interview with Steve West, September 11, 2015.

Chapter 38   Home Sweet Home
1   "*...echo and whisper of your days...*" Note from Sister Sid Oakes to Ellie Colton, date unknown.
2   *"President Colton was cool..."* Kenney C. Higley, Canada Vancouver Mission 1995-1998, a Facebook file for missionaries who served in the Colton years.
3   "*Sister Mary Jones served...*" Interview with Mary Jones, October 5, 2016.
4   *"Our mission mom always had a kind word ..."* Interview with Krista Smith Worth, October 17, 2016.
5   *"President Colton was so eager to serve..."* Interview with Tom Hawes, October 18, 2016.

Chapter 39   Safari in Southern Africa
1   *"They just went for it ..."* Interview with Fred Daniels, August 15, 2015.

Chapter 40   President, Matron of Washington D.C. Temple
1   *"There never was an issue..."* Interview with Ed Scholz, October 17, 2016.
2   *"He wanted to be very specific..."* Interview with Chuck Eckery, October 12, 2016.
3   *"Ellie divided the work..."* Interview with Marlene Eckery, October 12, 2016.

Chapter 41   Angels in White
1   *"Many have grandchildren..." The Washington Post*, January 11, 2001.

Chapter 42   Faith of a Patriarch

1   *"Sterling was one of the people…"* Interview with W. Cole Durham, Jr., October 10, 2016.

2   *"…the voice of the Lord…"* Interview with Ralph Hardy, September 8, 2015.

Chapter 43   Traveling the World

1   *"Sterling has had a profound impact…"* Email from Julie Jensen Colton to the author, May 6, 2015.

2   *"the most romantic sailing ship…"* Berlitz Complete Guide to Cruising & Cruise Ships.

3   *"…honored to be married to Sterling."* Interview with Ronald Harrison, February 4, 2016.

Index

Abzug, Bella 232
Adams, Annette 86, 280, 369, 468, 477
Africa ix, 193, 211, 316, 415-416, 418, 442, 481
Alaska 321-322, 351, 365, 367, 392, 433, 455
Alberta, Canada 121, 262
Alleman, Matthew Kurt 468
Alleman, Rebecca (Becca) Colton 259, 260, 280, 328, 333, 344, 345, 356, 397, 403, 412
Alpha Chi Omega 92, 94
Ambrose, Stephen 31, 486
Andrew, Howard 56
Andrew, Vie Ricks (Annie and Emerson's daughter) 94
Andria Doria 139
Anfinson, Gene 386, 387
Anfinson, Lynell 386
Archibald, Nolan 436
Army Judge Advocate General (JAG) Corps 117-119, 123, 125, 131-132, 134-135, 137, 146
Army Reserve 91, 98, 151
Arroyo Grande 25

Ashley Valley 4-5, 12, 14, 19, 23, 83
Ashton Avenue 145
Ashton, Marvin J. 319
Ballard, M. Russell 87, 301
Barker, Des 91
Bednarz, Ed 201
Bella Coola, British Columbia 386-387
Bengston, Marilyn Pond 55, 57, 60-61, 488
Bennion, Lowell L. 110, 489
Bennion, Steve 368
Berchtesgaden 132, 134
Berlin 34, 97, 134, 246, 298
Berrett, Shirley Stanger 58, 121, 488
Beta Gamma Sigma 88
Bethesda, MD 247-248, 250-252, 255-256, 259-260, 344, 348, 350, 352-353, 451-452, 456, 459, 461
bird-watching 323, 396, 456
birds 49, 52, 93, 111, 156, 185, 323-324, 329, 397, 414-415, 418, 440-441
Black, Ethan Wallace 328, 471
Black, Jane Elizabeth Colton 280, 328, 347, 352, 403, 438, 450-452, 455, 456, 471

Blackcomb Mountain 396
"Blue Moon" 91
Bollenbach, Steve 191, 275, 307, 309, 312, 463
Bonneville Ward 147, 160
Book of Mormon 186, 224, 262, 288, 336, 356, 362-363, 377-379, 399, 401, 412, 446
Bradley, Nancy Colton 15-16, 25, 29, 68, 89-90, 267, 490, 493
Bradley, Nancy Elizabeth (Merians) 198, 267, 490, 493
Bradley, Robert (Bob) Louis 137-138, 257, 267, 340, 352
Bradley, Robert (Bobby) Louis Jr. 138, 198, 267
Bradley, Robin (Sitar) 52, 141, 160, 198, 267, 385, 443
Brewer, Mauri Lyn Colton 256, 279, 283, 284, 327, 333, 345, 347, 352, 420, 455, 466
Brewer, Nathanael (Nathan) Warren 466
Brigham Young 2, 7-8, 15, 35-39, 85, 89, 261, 270, 328, 332, 398, 485, 487
Brigham Young University 7, 15, 39, 85, 89, 261, 270, 328, 332, 398, 485, 487
Brinton, Marilyn Rolapp 239, 267, 493
British Columbia 322, 335-336, 338, 357-358, 360, 362-363, 365, 367-368, 370, 373, 377-379, 387, 389, 396, 402-404, 408, 411, 413, 440, 463, 495-496
Brown, Kathi Ann 396, 484, 491
Brush Creek 5, 126
Bryan, Bradford (Brad) 201, 203, 285, 492
Buchanan, Angela Marie (Bay) 212, 213

Bucharest 303, 342
Buckley, Gladys 65
bungee-jump 324
Burke, Jack 295
Burnett, Jay 369
Burnett, Yvonne 369
Cabo San Lucas, Mexico 432
Cache Valley, UT 7-8, 38, 40
Caffey, Eugene 118
Cairo Marriott 244, 256, 268, 271
Caldwell, Lowell 80, 488
Caldwell, Wallace 20, 80-81
Cambodia 433-435
Camp San Luis Obispo 25
Campbell, Beverly 301
Canada Vancouver Mission 335, 418, 447, 496-497
Carlson Hall 86, 89-91, 114, 163
Casey 156-157, 183, 189
Cash, Francis W. (Butch) 243
Cash, Judy 281, 285, 300, 345, 355, 494
Central Elementary School 18
Chalmers Graham Scholarship 102
Chariot 307-314
Checchi, Al 275
Christ Episcopal Day School 244-245
Church of Jesus Christ of Latter-day Saints (Mormon) 1-3, 62, 93, 132-133, 139, 142, 167, 186, 212, 223-224, 233, 235-236, 238-239, 261-262, 288, 303, 332, 336, 343, 356, 360, 362-363, 370, 372, 377-379, 398-399, 401, 412-413, 437, 446, 493
Churchill High School 216, 261-263, 267
Claudia 332, 495
Clayton, Richard 92
Colorado River 286-287

INDEX

Colton, Barbara (Bobby) Snyder 197, 299, 341
Colton, Bradley (Brad) Hugh 148, 151, 154, 155, 159, 160, 162, 184, 186, 194, 213-216, 219-221, 228, 262, 266-268, 280, 321, 326, 330, 331, 355, 360, 403, 436, 442, 443
Colton, Bradley Scott 280, 355, 443, 469
Colton, Brandon Cash 281, 328, 329, 438, 450, 452, 455, 475
Colton, Brittany Pierce 469
Colton, Carolyn xi, 142, 143, 147, 152, 153, 155, 157, 158, 160, 161, 184, 194, 216, 222, 233, 239, 279, 280, 293, 319, 331, 339, 340, 394, 400, 403, 436
Colton, Colleen Simper 197, 257, 355, 361
Colton, Darla Burnett 263, 279, 283, 319, 326, 339, 355, 439
Colton, Don B. (Byron) 11, 16
Colton, Eden Jensen 473
Colton, (Quartermaster) George 1, 485
Colton, Grace Stringham 12, 16-18, 141, 201, 481
Colton, Holly Christine 465
Colton, Hugh Maughan 15, 16, 25, 29, 80, 90, 96, 120, 121, 140, 197, 263, 299, 355, 361, 386-388 436
Colton, Hugh Wilkins (Sterling's father) 1, 3, 6, 7, 9-17, 19, 20, 21-34, 79-81, 83, 86, 103, 116, 118, 121, 126, 152, 158, 177, 178, 187, 197, 213, 221, 241, 245, 271, 286, 287, 293, 294, 297, 298-301
Colton, Jane Elizabeth (see Black, Jane Elizabeth Colton)

Colton, Jared Cash 281, 328, 333, 346, 347, 350, 443, 452, 455, 473
Colton, Jenna Arlene (see Jarvis, Jenna Arlene Colton)
Colton, Jeri Cash xi, 280, 281, 294, 328, 294, 328, 339, 355, 361, 391, 443
Colton, John Phillip (Phil) 15, 16, 29 80, 90, 121, 126, 148, 197, 214, 299, 300, 339, 341, 342, 386, 434, 435
Colton, Julie Jensen 326, 439, 442, 443
Colton, Kevin Cash 281, 328, 329, 438, 450, 452, 455, 460, 476
Colton, Marguerite Maughan (Sterling's mother) 7-12, 15, 17, 25, 26, 29, 80, 91, 93, 126, 139, 140, 152, 156, 178, 183, 197, 293, 294, 297, 299, 300, 361, 387, 388
Colton, Mauri Lyn (see Brewer, Mauri Lyn Colton)
Colton, Melanie Farrell 186, 228, 266, 267, 280, 321, 328, 338, 339, 355, 360, 361, 403, 442, 443
Colton, Meredith Cash (see Udvar-Hazy, Meredith Cash Colton)
Colton, Nancy Wilkins 6
Colton, Philander 1-2, 398
Colton, Polly Matilda Merrill 1-2, 398, 485
Colton, Rebecca Anne (see Alleman, Rebecca (Becca) Colton)
Colton, Sterling Daniel 255, 259, 264, 279, 317, 321, 322, 326, 329, 333, 338, 345, 398, 465
Colton, Sterling David 134, 136, 139, 142, 145, 149, 151, 154, 157-159, 161, 184, 185, 189, 194, 207, 208, 211, 213, 216, 261, 263, 279, 319, 321, 325-327, 330, 331, 334, 339, 355, 397, 436, 439, 442, 443

Colton, Sterling Driggs 3-6, 11, 18, 485
Colton, Steven (Steve) Ricks 150-155, 162, 184, 189, 208, 211, 213, 216, 219, 222, 233, 262, 263, 268, 271, 280, 281, 294, 319, 321, 328, 330, 331, 361, 391, 432, 443
Colton, Thomas James 280, 321, 328, 329, 403, 438, 452, 455, 472
Condie, Spencer J. 362, 365
Cook, Marianne (Muffy) Evans 226, 227, 383, 384, 385, 392
Cooper, Suzanne Glassman 228, 229, 324, 445
Cooper, Ward 201, 492
Cosic, Kresimir 342, 343
Croitoru, Anca 303, 304, 342, 348, 494
Croitoru, Carina 304, 342, 348
Croitoru, Cristian 304, 342
Croitoru, Verona 303
Curtis, Theodore 132, 142
Daniels, Fred 414, 430-431, 444, 452, 497
Diamond Mountain 17, 21, 83, 126
Droege, Bob 292
Durbin, James 242
Durham, Cole 435, 498
Earl, Joan Douglas 93, 96, 488, 490
Eastern States Mission 7, 16
Eckery, Charles (Chuck) 421-422, 424, 497
Eckery, Marlene 421, 424, 497
Edison School 116
Edwards, Howard 287, 494
Egypt 243-245, 254, 256, 271, 341
Ehrlich, Clifford J. 242, 492-493
Eisenhower, Dwight D. 27, 31, 34, 79, 149, 287
Equal Rights Amendment (ERA) 104, 131, 135, 192, 231-240, 439, 493

Esplin, Annette Adams 375, 496
Evans, Marianne (Muffy) (see Cook, Marianne (Muffy) Evans)
Eyring, Henry B. 365
family vacations 146, 159, 213, 333
Farrell's Ice Cream Parlour 209, 291
Faust, James E. 362, 364, 436
Fort Belvoir 25
Fort Douglas 79, 86, 146
Fort Lewis 26-29
Fort Sill 99, 116-117, 122-123, 166
Foulger, Clayton 223, 225, 492
France 29-30, 32, 79, 97, 124, 138, 244, 339-340, 367, 352-353, 367
Future Farmers of America (FFA) 82, 83
Garff, Andrew 445
Garff, Dennis 228-230
Garff, Peter Royal 445
Garn, Jake 87, 338
Germany 23, 30-33, 79, 82, 97, 109, 123-126, 130, 132-133, 136, 142-143, 167-168, 197, 223, 283, 317, 326, 341, 421, 440, 486
Glassman, Jay 324
Greentree Road 185, 189, 220, 332, 403, 414, 430
Hahn, Richard Gillis (Gil) 62
Haight, Bruce 99, 105
Haight, David B. 364, 372
Hall, Clara 12, 485-486
Hardy, Ralph 223, 252, 255, 325, 438
Harrison, Debbie Marriott 227, 493
Harrison, Ron 199, 227-228, 444, 485, 491
Hatch, Orrin 235-236, 493
Hawaii 186, 318-320, 333, 442, 350, 495
Hawes, Tom 373, 406, 410, 411, 496, 497

Index

Heaton, Elayne 58, 60, 64
Henry Newell Scholarship 101
Hester, Phyllis 209, 437
Hibbard 35, 40-45, 47-48, 73-75, 487
Highland Park Ward 145
Higley, Kenney 409, 497
Hinckley, Gordon B. 294, 335, 356, 362, 365, 377, 418, 496
Hollingshead, Kristi 376, 496
horses 4-7, 10, 19, 21, 29, 38-39, 46, 81, 122, 134, 151-152, 158, 186, 213, 271, 287, 293, 297, 300, 323, 419, 443
Host Marriott Corp. 308, 309, 311, 312
Howard Johnson 295
Hugh W. Colton Administration Building 300
Hugh W. Colton Professorship 297, 299, 485
Huguely, Sue 285, 496
Hunter, Howard W. 335, 362, 350, 496
Hutchings, William Willard Jr. 41
Idaho Falls, ID 76-78, 165, 169
Idaho Falls High Pep Club 58, 64, 78, 83
Idaho Falls High School 62, 78, 89
Idaho Falls Temple 118, 121, 139, 165, 425
Israel 243, 268, 325, 425
J. Reuben Clark Law School 279, 297, 435
J. Willard Marriott Award of Excellence 337
Jackman, Elden 369
Jackman, LaDawn 369
Jackson, Robert 13, 486
Janapaul, Dick 115, 164
Jaques, Alpha R. 59, 60
Jaques, Annie Hutchings Ricks (Ellie's mother) xiv, 41-47, 49-52, 55, 56, 59-61, 89, 94, 95, 112, 118, 133, 157, 196
Jarrard, Michael (Mike) 202, 492
Jarvis, Jared Vernon 467
Jarvis, Jenna Arlene Colton 260, 279, 327, 333, 345, 347, 350, 397, 455, 467
Jensen, Benjamin Greg 326, 439, 477
Jensen, Brooke Anne 477
Jensen, David Cannon 326, 439, 478
Jensen, Elizabeth (Lizzy) Ann 478
Jensen, Julie Claire Haycock (see Colton, Julie Jensen)
Jensen, Marcus 17
Jensen, Niels Christian 326, 327, 439, 479
Jensen, Sara Toolson 477
Jensen, Susan (Susie) Margaret 479
Jensen, Trevor Michael 326, 327, 439, 477
Jerusalem 256, 268-270
Johnson, Brian 223, 254
Johnson, Frank 246, 415, 418, 432, 453
Johnson, Gregory (Greg) 392
Johnson, Sally 415, 418, 432, 453
Johnson, Sonia 235-239
Jones, Clay 374, 496
Jones, Mary 392, 410, 497
Jones, Vince 115, 164
Junior Prom (at the "U") 91, 114, 283
Kafes, Bill 204, 306, 308, 492, 495
Kappa Kappa Gamma 91, 93, 95, 109-110
Kashiwagi, Aaron 375, 495-496
Kelly of Shannon 189, 248
Kentucky Derby 271
Keogh, William (Bill) 117
Khayyam, Omar 105, 244

Killpack, William L. 121
Kimball, Frank C. 187
Kimball, Spencer W. 231, 239
Koch, Ed 273, 277
Korologos, Joy 302
Ladd, Tom 220
Ladd, W. Donald 232
Lake Winnipesaukee 186, 293-294
Langston, Abram (Abe) Clinton 481
Langston, Elizabeth (Lizzie) Jensen 326, 481
LDS Serviceman's Branch (Stuttgart) 132, 135, 142, 143, 167, 223
Lindholm, Doretha Ricks 43, 45, 76-77, 169, 442
Little Brush Creek 126
MacGarry, Mac 224
Maeser 81, 267, 436
Malek, Fred 251, 292, 494
Manwaring, Arthur 20
Marriott, Alice (Allie) Sheets 10, 177-178, 181, 183, 205, 241, 294, 491
Marriott, Donna Garff 183-184, 186, 209, 227, 258, 300, 338, 360, 412, 440, 457
Marriott, J. Willard (Bill, J.W.) Sr. 1, 7, 177, 178, 181, 183, 184, 491
Marriott, J. Willard (Bill, J.W.) Jr. 87, 99, 105, 177, 178, 181, 182, 184, 187, 199-201, 204, 208, 241, 242, 274, 277, 282, 290-292, 305, 306, 308, 309, 311, 313, 337
Marriott Fairfield Farm 186, 194, 196, 301
Marriott Hot Shoppes 10, 96, 99, 178-180, 187, 188, 195, 489
Marriott hotels 1, 42, 115, 121, 134, 141, 180-181, 188, 192, 195, 200-201, 203, 239, 242-244, 263, 271, 273-274, 276-278, 285, 289-291, 305-307, 310-311, 314, 319, 339, 342, 374, 395, 397, 402, 417, 464, 484
Marriott In-Flite 179, 188, 195, 200, 210, 296
Marriott International 1, 87, 177, 300, 308-309, 311-313, 360, 463, 484
Marriott Legal Department 187, 188, 199, 200, 204, 205, 276, 280, 306, 307
Marriott Marquis, New York 203, 273-277, 290, 339
Marriott, Nancy Peery 104, 183, 186, 283, 302, 337, 489, 491
Marriott, Richard E. (Dick) 104, 178, 186, 251, 294, 298, 302, 308, 337, 338
"Marriott's Great America" theme parks 210, 241, 291, 292
Marriott Sun Line cruises 209-210, 241, 271, 292
Martindale-Hubbell 290, 494
Matheson, Norma Warenski 87, 93, 102, 103, 351, 488, 489
Matheson, Scott 87, 93, 102-103
Maughan, Peter 7-8
Maughan, William H. 7-8
Maughan, William H. Jr. 8
McGlockton, Joan 205, 492
McKay, David O. 139, 320
McKenna, Steve 203, 276, 354
Mecham, Barbara 189, 267, 338, 491
Mecham, Ralph 88, 189-190, 452, 491
Mella, Lynne 285, 494
Merkley, Nyle 101
Miller, Marvin Gregory 412
Missionary Training Center 336, 361
Monson, Thomas S. 320, 335, 362, 463, 496

Index

Montgomery County, MD 179, 183, 185, 190, 197, 492
Morgan, Barbara 8
Mormon Battalion 2, 398
Mortensen, Jared 380, 496
Nanaimo British Columbia Stake 370
National Guard 23-25, 99
National Honor Society 263
Nauvoo, IL 1-2, 7, 35, 239, 425
Neslen, Cannon 371-372, 398, 406, 412
Neuber, Mae 65
New Zealand 318, 324, 351
North Atlantic Treaty Organization (NATO) 124
O. E. Bell Junior High School 55, 60
O'Connor, Sandra Day 102, 143
Oakes, Don 369-370, 409, 497
Oakes, Sid 369-370, 409, 497
Oaks, Dallin H. 15, 85, 99, 227, 299, 320, 488
Oaks, June 320
Oaks, Stella Harris 15, 85
oil fields 100, 208
Onondaga Avenue 183
Osborne, George 102
pack trips 87, 158-159, 213, 294, 440
Packer, Boyd K. 294, 363
Pagley, Beth 212
Palm Springs, CA 115, 164, 285
Palo Alto, CA 101, 104-105, 107, 113, 364
Parker, Joseph (Joe) 44, 52, 95
Parker, Vie Ricks (Annie's sister) 44
Parkinson's disease 443
Pearl Harbor 25
Perry, Anne 369
Perry, Walter 369
Peterson, H. Burke 145

Peterson, Richard 84
Peterson, Steven 392
Phi Eta Sigma 87
Pickerell, Dolly 414
poetry 65, 107, 112, 239-240
Polynesian Cultural Center 317, 320, 350
Pond, Marilyn (see Bengston, Marilyn Pond)
Portman, John Jr. 274
Potomac South Ward 225-226, 229, 403, 413, 496
Potomac Ward 190, 221, 225-226, 229, 252, 403, 413, 425, 496
Potter, Glenn 287, 494
Prince, Greg 223, 254
Princeton Avenue 146, 148-149, 154-155, 174 183
Rawlins, Jeffrey 379, 496
Rehnquist, William 102, 143
Relief Society (LDS) 51, 184, 223, 226, 231, 233, 239, 252
Reserve Officers' Training Corps (ROTC) 91, 92, 98, 99, 102, 107, 116, 140
Richards, Frank 287
Richards, Merlon 284
Richins, Nantie 11
Ricks, Annie (see Jaques, Annie Hutchings)
Ricks, Emerson Lloyd (Ellie's brother) 44, 119, 121, 169, 487
Ricks, Jean Hart 169
Ricks, Margaret Archibald 48, 419
Ricks, Opal 52
Ricks, Orson (Ellie's grandfather) 40, 43, 46-48, 50, 95, 419
Ricks, Thomas E. 35, 36, 38-40, 398, 487
Ricks, Thomas E., Jr. 38, 39

Ricks, Thomas Emerson (Ellie's father) 40, 41-44, 46-50, 95
Rigby, Joseph 43
Riverside Elementary School 51
Rona, Daniel 268
Roosevelt, Franklin D. 16, 23, 83
Rottman, Ethel 65
Rubaiyat 105
safari 322, 413, 453, 481, 497
Salisbury, Carol 253, 422
Salisbury, David 87, 102, 143, 158, 255, 287, 490
San Luis Obispo 25
Scholz, Ed 421-422, 424, 429, 497
Scholz, Lois 421, 424
Scott, Richard G. 364
Sea Cloud 440-441, 457
Seiberling, Steve 223
Seven Locks Elementary School 185
Shakespeare, William 116, 128, 133, 186, 265-266, 316, 470
Shepherd, Fred 219-220, 492
Shirley, Andrew 368, 391, 411, 496-497
Shupe, Elizabeth Jane 40
Sigma Chi Fraternity 87, 90, 91, 94, 99, 102, 104, 114, 116, 120, 163, 164, 178
Simmons, Dennis 225
skiing 147, 158, 186, 229, 454
Smart, Dorotha Sharp 90, 94, 348, 433
Smith, Joseph 1, 35, 40, 262, 356, 362, 378, 394, 400, 408
Smith, Krista 410, 497
Snake River Valley 35, 38, 66, 487
Sowards, Glade 83, 86-87
Stanford Law School 97, 101, 109, 112, 360, 484, 489
Stanford University 101, 433, 439, 441

Stanger, Paula (see Stanley, Paula Stanger)
Stanger, Shirley (see Berrett, Shirley Stanger)
Stanley, Paula Stanger 58, 60, 62, 64, 65, 91, 121, 488
Sterling and Eleanor Colton Chair in Law and Religion 435
Stewart, Chuck 115, 164
Stringham, Bea 18, 67
Switzerland Temple 139
Tau Kappa Alpha 92
tennis 84, 86, 115-116, 173, 219, 224, 282, 284-285, 310, 316, 319-320, 329-330, 344, 361, 395-396, 413, 417, 431, 433
Terry, David Ryan 480
Terry, Sarah Marie Jensen 327, 439, 480
"Tex" Henry 100
The New York Times 273, 278, 300, 493, 495
The Salt Lake Tribune 143, 488-490
The Washington Post 234, 300, 311, 427, 491, 493, 495, 497
Thurgood, Troy 373, 496
Times Square 203, 273-277, 289, 493
Times Square Marriott hotel (see Marriott Marquis, New York)
trips 42, 115, 137, 139, 144, 195, 209, 219, 270, 308, 320-321, 367, 370, 376, 433, 437, 440, 443
Udvar-Hazy, Meredith Cash Colton 281, 328, 329, 347, 348, 350, 352, 391, 450, 452, 455-456, 460, 474
Udvar-Hazy, Trenton (Trent) Scott 474
Uinta Mountains xv, 121, 152, 158, 159, 213, 286, 287, 294, 322, 440

Index

Uintah Basin 4, 6-8, 14, 20, 24, 72, 191, 197, 287, 298, 359, 486, 489
Uintah High School 27, 80, 82, 284
University of Utah 9, 86, 89, 92-93, 95, 103, 110-111, 146, 160, 163, 177-178, 189, 197, 255, 261, 328, 389, 414, 483, 489
University of Utah Law School 103
U.S. Army 27, 79, 98, 135, 138, 143, 179, 398, 486
U.S. Army Artillery School 98
U.S. Army Hospital 27, 79, 135
U.S. Seventh Army 124, 125, 126, 132
U.S. War Department 24, 25
Utah National Guard 24, 99
Utah State Bar 151
Utah State University 89, 91, 212
Utonian 93, 109, 483, 489
V-E Day 79, 82
V-J Day 80
Vaihingen, Germany 126, 132, 135, 139-141
Van Cott, Bagley, Cornwall & McCarthy 143, 145, 279, 287, 331, 484, 490
Vancouver, Canada 322, 335-336, 360, 367, 369-370, 381-382, 384-386, 395-400, 409, 412, 418, 447-450, 463, 484, 496-497
Vancouver Temple 412
Veasy, George 148
Vencura, Frau 132, 139, 142
Vernal, UT 5-7, 10-12, 14-18, 20-21, 24-27, 34-35, 67-72, 79-82, 84, 86-87, 89-90, 99-101, 107, 116, 118-119, 122, 125-126, 140, 144, 151-152, 157-158, 183, 196-197, 257, 263, 267, 282, 284, 286, 293, 299, 320, 355, 361, 386-387, 408, 436, 485-486, 488, 490

Walele, Abdul 211
Walker, Myron 202, 354, 492
Walker, Olene 149
walking 57, 81, 160, 191, 211, 269, 274, 282-283, 321, 426, 443-444, 494
Warenski, Norma (see Matheson, Norma Warenski)
Washington, D.C. North Mission 225
Washington, D.C. Stake 185, 217, 231-232, 249, 436
Washington, D.C. Temple 263, 280, 337, 403, 411, 415, 418, 421-423, 427, 453, 475, 497
West, Martha 361, 447
West, Stephen A. (Steve) 202, 205, 292, 402, 354, 497
Whistler Blackcomb 368, 395
Wildrick, Richard 422
Wildrick, Ruth 422
Williams, David 376, 412, 496
Williams, W.G. 24
Wilson, Gary 181, 242, 251, 274-275, 487, 491, 493
Wirthlin, Joseph B. 147, 320
Women's International Committee 301
World War II, 23, 28, 31-32, 53, 77, 82, 86, 90, 96-98, 117, 124, 134, 179, 245, 297, 300, 316
Yellowstone National Park 56, 419
Young Women's program 160, 216-217
Zak, Ahmed 244